Betty Crocker's

COOKING BASICS

Betty Crocker

BASICS

HOW TO COOK AND ENTERTAIN WITH CONFIDENCE

Wiley Publishing, Inc.

For general information on our other products and services or to obtain technical support please contact our Customer Care Department within the U.S. at 800-762-2974, outside the U.S. at 317-572-3993 or fax 317-572-4002.

Wiley also publishes its books in a variety of electronic formats. Some content that appears in print may not be available in electronic books.

Cataloging-in-Publication Data is available upon request.

ISBN 0-7645-9645-4

GENERAL MILLS
Director, Book and Online Publishing: Kim Walter

Manager, Cookbook Publishing: Lois Tlusty

Recipe Development and Testing: Betty Crocker Kitchens

Photography and Food Styling: General Mills Photography Studios

WILEY PUBLISHING, INC.
Publisher: Natalie Chapman

Executive Editor: Anne Ficklen

Manufacturing Manager: Kevin Watt

For consistent baking results, the Betty Crocker Kitchens recommend Gold Medal Flour.

The Betty Crocker Kitchens seal guarantees success in your kitchen. Every recipe has been tested in America's Most Trusted Kitchens™ to meet our high standards of reliability, easy preparation and great taste.

Find more great ideas and shop for name-brand housewares at *BettyCrocker*.com

Manufactured in the United States of America

10 9 8 7 6 5 4 3 2 1

First Edition

INTRODUCTION

Have you been wanting to cook something new, or just learn to cook with more fun and confidence? Then let BETTY CROCKER'S COOKING BASICS be your guide! We've heard from so many people that cooking a simple supper, bringing a dish to a friend's house, or cooking a treat for dessert is something they would like to do, but there doesn't seem to be a book that shows new cooks how to cook with confidence. Until now, that is!

We heard those requests, so we went out and asked you exactly what you'd like to make cooking clear, easy and stress-free. . . . You told us pictures were important, so every recipe has a photo, plus photos that show techniques used in the recipe—nothing is a mystery.

You told us to make the recipes simple to follow, and not to overload them with unnecessary information. No problem! These recipes are easy to read and a cinch to follow. We asked you to tell us exactly what you wanted to cook. The 100 recipes are just what you asked for, from how to cook a perfect hamburger to elegant Chicken Breasts with Orange Glaze.

We heard that many of you yearned to cook Thanksgiving dinner—or at least bring a dish to a friend's house or family gathering. Great idea! We included a complete Thanksgiving menu, plus an easy-to-use timetable, so you can sit down to your feast right when you want to. And everyone wants a simple way to entertain friends. The answer? A hearty do-ahead meal of Vegetable Lasagna that even the busiest person can make the night before and serve up the next day.

Then, you told us that setting up a kitchen seemed very expensive, not to mention confusing. What is a zester anyway? Betty Crocker guides you through kitchen equipment—what you really need, what's less critical, though nice to have. Every item is pictured, so there's no more wondering what that thing is you found in the back of the kitchen drawer.

And, we explain all the cooking terms you need to know, give you the scoop on herbs and spices, pass on advice for what foods to have on hand and how to store food safely. We added great information on grilling, as well as how to set your table, even have a buffet. What's left? Common cooking techniques, such as dicing, slicing and peeling. We gave you a photo of each, so you can do it confidently in your own kitchen.

Want to cook something? Go right ahead. With Betty Crocker, you can be confident that it's easy, it's delicious and it's just what you want.

Betty Crocker

CONTENTS

CHAPTER 1

THE BASICS OF GETTING STARTED

UNDERSTANDING THE RECIPE

You will feel confident, organized and well prepared when trying a recipe for the first time if you read through the entire recipe before starting to cook. This will give you an opportunity to ask an experienced cook for help if there is a direction that isn't clear. Also, you will have time to make sure you have all the ingredients, utensils and pans needed to prepare the recipe. And you'll know if the recipe makes as many servings as you need and how much time the food needs to cook or bake. After reviewing the recipe, you'll be ready to cook with confidence.

Some ingredients need to be prepared before they can be added to a recipe. This might involve slicing a carrot or draining the liquid from a can of black beans. The recipe is easier to assemble if you prepare each ingredient first, so it is ready to use when you need it. If you will be using the oven or broiler, check the shelves or racks in the oven to be sure they are in the right place before turning on the heat. For most baked recipes, the oven shelf should be near the middle. For broiling, you will need to place the shelf closer to the heating element, which is usually at the top of the oven. A recipe requiring broiling usually will tell you how far from the heat to broil the food.

In this book, equipment that is absolutely necessary for preparation is identified at the top of each recipe. For example, the equipment could be a baking pan, electric mixer or a blender. You may need to use additional equipment or utensils other than those listed to complete the recipe, but their exact size is not always critical. We also tell you at the top of each recipe how long the food needs to cook, bake, chill or stand, so you can plan your time more easily. The time needed to prepare the ingredients is not included because this will vary, depending on your cooking experience.

The first time you make a recipe, it's a good idea to follow the directions exactly and use the ingredients called for. Often the results will be just what you wanted, but sometimes a certain flavor may seem too strong or be one you don't like. If that happens, the next time you make the recipe, try adjusting the flavorings, herbs and spices slightly. Put a reminder near the recipe of changes you'd like to try. As you gain cooking experience, you'll learn more about ingredients and how to make changes to suit your taste.

Finally, cleanup will be easy if you wash utensils or rinse and put them in the dishwasher, as you use them. This way, cooking and baking will be enjoyable and rewarding.

Cooking or
Baking Time

ROASTED GARLIC

MAKES 2 to 8 servings · **BAKE: 50 minutes**

INGREDIENTS

Easy
Step-by-Step
Directions

ESSENTIAL EQUIPMENT:
*aluminum foil; baking pan
or pie plate*

1 to 4 garlic bulbs

**2 teaspoons olive or
vegetable oil for each
garlic bulb**

Salt and pepper to taste

Suggestions
for Serving

**Sliced French bread,
if desired**

DIRECTIONS

1 Heat the oven to 350°.

2 Carefully peel the paperlike skin from around each bulb of
garlic, leaving just enough to hold the cloves together. Cut a 1/4-
to 1/2-inch slice from the top of each bulb to expose the cloves.
Place bulb, cut side up, on a 12-inch square of aluminum foil.

3 Drizzle 2 teaspoons oil over each bulb. Sprinkle with salt
and pepper. Wrap foil securely around the bulb. Place in the
baking pan or pie plate.

4 Bake 45 to 50 minutes or until garlic is tender when pierced
with a toothpick or fork. Cool slightly. To serve, gently squeeze
one end of each clove to release the roasted garlic. Spread on
slices of bread.

1 SERVING. Calories 75 (Calories from Fat 45); Fat 5g (Saturated 1g); Cholesterol 0mg;
Sodium 75mg; Carbohydrate 6g (Dietary Fiber 0g); Protein 1g

Nutrition
Information

TiP **GARLIC BECOMES** rich and
mellow when roasted.

Tips and
Useful
Information

TiP **GARLIC BULBS,** sometimes called "heads" of garlic, are made up of as many as fifteen sections called "cloves," each
of which is covered with a thin skin. You can find garlic bulbs in the produce section of the supermarket.

Helpful
How-To
Photographs

Preparing Garlic for Roasting

Carefully peel
paperlike skin from
around each garlic
bulb, leaving just
enough to hold the
cloves together. Cut
a 1/4- to 1/2-inch
slice from top of
each bulb to expose
cloves.

Wrapping Garlic for Roasting

Place bulb, cut side
up, on 12-inch
square of aluminum
foil. Drizzle 2 tea-
spoons oil over each
bulb. Sprinkle with
salt and pepper.
Wrap foil securely.

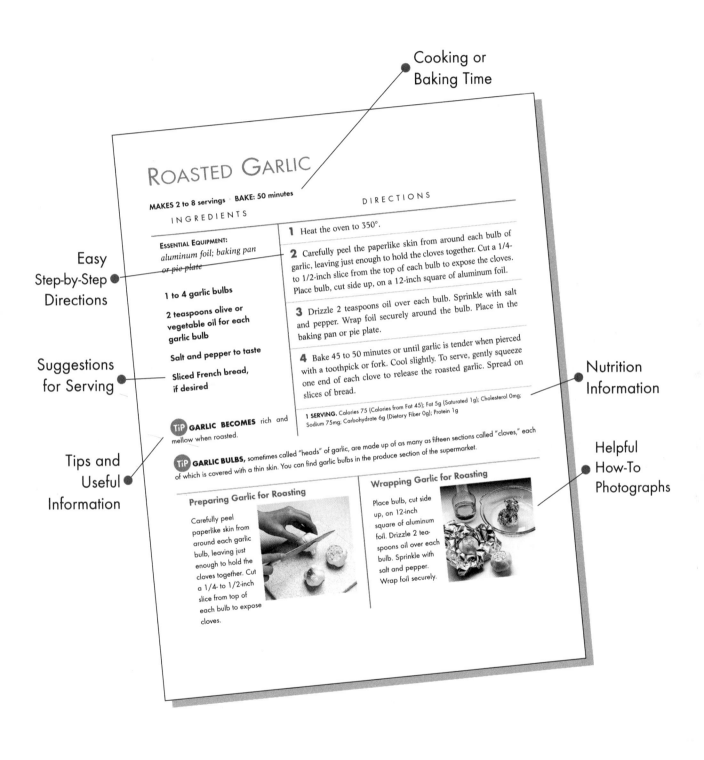

COMMON ABBREVIATIONS

Be prepared. In our recipes we don't use abbreviations, but other recipes do, so we've rounded up some common abbreviations to help you out.

t	=	teaspoon
tsp	=	teaspoon
T	=	tablespoon
Tbsp	=	tablespoon
c	=	cup
oz	=	ounce
pt	=	pint
qt	=	quart
gal	=	gallon
lb	=	pound
#	=	pound

MEASURING GUIDE

What's different, yet exactly the same? All these measurements! In our recipes, we have used the larger measurement—1/4 cup, not 4 tablespoons—but this equivalency chart will help you out for the other measuring you do in the kitchen.

3 teaspoons	=	1 tablespoon
4 tablespoons	=	1/4 cup
5 tablespoons + 1 teaspoon	=	1/3 cup
8 tablespoons	=	1/2 cup
1 cup	=	1/2 pint
2 cups	=	1 pint
4 cups (2 pints)	=	1 quart
4 quarts	=	1 gallon
16 ounces	=	1 pound
Dash or pinch	=	less than 1/8 teaspoon

HOW TO MEASURE INGREDIENTS

Successful cooking starts with measuring correctly. Not all ingredients are measured the same way or with the same type of cups or spoons. Here are some tips to help you measure successfully.

MEASURING CUPS: For liquids usually are glass. They have a spout for pouring and space above the top measuring line. They can be purchased in 1-, 2-, 4- and 8-cup sizes.

Dry ingredients and solid ingredients such as shortening are measured using a set of cups that stack or "nest" inside one another. These cups are made to hold an exact amount when filled to the top. They are purchased as a set that contains 1/4-, 1/3-, 1/2- and 1-cup sizes. Some sets also may have a 1/8-cup (2 tablespoons) and/or a 2-cup size.

MEASURING SPOONS: Are sold as a set that includes 1/4-, 1/2- and 1-teaspoon sizes plus a 1-tablespoon size. Some sets may have a 1/8-teaspoon size. These special spoons are designed for measuring and should be used instead of spoons intended for eating. They are used for both liquid and dry ingredients.

LIQUIDS: When measuring liquids, use the smallest measuring cup size you have that is large enough to hold the amount needed. For example, to measure 1/2 cup milk, you'd use a 1-cup measuring cup instead of a 2-cup measuring cup. Place the cup on a level surface, then bend down to check the amount at eye level. To measure sticky liquids such as honey, molasses and corn syrup, lightly spread the cup with oil first, or spray with cooking spray, so the liquid will be easier to remove.

DRY: For dry ingredients, gently fill the measuring cup to heaping, using a large spoon. Do not shake the cup or pack down the ingredients. While holding the cup over the canister or storage container to catch the excess of the ingredient, level the cup off, using something with a straight edge, such as a knife or the handle of a wooden spoon.

SOLID FATS AND BROWN SUGAR: Fill the measuring cup, using a spoon or rubber spatula. Pack down the ingredient, and level off if necessary.

SHREDDED CHEESE, CEREAL, CHOPPED NUTS: Fill the measuring cup lightly without packing down the ingredient, and level off.

MARGARINE AND BUTTER IN STICKS: Cut off the amount needed, following guideline marks on the wrapper, using a sharp knife. An entire 1/4-pound stick equals 1/2 cup, half a stick is 1/4 cup, an eighth of a stick is 1 tablespoon.

SALT, PEPPER, HERBS AND SPICES: Fill measuring spoon with salt, pepper or a ground spice such as cinnamon; level off. For dried herbs, lightly fill the spoon to the top.

ESSENTIAL EQUIPMENT AND TOOLS

Having the right equipment makes cooking easier and fun. The following are the basic tools you should consider having for your kitchen. You may already have many of these things, and sometimes you can improvise by using another tool.

CAN OPENER: Purchase one that's easy to wash after each use.

COLANDER: For draining pasta and other foods after cooking and for draining fresh produce after washing. If you are purchasing a new colander, choose one that will be easy to clean.

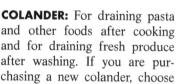

CUTTING BOARD: Plastic boards can be easily and thoroughly washed. Wash them immediately after cutting raw meat, poultry or fish.

GRATER: A box grater has different size openings on each side for shredding cheeses or vegetables and for grating fruit peels. Other types are available, but all should have several sizes of openings for a variety of shredding and grating.

KITCHEN SCISSORS OR SHEARS: Good for snipping fresh herbs and for all-purpose cutting and trimming of ingredients.

KNIVES: With three good knives—paring, chef's and all-purpose—cutting, slicing, dicing and chopping are easy. (See page 9.)

MEASURING CUPS AND SPOONS: Measuring accurately ensures recipe success. (See page 5.)

MIXING BOWLS: Choose two or three deep bowls in different sizes. A large mixing bowl can double as a salad bowl.

POTATO MASHER: You'll need this for making mashed potatoes or twice-baked potatoes.

SPATULA, WIDE METAL OR PLASTIC, OR PANCAKE TURNER: Not just for pancakes, it's great for turning chicken breasts and fish fillets as well as serving lasagna and desserts.

SPATULA, RUBBER: For scraping the last bit of food out of mixing bowls or measuring cups.

SPOON, LARGE METAL: Use to stir mixtures and to spoon juices over meats or poultry as they roast. Use also to lift large pieces of meat from the cooking pan to the serving plate.

SPOON, SLOTTED: Use to lift solid foods out of cooking liquids.

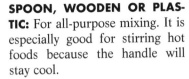

SPOON, WOODEN OR PLASTIC: For all-purpose mixing. It is especially good for stirring hot foods because the handle will stay cool.

STRAINER: For draining cans of fruit or vegetables and for draining the liquid off cooked foods.

THERMOMETER, MEAT: An easy way to be sure meats, poultry and fish are cooked properly.

TIMER: To ensure that your foods are cooked to perfection. If the recipe gives a range of time, set the timer for the minimum time to check for doneness.

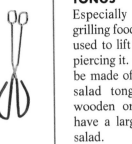

TONGS FOR COOKING: Especially good to use when grilling foods, but can also can be used to lift or turn food without piercing it. Cooking tongs should be made of metal, in contrast to salad tongs, which might be wooden or plastic and usually have a larger end for tossing a salad.

VEGETABLE BRUSH: Use to clean celery and potatoes.

VEGETABLE PEELER: Much easier to use than a knife to remove a thin peel from apples, potatoes and carrots.

WIRE WHISK: Great for beating eggs and preparing sauces and dressings as well as for all-purpose mixing.

NOT ESSENTIAL, BUT NICE TO HAVE

BLENDER: Can be used for certain types of chopping as well as to whirl smoothies and puree vegetables for creamy soups.

FORK, LONG-HANDLED: Great for holding meat and poultry in place while it is being sliced or carved.

JUICER: To squeeze fresh juice from oranges, lemons, limes and other citrus fruits.

LADLE: A large ladle is best to dish up soups, stews and chili.

ELECTRIC MIXER: An easy way to whip cream and beat cakes and other desserts. It also can be used to mash potatoes.

HAND BEATER: Also called an egg beater or a rotary beater.

PASTRY BLENDER: Used to mix shortening, butter or margarine with dry ingredients such as flour and sugar to produce a crumbly mixture.

SPATULA, NARROW METAL: When measuring dry ingredients, this spatula is handy to use to level off the measuring cup. It's also helpful when frosting a cake.

SPATULA, WOODEN, OR SPECIALLY COATED UTENSILS: Use to stir when cooking or frying in a nonstick pan to protect the surface of the pan.

STEAMER BASKET: Use to suspend vegetables above boiling water. It adapts to many pan sizes and folds for easy storage.

ALL ABOUT KNIVES

Invest in good knives to make food preparation easy, fast and efficient. Before purchasing a knife, pick it up. It should fit your hand and feel comfortable to use. The blade of a good knife extends through the full length of the knife handle. If this extension, called the tang, is not visible, make sure the knife has three rivets, which indicate that the blade is inside the handle.

Good knives are expensive but will last for a very long time if they are cared for properly. Storing them in a block of wood designed for knife storage is perfect, but the cardboard sleeve the knife was packaged in works well, too. The idea is to keep knives from getting dull edges by bumping into other utensils in a drawer. Preserve knife handles by washing and drying knives by hand instead of in the dishwasher. If knives become too soaked with water, wooden handles will dry and warp and the blades may loosen. Sharp knives are the easiest and safest to use. Refer to manufacturers' recommendations for keeping your knives sharp.

Slicing, dicing, cutting and chopping can be done easily, quickly and correctly if you have three good knives. You'll need a paring knife, a chef's knife and a multipurpose knife with a serrated edge.

THREE ESSENTIAL KNIVES

PARING KNIFE: Has a small blade, about 2 1/2 to 3 inches long, and a rounded or pointed tip. If you plan to have only one paring knife, choose one with a pointed tip. You'll need it to cut up fruits and vegetables, cut fat from a steak or a pork chop, cut into meats and poultry to check for doneness and for many other uses.

CHEF'S KNIFE: Has a heavy, triangular blade, anywhere from 6 to 12 inches long. A medium-size blade, about 8 to 10 inches, is the most versatile size. It is used for chopping, slicing and dicing as well as for crushing a clove of garlic. This knife also is called a cook's knife.

MULTIPURPOSE KNIFE: Has a scalloped or serrated edge and comes in several sizes, but the most helpful one has a blade that is at least 7 to 8 inches long. It may be called a bread knife, a slicer, or a carver and its uses include slicing bread, tomatoes, cooked meats and carving a turkey.

# POTS AND PANS FOR COOKING

You'll be able to make most recipes if you have a small collection of pans with lids, in sizes ranging from 1 to 4 quarts, and a large skillet. Pans can be purchased in large sets, but if you don't need everything in the set, you can collect some unmatched pots and pans that will work just as well.

THREE ESSENTIAL SAUCEPANS

SAUCEPANS (1-, 2-, 3-QUART): Essential for cooking or reheating foods on a range top. Although one or two saucepans may be adequate, a collection of saucepans will make cooking more efficient. Each pan should have a tight-fitting lid, which is important when cooking dishes that require the retention of moisture. Pans with a non-stick finish require plastic or coated utensils to prevent scratching the surface of the pan.

MORE ESSENTIAL SAUCEPANS

SKILLET: Used for sautéing vegetables, panfrying meats and stir-frying almost any food. Available in an assortment of materials and sizes. When purchasing a skillet, look for a solid, thick-bottomed pan that will transmit heat evenly and that has a tight-fitting lid. Although a 10-inch skillet is used most often, some recipes work better in a skillet that is slightly larger. A smaller skillet, about 8 inches in diameter, is nice to have when cooking smaller quantities.

DUTCH OVEN (4 QUARTS OR LARGER): A large pot that is used most often on top of the range to prepare a large batch of soup or chili or to cook pasta. It should have a tight-fitting lid. Many Dutch ovens are ovenproof and can be used when cooking pot roast or stew in the oven.

PANS FOR BAKING

You will need a few baking pans for meats, vegetables and main dishes as well as for cakes, cookies and other desserts. The dimensions of a pan are often given on its bottom. If the dimensions are not there, measure across the bottom to determine the size. Some baking pans have a nonstick finish or lining. This surface will scratch easily, so use care when cutting main dishes or desserts that are served from the pan, and wash the pans with a nonabrasive or plastic scrubber.

SQUARE BAKING PAN: An 8- or 9-inch square pan that can be used for main dishes, such as lasagna, as well as for cakes, bar cookies and other desserts.

13×9-INCH RECTANGULAR PAN: A popular pan size for baking brownies, bars and cakes. Some main dishes, vegetables and casseroles also can be prepared in this pan.

9-INCH ROUND PAN: One of the most popular sizes for baking layer cakes. Most layer cakes require two of these pans.

COOKIE SHEET: Available in an assortment of sizes. To ensure proper heat circulation, select one that is at least 2 inches narrower on each side than your oven. Although a cookie sheet may have a small lip edge, it should not have straight sides that are 1 inch or more in height. (A large rectangular pan with 1-inch sides is usually called a jelly roll pan rather than a cookie sheet and will not bake or brown cookies in the same way that a cookie sheet does.)

9-INCH PIE PAN: Not only is a pie pan essential for making pies, it also can be used to bake a meat loaf or small cuts of meat and poultry. If you are uncertain about the size of your pie pan, measure across the top of the pan, excluding the lip edge.

CHAPTER 2

BEEF AND PORK MAIN DISHES

Juicy Hamburgers—Three Ways

BROILING, GRILLING AND PANFRYING

MAKES 4 servings

INGREDIENTS

1 pound regular or lean ground beef

3 tablespoons water

1/2 teaspoon salt

1/4 teaspoon pepper

4 hamburger buns

DIRECTIONS

BROILING HAMBURGERS

1 You may need to move the oven rack so it is 5 to 6 inches below the broiler. Set the oven control to broil.

2 Mix the beef, water, salt and pepper in a bowl. Shape the mixture into 4 uniform, flat patties, each about 3/4 inch thick. Handle the patties as little as possible. The more the beef is handled, the less juicy the burgers will be.

3 Place the patties on the rack in a broiler pan. (For easy cleanup, line the bottom of the broiler pan with aluminum foil before placing patties on rack.)

4 Broil patties with tops about 3 inches from heat 5 to 7 minutes on each side for doneness, turning once, until no longer pink in center and juice is clear. Serve on buns.

CHEESEBURGERS: About 1 minute before the hamburgers are done, top each burger with 1 slice (1 ounce) American, Cheddar, Swiss or Monterey Jack cheese. Broil until cheese is melted and bubbling.

GRILLING HAMBURGERS

1 Prepare the coals or a gas grill for direct heat (pages 236–237). Heat to medium heat, which will take about 40 minutes for charcoal or about 10 minutes for a gas grill.

2 Shape the hamburger patties as described in step 2 of Broiling Hamburgers.

3 Place the patties on the grill about 4 inches from medium heat. Grill uncovered 7 to 8 inches on each side for doneness, turning once, until no longer pink in center and juice is clear. Loosen patties gently with a turner to prevent crumbling. Serve on buns.

PANFRYING HAMBURGERS

1 Shape the hamburger patties as described in step 2 of Broiling Hamburgers.

2 Cook the patties in a skillet over medium heat about 10 minutes for doneness, turning occasionally, until no longer pink in center and juice is clear. Serve on buns.

Shaping Patties

Shaping the patties to have smooth edges will keep them together during cooking and result in uniform doneness. Gently pinch to close any cracks in the patty.

TiP DON'T PRESS THE BEEF PATTIES with a spatula while cooking. Pressing squeezes natural juices out and makes the burgers dry and less tender.

TiP FOR MORE FLAVOR and better burgers, use lean or regular ground beef; hamburgers made with extra-lean ground beef may crumble when broiled. For a moister hamburger, use coarsely ground instead of finely ground beef.

✔ **STORE THE UNCOOKED MEAT** immediately in the coldest part of your refrigerator, or freeze as soon as possible. Ground meat deteriorates more quickly than other cuts, so it should be used promptly.

MEAT LOAF

MAKES 4 servings • **BAKE: 1 hour** • **LET STAND: 5 minutes**

INGREDIENTS

DIRECTIONS

ESSENTIAL EQUIPMENT: *baking pan, such as 8-inch square pan or 9-inch pie pan*

1 pound lean ground beef

1 clove garlic or 1/8 teaspoon garlic powder

1 small onion

2 slices bread with crust

1/4 cup milk

2 teaspoons Worcestershire sauce

1 teaspoon chopped fresh or 1/4 teaspoon dried sage leaves

1/4 teaspoon salt

1/4 teaspoon ground mustard (dry)

1/8 teaspoon pepper

1 egg

1/3 cup ketchup, chili sauce or barbecue sauce

1 Heat oven to 350°. Break up the beef into small pieces in a large bowl, using a fork or spoon.

2 Peel and finely chop the garlic. Peel the onion, and chop enough of the onion into small pieces to measure 3 tablespoons. Wrap remaining piece of onion, and refrigerate for another use. Add the garlic and onion to the beef.

3 Tear the bread into small pieces and add to beef mixture.

4 Add the milk, Worcestershire sauce, sage, salt, mustard, pepper and egg to the beef mixture. Mix with a fork, large spoon or your hands until the ingredients are well mixed.

5 Place the beef mixture in the ungreased baking pan. Almost any size pan will work; just be sure the pan has sides on it to catch the juices that will accumulate while the meat loaf bakes. Shape the mixture into an 8×4-inch loaf in the pan, and spread ketchup over the top.

6 Bake uncovered 50 to 60 minutes or until beef in center of loaf is no longer pink. A meat thermometer inserted in the center of the loaf should read 160°. Let the loaf stand 5 minutes, so it will be easier to remove from the pan. Cut the loaf into slices.

1 SERVING: Calories 320 (Calories from Fat 160); Fat 18g (Saturated 7g); Cholesterol 120mg; Sodium 550mg; Carbohydrate 15g (Dietary Fiber 0g); Protein 25g

MEAT LOAF For 12 grams of fat and 270 calories per serving, substitute ground turkey for the ground beef, substitute 1/4 cup fat-free cholesterol-free egg product for the egg and use skim milk. Bake until 180°.

TiP **FOR MORE FLAVOR,** purchase a meat loaf mixture of ground beef, lamb and pork, already prepared in your supermarket meat case.

TiP **TO SAVE TIME,** purchase fresh garlic already chopped or crushed. You'll find it in the produce section of the supermarket. Store it in the refrigerator after opening the jar.

Checking for Doneness

Cut a small slit near center of loaf; meat and juices should no longer be pink.

Meat Loaf, Dilled Carrots with Pea Pods (page 182)

MEXICAN BEEF AND BEAN CASSEROLE

MAKES 4 servings • BAKE: 50 minutes

INGREDIENTS

ESSENTIAL EQUIPMENT: *10-inch skillet; 2-quart baking pan or casserole*

1 pound ground beef

2 cans (15 to 16 ounces each) pinto beans

1 can (8 ounces) tomato sauce

1/2 cup mild chunky-style salsa

1 teaspoon chili powder

1 cup shredded Monterey Jack cheese (4 ounces)

DIRECTIONS

1 Heat the oven to 375°.

2 Cook the beef in the skillet over medium heat 8 to 10 minutes, stirring occasionally, until brown; drain.

3 Rinse and drain the beans in a strainer. Mix the beef, beans, tomato sauce, salsa and chili powder in the ungreased baking pan.

4 Cover with lid or aluminum foil and bake 40 to 45 minutes, stirring once or twice, until hot and bubbly. Carefully remove the lid, and sprinkle cheese over the top. Continue baking uncovered about 5 minutes or until the cheese is melted.

1 SERVING: Calories 520 (Calories from Fat 235); Fat 26g (Saturated 12g); Cholesterol 90mg; Sodium 1020mg; Carbohydrate 45g (Dietary Fiber 14g); Protein 41g

Lighter **MEXICAN BEEF AND BEAN CASSEROLE:** For 18 grams of fat and 465 calories per serving, substitute ground turkey for the beef and reduced-fat Cheddar cheese for the Monterey Jack cheese.

TiP FOR A FLAVOR WITH MORE ZIP, use Monterey Jack cheese with jalapeño peppers or, as it's also known, pepper Jack cheese.

TiP TO SPICE UP THE FLAVOR, next time try a higher spice level of salsa. If it is too hot, cool it with sour cream. Salsa comes in mild, hot and extra-hot.

Rinsing Pinto Beans

Rinse and drain the beans in a strainer. Rinsing canned beans results in a cleaner taste and can reduce digestive problems.

Mexican Beef and Bean Casserole

CHILI

MAKES 4 servings • **COOK: 1 hour 20 minutes**

INGREDIENTS

ESSENTIAL EQUIPMENT: *3-quart saucepan or 12-inch skillet with high side*

1 large onion

2 cloves garlic

1 pound ground beef

1 tablespoon chili powder

2 teaspoons fresh chopped or 1 teaspoon dried oregano leaves

1 teaspoon ground cumin

1/2 teaspoon salt

1/2 teaspoon red pepper sauce

1 can (16 ounces) whole tomatoes, undrained

1 can (15 to 16 ounces) red kidney beans, undrained

DIRECTIONS

1 Peel and chop the onion. Peel and crush the garlic.

2 Cook the beef, onion and garlic in the saucepan over medium heat 8 to 10 minutes, stirring occasionally, until beef is brown; drain.

3 Stir in the chili powder, oregano, cumin, salt, pepper sauce and tomatoes with their liquid, breaking up the tomatoes with a spoon or fork.

4 Heat the mixture to boiling over high heat. Once mixture is boiling, reduce heat just enough so mixture bubbles gently. Cover and cook 1 hour, stirring occasionally.

5 Stir in the beans with their liquid. Heat to boiling over high heat. Once mixture is boiling, reduce heat just enough so mixture bubbles gently. Cook uncovered about 20 minutes, stirring occasionally, until desired thickness.

1 SERVING: Calories 350 (Calories from Fat 155); Fat 17g (Saturated 7g); Cholesterol 65mg; Sodium 920mg; Carbohydrate 27g (Dietary Fiber 7g); Protein 29g

CINCINNATI-STYLE CHILI: For each serving, spoon about 3/4 cup beef mixture over 1 cup hot cooked spaghetti. Sprinkle each serving with 1/4 cup shredded Cheddar cheese and 2 tablespoons chopped onion. Top with sour cream if desired.

TiP **TO SAVE TIME,** increase chili powder to 2 tablespoons, and omit the cumin, oregano and pepper sauce.

TiP **IF YOU REALLY LIKE IT HOT,** top chili with sliced fresh jalapeño chilies.

Breaking up Tomatoes

Break up tomatoes with a spoon or fork. This distributes the tomatoes evenly throughout the chili and makes serving the chili easier.

Chili

Quick Lasagna

MAKES 4 servings • BAKE: 40 minutes • LET STAND: 10 minutes

INGREDIENTS

DIRECTIONS

ESSENTIAL EQUIPMENT: *10-inch skillet; 8- or 9-inch square pan*

1 clove garlic

1/2 pound ground beef

1 teaspoon Italian seasoning

1 cup spaghetti sauce

6 purchased precooked or oven-ready lasagna noodles (each about 7 × 3 inches)

1 container (12 ounces) reduced-fat cottage cheese (1 1/2 cups)

1 cup shredded mozzarella cheese (4 ounces)

2 tablespoons grated Parmesan cheese

1 Heat the oven to 400°. Peel and finely chop the garlic. Cook the beef and garlic in the skillet over medium heat about 5 minutes, stirring occasionally, until the beef is brown; drain.

2 Stir the Italian seasoning and spaghetti sauce into the beef. Spread 1/4 cup of the beef mixture in the ungreased square pan.

3 Top with 2 noodles, placing them so they do not overlap or touch the sides of the pan because they will expand as they bake. Spread about 1/2 cup of the remaining beef mixture over the noodles.

4 Spread about 1/2 cup of the cottage cheese over the beef mixture. Sprinkle with about 1/3 cup of the mozzarella cheese.

5 Repeat layering twice more, beginning with 2 more noodles and following directions in steps 3 and 4 Sprinkle with the Parmesan cheese.

6 Cover with aluminum foil and bake 30 minutes. Carefully remove the foil, and continue baking about 10 minutes longer or until lasagna is bubbly around the edges and looks very hot. Let stand 10 minutes, so the lasagna will become easier to cut and serve.

1 SERVING: Calories 430 (Calories from Fat 160); Fat 18g (Saturated 8g); Cholesterol 55mg; Sodium 980mg; Carbohydrate 33g (Dietary Fiber 2g); Protein 36g

TiP **TO MAKE AHEAD,** assemble the lasagna, but do not bake it. Cover with aluminum foil and refrigerate no longer than 24 hours. Bake as directed in step 6, increasing the first bake time to 40 minutes.

TiP **YOU CAN SUBSTITUTE** ricotta cheese for the cottage cheese. Ricotta is drier in texture than cottage cheese. Look for it in the dairy case near the cottage cheese.

Layering Beef and Noodles

Spread 1/4 cup beef mixture in pan; top with noodles. Spread 1/2 cup beef mixture over noodles.

Layering Cheese

After beef mixture and noodles are layered, spread 1/2 cup cottage cheese over beef mixture. Sprinkle with 1/3 cup mozzarella cheese.

Quick Lasagna

GREAT STEAK—THREE WAYS

BROILING, GRILLING AND PAN FRYING

TYPES OF STEAK

Porterhouse   *Rib Eye*   *Sirloin*   *T-Bone*   *Tenderloin*

Select a steak that is bright red in color. Vacuum-packed beef will have a darker, purplish red color because the meat is not exposed to air. These cuts of steak, porterhouse, rib eye, sirloin, T-bone and tenderloin, are the most tender and are best for broiling, grilling and panfrying.

BROILING A STEAK

1 Select a 3/4- to 1-inch-thick steak from those shown in the photos.

2 You may need to move the oven rack so it is 5 to 6 inches below the broiler. Set the oven control to broil.

3 To prevent the steak from curling during broiling, cut outer edge of fat on steak diagonally at 1-inch intervals with a sharp knife. Do not cut into the meat or it will dry out during broiling.

4 Place steak on the rack in a broiler pan. (For easy cleanup, line the bottom of the broiler pan with aluminum foil before placing steak on rack.) Place in oven with the top of the steak the number of inches from heat listed in the chart.

5 Broil uncovered for about half the time listed in the chart or until the steak is brown on one side.

6 Turn the steak and continue cooking until desired doneness. To check doneness, cut a small slit in the center of boneless cuts or in the center near the bone of bone-in cuts. Medium-rare is very pink in the center and slightly brown toward the edges. Medium is light pink in center and brown toward the edges. Or insert a meat thermometer in the center of the steak to check for desired doneness. Sprinkle salt and pepper over both sides of steak after cooking if desired. Serve immediately.

Cutting Fat

Cut fat diagonally at 1-inch intervals with sharp knife.

GRILLING A STEAK

1 Select a 3/4- to 1-inch-thick steak from those shown in the photos.

2 Prepare the coals or a gas grill for direct heat (pages 236–237). Heat to medium heat, which will take about 40 minutes for charcoal or about 10 minutes for a gas grill.

3 Cut edges of fat on steak as described in step 3 of Broiling a Steak.

4 Place steak on the grill the number of inches from heat listed in the chart.

5 Turn the steak and continue cooking until desired doneness. Check for doneness as described in step 6 of Broiling a Steak.

TiP **MARBLING IN MEATS,** refers to the small flecks of fat throughout the lean meat. The flavor and juiciness of the meat is improved with marbling.

TiP **SOME STEAKS ARE AGED;** aging is a process done by a butcher and results in meat with firmer texture and a more concentrated beef flavor. Aged steaks are usually more expensive.

TIMETABLE FOR BROILING OR GRILLING STEAKS

Type of Steak	Inches from Heat	Approximate Total Broiling Time in Minutes		Approximate Total Grilling Time in Minutes	
		145° *(medium-rare)*	*160°* *(medium)*	*145°* *(medium-rare)*	*160°* *(medium)*
Porterhouse and T-Bone	3 to 4	10	15	19	14
Rib Eye	2 to 4	8	15	7	12
Sirloin (boneless)	2 to 4	10	21	12	16
Tenderloin	2 to 3	10	15	11	13

PANFRYING A STEAK

1 Select a 1/2- to 1-inch-thick steak from those shown in the photos.

2 If the steak is very lean and has little fat, coat a heavy skillet or frying pan with a small amount of vegetable oil, or spray it with cooking spray. Or use a nonstick skillet.

3 If the steak is more than 1/2 inch thick, heat the skillet over medium-low to medium heat 1 to 2 minutes. If the steak is 1/2 inch, use medium to medium-high heat.

4 Place the steak in the hot skillet. You do not need to add oil or water or cover the skillet; covering will cause the steak to be steamed rather than panfried.

5 Cook for the time listed in the chart. If the steak has extra fat on it, fat may accumulate in the skillet; remove this fat with a spoon as it accumulates. Turn steaks thicker than 1/2 inch occasionally, turn steaks that are 1/2 inch thick once, until brown on both sides and desired doneness. To check doneness, cut a small slit in the center of boneless cuts or in the center near the bone of bone-in cuts. Medium-rare is very pink in center and slightly brown toward the edges. Medium is light pink in center and brown toward the edges. Or insert a meat thermometer in the center of the steak to check for desired doneness. Sprinkle salt and pepper over both sides of steak after cooking if desired. Serve immediately.

TIMETABLE FOR PANFRYING STEAKS

Type of Steak	Thickness in Inches	Range-top Temperature	Approximate Total Cooking Time in Minutes 145° to 160° (medium-rare to medium)
Porterhouse and T-Bone	1/2	Medium	8 to 10
Rib Eye	1/2	Medium-high	3 to 5
Sirloin (boneless)	3/4 to 1	Medium-low to Medium	10 to 12
Tenderloin	3/4 to 1	Medium	6 to 9

T-Bone Steak, Corn (page 163), Baked Potato Wedges (page 172)

BEEF WITH PEA PODS

MAKES 4 servings · **COOK: 8 minutes**

INGREDIENTS

ESSENTIAL EQUIPMENT: *2-quart saucepan; 10-inch skillet or wok*

1 pound beef boneless sirloin steak

1 clove garlic

Hot Cooked Rice (below)

1 tablespoon vegetable oil

1/4 teaspoon salt

Dash of pepper

2/3 cup beef broth

1 tablespoon cornstarch

2 tablespoons water

1 tablespoon soy sauce

1 teaspoon finely chopped gingerroot or 1/4 teaspoon ground ginger

1 package (6 ounces) frozen snow (Chinese) pea pods, thawed

HOT COOKED RICE

1 cup uncooked regular long-grain white rice

2 cups water

DIRECTIONS

1 Cut and discard most of the fat from the beef. Cut the beef with the grain into 2-inch strips, then cut the strips across the grain into 1/4-inch slices. Peel and finely chop the garlic.

2 Prepare Hot Cooked Rice. While the rice is cooking, continue with the recipe.

3 Heat the skillet over high heat 1 to 2 minutes. Add the oil to the hot skillet. If using a wok, rotate it to coat the side with oil. Add the beef and garlic to the skillet. Stir-fry with a turner or large spoon about 3 minutes, lifting and stirring constantly, until beef is brown.

4 Sprinkle salt and pepper over beef, and stir in the broth. Heat to boiling over high heat.

5 Mix the cornstarch, water and soy sauce, and stir into the beef mixture. Cook, stirring constantly, until the mixture thickens and boils. Continue boiling 1 minute, stirring constantly. The sauce will be thin.

6 Stir in the gingerroot and pea pods. Cook uncovered about 2 minutes, stirring occasionally, until pea pods are crisp-tender when pierced with a fork. Serve over rice.

HOT COOKED RICE Heat the rice and water to boiling in the saucepan over high heat, stirring occasionally to prevent sticking. Once mixture is boiling, reduce heat just enough so mixture bubbles gently. Cover and cook about 15 minutes or until rice is fluffy and tender.

1 SERVING: Calories 345 (Calories from Fat 65); Fat 7g (Saturated 2g); Cholesterol 55mg; Sodium 620mg; Carbohydrate 46g (Dietary Fiber 1g); Protein 26g

Lighter

BEEF WITH PEA PODS: For 4 grams of fat and 320 calories per serving, omit the oil and use a non-stick skillet or wok. Spray the room-temperature skillet or wok with cooking spray before heating in step 3.

TiP **FOR EASY PREPARATION,** place beef in the freezer for 1 hour before slicing; it will be easier to slice when partially frozen.

TiP **FOR MORE FLAVOR,** use any leftover beef broth to replace part of the water used for cooking the rice.

Slicing Beef

Cut beef with grain into 2-inch strips; cut strips across grain into 1/4-inch slices.

Thawing Frozen Pea Pods

Place frozen pea pods in a strainer, then run cold water over them until the pea pods can be separated easily.

Beef with Pea Pods

BEEF STROGANOFF

MAKES 6 servings • COOK: 20 minutes

INGREDIENTS

ESSENTIAL EQUIPMENT: *10-inch skillet; 3-quart saucepan*

1 1/2 pounds beef boneless top loin steak, about 1 inch thick

2 tablespoons margarine or butter

Hot Cooked Noodles (below)

1 clove garlic

1 1/2 cups beef broth

2 tablespoons ketchup

1 teaspoon salt

1 medium onion

1/2 pound mushrooms

3 tablespoons all-purpose flour

1 cup sour cream or plain yogurt

HOT COOKED NOODLES

6 cups water

3 cups uncooked egg noodles (6 ounces)

DIRECTIONS

1 Cut the beef across the grain into about 1/8-inch strips. Cut longer strips crosswise in half.

2 Melt the margarine in the skillet over medium-high heat. Cook the beef in the margarine 8 to 10 minutes, stirring occasionally, until brown. While the beef is cooking, heat the water for Hot Cooked Noodles and continue with step 3.

3 Peel and finely chop the garlic. Reserve 1/3 cup of the beef broth. Stir the remaining broth, the ketchup, salt and garlic into beef. Heat to boiling over high heat. Once mixture is boiling, reduce heat just enough so mixture bubbles gently. Cover and cook about 10 minutes or until beef is tender.

4 While the beef is cooking, peel and chop the onion and cut the mushrooms into slices. Finish preparing the noodles.

5 Stir the onion and mushrooms into the beef mixture. Cover and cook about 5 minutes or until onion is tender.

6 Shake the reserved 1/3 cup beef broth and the flour in a tightly covered jar or container. Gradually stir this mixture into beef mixture. Heat to boiling over high heat, stirring constantly. Continue boiling 1 minute, stirring constantly, until thickened. Reduce heat just enough so mixture bubbles gently.

7 Stir in the sour cream. Cook until hot, but do not heat to boiling or the mixture will curdle. Serve over noodles.

HOT COOKED NOODLES Heat water to boiling in the saucepan over high heat. Stir in the noodles. Boil vigorously 8 to 10 minutes, stirring occasionally to prevent sticking, until noodles are tender. Boiling vigorously allows pasta to move freely so it cooks evenly, but watch carefully so the water doesn't boil over. Drain noodles in a strainer or colander.

1 SERVING: Calories 390 (Calories from Fat 170); Fat 19g (Saturated 8g); Cholesterol 105mg; Sodium 820mg; Carbohydrate 28g (Dietary Fiber 1g); Protein 28g

TiP **FOR A BIT OF COLOR** and fresh flavor, sprinkle freshly chopped parsley over the noodles.

TiP **FOR A MORE FLAVORFUL** and exotic version, use chanterelle, morel or shiitake mushrooms instead of regular white mushrooms.

Cleaning and Slicing Mushrooms

Rinse mushrooms, and cut off the stem ends. Cut mushrooms into 1/4-inch slices.

Thickening the Stroganoff

Stir broth-and-flour mixture gradually into beef mixture. For the right consistency, it is important to boil and stir 1 minute.

Beef Stroganoff

SPICY BEEF SALAD

MAKES 6 servings • COOK: 5 minutes • REFRIGERATE: 30 minutes plus 1 hour

INGREDIENTS

DIRECTIONS

ESSENTIAL EQUIPMENT: *10-inch nonstick skillet or wok*

1 pound beef boneless sirloin steak

2 tablespoons dry sherry or apple juice

1 tablespoon soy sauce

2 teaspoons sugar

1 small head lettuce

8 medium green onions with tops

2 medium tomatoes

3/4 pound mushrooms

Spicy Dressing (below)

SPICY DRESSING

1 clove garlic

1/4 cup rice vinegar or white wine vinegar

2 tablespoons soy sauce

1 teaspoon finely chopped gingerroot

1 teaspoon sesame oil

1/8 teaspoon ground red pepper (cayenne)

1 Cut and discard most of the fat from the beef. Cut the beef with the grain into 2-inch strips, then cut the strips across the grain into 1/8-inch slices. (For easier cutting, partially freeze beef about 1 hour.)

2 To marinate the beef, toss the beef, sherry, soy sauce and sugar in a glass or plastic bowl. Cover and refrigerate 30 minutes.

3 Wash the lettuce, and let drain. Peel and cut the green onions into 1/8-inch slices. Coarsely chop the tomatoes. Cut the mushrooms into slices. Tear or shred the lettuce into bite-size pieces.

4 Heat the skillet over medium-high heat 1 to 2 minutes. Add half of the beef to the hot skillet. Stir-fry with a turner or large spoon about 3 minutes, lifting and stirring constantly, until beef is brown. Remove beef from the skillet; drain. Repeat with remaining beef.

5 Toss the beef and green onions in a large salad or serving bowl. Layer the tomatoes, mushrooms and lettuce on the beef. Cover and refrigerate at least 1 hour but no longer than 10 hours.

6 Prepare Spicy Dressing. Pour the dressing over the salad, then toss until well coated.

SPICY DRESSING Peel and finely chop the garlic. Shake garlic and remaining ingredients in a tightly covered jar or container.

1 SERVING: Calories 120 (Calories from Fat 25); Fat 3g (Saturated 1g); Cholesterol 35mg; Sodium 430mg; Carbohydrate 9g (Dietary Fiber 2g); Protein 16g

TiP **TO SAVE TIME,** purchase fresh mushrooms that are already sliced.

TiP **SESAME OIL** is an Asian oil with a strong flavor and fragrance. It's usually with the Asian foods, but if you can't find it, you can substitute vegetable oil. Also, if you don't have rice or white wine vinegar, regular white vinegar will do.

Cutting Grain of Meat

The "grain" of meat refers to the muscle fibers that run the length of a cut of meat. Cut with the grain into 2-inch strips, then cut across the grain into 1/8-inch slices.

Preparing Gingerroot

Peel gingerroot with a paring knife, cut into thin slices and chop finely.

Spicy Beef Salad

ITALIAN BEEF KABOBS

MAKES 2 servings • REFRIGERATE: 1 hour • BROIL: 8 minutes

INGREDIENTS

ESSENTIAL EQUIPMENT: *four 10-inch metal or bamboo skewers; broiler pan with rack*

3/4 pound beef bone-in sirloin or round steak, 1 inch thick

2 cloves garlic

1/4 cup balsamic vinegar

1/4 cup water

1 tablespoon chopped fresh or 1 teaspoon dried oregano leaves

2 tablespoons olive or vegetable oil

1 1/2 teaspoons chopped fresh or 1/2 teaspoon dried marjoram leaves

1 teaspoon sugar

DIRECTIONS

1 Cut and discard most of the fat and the bone from the beef. Cut beef into 1-inch pieces.

2 Peel and finely chop the garlic. Make a marinade by mixing the vinegar, water, oregano, oil, marjoram, sugar and garlic in a medium glass or plastic bowl. Stir in the beef until coated. Cover and refrigerate, stirring occasionally, at least 1 hour but no longer than 12 hours. If you are using bamboo skewers, soak them in water 30 minutes before using to prevent burning.

3 You may need to move the oven rack so it is near the broiler. Set the oven control to broil.

4 Remove the beef from the marinade, reserving the marinade. Thread the beef on the skewers, leaving a 1/2-inch space between each piece. Brush the kabobs with the marinade.

5 Place the kabobs on the rack in the broiler pan. Broil kabobs with tops about 3 inches from heat 6 to 8 minutes for medium-rare to medium doneness, turning and brushing with marinade after 3 minutes. Discard any remaining marinade.

1 SERVING: Calories 195 (Calories from Fat 70); Fat 8g (Saturated 2g); Cholesterol 80mg; Sodium 60mg; Carbohydrate 1g (Dietary Fiber 0g); Protein 30g

TiP TO SAVE TIME, omit the garlic, vinegar, water, oregano, oil, marjoram and sugar, and instead, marinate the beef in 2/3 cup purchased Italian dressing in step 2.

✔**ALTHOUGH YOU MIGHT BE TEMPTED** to serve the extra marinade with the cooked kabobs, you should discard any marinade that has been in contact with raw meat. Bacteria from the raw meat could transfer to the marinade.

Broiling

The distance from the heat to the food is important. If the food is too close to the heat, it will burn.

Italian Beef Kabobs

BEEF STEW

MAKES 4 servings • COOK: 3 hours 20 minutes

INGREDIENTS

ESSENTIAL EQUIPMENT: *12-inch skillet or Dutch oven (about 4-quart size)*

1 pound beef boneless chuck, tip or round roast

1 tablespoon vegetable oil or shortening

3 cups water

1/2 teaspoon salt

1/8 teaspoon pepper

2 medium carrots

1 large potato

1 medium green bell pepper

1 medium stalk celery

1 small onion

1 teaspoon salt

1 dried bay leaf

1/2 cup cold water

2 tablespoons all-purpose flour

DIRECTIONS

1 Cut and discard most of the fat from the beef. Cut the beef into 1-inch cubes.

2 Heat the oil in the skillet over medium heat 1 to 2 minutes. Cook the beef in the oil about 15 minutes, stirring occasionally, until brown on all sides.

3 Remove the skillet from the heat, then add the water, 1/2 teaspoon salt and the pepper. Heat to boiling over high heat. Once mixture is boiling, reduce heat just enough so mixture bubbles gently. Cover and cook 2 to 2 1/2 hours or until beef is almost tender.

4 Peel the carrots, and cut into 1-inch pieces. Scrub the potato thoroughly with a vegetable brush, but do not peel. Cut the potato into 1 1/2-inch pieces. Cut the bell pepper lengthwise in half, and cut out seeds and membrane. Cut the bell pepper into 1-inch pieces. Cut the celery into 1-inch pieces. Peel and chop the onion; cut in half.

5 Stir the vegetables, 1 teaspoon salt and bay leaf into the beef mixture. Cover and cook about 30 minutes or until vegetables are tender when pierced with a fork. Remove and discard bay leaf.

6 Shake the cold water and flour in a tightly covered jar or container. Gradually stir this mixture into beef mixture. Heat to boiling over high heat, stirring constantly. Continue boiling 1 minute, stirring constantly, until thickened.

1 SERVING: Calories 310 (Calories from Fat 145); Fat 16g (Saturated 5g); Cholesterol 65mg; Sodium 950mg; Carbohydrate 21g (Dietary Fiber 3g); Protein 24g

TiP TO SAVE TIME, use a 16-ounce bag of frozen mixed vegetables instead of the carrots, potato, bell pepper, celery and onion. There's no need to thaw the vegetables; just stir them into the beef mixture in step 5.

TiP TO SAVE TIME, cut up the vegetables about 1 hour in advance, putting the potato pieces in cold water to keep them from turning brown.

Browning the Beef

Cook the beef in the oil about 15 minutes, stirring occasionally, until brown on all sides. Browning helps develop the flavor of the stew.

Beef Stew

NEW ENGLAND POT ROAST

MAKES 4 servings • COOK: 3 hours

INGREDIENTS

ESSENTIAL EQUIPMENT: *Dutch oven (about 4-quart size) or 12-inch skillet*

2- to 2 1/2-pound beef arm, blade or cross rib pot roast

3/4 teaspoon salt

1/2 teaspoon pepper

1/2 cup prepared horseradish

1/2 cup water

8 small potatoes

6 medium carrots

4 small onions

Pot Roast Gravy (below)

POT ROAST GRAVY

Water

1/4 cup cold water

2 tablespoons all-purpose flour

DIRECTIONS

1 Place the pot roast in the room-temperature Dutch oven. Cook over medium heat, turning about every 6 minutes, until all sides are brown. Browning is important because it helps develop the rich flavor of the roast. If the roast sticks to the Dutch oven, loosen it carefully with a fork or turner. Remove the Dutch oven from the heat.

2 Sprinkle the salt and pepper over the roast. Spread the horseradish on top of the roast. Pour the water into the Dutch oven along the side of the roast, leaving the horseradish on top. Heat to boiling over high heat. Once water is boiling, reduce heat just enough so water bubbles gently. Cover and cook 2 hours. If more water is needed to keep the Dutch oven from becoming dry, add it 2 tablespoons at a time.

3 After the roast has been cooking for 1 1/2 hours, scrub the potatoes thoroughly with a vegetable brush, but do not peel. Cut each potato in half. Peel the carrots, and cut each into 4 equal lengths. Peel the onions and cut each in half. Add the potatoes, carrots and onions to the Dutch oven. Cover and cook about 1 hour or until the roast and vegetables are tender when pierced with a fork. Vegetables that are in the cooking liquid will cook more quickly, so you may want to move some of the vegetables from the top of the roast into the liquid to cook all uniformly.

4 Remove the roast and vegetables to a warm ovenproof platter or pan; keep warm by covering with aluminum foil or placing in oven with the temperature set at 200° or lower for no longer than 10 minutes. Prepare Pot Roast Gravy.

5 While keeping the gravy warm over low heat, cut the roast into 1/4-inch slices. Serve with the gravy and vegetables.

POT ROAST GRAVY Gravy is easy if you measure the water and flour accurately. Remove all but about 1 tablespoon of fat from the Dutch oven by skimming off the liquid with a large spoon and discarding the fat. Add enough water to the liquid to measure 1 cup. Shake 1/4 cup water and the flour in a tightly covered jar. Gradually stir this mixture into the liquid. Heat to boiling over high heat, stirring constantly. Continue boiling 1 minute, stirring constantly, until thickened.

1 SERVING: Calories 555 (Calories from Fat 190); Fat 21g (Saturated 8g); Cholesterol 90mg; Sodium 590mg; Carbohydrate 66g (Dietary Fiber 9g); Protein 35g

TiP CUT LEFTOVER COLD POT ROAST into slices, for a hearty sandwich.

TiP LOOK FOR PREPARED HORSERADISH in glass jars in the condiment section of your supermarket.

Browning the Pot Roast

Start the pot roast in a room-temperature Dutch oven. If it sticks during browning, loosen carefully with a fork or turner.

Making Pot Roast Gravy

Remove excess fat from the liquid; keep 1 tablespoon. Heat the liquid and flour-water mixture to boiling, then boil and stir 1 minute.

New England Pot Roast

SUCCULENT PORK CHOPS—THREE WAYS

BROILING, GRILLING AND PANFRYING

Loin or Rib Chop

Loin Chop, boneless

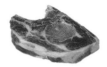

Blade Chop

Fresh, lean pork should be grayish pink in color and fine grained in texture.

BROILING OR GRILLING PORK CHOPS

1 Select pork chop from those shown in the photos.

2 To Broil: You may need to move the oven rack so it is 5 to 6 inches below the broiler. Set the oven control to broil.

To Grill: Prepare the coals or a gas grill for direct heat (pages 236–237). Heat to medium heat, which will take about 40 minutes for charcoal or about 10 minutes for a gas grill.

3 To Broil: Place pork chop on the rack in a broiler pan. (For easy cleanup, line the bottom of the broiler pan with aluminum foil before placing pork on rack.) Place in oven with the top of the pork chop the number of inches from heat listed in the chart.

To Grill: Place pork chop on the grill the number of inches from heat listed in the chart.

4 Broil or **Grill** uncovered for about half the time listed in the chart or until pork chop is brown on one side.

5 Turn the pork chop and continue cooking until the doneness listed in the chart.* To check doneness, cut a small slit in the center of boneless cuts or in the center near the bone of bone-in cuts. Medium pork is slightly pink in center. Well-done pork is no longer pink in center. Or insert a meat thermometer in the center of the pork chop to check for desired doneness. Sprinkle salt and pepper over both sides of pork chop after cooking if desired. Serve immediately.

Well-done pork, although a little less juicy, is recommended for some cuts because the pork will be more flavorful.

TIMETABLE FOR BROILING OR GRILLING PORK CHOPS

Pork Cut	Approximate Thickness	Inches from Heat	Approximate Doneness	Approximate Total Broiling Time in Minutes	Total Grilling Time in Minutes
Loin or Rib Chops (bone-in)	3/4 inch	3 to 4	160° (medium)	8 to 11	6 to 8
	1 1/2 inches	3 to 4	160° (medium)	19 to 22	12 to 16

Pork Cut	Approximate Thickness	Inches from Heat	Approximate Doneness	Approximate Total Broiling Time in Minutes	Total Grilling Time in Minutes
Loin Chop (boneless)	1 inch	3 to 4	160° (medium)	11 to 13	8 to 10
Blade Chop (bone-in)	3/4 inch	3 to 4	170° (well)	13 to 15	11 to 13
	1 1/2 inches	3 to 4	170° (well)	26 to 29	19 to 22

PANFRYING PORK CHOPS

1 Select pork chop from those shown in the photos.

2 If the pork is very lean and has little fat, coat a heavy skillet or frying pan with a small amount of vegetable oil, or spray it with cooking spray. Or use a nonstick skillet.

3 Heat the skillet over medium heat 1 to 2 minutes.

4 Place the pork chop in the hot skillet. You do not need to add oil or water or cover the skillet; covering will cause the pork chop to be steamed rather than panfried.

5 Cook for the time listed in the chart, turning pork chop occasionally. If the pork chop has extra fat on it, fat may accumulate in the skillet; remove this fat with a spoon as it accumulates. Cook until brown on both sides and the doneness listed in chart.* To check doneness, cut a small slit in the center of boneless cuts or in the center near the bone of bone-in cuts. Medium pork is slightly pink in center. Well-done pork is no longer pink in center. Or insert a meat thermometer in the center of the pork chop to check for desired doneness. Sprinkle salt and pepper over both sides of pork chop after cooking if desired. Serve immediately.

Well-done pork, although a little less juicy, is recommended for some cuts because the pork will be more flavorful.

 ## TIMETABLE FOR PANFRYING PORK CHOPS

Pork Cut	Thickness in Inches	Pork Doneness	Approximate Total Cooking Time in Minutes
Loin or Rib Chops (bone-in)	1/2	160° (medium)	7 to 8
	1	160° (medium)	12 to 14
Loin Chops (boneless)	1/2	160° (medium)	7 to 8
	1	160° (medium)	10 to 12

PORK CHOPS AND APPLES

MAKES 2 servings • **BAKE: 45 minutes**

INGREDIENTS

ESSENTIAL EQUIPMENT: *1 1/2-quart casserole; small non-stick skillet (8- or 10-inch size)*

1 medium apple, such as Granny Smith, Wealthy or Rome Beauty

2 tablespoons packed brown sugar

1/4 teaspoon ground cinnamon

2 pork rib chops, 1/2 to 3/4 inch thick (about 1/4 pound each)

Cooking spray

DIRECTIONS

1 Heat the oven to 350°.

2 Cut the apple into fourths, and remove the seeds. Cut each fourth into 3 or 4 wedges. Place apple wedges in the casserole. Sprinkle the brown sugar and cinnamon over the apples.

3 Cut and discard most of the fat from the pork chops. Spray the skillet with cooking spray, and heat over medium heat 1 to 2 minutes. Cook pork chops in hot skillet about 5 minutes, turning once, until light brown.

4 Place the pork chops in a single layer on the apple wedges. Cover with lid or aluminum foil and bake about 45 minutes or until pork is slightly pink when you cut into the center and apples are tender when pierced with a fork.

1 SERVING: Calories 200 (Calories from Fat 55); Fat 6g (Saturated 2g); Cholesterol 45mg; Sodium 30mg; Carbohydrate 24g (Dietary Fiber 2g); Protein 15g

TiP SERVE WITH baked Acorn Squash (page 165) and a green salad with Honey-Dijon Dressing (page 148).

TiP FOLLOW COOK TIMES for pork carefully. Today's pork is lean and requires shorter cooking times. Overcooking pork will make it tough.

Cutting Fat from Pork Chop

Use a sharp knife to cut most of the fat from pork chop, being careful not to cut into the meat.

Slicing Apple

Cut apple into fourths, and remove seeds. Cut each fourth into wedges.

Pork Chops and Apples

ORANGE-GLAZED PORK CHOPS

MAKES 4 servings • COOK: 15 minutes

INGREDIENTS

ESSENTIAL EQUIPMENT: *10-inch skillet*

4 pork loin or rib chops, about 1/2 inch thick (about 1 1/4 pounds total)

Cooking spray

1/4 teaspoon salt

1/8 teaspoon pepper

1/2 cup orange juice

1/4 cup dry white wine or chicken broth

1 tablespoon chopped fresh or 1/2 teaspoon dried tarragon leaves

1 tablespoon cornstarch

2 tablespoons water

DIRECTIONS

1 Cut and discard most of the fat from the pork chops. Spray the room-temperature skillet with cooking spray, and heat over medium heat 1 to 2 minutes. Sprinkle salt and pepper over both sides of pork chops. Cook pork chops in hot skillet about 5 minutes, turning once, until light brown. Remove the skillet from the heat.

2 Add the orange juice, wine and tarragon to the skillet. Heat to boiling over high heat. Once mixture is boiling, reduce heat just enough so mixture bubbles gently. Cover and cook 10 to 15 minutes, stirring occasionally, until pork is slightly pink when you cut a small slit near the bone.

3 While the pork chops are cooking, mix the cornstarch and water.

4 When the pork chops are done, remove from the skillet to a serving platter. Cover with aluminum foil or lid to keep warm. Stir cornstarch mixture into orange juice mixture in skillet. Cook over medium heat, stirring constantly, until mixture thickens and boils. Continue boiling 1 minute, stirring constantly. Pour over pork chops.

1 SERVING: Calories 180 (Calories from Fat 70); Fat 8g (Saturated 3g); Cholesterol 65mg; Sodium 190mg; Carbohydrate 5g (Dietary Fiber 0g); Protein 22g

TiP **SERVE WITH** roasted sweet potatoes: Scrub fresh medium sweet potato with a vegetable brush, and pierce with fork or knife. Bake at 350° about 1 hour or until tender when pierced with a fork. Serve with butter.

TiP **FOR RECIPE SUCCESS,** stir the cornstarch mixture constantly while you are heating it; otherwise, the consistency will be lumpy and uneven.

Thickening the Glaze

Stir cornstarch mixture into skillet. Cook over medium heat, stirring constantly, until mixture thickens and boils.

Checking Pork for Doneness

Cut a small slit in the center near the bone of the pork chop. The meat should be just slightly pink.

Orange-Glazed Pork Chops

STIR-FRIED BROCCOLI AND PORK

MAKES 4 servings · REFRIGERATE: 20 minutes · COOK: 10 minutes

INGREDIENTS

ESSENTIAL EQUIPMENT: *2-quart saucepan; 12-inch skillet or wok*

1 pound pork boneless loin or leg

1 clove garlic

2 small onions

1 can (8 ounces) whole water chestnuts

1 tablespoon soy sauce

2 teaspoons cornstarch

1/2 teaspoon ground red pepper (cayenne)

Hot Cooked Rice (below)

2 tablespoons vegetable oil

3 cups broccoli flowerets or 1 bag (16 ounces) frozen broccoli cuts, thawed

1/4 cup chicken broth

1/2 cup peanuts

HOT COOKED RICE

1 cup uncooked regular long-grain white rice

2 cups water

DIRECTIONS

1 Cut and discard most of the fat from the pork. Cut pork into 2×1×1/8-inch slices. Peel and finely chop the garlic. Peel the onions, and cut each into 8 pieces; set aside. Drain the water chestnuts in a strainer.

2 To make a marinade, mix the garlic, soy sauce, cornstarch and red pepper in a glass or plastic bowl. Stir in pork. Cover and refrigerate 20 minutes.

3 While the pork is marinating, prepare Hot Cooked Rice.

4 About 10 minutes before rice is done, heat the skillet over high heat 1 to 2 minutes. Add the oil to the hot skillet, then the pork. Stir-fry with a turner or large spoon 5 to 6 minutes, lifting and stirring constantly, until pork is no longer pink.

5 Add the onions, broccoli and water chestnuts to pork mixture. Stir-fry 2 minutes.

6 Stir in the broth, and heat to boiling over high heat. Stir in the peanuts. Serve pork mixture with rice.

HOT COOKED RICE Heat the rice and water to boiling in the saucepan over high heat, stirring occasionally to prevent sticking. Once mixture is boiling, reduce heat just enough so mixture bubbles gently. Cover and cook about 15 minutes or until rice is fluffy and tender.

1 SERVING: Calories 570 (Calories from Fat 225); Fat 25g (Saturated 5g); Cholesterol 70mg; Sodium 200mg; Carbohydrate 56g (Dietary Fiber 5g); Protein 35g

TiP **SAVE A FEW MINUTES** by buying broccoli at the salad bar. It's already cut up, and you can buy only what you need.

TiP **FOR MORE FLAVOR AND VARIETY,** substitute fried rice from the deli or frozen food case for the Hot Cooked Rice.

Marinating Pork

For easier marinating, use a resealable plastic bag. The bag makes it much easier to turn the pork to coat all sides.

Stir-Frying Pork

Because stir-frying is done over high heat, you must constantly lift and turn the pork to prevent scorching and to cook evenly.

Stir-Fried Broccoli and Pork

TERIYAKI PORK TENDERLOIN

MAKES 3 servings • REFRIGERATE: 1 hour • BAKE: 30 minutes

INGREDIENTS

DIRECTIONS

ESSENTIAL EQUIPMENT: *baking pan, such as 8-inch square or 11×7-inch rectangle*

1 clove garlic

2 tablespoons soy sauce

1 tablespoon water

1 teaspoon packed brown sugar

2 teaspoons lemon juice

2 teaspoons vegetable oil

1/8 teaspoon coarsely ground pepper

1 pork tenderloin (about 3/4 pound)

Cooking spray

1 Peel and finely chop the garlic. To make a teriyaki marinade, mix the garlic, soy sauce, water, brown sugar, lemon juice, oil and pepper in a shallow glass or plastic dish. Add pork, and turn to coat with marinade. Cover and refrigerate, turning occasionally, at least 1 hour but no longer than 24 hours.

2 Heat the oven to 425°. Spray the baking pan with cooking spray. Remove the pork from the marinade, and discard marinade. Place pork in the sprayed pan.

3 Bake uncovered 27 to 30 minutes or until meat thermometer inserted in thickest part of pork reads 160° or pork is slightly pink when you cut into the center. Cut pork crosswise into thin slices.

1 SERVING: Calories 155 (Calories from Fat 45); Fat 5g (Saturated 2g); Cholesterol 70mg; Sodium 220mg; Carbohydrate 1g (Dietary Fiber 0g); Protein 26g

✔**FOR FOOD SAFETY,** be sure to use a glass or plastic dish to marinate the pork. Acidic ingredients such as lemon juice can react with a metal pan, causing discoloration of the pan and an off flavor. You also can use a tightly sealed plastic bag for marinating.

TiP **SERVE WITH** Garlic Mashed Potatoes (page 167) and Brown Sugar-Glazed Carrots (page 85) for an impressive and quick dinner.

Slicing Pork

Use a sharp knife to cut pork crosswise into thin slices.

Teriyaki Pork Tenderloin, Garlic Mashed Potatoes, Brown Sugar-Glazed Carrots

PORK TENDERLOIN WITH ROSEMARY

MAKES 3 servings • BAKE: 30 minutes

INGREDIENTS

ESSENTIAL EQUIPMENT: *baking pan, such as 8-inch square or 11×7-inch rectangle*

Cooking spray

1 clove garlic

1/4 teaspoon salt

1/8 teaspoon pepper

1 pork tenderloin (about 3/4 pound)

1 1/2 teaspoon finely chopped rosemary or 1/2 teaspoon dried rosemary leaves, crumbled

DIRECTIONS

1 Heat the oven to 425°. Spray the baking pan with cooking spray.

2 Peel and crush the garlic. Sprinkle salt and pepper over all sides of the pork tenderloin. Rub rosemary and garlic on all sides of pork. Place pork in the sprayed pan.

3 Bake uncovered 27 to 30 minutes or until meat thermometer inserted in thickest part of pork reads 160° or pork is slightly pink when you cut into the center. Cut pork crosswise into thin slices.

1 SERVING: Calories 140 (Calories from Fat 35); Fat 4g (Saturated 2g); Cholesterol 70mg; Sodium 100mg; Carbohydrate 0g (Dietary Fiber 0g); Protein 26g

TiP SERVE WITH Stir-Fried Green Beans and Pepper (page 180), which you can easily prepare while the pork is baking.

Crushing Garlic

Garlic can be crushed in a special tool, called a garlic press, or by pressing with the side of a knife or mallet to break into small pieces.

Crumbling Rosemary Leaves

When using dried rosemary, crumble the herbs in the palm of your hand to release more flavor before rubbing them onto the pork.

Pork Tenderloin with Rosemary, Stir-Fried Green Beans and Pepper

Barbecued Ribs

MAKES 6 servings • BAKE: 1 hour 45 minutes

INGREDIENTS

Essential Equipment: *shallow roasting pan (about 13 × 9-inch rectangle); 1-quart saucepan or 1 cup microwavable measuring cup*

4 1/2 pounds pork spareribs

Spicy Barbecue Sauce (below)

Spicy Barbecue Sauce

1/3 cup margarine or butter

2 tablespoons white vinegar

2 tablespoons water

1 teaspoon sugar

1/2 teaspoon garlic powder

1/2 teaspoon onion powder

1/2 teaspoon pepper

Dash of ground red pepper (cayenne)

DIRECTIONS

1 Heat the oven to 325°.

2 Cut the ribs into 6 serving pieces. Place the ribs, meaty sides up, in the roasting pan.

3 Bake uncovered 1 hour. While the ribs are baking, prepare Spicy Barbecue Sauce.

4 Brush the sauce over the ribs. Bake uncovered about 45 minutes longer, brushing frequently with sauce, until tender.

SPICY BARBECUE SAUCE Heat all ingredients in the saucepan over medium heat, stirring frequently, until margarine is melted. Or microwave all ingredients in a 1-cup microwavable measuring cup on high about 30 seconds or until margarine is melted.

1 SERVING: Calories 615 (Calories from Fat 450); Fat 50g (Saturated 17g); Cholesterol 160mg; Sodium 240mg; Carbohydrate 2g (Dietary Fiber 0g); Protein 39g

COUNTRY-STYLE SAUCY RIBS: Use 3 pounds pork country-style ribs. Cut the ribs into 6 serving pieces. Place in 13 × 9-inch rectangular pan. Cover with aluminum foil and bake at 325° for 2 hours; drain. Pour Spicy Barbecue Sauce over the ribs. Bake uncovered about 30 minutes longer or until tender.

TiP **SERVE WITH** Creamy Coleslaw (page 150) and crusty rolls from your favorite bakery.

TiP **TO SERVE SAUCE WITH RIBS,** heat any remaining sauce to boiling, stirring constantly. Continue boiling 1 minute, stirring constantly.

Cutting Ribs

Using a sharp knife or kitchen scissors, cut pork ribs into serving-size pieces.

Brushing on Sauce

Coat the ribs liberally with sauce, using a pastry brush. Turn ribs with tongs, and brush the other side.

Barbecued Ribs

GLAZED BAKED HAM

INGREDIENTS

ESSENTIAL EQUIPMENT: *shallow roasting pan (about 13×9-inch rectangle), and rack*

BROWN-SUGAR GLAZE

1/2 cup packed brown sugar

2 tablespoons orange or pineapple juice

1/2 teaspoon ground mustard (dry)

TiP FOR EASY CLEANUP, line bottom of roasting pan with aluminum foil before placing ham on rack.

TiP FOR MORE FLAVOR, use dark brown sugar instead of light.

DIRECTIONS

1 Select a fully cooked ham from those listed in Timetable for Roasting Ham (right). Allow about 1/3 pound ham per person, slightly less for a boneless ham and slightly more for ham with a bone.

2 Place the ham, fat side up, on a rack in the roasting pan. The rack keeps the ham out of the drippings and prevents scorching. It is not necessary to brush the ham with pan drippings while it bakes.

3 Insert a meat thermometer so the tip is in the thickest part of the ham and does not touch bone or rest in fat.

4 Bake uncovered in 325° oven for the time listed in the chart. It is not necessary to preheat the oven. While the ham is baking, prepare Brown Sugar Glaze (below).

5 Remove the ham from the oven 30 minutes before it is done. Remove any skin from the ham. Make cuts about 1/2 inch apart in a diamond pattern in the fat surface of the ham, not into the meat. Insert a whole clove in the corner of each diamond if desired. Pat or spoon glaze over the ham.

6 Bake uncovered about 30 minutes longer or until thermometer reads 135°. Cover the ham with a tent of aluminum foil and let stand 15 to 20 minutes or until thermometer reads 140°. (Temperature will continue to rise about 5° and roast will be easier to carve as juices set up.)

BROWN-SUGAR GLAZE Mix all ingredients. Makes enough for a 4- to 8-pound ham.

1 SERVING. Calories 240 (Calories from Fat 110); Fat 12g (Saturated 4g); Cholesterol 75mg; Sodium 1930mg; Carbohydrate 4g (Dietary Fiber 0g); Protein 29g

Cutting Diamond Pattern in Ham

Make cuts about 1/2 inch apart and 1/4 inch deep in diamond pattern in fat surface of ham, not into the meat.

Carving Ham

Place ham, fat side up and bone to your right, on carving board. Cut a few slices from thin side. Turn ham cut side down, so it rests firmly. Make vertical slices down to the leg bone, then cut horizontally along bone to release slices.

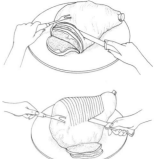

TIMETABLE FOR ROASTING HAM

Fully Cooked Smoked Ham	Oven Temperature	Approximate Weight in Pounds	Approximate Cooking Time in Minutes per Pound
Boneless Ham	325°	1 1/2 to 2	29 to 33
		3 to 4	19 to 23
		6 to 8	16 to 20
		9 to 11	12 to 16
Bone-in Ham	325°	6 to 8	13 to 17
		14 to 16	11 to 14

Glazed Baked Ham

POULTRY AND SEAFOOD MAIN DISHES

Fast and Flavorful Chicken Breasts—Three Ways

BROILING, GRILLING AND PANFRYING

Broiling or Grilling Chicken Breasts

1 Select skinless, boneless chicken breast halves (about 1/4 pound each) or skinless bone-in chicken breast halves (about 1/2 pound each). If the chicken is frozen, place it in the refrigerator the night before you plan to use it or for at least 12 hours. Cut and discard fat from chicken with kitchen scissors or knife. Rinse chicken under cold water, and pat dry with paper towels.

2 To Broil: You may need to move the oven rack so it is 5 to 7 inches below the broiler. Brush the rack of broiler pan with vegetable oil, or spray it with cooking spray. Set the oven control to broil.

To Grill: Brush the grill rack with vegetable oil, or spray it with cooking spray. Prepare the coals or a gas grill for direct heat (pages 236–237). Heat to medium heat, which will take about 40 minutes for charcoal or about 10 minutes for a gas grill.

3 To Broil: Place the chicken breast on the rack in a broiler pan.

To Grill: Place the chicken breast on the grill 4 to 6 inches from heat.

4 Broil or **Grill** uncovered for the time listed in the chart, turning frequently with tongs. If desired, brush the chicken breasts with prepared barbecue or teriyaki sauce from your supermarket during the last 15 to 20 minutes for bone-in chicken or the last 10 minutes for boneless chicken.

Cutting Fat from Chicken

Cut fat from chicken with kitchen scissors or knife.

Rinsing Chicken

Rinse chicken under cold water; pat dry with paper towels.

TIMETABLE FOR BROILING AND GRILLING CHICKEN BREASTS

Cut of Chicken	Approximate Broiling Time	Approximate Grilling Time	Doneness
Breast halves (bone in)	25 to 35 minutes, turning once (7 to 9 inches from heat)	20 to 25 minutes	Cook until juice of chicken is no longer pink when centers of thickest pieces are cut.
Breast halves (boneless)	15 to 20 minutes, turning once (4 to 6 inches from heat)	15 to 20 minutes	Cook until juice of chicken is no longer pink when centers of thickest pieces are cut.

PANFRYING CHICKEN BREASTS

1 Select skinless, boneless chicken breast halves (about 1/4 pound each) or skinless, bone-in chicken breast halves (about 1/2 pound each). If the chicken is frozen, place it in the refrigerator the night before you plan to use it or for at least 12 hours. Cut and discard fat from chicken with kitchen scissors or knife. Rinse chicken under cold water, and pat dry with paper towels.

2 Heat 1 teaspoon vegetable oil in a 8-inch nonstick skillet over medium heat 1 to 2 minutes. If you are preparing 3 to 4 chicken breast halves, use a 10- or 12-inch skillet. Add the chicken.

3 Cook 8 to 10 minutes, turning chicken over once with tongs, until outside of chicken is golden brown and the juice is no longer pink when you cut into the center of the thickest piece. Larger chicken breast halves may take 2 to 3 minutes longer. If desired, sprinkle with salt, pepper and paprika.

TiP **FOR MORE FLAVOR,** chicken breasts can be marinated before broiling, grilling or panfrying. A wide array of marinades are available in your supermarket, or you may wish to make your own. Allow about 1/4 to 1/2 cup marinade for each 1 to 2 pounds of chicken. Marinate chicken covered in the refrigerator for 15 minutes to 2 hours.

Chicken Breasts with Orange Glaze

MAKES 2 servings • COOK: 25 minutes

INGREDIENTS

ESSENTIAL EQUIPMENT: *8-inch skillet or 3-quart saucepan*

2 skinless, boneless chicken breast halves (about 1/4 pound each)

1 tablespoon margarine or butter

1/2 teaspoon cornstarch

1/4 teaspoon ground mustard (dry)

1/4 cup orange juice

2 tablespoons orange marmalade

1 tablespoon soy sauce

DIRECTIONS

1 If the chicken is frozen, place it in the refrigerator the night before you plan to use it or for at least 12 hours. Cut and discard fat from chicken with kitchen scissors or knife. Rinse chicken under cold water, and pat dry with paper towels.

2 Melt the margarine in the skillet over medium heat. Cook chicken in margarine about 15 minutes, turning chicken over once with tongs, until juice of chicken is no longer pink when you cut into the center of the thickest piece.

3 While the chicken is cooking, mix the cornstarch and mustard in a small bowl. Stir in the orange juice, orange marmalade and soy sauce, mixing well.

4 Place the chicken on a serving plate, and cover with aluminum foil or a pan lid to keep it warm. Discard any juices left in the skillet.

5 To make the glaze, pour the orange mixture into the same skillet. Heat to boiling over medium heat, stirring constantly. Continue boiling about 1 minute, stirring constantly, until the sauce is thickened. Pour the glaze over chicken on serving plate.

1 SERVING: Calories 255 (Calories from Fat 80); Fat 9g (Saturated 2g); Cholesterol 65mg; Sodium 650mg; Carbohydrate 17g (Dietary Fiber 0g); Protein 27g

TiP **YOU CAN SUBSTITUTE** apricot, peach or pineapple preserves for the orange marmalade in the glaze.

✔**PREVENT POULTRY FROM** contaminating any foods in your grocery cart by putting it in plastic bags and placing it in the cart so that juices do not drip on other foods.

Making Orange Glaze

For smooth orange glaze, heat to boiling, stirring constantly. Boil and stir 1 minute.

Chicken Breasts with Orange Glaze

PARMESAN-DIJON CHICKEN

MAKES 6 servings • BAKE: 30 minutes

INGREDIENTS

ESSENTIAL EQUIPMENT: *shallow microwavable dish or pie pan; rectangular pan (about 13×9 inches)*

6 skinless, boneless chicken breast halves (about 1/4 pound each)

1/4 cup (1/2 stick) margarine or butter

3/4 cup dry bread crumbs

1/4 cup grated Parmesan cheese

2 tablespoons Dijon mustard

DIRECTIONS

1 If the chicken is frozen, place it in the refrigerator the night before you plan to use it or for at least 12 hours. Cut and discard fat from chicken with kitchen scissors or knife. Rinse chicken under cold water, and pat dry with paper towels.

2 Heat the oven to 375°. Either place the margarine in the shallow microwavable dish and microwave uncovered on High about 15 seconds until melted, or place the margarine in a pie pan and place in the oven about 1 minute until melted.

3 Mix the bread crumbs and cheese in a large plastic bag. Stir the mustard into the melted margarine until well mixed.

4 Dip the chicken, one piece at a time, into the margarine mixture, coating all sides. Then place in the bag of crumbs, seal the bag and shake to coat with crumb mixture. Place the chicken in a single layer in the ungreased rectangular pan.

5 Bake uncovered 20 to 30 minutes, turning chicken over once with tongs, until juice of chicken is no longer pink when you cut into the center of the thickest pieces. If chicken sticks to the pan during baking, loosen it gently with a turner or fork.

1 SERVING: Calories 275 (Calories from Fat 115); Fat 13g (Saturated 3g); Cholesterol 70mg; Sodium 390mg; Carbohydrate 10g (Dietary Fiber 0g); Protein 30g

TiP **FOR RECIPE SUCCESS,** pat rinsed chicken until it's very dry before dipping it into the margarine mixture, or the coating will not adhere.

TiP **SERVE WITH** Twice-Baked Potatoes (page 170), which can bake at the same time as the chicken. Put the potatoes in the oven before you begin preparing the chicken.

Making Dry Bread Crumbs

Place 4 pieces of bread on a cookie sheet and heat in a 200° oven about 20 minutes or until dry; cool. Crush into crumbs with a rolling pin or clean bottle.

Coating Chicken

Dip chicken into margarine mixture, then shake in bag of crumb coating.

Parmesan-Dijon Chicken, Twice-Baked Potatoes

RANCH CHICKEN

MAKES 4 servings • **COOK: 15 minutes**

INGREDIENTS

ESSENTIAL EQUIPMENT: *shallow bowl or pie pan; 10- or 12-inch nonstick skillet*

4 skinless, boneless chicken breast halves (about 1/4 pound each)

1/4 cup ranch dressing

1/3 cup seasoned dry bread crumbs

2 tablespoons olive or vegetable oil

TiP **YOU CAN USE** reduced-fat ranch dressing in this recipe.

DIRECTIONS

1 If the chicken is frozen, place it in the refrigerator the night before you plan to use it or for at least 12 hours. Cut and discard fat from chicken with kitchen scissors or knife. Rinse chicken under cold water, and pat dry with paper towels.

2 Pour the dressing into the shallow bowl or pie pan. Place the bread crumbs on waxed paper or a plate.

3 Dip the chicken, one piece at a time, into the dressing, coating all sides. Then coat all sides with bread crumbs.

4 Heat the oil in the skillet over medium-high heat 1 to 2 minutes. Cook chicken in oil 12 to 15 minutes, turning chicken over once with tongs, until outside is golden brown and the juice is no longer pink when you cut into the center of the thickest pieces. If the chicken sticks to the pan, loosen it gently with a turner or fork.

1 SERVING: Calories 290 (Calories from Fat 145); Fat 16g (Saturated 3g); Cholesterol 70mg; Sodium 260mg; Carbohydrate 8g (Dietary Fiber 0g); Protein 28g

TiP **SERVE WITH** a big bowl of cooked pasta sprinkled with olive oil, grated Parmesan cheese and chopped fresh oregano. Round out the meal with a marinated-vegetable salad from the deli.

Selecting Chicken

When you select packaged chicken, buy trays or bags that have very little or no liquid in the bottom. Avoid torn and leaking packages.

Thawing Chicken in the Microwave

Uncooked frozen chicken can be thawed in the microwave oven, following the microwave manufacturer's directions.

Ranch Chicken

CREAMY CHICKEN AND DUMPLINGS

MAKES 4 servings • COOK: 30 minutes

INGREDIENTS

DIRECTIONS

ESSENTIAL EQUIPMENT: *Dutch oven (about 4-quart size) or 3-quart saucepan*

1 pound skinless, boneless chicken breast halves

1 tablespoon vegetable oil

1 3/4 cups water

1 cup milk

1 envelope (about 1 ounce) chicken gravy mix

2 teaspoons chopped fresh or 3/4 teaspoon dried marjoram leaves

1/2 teaspoon salt

1 bag (16 ounces) frozen broccoli, cauliflower and carrots

Dumplings (below)

DUMPLINGS

1 2/3 cups Bisquick® Original baking mix

1/2 cup milk

1 If the chicken is frozen, place it in the refrigerator the night before you plan to use it or for at least 12 hours. Cut and discard fat from chicken with kitchen scissors or knife. Rinse chicken under cold water, and pat dry with paper towels. Cut chicken into 1-inch pieces.

2 Heat the oil in the Dutch oven over medium heat. Cook chicken in oil 5 to 7 minutes, stirring frequently, until golden brown. Remove the Dutch oven from the heat.

3 Stir in the water, milk, gravy mix (dry), marjoram, salt and frozen vegetables. Although thawing the vegetables is not necessary, stir them into the chicken mixture to allow them to cook uniformly.

4 Heat chicken mixture to boiling over high heat. Once mixture is boiling, reduce heat just enough so mixture bubbles gently.

5 Prepare Dumplings. With the chicken mixture boiling gently with bubbles breaking the surface continually, drop the dumpling dough by 12 spoonfuls onto hot chicken mixture. The dumplings will cook completely through when they are dropped onto the chicken mixture rather than into the liquid. If they are dropped directly into the liquid, the dumplings will be doughy and will not cook through.

6 Cook uncovered 10 minutes. Cover and cook 10 minutes longer.

DUMPLINGS Mix baking mix and milk in small or medium bowl with a fork until baking mix is completely moistened and a soft dough forms.

1 SERVING: Calories 435 (Calories from Fat 135); Fat 15g (Saturated 4g); Cholesterol 70mg; Sodium 1460mg; Carbohydrate 45g (Dietary Fiber 3g); Protein 33g

TiP **YOU CAN SUBSTITUTE** 1 pound skinless, bone-less chicken thighs for the chicken breast halves.

TiP **FOR RECIPE SUCCESS,** mix the dumpling dough only until the baking mix and milk form a soft dough; overmixing will cause tough dumplings.

Mixing Dumpling Dough

Mix baking mix and milk with fork until a soft dough forms.

Dropping Dumplings onto Chicken Mixture

Drop dumpling dough by spoon-fuls onto hot chicken mixture.

Creamy Chicken and Dumplings

TERIYAKI CHICKEN STIR-FRY

MAKES 4 servings • COOK: 10 minutes

INGREDIENTS

ESSENTIAL EQUIPMENT: *12-inch skillet or wok; 2-quart saucepan*

1 pound skinless, boneless chicken breast halves

1 tablespoon vegetable oil

1/2 cup teriyaki baste and glaze

3 tablespoons lemon juice

1 bag (16 ounces) frozen broccoli, carrots and water chestnuts

Hot Cooked Couscous (below)

HOT COOKED COUSCOUS

2 cups water

1/2 teaspoon salt

1 tablespoon olive or vegetable oil

1 1/2 cups uncooked couscous

DIRECTIONS

1 If the chicken is frozen, place it in the refrigerator the night before you plan to use it or for at least 12 hours. Cut and discard fat from chicken with kitchen scissors or knife. Rinse chicken under cold water, and pat dry with paper towels. Cut into 1-inch pieces.

2 Heat the skillet over high heat 1 to 2 minutes. Add the oil to the hot skillet. If using a wok, rotate it to coat the side with oil.

3 Add the chicken. Stir-fry with a turner or large spoon 3 to 4 minutes, lifting and stirring constantly, until chicken is no longer pink in center.

4 Stir in the teriyaki glaze, lemon juice and frozen vegetables. Although thawing the vegetables is not necessary, stir them into the chicken mixture to allow them to cook uniformly.

5 Heat the mixture to boiling over high heat, stirring constantly. Reduce heat just enough so mixture bubbles gently. Cover and cook about 6 minutes or until vegetables are crisp-tender when pierced with a fork.

6 While chicken mixture is cooking, prepare Hot Cooked Couscous. Serve chicken mixture with couscous.

HOT COOKED COUSCOUS Heat the water, salt and oil just to boiling in the saucepan over high heat. Stir in the couscous. Cover and remove from heat. Let stand 5 minutes. Fluff couscous lightly with a fork before serving.

1 SERVING: Calories 490 (Calories from Fat 100); Fat 11g (Saturated 2g); Cholesterol 60mg; Sodium 1770mg; Carbohydrate 66g (Dietary Fiber 6g); Protein 38g

TiP **TRY A FLAVORED COUSCOUS,** such as roasted garlic and olive, herbed chicken or wild mushroom.

✔**WHEN CUTTING RAW POULTRY,** use hard-plastic cutting boards. They are less porous than wooden cutting boards and are easily cleaned or washed in a dishwasher.

Stir-Frying Chicken

Stir-fry chicken over high heat with a turner or large spoon, lifting and stirring constantly.

Fluffing Couscous

Use a fork to fluff and lift the couscous after it cooks, which prevents the couscous from clumping and sticking.

Teriyaki Chicken Stir-Fry

QUICK CHICKEN SOUP

MAKES 6 servings • COOK: 15 minutes

INGREDIENTS

DIRECTIONS

ESSENTIAL EQUIPMENT: *Dutch oven (about 4-quart size)*

3/4 pound cooked chicken (about 2 cups cut up)

2 medium stalks celery

2 medium carrots

1 medium onion

2 cloves garlic

4 cans (14 1/2 ounces each) ready-to-serve 1/3-less-sodium chicken broth

1 cup frozen green peas

1 tablespoon chopped fresh parsley or 1 teaspoon parsley flakes

1 tablespoon chopped fresh or 1 teaspoon dried thyme leaves

1/4 teaspoon pepper

1 dried bay leaf

1 cup uncooked gemelli or rotini pasta (4 ounces)

1 Cut the chicken into 1/2-inch pieces. Slice the celery. Peel and slice the carrots. Peel and chop the onion. Peel and finely chop the garlic.

2 Heat the chicken, celery, carrots, onion, garlic, broth, frozen peas, parsley, thyme, pepper and bay leaf to boiling in the Dutch oven over high heat. Stir in the pasta. Heat to boiling over high heat, stirring occasionally to prevent sticking. Once mixture is boiling, reduce heat just enough so mixture bubbles gently.

3 Cook uncovered 10 to 15 minutes, stirring occasionally, until pasta is tender and vegetables are tender when pierced with a fork. Remove and discard bay leaf.

1 SERVING: Calories 255 (Calories from Fat 55); Fat 6g (Saturated 2g); Cholesterol 45mg; Sodium 650mg; Carbohydrate 26g (Dietary Fiber 3g); Protein 27g

TiP **LEFTOVER CHICKEN SOUP** freezes well. Place it in a moistureproof and vaporproof container such as a plastic container with tight-fitting lid; label and date before freezing.

✔ **FOR FOOD SAFETY**—and the best flavor—cooked poultry should be wrapped tightly and refrigerated no longer than 2 days.

Chopping Fresh Parsley and Thyme

Remove stems from parsley leaves. Place leaves in small bowl or measuring cup. Cut into very small pieces with kitchen scissors. Repeat with thyme.

Chopping Garlic

Hit garlic clove with flat side of heavy knife to crack the skin, which will then slip off easily. Finely chop garlic with knife.

Quick Chicken Soup

OVEN-FRIED CHICKEN

MAKES 6 servings • **BAKE: 1 hour**

INGREDIENTS

ESSENTIAL EQUIPMENT: *13×9-inch rectangular pan*

3- to 3 1/2-pound cut-up broiler-fryer chicken

1/4 cup (1/2 stick) margarine or butter

1/2 cup all-purpose flour

1 teaspoon paprika

1/2 teaspoon salt

1/4 teaspoon pepper

DIRECTIONS

1 If the chicken is frozen, place it in the refrigerator the night before you plan to use it or for at least 12 hours. Cut and discard fat from chicken with kitchen scissors or knife. Rinse chicken under cold water, and pat dry with paper towels.

2 Heat the oven to 425°. Place the margarine in the rectangular pan, and melt in the oven, which will take about 3 minutes.

3 Mix the flour, paprika, salt and pepper in a large plastic bag. Place the chicken, a few pieces at a time, in the bag, seal the bag and shake to coat with flour mixture. Place the chicken, skin sides down, in a single layer in margarine in pan.

4 Bake uncovered 30 minutes. Remove chicken from oven, and turn pieces over with tongs. Continue baking uncovered about 30 minutes longer or until juice of chicken is no longer pink when you cut into the center of the thickest pieces. If chicken sticks to the pan, loosen it gently with a turner or fork.

1 SERVING: Calories 245 (Calories from Fat 125); Fat 14g (Saturated 4g); Cholesterol 85mg; Sodium 120mg; Carbohydrate 2g (Dietary Fiber 0g); Protein 28g

Lighter **OVEN-FRIED CHICKEN:** For 6 grams of fat and 160 calories per serving, remove the skin from chicken before cooking. Do not melt margarine in pan; instead, spray pan with cooking spray. Decrease margarine to 2 tablespoons; melt the margarine, and drizzle over chicken after turning in step 4.

TiP **SERVE WITH** Garlic Mashed Potatoes (page 167). Peel potatoes after chicken goes into the oven to bake. Start to cook the potatoes and garlic just before turning the chicken.

Removing Chicken Skin

Remove chicken skin by lifting and pulling skin away from chicken. Loosen and cut away connective membrane with kitchen scissors or knife.

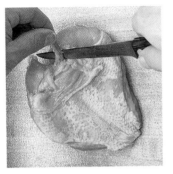

Turning Chicken Pieces

Chicken is baked skin sides down for the first 30 minutes; turn chicken with tongs or a turner. If chicken sticks to the pan, gently loosen it.

Oven-Fried Chicken

OVEN-BARBECUED CHICKEN

MAKES 6 servings • BAKE: 1 hour

INGREDIENTS

DIRECTIONS

ESSENTIAL EQUIPMENT: *13×9-inch rectangular pan*

3- to 3 1/2-pound cut-up broiler-fryer chicken

3/4 cup chili sauce

2 tablespoons honey

2 tablespoons soy sauce

1 teaspoon ground mustard (dry)

1/2 teaspoon prepared horseradish

1/2 teaspoon red pepper sauce

1 If the chicken is frozen, place it in the refrigerator the night before you plan to use it or for at least 12 hours. Cut and discard fat from chicken with kitchen scissors or knife. Rinse chicken under cold water, and pat dry with paper towels.

2 Heat the oven to 375°.

3 Place the chicken, skin sides down, in a single layer in the ungreased pan. Cover with aluminum foil and bake 30 minutes.

4 While the chicken is baking, mix the chili sauce, honey, soy sauce, mustard, horseradish and pepper sauce in a small bowl. Remove chicken from oven, and turn pieces over with tongs. Pour sauce over chicken, spooning sauce over chicken pieces if necessary to coat them completely.

5 Continue baking uncovered about 30 minutes longer or until juice of chicken is no longer pink when you cut into the center of the thickest pieces. Spoon remaining sauce over chicken before serving.

1 SERVING: Calories 280 (Calories from Fat 110); Fat 12g (Saturated 3g); Cholesterol 85mg; Sodium 790mg; Carbohydrate 15g (Dietary Fiber 0g); Protein 28g

TiP TO SAVE TIME, omit sauce ingredients and use 1 cup purchased barbecue sauce.

✔**WHEN HANDLING** uncooked poultry, be sure to keep your hands, utensils and countertops soap-and-hot-water clean. When cleaning up after working with raw poultry, be sure to use disposable paper towels.

Turning Chicken

To retain juices
and keep
chicken from
becoming dry,
turn pieces with
tongs instead of
a fork.

Adding Sauce

The sauce is added
the last 30 minutes.
For uniform flavor
and juiciness, be
certain all pieces of
chicken are coated
with sauce.

Oven-Barbecued Chicken

Thyme-Baked Chicken with Vegetables

MAKES 6 servings • BAKE: 1 1/2 to 2 hours

INGREDIENTS

ESSENTIAL EQUIPMENT: *shallow roasting pan (about 13×9-inch rectangle)*

3- to 3 1/2-pound whole broiler-fryer chicken

6 medium carrots

4 medium stalks celery

3 medium baking potatoes (russet or Idaho), 8 to 10 ounces each

3 medium onions

2 tablespoons margarine or butter

1 tablespoon chopped fresh or 1 teaspoon dried thyme leaves

TiP FOR EASY CLEANUP, use a disposable aluminum pan. For easier handling of the heavy chicken and vegetables, buy a heavy-duty pan or use two lighter-weight pans.

TiP TO KEEP VEGETABLES HOT while you are carving the chicken, place them on an ovenproof serving platter or baking pan. Cover with aluminum foil and return to the still-warm oven, which has been turned off.

DIRECTIONS

1 Heat the oven to 375°. Rinse the chicken under cold water, and pat dry with paper towels. Pat the inside of the chicken with paper towels. Fold the wings of chicken across the back so tips are touching. There may be a little resistance, but once they are in this position, they will stay. Tie the drumsticks to the tail with string, but if the tail is missing, tie the drumsticks together.

2 Place the chicken, breast side up, in the roasting pan. Insert a meat thermometer so the tip is in the thickest part of inside thigh muscle and does not touch bone. Roast chicken uncovered 45 minutes.

3 While the chicken is roasting, prepare the vegetables. Peel the carrots, and cut into 1-inch pieces. Cut the celery into 1-inch pieces. Scrub the potatoes thoroughly with a vegetable brush or peel the potatoes, and cut into 1 1/2-inch pieces. Peel the onions, and cut into wedges.

4 Remove the chicken from the oven. Arrange the carrots, celery, potatoes and onions around the chicken. Melt the margarine. Stir the thyme into the margarine. Drizzle this mixture over the chicken and vegetables.

5 Cover the chicken and vegetables with aluminum foil and bake 45 to 60 minutes longer or until the thermometer reads 180°, the juice of chicken is no longer pink when you cut into the center of the thigh and the vegetables are tender when pierced with a fork. Another way to test for doneness is to wiggle the drumstick; if it moves easily, the chicken is done.

6 Remove the vegetables from the pan, and cover with aluminum foil to keep warm while carving the chicken. If you have an ovenproof platter, place the vegetables on the platter, cover with aluminum foil and place in the oven, which has been turned off.

7 Place chicken on a stable cutting surface, such as a plastic cutting board or platter. Place chicken, breast up and with its legs to your right if you're right-handed or to the left if left-handed. Remove ties from drumsticks. To carve chicken, see Carving the Turkey (page 87).

1 SERVING: Calories 350 (Calories from Fat 145); Fat 16g (Saturated 4g); Cholesterol 85mg; Sodium 170mg; Carbohydrate 25g (Dietary Fiber 4g); Protein 30g

Folding Wings of Chicken

Fold wings of the chicken across its back so that tips are touching.

Tying Drumsticks

Cross the drumsticks, and tie them to the tail with clean string.

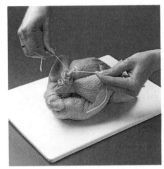

Thyme-Baked Chicken with Vegetables

TURKEY SALAD WITH FRUIT

MAKES 4 servings • REFRIGERATE: 2 hours

INGREDIENTS

DIRECTIONS

ESSENTIAL EQUIPMENT: *large serving bowl*

Mixed salad greens to line salad plates

10 ounces cooked turkey (about 2 cups cut up)

2 medium stalks celery

1 medium green onion with top

1 can (11 ounces) mandarin orange segments

1 can (8 ounces) sliced water chestnuts

1 container (6 ounces) peach, orange or lemon yogurt (2/3 cup)

1/4 teaspoon ground ginger

1 cup seedless green grapes

1 Wash the salad greens, let drain and refrigerate.

2 Cut the turkey into 1/2-inch pieces. Thinly slice the celery. Peel and cut the green onion into 1/8-inch slices. Drain the orange segments and water chestnuts in a strainer.

3 Mix the yogurt and ginger in the bowl. Stir in the turkey, celery, onion, orange segments, water chestnuts and grapes. Cover and refrigerate at least 2 hours. Arrange salad greens on 4 plates. Top greens with turkey salad.

1 SERVING: Calories 265 (Calories from Fat 45); Fat 5g (Saturated 2g); Cholesterol 60mg; Sodium 110mg; Carbohydrate 33g (Dietary Fiber 2g); Protein 24g

TiP **TO SAVE TIME,** purchase cooked turkey or chicken at the deli counter of your favorite supermarket.

TiP **SERVE WITH** Garlic Bread (page 142) or toasted pita breads, cut into wedges.

Cutting up Turkey

Cut turkey into 1/2-inch pieces. Some pieces will be irregular in shape.

Turkey Salad with Fruit

THANKSGIVING DINNER

You've always wanted to prepare and serve a traditional and delicious Thanksgiving dinner just like Grandma's—and now you can, with the help of this timetable and some planning. We provide dishes you can prepare in advance of the big day as well as help in dovetailing the preparations for this family-and-friends feast. If you receive offers of help, take them! Everyone likes to pitch in with this special dinner. So go ahead and send those dinner invitations with confidence.

This timetable was created for an 8- to 12-pound turkey, so you'll need to adjust the schedule slightly if your turkey is larger or smaller. To start off, we suggest a light and easy appetizer that doubles as the salad, to leave room for turkey and stuffing. Any apple and pear combination works for the appetizer. Purchase the dinner rolls from your favorite bakery. If time is really crunched, purchase the cranberry sauce and pumpkin pie, too. Or let a guest bring the pie.

There's no need to worry about matching linens. Select from the array of bright, colorful paper napkins and place mats available. Short on serving bowls? Try inexpensive sturdy plastic bowls available in the housewares or party supply section of your favorite store. For a stunning and colorful centerpiece, fill a large bowl or vegetable dish with chrysanthemums. Avoid last-minute frenzy by asking others to help you in carving the turkey and mashing the potatoes. Then sit down and enjoy a Thanksgiving dinner certain to bring well-deserved rave reviews.

SERVES EIGHT

Granny Smith Apple and Red Anjou Pear Appetizer

Roast Turkey with Bread Stuffing

Mashed Potatoes with Turkey Gravy

Brown Sugar-Glazed Carrots

Cranberry Sauce

Dinner Rolls with Butter

Pumpkin Pie with Whipped Cream (page 218)

Coffee and Tea

Wine, if desired

READY, SET, GO

3 days before dinner

- Purchase groceries.
- Wrap rolls in aluminum foil and freeze to keep them fresh.

2 days before dinner

- **Thaw turkey,** if frozen, in refrigerator.
- Make Cranberry Sauce (page 85); cover and refrigerate.
- Whip cream for Pumpkin Pie (page 218); freeze as directed in recipe.
- Purchase flowers for centerpiece, order a floral centerpiece or purchase a low, pretty pot of mums for the table.

1 day before dinner

- Make Bread Stuffing (page 83); cover and refrigerate immediately.
- Peel, slice and cook carrots; cover and refrigerate.
- Chill wine.
- Set the table, and select serving dishes.
- Make Pumpkin Pie (page 218), or purchase from your favorite bakery.

Morning of the dinner

- Remove rolls from freezer.
- Wash apples and pears; core and slice. Dip into lemon juice to keep them from turning brown. Arrange apple and pear slices on a serving plate with lemon yogurt as the dip. Cover with plastic wrap and refrigerate.
- Prepare glaze ingredients for Brown Sugar-Glazed Carrots (page 85); place in skillet and leave at room temperature until ready to finish.

5 hours before dinner

- Wash turkey; pat dry with paper towels. Stuff with Bread Stuffing (page 83).
- Place turkey in oven for roasting immediately after stuffing.

- Peel potatoes for Mashed Potatoes (page 84); cover with cold water in saucepan to keep them from turning brown.

1 hour before dinner

- Place butter and Cranberry Sauce on the table.

45 minutes before dinner

- Begin cooking potatoes.
- Prepare coffee.
- Serve appetizer.
- Fill water glasses.

30 minutes before dinner

- Remove turkey from oven; place on carving board or platter and cover with aluminum foil to keep warm.
- Place rolls in aluminum foil in oven to heat.
- Remove stuffing from turkey; place in serving bowl and cover with aluminum foil to keep warm.
- Make Turkey Gravy (page 86).
- Mash the potatoes. The potatoes can stand for about 5 minutes but no longer than 10 minutes after they are mashed; keep them in a covered saucepan so they stay warm.
- Carve the turkey and arrange on a platter. If you aren't serving immediately, cover with aluminum foil to keep warm, and serve within 10 minutes.

10 minutes before dinner

- Heat the glaze for the carrots; add carrots.
- Remove whipped cream from freezer, and place in refrigerator.
- Make tea.
- Remove rolls from oven, and place in serving basket.
- Place carrots and gravy in serving bowls. Place the food on the table.
- Serve wine.

Roast Turkey

1 Select a turkey that is plump and meaty with smooth, moist-looking skin. The skin should be creamy colored. The cut ends of the bones should be pink to red in color.

2 If the turkey is frozen, thaw it slowly in the refrigerator, in cold water or quickly in the microwave, following the manufacturer's directions. A turkey weighing 8 to 12 pounds will thaw in about 2 days in the refrigerator. A turkey weighing 20 to 24 pounds will thaw in about 5 days in the refrigerator. A whole frozen turkey can be safely thawed in cold water. Leave the turkey in its original wrap, free from tears or holes. Place in cold water, allowing 30 minutes per pound for thawing, and change the water often.

3 Remove the package of giblets (gizzard, heart and neck), if present, from the neck cavity of the turkey, and discard. Rinse the cavity, or inside of the turkey, with cool water; pat dry with paper towels. Rub the cavity of turkey lightly with salt if desired. Do not salt the cavity if you will be stuffing the turkey.

4 Stuff the turkey just before roasting—not ahead of time. See Bread Stuffing (page 83). Fill the wishbone area (the neck) with stuffing first. Fasten the neck skin to the back of the turkey with a skewer. Fold the wings across the back so the tips are touching. Fill the body cavity lightly with stuffing. It is not necessary to pack the stuffing because it will expand during roasting. Tuck the drumsticks under the band of skin at the tail, or tie or skewer the drumsticks to the tail.

5 Place the turkey, breast side up, on a rack in a shallow roasting pan. Brush with melted margarine or butter. It is not necessary to add water or to cover the turkey. Place a meat thermometer in the thickest part of thigh muscle, so thermometer does not touch bone. Follow Timetable (below) for approximate roasting time. Place a tent of aluminum foil loosely over the turkey when it begins to turn golden. When two thirds done, cut the band or remove the skewer holding the drumsticks; this will allow the interior part of the thighs to cook through.

6 Roast until the thermometer reads 180° (for a whole turkey) and the juice is no longer pink when you cut into the center of the thigh. The drumstick should move easily when lifted or twisted. When the turkey is done, remove it from the oven and let it stand about 15 minutes for easiest carving. Keep turkey covered with aluminum foil so it will stay warm.

 ## Timetable for Roasting Turkey

	Ready-to-Cook Weight	Oven Temperature	Roasting Time*
Whole Turkey	8 to 12 pounds	325°	3 to 3 1/2 hours
(stuffed)	12 to 14 pounds	325°	3 1/2 to 4 hours
	14 to 18 pounds	325°	4 to 4 1/4 hours
	18 to 20 pounds	325°	4 1/4 to 4 3/4 hours
	20 to 24 pounds	325°	4 3/4 to 5 1/4 hours

Begin checking turkey for doneness about one hour before end of recommended roasting time. For prestuffed turkeys, follow package directions very carefully—do not use this timetable.

BREAD STUFFING

MAKES 10 servings, about 1/2 cup each • **PREPARE:** 30 minutes

INGREDIENTS	DIRECTIONS

ESSENTIAL EQUIPMENT: *Dutch oven (about 4-quart size) or 12-inch skillet*

2 large celery stalks with leaves

1 medium onion

3/4 cup (1 1/2 sticks) margarine or butter

9 cups soft bread cubes

1 1/2 teaspoons chopped fresh or 1/2 teaspoon dried thyme leaves

1 teaspoon salt

1/2 teaspoon ground sage

1/4 teaspoon pepper

1 Chop the celery, including the leaves. Peel and chop the onion.

2 Melt the margarine in the Dutch oven over medium-high heat. Cook the celery and onion in margarine 6 to 8 minutes, stirring occasionally, until tender when pierced with a fork. Remove the Dutch oven from the heat.

3 Gently toss the celery mixture with the bread cubes, thyme, salt, sage and pepper, using a spoon, until bread cubes are evenly coated.

Lighter

BREAD STUFFING For 6 grams of fat and 130 calories per serving, decrease margarine to 1/4 cup. Heat margarine and 1/2 cup chicken broth to boiling in Dutch oven over medium-high heat. Cook celery and onion in broth mixture.

Filling Wishbone Area

Fill wishbone area with stuffing. Fasten neck skin to back with skewer. Fold wings across back with tips touching.

Filling Body Cavity

Fill body cavity lightly with stuffing. Do not pack; stuffing will expand. Tuck drumsticks under band of skin at tail, or skewer to tail.

MASHED POTATOES

MAKES 4 to 6 servings • COOK: 25 minutes

INGREDIENTS

ESSENTIAL EQUIPMENT: *large saucepan (about 3-quart size); potato masher or electric mixer*

6 medium potatoes (about 2 pounds)

1/4 cup (1/2 stick) margarine or butter at room temperature

1/4 teaspoon salt, if desired

1/2 cup milk

1/2 teaspoon salt

Dash of pepper

DIRECTIONS

1 Wash and peel the potatoes, and cut into large pieces. Remove the margarine from the refrigerator so it can soften while the potatoes cook.

2 Add 1 inch of water (and the 1/4 teaspoon salt if desired) to the saucepan. Cover and heat to boiling over high heat. Add potato pieces. Cover and heat to boiling again. Once water is boiling, reduce heat just enough so water bubbles gently.

3 Cook covered 20 to 25 minutes or until tender when pierced with a fork. The cooking time will vary, depending on the size of the potato pieces and the type of potato used. Drain potatoes in a strainer.

4 Return the drained potatoes to the saucepan, and cook over low heat about 1 minute to dry them. While cooking, shake the pan often to keep the potatoes from burning, which can happen very easily once the water has been drained off.

5 Place the potatoes in a medium bowl to be mashed. You can mash them in the same saucepan they were cooked in if the saucepan will not be damaged by the potato masher or electric mixer.

6 Mash the potatoes with a potato masher or electric mixer until no lumps remain. Add the milk in small amounts, beating after each addition. You may not use all the milk because the amount needed to make potatoes smooth and fluffy depends on the type of potato used. Add the margarine, 1/2 teaspoon salt and the pepper. Beat vigorously until potatoes are light and fluffy.

BROWN SUGAR-GLAZED CARROTS

MAKES 8 servings • COOK: 15 minutes

INGREDIENTS

ESSENTIAL EQUIPMENT: *3-quart saucepan; 10- or 12-inch skillet*

2 pounds carrots (6 to 7 medium)

1/2 teaspoon salt, if desired

2/3 cup packed brown sugar

1/4 cup margarine or butter

1 teaspoon grated orange peel

1/2 teaspoon salt

DIRECTIONS

1 Peel the carrots, and cut into 1/4-inch slices. Heat 1 inch water to boiling in the saucepan over high heat. Add the 1/4 teaspoon salt if desired. Add the carrot slices. Cover and heat to boiling again. Reduce heat just enough so water bubbles gently. Cook covered 12 to 15 minutes or until carrots are tender when pierced with a fork.

2 While carrots are cooking, heat the brown sugar, margarine, orange peel and 1/2 teaspoon salt in the skillet over medium heat, stirring constantly, until sugar is dissolved and mixture is bubbly. Be careful not to overcook or the mixture will taste scorched. Remove the skillet from the heat.

3 Drain carrots in a strainer, then stir them into the brown sugar mixture. Cook over low heat about 5 minutes, stirring occasionally and gently, until carrots are glazed and hot.

CRANBERRY SAUCE

MAKES 16 servings • COOK: 20 minutes • REFRIGERATE: 3 hours

INGREDIENTS

ESSENTIAL EQUIPMENT: *3-quart saucepan*

4 cups 1 pound fresh or frozen cranberries (4 cups)

2 cups water

2 cups sugar

DIRECTIONS

1 Rinse the cranberries in a strainer with cool water, and remove any stems or blemished berries.

2 Heat the water and sugar to boiling in the saucepan over medium heat, stirring occasionally. Continue boiling 5 minutes longer, stirring occasionally.

3 Stir in the cranberries. Heat to boiling over medium heat, stirring occasionally. Continue boiling about 5 minutes longer, stirring occasionally, until cranberries begin to pop. Remove the saucepan from the heat, and pour the sauce into a bowl or container. Refrigerate about 3 hours or until chilled.

TURKEY GRAVY

MAKES 1 cup gravy • COOK: 5 minutes

INGREDIENTS

ESSENTIAL EQUIPMENT: *the pan the turkey was roasted in*

2 tablespoons turkey drippings (fat and juices)

2 tablespoons all-purpose flour

1 cup liquid (turkey juices, broth or water)

Browning sauce, if desired

Salt and pepper to taste

TiP **THIS RECIPE CAN EASILY** be doubled or tripled if there are enough drippings. Sprinkle carefully with salt and pepper, though; they do not need to be doubled or tripled.

DIRECTIONS

1 Place the turkey on a carving board or warm platter, and cover with aluminum foil while preparing gravy. Pan and drippings will be hot, so be careful when handling. Pour drippings from roasting pan into a bowl, leaving the brown particles in the pan. Return 2 tablespoons of the drippings to the roasting pan. Measuring accurately is important because too little fat makes the gravy lumpy and too much fat makes the gravy greasy.

2 Stir the flour into the drippings in the pan, using a long-handled fork or spoon. Cooking with the roasting pan on top of the burner may be unwieldy, so keep a pot holder handy to steady the pan. Cook over low heat, stirring constantly, until the mixture is smooth and bubbly. As you stir, the brown particles will be loosened from the bottom of the pan; they add more flavor to the gravy. Remove the pan from the heat.

3 Stir in the 1 cup liquid (turkey juices, broth or water). Heat to boiling over high heat, stirring constantly. Continue boiling 1 minute, stirring constantly. Stir in a few drops of browning sauce if you want the gravy to have a richer, deeper color. Taste the gravy, and add a desired amount of salt and pepper.

Returning Drippings to the Pan

Return 2 tablespoons drippings to the roasting pan.

Thickening Gravy

Stir in the 1 cup turkey juices. Heat to boiling, stirring constantly. Continue boiling 1 minute, stirring constantly.

CARVING THE TURKEY

Use a sharp carving knife for best results when carving a whole turkey. While carving, keep the turkey from moving by holding it in place with a meat fork. Carve on a stable cutting surface, such as a plastic cutting board or platter. Carving is easier if the turkey is allowed to stand for about 15 minutes after roasting.

1 Place the turkey, breast up and with its legs to your right if you're right-handed or to the left if left-handed. Remove the ties or skewers.

2 While gently pulling the leg and thigh away from the body, cut through the joint between leg and body. Separate the drumstick and thigh by cutting down through the connecting joint. Serve the drumstick and thighs whole, or carve them.

3 Make a deep horizontal cut into the breast just above the wing. Insert a fork in the top of the breast as shown, and starting halfway up the breast, carve thin slices down to the horizontal cut, working upward. Repeat steps 1 through 3 on the other side of the turkey.

Thanksgiving Dinner

Fabulous Fish—Four Ways

BROILED, GRILLED, PANFRIED AND BAKED

Fish is easy to fix and so good for you. Here are four simple and delicious ways to prepare it. Fish is available whole, drawn and pan-dressed, but you'll find it most often in steaks or fillets. You can purchase fish fresh or frozen. When you select fresh fish, the scales should be bright with a sheen, the flesh should be firm and elastic and there should be no odor. Frozen fish should be tightly wrapped and frozen solid; there should be no discoloration and no odor.

CUTS OF FISH

Fish Steaks

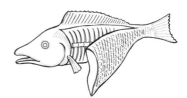

Fish Fillets

FISH STEAKS are the cross section of a large pan-dressed fish. Steaks are 1/2 to 3/4 inch thick. Allow 1/4 to 1/3 pound per serving.

FISH FILLETS are the sides of the fish, cut lengthwise from the fish. They can be purchased with or without skin. Fillets usually are boneless; however, small bones, called *pins,* may be present. Allow 1/4 to 1/3 pound per serving.

BROILED FISH STEAK

MAKES 1 serving	BROIL: 10 minutes

ESSENTIAL EQUIPMENT: *broiler pan with rack*

Fish steak, about 3/4 inch thick (1/4 to 1/3 pound)
Salt and pepper to taste
2 teaspoons margarine or butter, melted

1 You may need to move the oven rack so it is 5 to 6 inches below the broiler. Set the oven control to broil.

2 Sprinkle both sides of the fish steak with salt and pepper. Brush both sides with half of the margarine.

3 Place fish steak on the rack in the broiler pan. Broil with top of fish steak about 4 inches from heat 5 minutes. Brush with margarine.

4 Carefully turn fish over with a turner. If fish sticks to the rack, loosen it gently with a turner or fork. Brush other side with margarine.

5 Broil 4 to 6 minutes longer or until the fish flakes easily with a fork.

BROILED FISH FILLETS: Substitute 1/4 to 1/3 pound fish fillets for the fish steak. Sprinkle with salt and pepper and brush with margarine as directed for fish steaks. Broil with tops about 4 inches from heat 5 to 6 minutes or until fish flakes easily with a fork. Turning the fillets is not necessary.

GRILLED FISH STEAK

MAKES 1 serving   **GRILL: 20 minutes**

ESSENTIAL EQUIPMENT: *grill*

Fish steak, about 3/4 inch thick (1/4 to 1/3 pound)
Salt and pepper to taste
1 tablespoon margarine or butter, melted
1 teaspoon lemon juice

1 Prepare the coals or a gas grill for direct heat (pages 236–237). Heat to medium heat, which will take about 40 minutes for charcoal or about 10 minutes for a gas grill.

2 Sprinkle both sides of the fish steak with salt and pepper. Mix the margarine and lemon juice.

3 Grill the fish steak uncovered about 4 inches from medium heat 7 to 10 minutes, brushing 2 or 3 times with the margarine mixture.

4 Carefully turn the fish steak with a turner. If fish sticks to the grill, loosen it gently with a turner. Brush other side with margarine mixture.

5 Grill uncovered 7 to 10 minutes longer or until the fish flakes easily with a fork. Brush with margarine mixture.

PANFRIED FISH FILLETS

MAKES 6 servings   **COOK: 10 minutes**

ESSENTIAL EQUIPMENT: *shallow bowl or pie pan; 10-inch skillet*

1 1/2 pounds lean fish fillets, about 3/4 inch thick
1/2 teaspoon salt
1/8 teaspoon pepper
1 egg
1 tablespoon water
1/2 cup all-purpose flour, cornmeal or grated Parmesan cheese
Vegetable oil or shortening

1 Cut the fish fillets into 6 serving pieces. Sprinkle both sides of fish with salt and pepper.

2 Beat egg and water in the shallow bowl or pie pan until well mixed. Sprinkle the flour on waxed paper or a plate. Dip both sides of fish pieces into egg, then coat completely with flour.

3 Heat the oil (1/8 inch) in the skillet over medium heat about 2 minutes. Fry the fish in the oil 6 to 10 minutes, turning fish over once, until the fish flakes easily with a fork and is brown on both sides. Drain on paper towels.

BAKED FISH FILLETS

MAKES 4 servings   **BAKE: 15 to 20 minutes**

ESSENTIAL EQUIPMENT: *shallow baking pan, such as 11×7-inch rectangle or 8-inch square*

Shortening to grease pan
1 pound lean fish fillets, about 3/4 inch thick
3 tablespoons margarine or butter, melted
1 tablespoon lemon juice
1/4 teaspoon salt
1/4 teaspoon paprika

1 Heat the oven to 375°. Grease the bottom of the baking pan with the shortening.

2 Cut the fish fillets into 4 serving pieces if needed. Place the pieces, skin sides down, in the greased pan.

3 Mix the margarine, lemon juice, salt and paprika. Drizzle this mixture over the fish.

4 Bake uncovered 15 to 20 minutes or until the fish flakes easily with a fork.

SOLE WITH ALMONDS

MAKES 4 servings • BAKE: 15 minutes

INGREDIENTS

ESSENTIAL EQUIPMENT: *shallow baking pan, such as 11×7-inch rectangle or 9-inch square*

Vegetable oil for greasing pan

1 pound sole or other lean fish fillets, about 3/4 inch thick

1/3 cup sliced almonds or chopped walnuts

3 tablespoons margarine or butter at room temperature

1 1/2 tablespoons grated lemon peel

1 1/2 tablespoons lemon juice

1/2 teaspoon salt

1/2 teaspoon paprika

DIRECTIONS

1 Heat the oven to 375°. Grease the bottom of the baking pan with the oil.

2 Cut the fish fillets into 4 serving pieces if needed. Place the pieces, skin sides down, in the greased pan.

3 Mix the almonds, margarine, lemon peel, lemon juice, salt and paprika. Spoon this mixture over the fish.

4 Bake uncovered 15 to 20 minutes or until the fish flakes easily with a fork.

1 SERVING: Calories 220 (Calories from Fat 125); Fat 14g (Saturated 2g); Cholesterol 55mg; Sodium 480mg; Carbohydrate 3g (Dietary Fiber 1g); Protein 21g

Lighter **SOLE WITH ALMONDS:** For 9 grams of fat and 170 calories per serving, decrease almonds to 2 tablespoons and margarine to 2 tablespoons.

TiP **GRATE ONLY THE YELLOW PORTION,** or the "zest," of the lemon peel. The bright yellow peel provides the best flavor without bitterness. Also, grate the lemon peel before you squeeze the lemon for juice.

TiP **SERVE WITH** Green Beans (page 159) and packaged rice pilaf for an easy and impressive dinner ready in one hour.

Grating Lemon Peel

Grate the lemon peel by rubbing the lemon across the small rough holes of a grater.

Checking Fish for Doneness

You can test fish for doneness by placing a fork in the thickest part of the fish, then gently twisting the fork. The fish will flake easily when it's done.

Sole with Almonds, Green Beans

BAKED FLOUNDER TERIYAKI

MAKES 6 servings • **REFRIGERATE: 1 hour** • **BAKE: 20 minutes**

INGREDIENTS

ESSENTIAL EQUIPMENT: *13×9-inch rectangular pan*

Cooking spray

1 1/2 pounds flounder (about 6 small fillets) or other lean fish fillets

1 medium green onion with top

2 cloves garlic

1/3 cup dry sherry or apple juice

3 tablespoons lemon juice

2 teaspoons finely chopped gingerroot

1 teaspoon vegetable oil

2 teaspoons honey

1/4 teaspoon pepper

DIRECTIONS

1 Spray the rectangular pan with cooking spray. Cut the fish fillets into 6 serving pieces if needed. Place the pieces in the sprayed pan. If the pieces have skin, place with skin sides down.

2 Peel and cut the green onion into 1/8-inch slices. Peel and finely chop the garlic.

3 Mix the onion, garlic, sherry, lemon juice, gingerroot, oil, honey and pepper. Spoon this mixture over the fish. Cover with aluminum foil and refrigerate 1 hour.

4 Heat the oven to 375°. Bake covered 15 to 20 minutes or until the fish flakes easily with a fork.

1 SERVING: Calories 120 (Calories from Fat 20); Fat 2g (Saturated 0g); Cholesterol 55mg; Sodium 90mg; Carbohydrate 5g (Dietary Fiber 0g); Protein 20g

TiP YOU CAN SUBSTITUTE other lean fish, such as halibut, orange roughy, ocean perch, red snapper or scrod, for the flounder.

TiP SERVE WITH Sautéed Mushrooms (page 164) and Asparagus (page 158) for a light and healthful supper.

Folding Fish Fillets

Fish fillets are naturally uneven in thickness, so for even cooking, fold the thin end under before you spoon onion mixture over fish.

Baked Flounder Teriyaki, Asparagus

STIR-FRIED SCALLOPS WITH BROCCOLI AND MUSHROOMS

MAKES 4 servings • COOK: 10 minutes

INGREDIENTS

ESSENTIAL EQUIPMENT: *2-quart saucepan; 3-quart saucepan or 12-inch skillet*

1/2 pound broccoli

1/4 pound mushrooms

1 pound scallops

1 jar (2 ounces) sliced pimientos

Hot Cooked Rice (below)

2 tablespoons margarine or butter

1 can (10 1/2 ounces) condensed chicken broth

3 tablespoons cornstarch

2 teaspoons soy sauce

HOT COOKED RICE

1 cup uncooked regular long-grain white rice

2 cups water

DIRECTIONS

1 Trim the large leaves from the broccoli, and cut off any tough ends of lower stems. Rinse broccoli with cool water. Cut stems and flowerets into bite-sized pieces. Cut stem ends from the mushrooms, and cut the mushrooms into 1/4-inch slices.

2 If the scallops are larger than 1 inch in diameter, cut each in half. Rinse with cool water, and pat dry with paper towels. Drain the pimientos in a strainer.

3 Prepare Hot Cooked Rice. While the rice is cooking, continue with the recipe.

4 Melt the margarine in the 3-quart saucepan over medium heat. Cook the mushrooms in the margarine about 5 minutes, stirring frequently, until tender when pierced with a fork.

5 Stir in the scallops, broccoli and pimientos. Cook 3 to 4 minutes, stirring frequently, until scallops are white. Remove the saucepan from the heat.

6 Gradually stir the chicken broth into the cornstarch until the mixture is smooth. Stir the broth mixture and soy sauce into the scallop mixture. Heat to boiling over high heat, stirring constantly. Continue boiling 1 minute, stirring constantly. Serve over rice.

HOT COOKED RICE Heat the rice and water to boiling in the 2-quart saucepan over high heat, stirring occasionally to prevent sticking. Once mixture is boiling, reduce heat just enough so mixture bubbles gently. Cover and cook about 15 minutes or until rice is fluffy and tender.

1 SERVING: Calories 425 (Calories from Fat 80); Fat 9g (Saturated 2g); Cholesterol 35mg; Sodium 1030mg; Carbohydrate 54g (Dietary Fiber 2g); Protein 34g

TiP **TO SAVE TIME,** buy broccoli and mushrooms that are already cleaned and sliced at the salad bar.

TiP **SERVE WITH** a fruit salad of sliced bananas and halved strawberries drizzled with a tablespoon of orange or pineapple juice.

Thickening with Cornstarch

Gradually stir the broth into the cornstarch until smooth. Heat to boiling, stirring constantly. Boil and stir 1 minute.

Testing Scallops for Doneness

Scallops are very tender and cook quickly, turning white and opaque when they are done. Longer cooking results in tough scallops.

Stir-Fried Scallops with Broccoli and Mushrooms

SHRIMP SCAMPI

MAKES 2 or 3 servings • COOK: 12 minutes

INGREDIENTS

ESSENTIAL EQUIPMENT: *3-quart saucepan; 10-inch skillet*

3/4 pound uncooked peeled and cleaned medium shrimp

1 medium green onion with top

1 clove garlic

4 ounces uncooked fettuccine

1 tablespoon olive or vegetable oil

2 teaspoons chopped fresh or 1/2 teaspoon dried basil leaves

2 teaspoons chopped fresh parsley or 3/4 teaspoon parsley flakes

1 tablespoon lemon juice

1/8 teaspoon salt

Grated Parmesan cheese, if desired

DIRECTIONS

1 Fill the saucepan about half full of water. Add 1/4 teaspoon salt if desired. Cover and heat over high heat until the water is boiling rapidly. While water is heating, continue with the recipe.

2 Rinse the shrimp with cool water, and pat dry with paper towels. If the shrimp have tails, remove tails with knife. Peel the green onion, and cut into 1/4-inch slices. Peel and finely chop the garlic.

3 Once the water is boiling, add the fettuccine and stir to prevent sticking. Heat to boiling again. Boil uncovered 10 to 13 minutes, stirring frequently, until tender.

4 When fettuccine has been cooking for 5 minutes, heat the oil in the skillet over medium heat 1 to 2 minutes. Cook the shrimp, onion, garlic, basil, parsley, lemon juice and salt in the oil 2 to 3 minutes, stirring frequently, until shrimp are pink and firm. Do not overcook the shrimp or they will become tough. Remove the skillet from the heat.

5 Drain the fettuccine in a strainer or colander. Toss fettuccine and shrimp mixture in skillet. Sprinkle with cheese.

1 SERVING: Calories 365 (Calories from Fat 90); Fat 10g (Saturated 2g); Cholesterol 290mg; Sodium 440mg; Carbohydrate 38g (Dietary Fiber 2g); Protein 33g

TiP **IF YOU USE FRESH FETTUCCINE** instead of dried, it will cook much faster. You will need to start the shrimp as soon as the fettuccine begins to cook.

✔**SHRIMP IS VERY PERISHABLE.** Store it uncooked in refrigerator no longer than 1 to 2 days.

Cooking Shrimp
Cook the shrimp only 2 to 3 minutes, stirring frequently. Shrimp will turn pink and become firm when done.

Shrimp Scampi

CHAPTER 4

PASTA AND MEATLESS MAIN DISHES

ITALIAN TOMATO SAUCE WITH PASTA

MAKES 4 servings • COOK: 35 minutes

INGREDIENTS

ESSENTIAL EQUIPMENT: *medium saucepan (about 2-quart size); Dutch oven (about 4-quart size)*

1 medium onion

1 large clove garlic

1 small green bell pepper

1 tablespoon olive or vegetable oil

1 can (14.5 ounces) whole tomatoes, undrained

1 can (8 ounces) tomato sauce

1 tablespoon chopped fresh or 1 teaspoon dried basil leaves

1 1/2 teaspoons chopped fresh or 1/2 teaspoon dried oregano leaves

1/4 teaspoon salt

1/4 teaspoon fennel seed

1/8 teaspoon pepper

7 or 8 ounces uncooked spaghetti, fettuccine or linguine

DIRECTIONS

1 Peel and chop the onion. Peel and finely chop the garlic. Cut the bell pepper lengthwise in half, and cut out seeds and membrane. Chop enough bell pepper to measure 1/4 cup. Wrap and refrigerate any remaining bell pepper.

2 Heat the oil in the saucepan over medium heat 1 to 2 minutes. Cook the onion, garlic and bell pepper in the oil 2 minutes, stirring occasionally.

3 Stir in the tomatoes with their liquid, and break them up with a fork. Stir in the tomato sauce, basil, oregano, salt, fennel seed and pepper. Heat to boiling over high heat. Once mixture is boiling, reduce heat just enough so mixture bubbles gently and does not spatter.

4 Cover and cook 35 minutes, stirring about every 10 minutes to make sure mixture is just bubbling gently and to prevent sticking. Lower the heat if the sauce is bubbling too fast.

5 After the tomato sauce has been cooking about 20 minutes, fill the Dutch oven about half full of water. Add 1/2 teaspoon salt if desired. Cover and heat over high heat until the water is boiling rapidly. Add the spaghetti. Heat to boiling again. Boil uncovered 8 to 10 minutes, stirring frequently, until tender. If using fettuccine or linguine, boil 9 to 13 minutes.

6 Drain the spaghetti in a strainer or colander. Serve with the tomato sauce.

1 SERVING: Calories 275 (Calories from Fat 45); Fat 5g (Saturated 1g); Cholesterol 0mg; Sodium 680mg; Carbohydrate 52g (Dietary Fiber 4g); Protein 9g

TiP **THE COOKING TIME** over low heat for the sauce allows the flavor to develop.

TiP **A TIGHTLY HELD BUNDLE** of spaghetti, about the diameter of a quarter, weighs about 4 ounces, which makes about 2 servings.

Simmering Tomato Sauce

Heat to boiling. Reduce heat just enough so mixture bubbles gently and does not spatter.

Italian Tomato Sauce with Pasta

PESTO WITH PASTA

MAKES 4 servings • COOK: 12 minutes

INGREDIENTS

DIRECTIONS

ESSENTIAL EQUIPMENT: *Dutch oven (about 4-quart size); blender or food processor*

3 cups uncooked rigatoni pasta (8 ounces)

1 cup fresh basil leaves

2 cloves garlic

1/3 cup grated Parmesan cheese

1/3 cup olive or vegetable oil

2 tablespoons pine nuts or walnut pieces

Grated Parmesan cheese, if desired

1 Fill the Dutch oven about half full of water. Add 1/2 teaspoon salt if desired. Cover and heat over high heat until the water is boiling rapidly. Add the pasta. Heat to boiling again. Boil uncovered 9 to 11 minutes, stirring frequently, until tender. While the water is heating and the pasta is cooking, continue with the recipe to make the pesto.

2 To measure basil, firmly pack basil leaves into a measuring cup. Use the style of cup designed for dry ingredients, usually made of metal instead of glass. Rinse the basil leaves with cool water, and pat dry thoroughly with a paper towel or clean, dry kitchen towel. Peel the garlic.

3 Place the basil leaves, garlic, 1/3 cup cheese, the oil and pine nuts in the blender. Cover and blend on medium speed about 3 minutes, stopping blender occasionally to scrape sides, until smooth.

4 Drain the pasta in a strainer or colander, and place in a large serving bowl or back in the Dutch oven. Immediately pour the pesto over the hot pasta, and toss until pasta is well coated. Serve with additional cheese.

CILANTRO PESTO: Substitute 3/4 cup firmly packed fresh cilantro leaves and 1/4 cup firmly packed fresh parsley leaves for the fresh basil.

SPINACH WINTER PESTO: Substitute 1 cup firmly packed fresh spinach leaves and 1/4 cup firmly packed fresh basil leaves, or 2 tablespoons dried basil leaves, for the 1 cup fresh basil.

1 SERVING: Calories 440 (Calories from Fat 215); Fat 24g (Saturated 4g); Cholesterol 5mg; Sodium 160mg; Carbohydrate 46g (Dietary Fiber 2g); Protein 12g

TiP **STORE PESTO AIRTIGHT** in the refrigerator up to 5 days or in the freezer up to 1 month. Cover and store immediately because its color will darken as it stands.

TiP **PESTO CAN BE USED** as a spread on sandwiches, mixed into salads or used as a topping for hot meats or vegetables.

Measuring Basil Leaves

Firmly pack basil leaves into a measuring cup.

Pesto with Pasta

FETTUCCINE ALFREDO

MAKES 6 servings • COOK: 15 minutes

INGREDIENTS

ESSENTIAL EQUIPMENT: *Dutch oven (about 4-quart size); medium saucepan (about 2-quart size)*

8 ounces uncooked fettuccine

1/2 cup (1 stick) margarine or butter

1/2 cup whipping (heavy) cream

3/4 cup grated Parmesan cheese

1/2 teaspoon salt

Dash of pepper

Chopped fresh parsley

DIRECTIONS

1 Fill the Dutch oven about half full of water. Add 1/2 teaspoon salt if desired. Cover and heat over high heat until the water is boiling rapidly. Add the fettuccine. Heat to boiling again. Boil uncovered 11 to 13 minutes, stirring frequently, until tender. To test fettuccine for doneness, cut a strand of fettuccine on the side of the Dutch oven. While fettuccine is cooking, continue with the recipe to make the Alfredo sauce.

2 Heat the margarine and whipping cream in the saucepan over low heat, stirring constantly, until margarine is melted. Stir in the cheese, salt and pepper until the mixture is smooth.

3 Drain the fettuccine in a strainer or colander, and place in a large serving bowl or back in the Dutch oven. Pour the sauce over the hot fettuccine, and stir until fettuccine is well coated. Sprinkle with parsley.

1 SERVING: Calories 370 (Calories from Fat 235); Fat 26g (Saturated 9g); Cholesterol 65mg; Sodium 570mg; Carbohydrate 26g (Dietary Fiber 1g); Protein 9g

FETTUCCINE ALFREDO: For 16 grams of fat and 290 calories per serving, decrease margarine to 1/3 cup, and substitute evaporated milk for the whipping cream.

TiP **FRESHLY GRATED PARMESAN** cheese will make a thinner sauce than will canned grated cheese.

TiP **OTHER PASTAS MAY BE** substituted for the fettuccine. The sauce will cling best to a flat, narrow shape, such as linguine or spaghetti.

Cooking Fettuccine

Boil until desired doneness. To test, cut a strand of fettuccine on the side of the Dutch oven.

Fettuccine Alfredo

PASTA PRIMAVERA

MAKES 4 servings • COOK: 15 minutes

INGREDIENTS

ESSENTIAL EQUIPMENT: *Dutch oven (about 4-quart size); 12-inch skillet*

8 ounces uncooked fettuccine or linguine

2 medium carrots

1 small onion

1 tablespoon olive or vegetable oil

1 cup broccoli flowerets

1 cup cauliflowerets

1 cup frozen green peas

1 container (10 ounces) refrigerated Alfredo sauce

Grated Parmesan cheese, if desired

DIRECTIONS

1 Fill the Dutch oven about half full of water. Add 1/2 teaspoon salt if desired. Cover and heat over high heat until the water is boiling rapidly. Add the fettuccine. Heat to boiling again. Boil uncovered 11 to 13 minutes, stirring frequently, until tender. While the water is heating and the fettuccine is cooking, continue with the recipe.

2 Peel the carrots, and cut crosswise into thin slices. Peel and chop the onion.

3 Heat the oil in the skillet over medium-high heat 1 to 2 minutes. Add the carrots, onion, broccoli flowerets, cauliflowerets and frozen peas. Stir-fry with a turner or large spoon 6 to 8 minutes, lifting and stirring constantly, until vegetables are crisp-tender when pierced with a fork.

4 Stir the Alfredo sauce into the vegetable mixture. Cook over medium heat, stirring constantly, until hot.

5 Drain the fettuccine in a strainer or colander. Stir the fettuccine into the vegetable mixture. Serve with cheese.

1 SERVING: Calories 520 (Calories from Fat 280); Fat 31g (Saturated 12g); Cholesterol 100mg; Sodium 690mg; Carbohydrate 51g (Dietary Fiber 6g); Protein 15g

---

TiP TO SAVE TIME, substitute a 16-ounce bag of fresh vegetables for stir-fry, available in the produce section of the supermarket, for the vegetables in this recipe.

TiP MANY SUPERMARKETS carry fresh broccoli flowerets and cauliflowerets already washed and ready to use. You'll find them in the produce department.

Stir-Frying Vegetables

Stir-fry with a turner or large spoon 6 to 8 minutes, lifting and stirring constantly, until vegetables are crisp-tender.

Pasta Primavera

STUFFED PASTA SHELLS

MAKES 6 servings • COOK: 12 minutes • BAKE: 30 minutes

INGREDIENTS

ESSENTIAL EQUIPMENT: *Dutch oven (about 4-quart size); large skillet (about 10-inch size); 8- or 9-inch square pan or baking dish*

12 uncooked jumbo pasta shells

1 medium onion

1 pound lean ground beef

1 1/2 teaspoons chili powder

1 package (3 ounces) cream cheese at room temperature

1/4 cup taco sauce

Cooking spray

1/2 cup taco sauce

1 cup shredded Colby-Monterey Jack cheese (4 ounces)

1/2 cup crushed corn chips

4 medium green onions with tops

1/2 cup sour cream

DIRECTIONS

1 Fill the Dutch oven about half full of water. Add 1/2 teaspoon salt if desired. Cover and heat over high heat until the water is boiling rapidly. Add the pasta shells. Heat to boiling again. Boil uncovered 11 to 13 minutes, stirring frequently, until tender. While the water is heating and the pasta shells are cooking, continue with the recipe.

2 Peel and chop the onion. Cook the ground beef and onion in the skillet over medium-high heat 5 to 6 minutes, stirring occasionally, until beef is brown; drain.

3 Stir the chili powder, cream cheese and 1/4 cup taco sauce into the beef in the skillet. Heat over medium-low heat 2 to 3 minutes, stirring occasionally, until cheese is melted. Remove the skillet from the heat.

4 Heat the oven to 350°. Spray the square pan with cooking spray.

5 Drain the pasta shells in a strainer or colander. Fill the shells with the beef mixture, using about 2 tablespoons for each shell. Place filled shells in the sprayed pan. Pour 1/2 cup taco sauce over the shells.

6 Cover with aluminum foil and bake 20 minutes. Remove the pan from the oven. Sprinkle the Colby-Monterey Jack cheese and corn chips over the shells. Bake uncovered about 10 minutes longer or until cheese is melted. Peel and slice the green onions. Garnish pasta shells with sour cream and green onions.

1 SERVING: Calories 585 (Calories from Fat 270); Fat 30g (Saturated 14g); Cholesterol 90mg; Sodium 340mg; Carbohydrate 53g (Dietary Fiber 3g); Protein 29g

STUFFED PASTA SHELLS: For 24 grams of fat and 540 calories per serving, use 1 pound lean ground turkey instead of the ground beef and use reduced-fat cream cheese (Neufchâtel), available in 8-ounce packages.

TiP **BE SURE TO PURCHASE** jumbo-size pasta shells, so they'll hold all the filling. Shells also come in small and medium sizes.

TiP **TO DO AHEAD,** cover and refrigerate pan of unbaked stuffed pasta shells up to 24 hours. Increase first bake time to 25 minutes.

Stuffing Jumbo Pasta Shells

Fill pasta shells with beef mixture, using about 2 tablespoons for each shell. Place in sprayed pan.

Stuffed Pasta Shells

DO-AHEAD
VEGETABLE LASAGNA DINNER

Whether cooking for family or friends, using do-ahead recipes makes dinner on a busy night easy and delicious. Invite friends over after work or the ball game to enjoy this special dinner, complete with dessert. Purchase the snacks, a 10-ounce bag of ready-to-eat salad greens, bottled dressing and a loaf of crusty bread from the supermarket along with the other ingredients you need, and let our timetable and recipes take away the guesswork. Your friends may offer to help set the table or toss the salad, which will make the dinner even easier for you. Plan to serve buffet-style from your kitchen counter.

SERVES FOUR

Peanuts or a purchased snack mix

Vegetable Lasagna

Crispy Green Salad

Crusty Bread

Creamy Lemon Dessert (page 216)

READY, SET, GO!

The night before dinner or up to 24 hours ahead

- Make Vegetable Lasagna, cover and refrigerate.
- Make Creamy Lemon Dessert, cover and refrigerate.

1 hour and 10 minutes before dinner

- Turn the oven to 400°, and allow to heat about 10 minutes.
- Set out a bowl of peanuts or snacks.
- Set the table, and select serving dishes for the salad and bread.

65 minutes before dinner

- Place Vegetable Lasagna in oven.
- Visit with your friends!

20 minutes before dinner

- Uncover lasagna, and continue baking 10 minutes.

10 minutes before dinner

- Remove lasagna from oven when it is bubbly around the edges and let stand 10 minutes.
- Place salad greens in a serving bowl, and toss with dressing.
- Cut wedges or slices of bread, and place in basket or on serving plate.
- Relax and enjoy your dinner!

After dinner

- Clear the table (accept help, if offered).
- Cut Creamy Lemon Dessert, and serve on small plates.

Vegetable Lasagna

MAKES 6 servings • BAKE: 55 minutes • LET STAND: 10 minutes

INGREDIENTS

ESSENTIAL EQUIPMENT: *8-inch or 9-inch square pan or baking dish*

1 medium zucchini

2 cups spaghetti sauce

1 package (10 ounces) frozen chopped spinach, thawed

1 1/2 cups reduced-fat cottage cheese or ricotta cheese (12 ounces)

1/3 cup grated Parmesan cheese

2 tablespoons chopped fresh or 1 1/2 teaspoons dried oregano leaves

1 can (4 ounces) mushroom stems and pieces

8 purchased precooked or oven-ready lasagna noodles (each about 7×3 inches)

2 cups shredded mozzarella cheese (8 ounces)

DIRECTIONS

1 Shred the zucchini by rubbing it across the largest holes of a shredder. You will need about 1 cup. Mix the spaghetti sauce and zucchini in a medium bowl.

2 Drain the thawed spinach in a strainer, then squeeze out the excess moisture from the spinach, using paper towels or a clean kitchen towel, until the spinach is dry.

3 Mix the spinach, cottage cheese, Parmesan cheese and oregano in a medium bowl. Drain the mushrooms in a strainer. Spread 1/2 cup of the sauce mixture in the ungreased square pan.

4 Top sauce mixture in pan with 2 noodles, placing them so they do not overlap or touch the sides of the pan because they will expand as they bake. Spread one fourth of the remaining sauce mixture (about 1/2 cup) over the noodles.

5 Drop one fourth of the spinach mixture by small spoonfuls over the sauce mixture; spread carefully, pulling with the tines of a fork if necessary. Sprinkle with one fourth of the mushrooms and 1/2 cup of the mozzarella cheese.

6 Repeat layering three more times, beginning with 2 more noodles and following directions in steps 4 and 5 Cover with plastic wrap and then with aluminum foil and refrigerate up to 24 hours. (The plastic wrap keeps the lasagna from touching the aluminum foil while being refrigerated.)

7 Heat the oven to 400°. Remove the plastic wrap from the lasagna, then cover the lasagna again with the aluminum foil. Bake 45 minutes. Carefully remove the foil, and continue baking about 10 minutes longer or until lasagna is bubbly around the edges. Remove from oven and let stand 10 minutes, so the lasagna will become easier to cut and serve.

1 SERVING: Calories 425 (Calories from Fat 115); Fat 13g (Saturated 6g); Cholesterol 30mg; Sodium 1030mg; Carbohydrate 53g (Dietary Fiber 4g); Protein 28g

TiP **TO COMPLETE THE LASAGNA** and serve just after assembling, heat oven to 400°. Cover with aluminum foil and bake as directed in step 7, decreasing the first bake time to 35 minutes.

TiP **PRECOOKED OR OVEN-READY** lasagna noodles are available with the other dried pastas in the supermarket.

Shredding Zucchini

Shred zucchini by rubbing it across the largest holes of a shredder.

Layering the Lasagna

Spread 1/2 cup sauce in the pan. Add 2 noodles, 1/2 cup sauce, one fourth of the spinach mixture, one fourth of the mushrooms and 1/2 cup mozzarella cheese.

Vegetable Lasagna

FRIED RICE

MAKES 4 servings • COOK: 30 minutes

INGREDIENTS

ESSENTIAL EQUIPMENT: *2-quart saucepan; 10-inch skillet*

Hot Cooked Rice (below)

1 cup bean sprouts

3 ounces mushrooms

2 medium green onions with tops

1 tablespoon vegetable oil

2 eggs

1 tablespoon vegetable oil

3 tablespoons soy sauce

Dash of pepper

HOT COOKED RICE

1 cup uncooked regular long-grain white rice

2 cups water

DIRECTIONS

1 Prepare Hot Cooked Rice. While the rice is cooking, continue with the recipe. If the rice is done before you need it, just remove the rice from the heat and let it stand a few minutes until you're ready.

2 Rinse the bean sprouts with cool water, and drain in a strainer. Cut off the ends of the mushroom stems, and slice the mushrooms. You should have about 1 cup. Peel and slice the green onions.

3 Heat 1 tablespoon oil in the skillet over medium heat 1 to 2 minutes. Cook the mushrooms in the oil about 1 minute, stirring frequently, until they are coated with oil.

4 Add the bean sprouts, onions and rice to the mushrooms. Stir-fry with a turner or large spoon, lifting and stirring constantly, until the mixture is hot. Remove the skillet from the heat.

5 Beat the eggs slightly in a small bowl with a fork. Push the rice mixture to one side of the skillet. Add 1 tablespoon oil to the cleared spot, then pour the eggs into this spot. Cook over medium heat, stirring constantly, until eggs are thickened and cooked but still moist.

6 Stir the eggs and rice mixture together. Stir in the soy sauce and pepper.

HOT COOKED RICE Heat the rice and water to boiling in the saucepan over high heat, stirring occasionally to prevent sticking. Once mixture is boiling, reduce heat just enough so mixture bubbles gently. Cover and cook about 15 minutes or until rice is fluffy and tender.

1 SERVING: Calories 320 (Calories from Fat 100); Fat 11g (Saturated 2g); Cholesterol 105mg; Sodium 810mg; Carbohydrate 45g (Dietary Fiber 1g); Protein 11g

TiP **COOK EXTRA RICE** the next time you are serving it with another meal. Refrigerate or freeze the leftover rice (you'll need about 3 cups) in an airtight container, and use it for Fried Rice.

TiP **SUBSTITUTE INGREDIENTS** in Fried Rice to suit your taste. Use chopped green bell pepper or sliced water chestnuts, or add leftover ham or chicken. Make it exactly as you like it.

Cooking Eggs in Fried Rice

Push the rice mixture to one side of the skillet. Add 1 tablespoon oil to the cleared spot, then pour eggs into this spot. Cook, stirring constantly, until eggs are thickened and cooked but still moist.

Fried Rice

SPANISH RICE

MAKES 4 servings • COOK: 30 minutes

INGREDIENTS

ESSENTIAL EQUIPMENT: *large skillet (about 10-inch size)*

1 medium onion

1 small green bell pepper

2 tablespoons vegetable oil

1 cup uncooked regular long-grain white rice

2 1/2 cups water

1 teaspoon salt

3/4 teaspoon chili powder

1/8 teaspoon garlic powder

1 can (8 ounces) tomato sauce

DIRECTIONS

1 Peel and chop the onion. Cut the bell pepper lengthwise in half, and cut out seeds and membrane. Chop the bell pepper.

2 Heat the oil in the skillet over medium heat 1 to 2 minutes. Cook the onion and uncooked rice in the oil about 5 minutes, stirring frequently, until rice is golden brown.

3 Remove the skillet from the heat. Stir in the bell pepper, water, salt, chili powder, garlic powder and tomato sauce. Heat to boiling over high heat, stirring occasionally.

4 Once mixture is boiling, reduce heat just enough so mixture bubbles gently. Cover and cook about 25 minutes, stirring occasionally, until rice is tender and tomato sauce is absorbed. You may have to lower the heat as the mixture becomes thicker.

1 SERVING: Calories 265 (Calories from Fat 65); Fat 7g (Saturated 1g); Cholesterol 0mg; Sodium 930mg; Carbohydrate 48g (Dietary Fiber 2g); Protein 5g

TiP **FOR EXTRA FLAVOR,** sprinkle 1/4 cup shredded Cheddar cheese over Spanish Rice just before serving.

TiP **SERVE WITH WARMED TORTILLAS** or toasted pita bread wedges and, for dessert, cool sherbet or sorbet.

Cooking Rice and Onion

Cook onion and rice in oil over medium heat about 5 minutes, stirring frequently, until rice is golden brown.

Cooking Spanish Rice

Reduce heat until rice mixture bubbles gently. Cover and cook about 25 minutes, stirring occasionally, until rice is tender and tomato sauce is absorbed. You may have to lower the heat as mixture becomes thicker.

Spanish Rice

QUESADILLAS

MAKES 6 servings • BAKE: 5 minutes

INGREDIENTS	DIRECTIONS
ESSENTIAL EQUIPMENT: *cookie sheet or large shallow baking pan (about 15×10 inches)*	**1** Heat the oven to 350°.
	2 Chop the tomato. Peel and chop the green onions.
1 small tomato	**3** Place the tortillas on a clean counter or on waxed paper. Sprinkle 1/3 cup of the cheese evenly over half of each tortilla. Top cheese with tomato, onions, chilies and cilantro, dividing ingredients so each tortilla has an equal amount.
3 medium green onions with tops	
6 flour tortillas (8 to 10 inches in diameter)	
2 cups shredded Colby or Cheddar cheese (8 ounces)	**4** Fold tortillas over filling, and place on the ungreased cookie sheet.
2 tablespoons chopped green chilies (from a 4-ounce can)	**5** Bake about 5 minutes or just until cheese is melted. Cut each quesadillas into wedges or strips, beginning cuts from the center of the folded side.
Chopped fresh cilantro or parsley, if desired	**1 SERVING:** Calories 280 (Calories from Fat 145); Fat 16g (Saturated 0g); Cholesterol 40mg; Sodium 470mg; Carbohydrate 26g (Dietary Fiber 1g); Protein 13g

 QUESADILLAS: For 10 grams of fat and 245 calories per serving, use reduced-fat cheese and reduced-fat tortillas.

TiP **QUESADILLAS CAN** be served as an appetizer or as a main dish. Add shredded cooked beef or chicken or refried beans to the filling for a heartier main dish.

TiP **IF NOT ALL** the tortillas will fit on your cookie sheet, bake just some of them at a time. Bake more as you need them, so they'll always be hot.

Chopping a Tomato

Cut tomato in half; place cut side down on cutting board, and chop into small pieces.

Quesadillas

CHEESE ENCHILADAS

MAKES 4 servings • COOK: 5 minutes • BAKE: 25 minutes

INGREDIENTS

ESSENTIAL EQUIPMENT: *rectangular baking dish or casserole (about 11×7 inches)*

1 small green bell pepper

1 clove garlic

1 medium onion

1 tablespoon chili powder

1 1/2 teaspoons chopped fresh or 1/2 teaspoon dried oregano leaves

1/4 teaspoon ground cumin

1 can (15 ounces) tomato sauce

2 cups shredded Monterey Jack cheese (8 ounces)

1 cup shredded Cheddar cheese (4 ounces)

1/2 cup sour cream

2 tablespoons chopped fresh parsley

1/4 teaspoon pepper

8 corn tortillas (5 or 6 inches in diameter)

Sour cream and chopped green onions, if desired

DIRECTIONS

1 Heat the oven to 350°. Cut the bell pepper lengthwise in half, and cut out seeds and membrane. Chop enough of the bell pepper to measure 1/3 cup. Wrap and refrigerate any remaining bell pepper. Peel and finely chop the garlic. Peel and chop the onion, and set aside.

2 Mix the bell pepper, garlic, chili powder, oregano, cumin and tomato sauce in a medium bowl, and set aside. Mix the onion, Monterey Jack cheese, Cheddar cheese, 1/2 cup sour cream, the parsley and pepper in a large bowl.

3 Place 2 tortillas between dampened microwavable paper towels or microwavable plastic wrap and microwave on High 15 to 20 seconds to soften them. Immediately spoon about 1/3 cup of the cheese mixture down one side of each softened tortilla to within 1 inch of edge. Roll tortilla around filling, and place seam side down in the ungreased baking dish. Repeat with the remaining tortillas and cheese mixture.

4 Pour the tomato sauce mixture over the tortillas.

5 Bake uncovered about 25 minutes or until hot and bubbly. Garnish with sour cream and chopped green onions.

1 SERVING: Calories 540 (Calories from Fat 305); Fat 34g (Saturated 20g); Cholesterol 105mg; Sodium 1290mg; Carbohydrate 38g (Dietary Fiber 5g); Protein 26g

QUICK CHEESE ENCHILADAS: Omit the bell pepper, garlic, chili powder, oregano, cumin and tomato sauce. Instead, use a 16-ounce jar of salsa, which is about 2 cups.

TiP **IF YOU LIKE ENCHILADAS** with a hotter flavor, seed and finely chop 2 green jalapeño chilies, and add to the tomato sauce mixture.

TiP **WHEN BUYING TORTILLAS,** check for freshness. They should not look dry or cracked around the edges.

Softening Tortillas

Place 2 tortillas between dampened paper towels or microwavable plastic wrap and microwave on High 15 to 20 seconds to soften them.

Filling Tortillas

Spoon about 1/3 cup of the cheese mixture down one side of each softened tortilla to within 1 inch of edge. Roll tortilla around filling, and place seam side down in baking dish.

Cheese Enchiladas

SOUTH-OF-THE-BORDER WRAPS

MAKES 4 servings • COOK: 3 minutes

INGREDIENTS

DIRECTIONS

ESSENTIAL EQUIPMENT: *9-inch square microwavable dish or dinner plate*

1 can (8 ounces) kidney beans

1 can (8 ounces) whole kernel corn

1 small bell pepper

1/2 cup chunky-style salsa

1 tablespoon chopped fresh cilantro or parsley

4 flour tortillas (8 to 10 inches in diameter)

1/2 cup shredded Cheddar cheese (2 ounces)

TiP **IF YOU HAVE** leftover rice from another dinner, stir 1/2 cup of it into the filling for these wraps.

1 Drain the kidney beans in a strainer, rinse with cool water and place in a bowl. Drain the corn in a strainer.

2 Cut the bell pepper lengthwise in half, and cut out seeds and membrane. Chop enough of the bell pepper to measure 1/4 cup. Wrap and refrigerate any remaining bell pepper.

3 Mix the beans, corn, bell pepper, salsa and cilantro.

4 Place the tortillas on a clean counter or on waxed paper. Spread about 1/2 cup of the bean mixture over each tortilla to within 1 inch of the edge. Sprinkle 2 tablespoons cheese over each tortilla.

5 Fold opposite sides of each tortilla up toward the center about 1 inch over the filling—the sides will not meet in the center. Roll up tortilla, beginning at one of the open ends. Place wraps, seam sides down, in the microwavable dish.

6 Microwave uncovered on High 1 minute. Rotate dish 1/4 turn. Microwave 1 minute to 1 minute 30 seconds longer.

1 SERVING: Calories 335 (Calories from Fat 90); Fat 10g (Saturated 4g); Cholesterol 15mg; Sodium 800mg; Carbohydrate 53g (Dietary Fiber 6g); Protein 14g

Filling Wraps

Fold opposite sides of each tortilla up toward the center about 1 inch over the filling—the sides will not meet in the center.

Rolling up Wraps and Placing in Dish

Roll up tortilla, beginning at one of the open ends. Place seam side down in microwavable dish.

South-of-the-Border Wraps

CHUNKY BROCCOLI SOUP

MAKES 4 servings • COOK: 10 minutes

INGREDIENTS

ESSENTIAL EQUIPMENT: *large saucepan (about 3-quart size)*

1 large or 2 small stalks broccoli (about 3/4 pound)

1 small carrot

1/4 teaspoon salt

1/8 teaspoon pepper

1 can (14 1/2 ounces) ready-to-serve chicken broth

2 tablespoons all-purpose flour

1/4 cup cold water

1 cup half-and-half

DIRECTIONS

1 Trim the large leaves from the broccoli, and cut off any tough ends of lower stems. Rinse broccoli with cool water. Cut flower end from stalk, and cut flowerets into bite-size pieces. Cut the stalk into small pieces, about 1/4- to 1/2-inch cubes. You should have about 3 cups of broccoli, including the flowerets, but having a little more or less is fine.

2 Peel and shred the carrot. Any size shreds is fine.

3 Heat the broccoli, shredded carrot, salt, pepper and chicken broth to boiling in the saucepan over high heat. Once mixture is boiling, reduce heat just enough so mixture bubbles gently. Cover and cook 6 to 8 minutes or until broccoli is tender when pierced with a fork.

4 Mix the flour and water in a small bowl or measuring cup with a fork or wire whisk until the flour is dissolved. Pour this mixture gradually into the broccoli mixture, stirring broccoli mixture constantly while pouring.

5 Heat to boiling over high heat, stirring constantly. Continue boiling 1 minute, stirring constantly.

6 Stir in the half-and-half. Cook, stirring occasionally, until hot. The soup should look hot and steamy, but do not let it boil.

1 SERVING: Calories 150 (Calories from Fat 70); Fat 8g (Saturated 5g); Cholesterol 20mg; Sodium 650mg; Carbohydrate 15g (Dietary Fiber 5g); Protein 9g

BROCCOLI-CHEESE SOUP: Make Chunky Broccoli Soup as directed. When soup is finished and very hot, gradually stir in 1 cup shredded Cheddar cheese until it is melted.

TiP **ONE 10-OUNCE PACKAGE** of frozen chopped broccoli may be substituted for the fresh broccoli. There's no need to thaw it before adding in step 3.

TiP **THE FLOUR MIXTURE** is used to thicken the broccoli soup. If it is not stirred constantly, it can form lumps instead of making the soup smooth and slightly thicker.

Thickening the Soup

Pour flour-and-water mixture gradually into broccoli mixture, stirring constantly.

Chunky Broccoli Soup

HOME-STYLE POTATO SOUP

MAKES 5 servings • COOK: 20 minutes

INGREDIENTS

ESSENTIAL EQUIPMENT: *large saucepan (about 3-quart size); potato masher or large fork*

3 medium potatoes (about 1 pound)

1 can (14 1/2 ounces) ready-to-serve chicken broth

2 medium green onions with tops

1 1/2 cups milk

1/4 teaspoon salt

1/8 teaspoon pepper

1/8 teaspoon dried thyme leaves

DIRECTIONS

1 Peel the potatoes, and cut into large pieces.

2 Heat the chicken broth and potatoes to boiling in the saucepan over high heat, stirring occasionally with a fork to make sure potatoes do not stick to the saucepan. Once mixture is boiling, reduce heat just enough so mixture bubbles gently. Cover and cook about 15 minutes or until potatoes are tender when pierced with a fork.

3 While the potatoes are cooking, peel and thinly slice the green onions. If you have extra onions, wrap them airtight and store in the refrigerator up to 5 days.

4 When the potatoes are done, remove the saucepan from the heat, but do not drain. Break the potatoes into smaller pieces with the potato masher or large fork. The mixture should still be lumpy.

5 Stir the milk, salt, pepper, thyme and onions into the potato mixture. Heat over medium heat, stirring occasionally, until hot and steaming, but do not let the soup boil.

1 SERVING: Calories 110 (Calories from Fat 20); Fat 2g (Saturated 1g); Cholesterol 5mg; Sodium 510mg; Carbohydrate 19g (Dietary Fiber 1g); Protein 5g

POTATO-CHEESE SOUP: Make Home-Style Potato Soup as directed. When soup is finished and very hot, gradually stir in 1 1/2 cups shredded Cheddar cheese until it is melted.

TiP **IF YOU REFRIGERATED** leftover soup and it seems too thick, just stir in some milk, a little at a time, while reheating it.

TiP **LOW-FAT OR NONFAT** milk can be used for this potato soup, but whole milk makes the soup a little richer and creamier.

Cutting Green Onions

Cut green onions into thin slices, using some of the green part. Throw away the tip with the stringy end.

Breaking up Potatoes

When potatoes are done, remove from heat, but do not drain. Break potatoes into smaller pieces using a potato masher or large fork.

Home-Style Potato Soup

BLACK BEAN SOUP

MAKES 4 servings • COOK: 30 minutes

INGREDIENTS

DIRECTIONS

ESSENTIAL EQUIPMENT: *medium or large saucepan (2- or 3-quart size)*

1 medium onion

1 large clove garlic

1 medium carrot

1 medium stalk celery

Parsley sprigs

1 slice bacon

1 can (14 1/2 ounces) ready-to-serve chicken broth

1/2 teaspoon dried oregano leaves

1/2 teaspoon crushed red pepper

1 can (15 ounces) black beans

4 lemon wedges

1 Peel and chop the onion. Peel and finely chop the garlic. Peel and coarsely chop the carrot. Coarsely chop the celery.

2 Rinse sprigs of parsley with cool water, and pat dry with a paper towel. Chop enough parsley leaves into small pieces on a cutting board using a chef's knife to measure about 2 table-spoons, or place the leafy portion of the parsley in a small bowl or cup and snip into very small pieces with kitchen scissors. Discard the stems.

3 Cut bacon slice crosswise into 1/2-inch strips. Cook the bacon strips in the saucepan over medium heat 1 minute, stir-ring constantly. Do not drain.

4 Add the onion and garlic to the bacon. Cook about 5 min-utes, stirring frequently, until onion is tender when pierced with a fork and beginning to turn yellow. Bacon will still be soft. Remove the saucepan from the heat.

5 Stir in the chicken broth, carrot, celery, parsley, oregano and red pepper. Heat to boiling over high heat. Once mixture is boil-ing, reduce heat just enough so mixture bubbles gently. Cover and cook 10 minutes.

6 While broth mixture is cooking, drain the black beans in a strainer, and rinse with cool water. Measure out 1/2 cup of the beans. Place the 1/2 cup beans in a small bowl, and mash them with a fork.

7 Stir the whole beans and the mashed beans into the broth mixture. Cook about 1 minute or until beans are heated. Serve soup with lemon wedges.

1 SERVING: Calories 140 (Calories from Fat 20); Fat 2g (Saturated 1g); Cholesterol 0mg; Sodium 670mg; Carbohydrate 27g (Dietary Fiber 7g); Protein 10g

TiP **TO MAKE** this a meatless soup, substitute 1 table-spoon vegetable oil for the bacon, and use vegetable broth instead of chicken broth.

TiP **THE BACON** will be easier to cut up if you place it in the freezer for 5 minutes first.

✔ **BEFORE ADDING** the chicken broth, remove the saucepan containing the hot bacon fat and onion from the heat to prevent spattering and steam.

Rinsing Beans

Empty beans into a strainer, and rinse with cool water.

Mashing Beans

Place 1/2 cup of the beans in a bowl, and mash with a fork.

Black Bean Soup

Vegetarian Chili

MAKES 4 servings • COOK: 17 minutes

INGREDIENTS | DIRECTIONS

ESSENTIAL EQUIPMENT: *Dutch oven (about 4-quart size)*

2 medium potatoes (about 10 ounces)

1 medium onion

1 small yellow bell pepper

1 can (15 to 16 ounces) garbanzo beans

1 can (15 to 16 ounces) kidney beans

1 can (28 ounces) whole tomatoes, undrained

1 can (8 ounces) tomato sauce

1 tablespoon chili powder

1 teaspoon ground cumin

1 medium zucchini

1 Scrub the potatoes thoroughly with a vegetable brush, but do not peel. Cut the potatoes into cubes that are 1/2 inch or slightly larger. Peel and chop the onion. Place the potatoes and onion in the Dutch oven.

2 Cut the bell pepper lengthwise in half, and cut out seeds and membrane. Chop the bell pepper into small pieces. Add to the Dutch oven.

3 Drain the garbanzo and kidney beans in a strainer, and rinse with cool water. Add to the Dutch oven.

4 Add the tomatoes with their liquid, the tomato sauce, chili powder and cumin to the Dutch oven. Heat to boiling over high heat, breaking up the tomatoes with a fork and stirring occasionally.

5 Once chili is boiling, reduce heat just enough so chili bubbles gently. Cover and cook 10 minutes.

6 While chili is cooking, cut the zucchini into 1/2 inch slices. Stir zucchini into chili. Cover and cook 5 to 7 minutes longer, stirring occasionally, until potatoes and zucchini are tender when pierced with a fork.

1 SERVING: Calories 315 (Calories from Fat 25); Fat 3g (Saturated 0g); Cholesterol 0mg; Sodium 1250mg; Carbohydrate 68g (Dietary Fiber 14g); Protein 18g

TiP **YOU MAY NOTICE** that zucchini comes in many sizes, with some homegrown ones reaching a foot or more in length. Choose a zucchini between 4 and 8 inches long because it will be younger and more tender than the bigger ones.

TiP **SUBSTITUTE** a green or red bell pepper if you can't find a yellow one. The flavor is similar.

Cubing Potatoes

Cut potatoes into cubes that are 1/2 inch or slightly larger.

Vegetarian Chili

EXCELLENT EGGS—FIVE WAYS

ALLOW 1 or 2 eggs per serving • COOK: Will vary with the method used

ESSENTIAL EQUIPMENT: *Saucepan or skillet large enough to hold desired number of eggs*

COOKED EGGS

HARD-COOKED EGGS: Place eggs in a saucepan. Add enough cold water until it is at least 1 inch above the eggs. Heat uncovered to boiling over high heat. Remove the saucepan from the heat. Cover and let stand 18 minutes. Immediately pour off the hot water from the eggs, then run cool water over them several seconds to prevent further cooking; drain. Tap egg lightly on kitchen counter to crackle the shell. Roll the egg between your hands to loosen the shell, then peel. If shell is hard to peel, hold egg under cold water while peeling.

SOFT-COOKED EGGS: Place eggs in a saucepan. Add enough cold water until it is at least 1 inch above the eggs. Heat uncovered to boiling over high heat. Remove the saucepan from the heat. Cover and let stand 3 minutes. Immediately pour off the hot water from the eggs, then run cool water over them several seconds to prevent further cooking; drain. Cut eggs lengthwise in half, and scoop eggs from shells.

FRIED EGGS

FRIED EGGS, SUNNY SIDE UP: Heat margarine or butter in a heavy skillet over medium heat until it begins to sizzle and look hot. Use enough margarine so when melted it is about 1/8 inch deep in the skillet. Break each egg into a custard cup or saucer. Slip the egg carefully into the skillet. Immediately reduce heat to low. You should still be able to see and hear the eggs sizzle as they cook. If they stop sizzling, turn the heat up a little. Cook uncovered 5 to 7 minutes, spooning margarine from the skillet over the eggs frequently, until the whites are set, a film forms over the yolks and the yolks are thickened.

FRIED EGGS, OVER EASY: Follow directions for Fried Eggs, Sunny Side Up (above), but after cooking 3 minutes, gently turn eggs over with a wide spatula and cook 1 to 2 minutes longer or until yolks are thickened.

SCRAMBLED EGGS

1 Using 1 tablespoon of milk, half-and-half or water for each egg, beat eggs and milk with a fork or wire whisk until well mixed. Add salt and pepper as desired. Heat margarine (about 1 tablespoon for 3 eggs) in a skillet over medium heat just until the margarine begins to sizzle.

2 Pour egg mixture into skillet. The egg mixture will become firm at the bottom and side very quickly. When this happens, gently lift the cooked portions around the edge with a spatula so that the thin, uncooked portion can flow to the bottom. Avoid constant stirring, but continue to lift the cooked portion and allow the thin uncooked portions to flow to the bottom.

3 Cook 3 to 4 minutes or until eggs are thickened throughout but still moist and creamy. Serve immediately.

TiP **STORE EGGS IN THEIR CARTON** in the refrigerator. Keeping them in the carton protects them from absorbing refrigerator odors.

TiP **WHETHER THE EGGSHELL** is white or brown depends on the breed and diet of the hen. Flavor, nutritive value and the way the egg cooks are the same for both kinds.

✔ **IF HARD-COOKED EGGS** are used for an egg hunt, avoid keeping them at room temperature for more than 2 hours. If you do, don't eat the eggs.

Peeling Hard-Cooked Eggs

Roll egg between hands to loosen shell, then peel. If shell is hard to peel, hold egg under cold water while peeling

Frying an Egg

Break each egg into a custard cup or saucer. Slip the egg carefully into the skillet.

Cooking Scrambled Eggs

Gently lift the cooked portions around the edge with a spatula so that the thin, uncooked portion can flow to the bottom.

OMELET

MAKES 1 serving • **COOK:** 5 minutes

INGREDIENTS

ESSENTIAL EQUIPMENT: *8-inch skillet*

2 eggs

2 teaspoons margarine or butter

Salt and pepper, if desired

DIRECTIONS

1 Beat the eggs in a small bowl with a fork or wire whisk until yolks and whites are well mixed.

2 Heat the margarine in the skillet over medium-high heat until margarine is hot and sizzling. As margarine melts, tilt skillet to coat bottom with margarine.

3 Quickly pour the eggs into the skillet. While sliding the skillet back and forth rapidly over the heat, quickly stir the eggs with a fork to spread them continuously over the bottom of the skillet as they thicken. When they are thickened, let stand over the heat a few seconds to lightly brown the bottom. Do not overcook—the omelet will continue to cook after being folded.

4 Tilt the skillet and run a spatula or fork under the edge of the omelet, then jerk the skillet sharply to loosen omelet from bottom of skillet. Fold the portion of the omelet nearest you just to the center. Allow for a portion of the omelet to slide up the side of the skillet. Turn the omelet onto a warm plate, flipping folded portion of omelet over so the far side is on the bottom. Tuck sides of omelet under if necessary. Sprinkle with salt and pepper.

1 SERVING: Calories 220 (Calories from Fat 160); Fat 18g (Saturated 5g); Cholesterol 425mg; Sodium 220mg; Carbohydrate 1g (Dietary Fiber 0g); Protein 13g

CHEESE OMELET: Before folding omelet, sprinkle with 1/4 cup shredded Cheddar, Monterey Jack or Swiss cheese or 1/4 cup crumbled blue cheese.

DENVER OMELET: Cook 2 tablespoons chopped fully cooked ham, 1 tablespoon finely chopped bell pepper and 1 tablespoon finely chopped onion in the margarine about 2 minutes, stirring frequently, before adding eggs.

TiP **TO WARM A PLATE** for serving the omelet, run hot water over the serving plate, then dry it thoroughly just before cooking the omelet.

TiP **USING A NONSTICK** skillet makes preparing an omelet easier.

Cooking an Omelet

Tilt skillet and run a spatula or fork under edge of omelet, then jerk skillet sharply to loosen omelet from bottom. Fold portion of omelet nearest you just to center.

Turning Omelet out of Skillet

Turn omelet onto warm plate, flipping folded portion of omelet over so the far side is on the bottom.

Omelet

ON THE SIDE

BLUEBERRY MUFFINS

MAKES 12 regular-size muffins • BAKE: 25 minutes

INGREDIENTS

DIRECTIONS

ESSENTIAL EQUIPMENT: *muffin pan with 12 regular-size muffin cups*

Shortening to grease muffin cups

1 cup fresh or canned blueberries

1 cup milk

1/4 cup vegetable oil

1/2 teaspoon vanilla

1 egg

2 cups all-purpose or whole wheat flour

1/3 cup sugar

3 teaspoons baking powder

1/2 teaspoon salt

1 Heat the oven to 400°. Grease just the bottoms of 12 regular-size muffin cups with the shortening, or line each cup with a paper baking cup.

2 If using canned blueberries, drain them in a strainer. Rinse fresh or canned blueberries with cool water, and discard any crushed ones. Break off any stems.

3 Beat the milk, oil, vanilla and egg in a large bowl with a fork or wire whisk until well mixed. Stir in the flour, sugar, baking powder and salt all at once just until the flour is moistened. The batter will be lumpy. If the batter is mixed too much, the muffins will have high peaks instead of being rounded.

4 Carefully stir in the blueberries. Spoon the batter into the greased muffin cups, dividing batter evenly among them. You can use an ice-cream scoop for this if you have one.

5 Bake 20 to 25 minutes or until golden brown. Immediately remove muffins from the pan to a wire cooling rack. Serve warm or cool.

1 MUFFIN: Calories 160 (Calories from Fat 55); Fat 6g (Saturated 1g); Cholesterol 20mg; Sodium 240mg; Carbohydrate 24g (Dietary Fiber 0g); Protein 3g

APPLE-CINNAMON MUFFINS: Omit blueberries. Stir in 1 cup chopped apple with the milk. Stir in 1/2 teaspoon ground cinnamon with the flour. Bake 25 to 30 minutes.

BLUEBERRY MUFFINS: For 3 grams of fat and 135 calories per serving, use skim milk, decrease the vegetable oil to 2 tablespoons and add 1/4 cup unsweetened applesauce.

TiP **SUBSTITUTE 3/4 CUP** frozen blueberries, thawed and well drained, for the fresh or canned blueberries if desired.

TiP **ALUMINUM FOIL** baking cups purchased at the supermarket can be used instead of a muffin pan. Place 12 foil cups on a cookie sheet or in a rectangular pan, and fill as directed.

Stirring Blueberries into Muffin Batter

Carefully stir blueberries into the muffin batter.

Filling Muffin Cups

Using an ice-cream scoop is an easy way to fill muffin cups.

Blueberry Muffins

CORN BREAD

MAKES 12 servings • BAKE: 25 minutes

INGREDIENTS

ESSENTIAL EQUIPMENT: *8-inch square pan or 9×1 1/2-inch round pan*

Shortening to grease pan

1 cup milk

1/4 cup (1/2 stick) stick margarine or butter, melted

1 egg

1 1/4 cups yellow, white or blue cornmeal

1 cup all-purpose flour

1/2 cup sugar

1 tablespoon baking powder

1/2 teaspoon salt

DIRECTIONS

1 Heat the oven to 400°. Grease the bottom and side of the pan with the shortening.

2 Beat the milk, margarine and egg in a large bowl with a fork or wire whisk until well mixed. Stir in the cornmeal, flour, sugar, baking powder and salt all at once just until the flour is moistened. The batter will be lumpy. Pour the batter into the greased pan.

3 Bake 20 to 25 minutes or until golden brown and when a toothpick inserted in the center comes out clean. Serve warm.

1 SERVING: Calories 175 (Calories from Fat 45); Fat 5g (Saturated 1g); Cholesterol 20mg; Sodium 280mg; Carbohydrate 29g (Dietary Fiber 1g); Protein 4g

CORN MUFFINS: Grease just the bottoms of 12 regular-size muffin cups with shortening, or line each cup with a paper baking cup. Fill each cup about 3/4 full with batter.

TiP IF USING MARGARINE, purchase regular margarine or a spread that contains at least 65 percent vegetable oil and is in a stick form. Spreads with less fat do not work well for cakes, cookies and other baked desserts.

TiP TO DO AHEAD, measure the cornmeal, flour, sugar, baking powder and salt into a plastic bag or a bowl ahead of time; seal or cover. Then finishing the cornbread at the last minute so it can be served warm will be as easy as using a mix.

Testing Corn Bread for Doneness

If corn bread is not fully baked, a toothpick inserted in the center will have uncooked batter clinging to it.

Corn Bread

GARLIC BREAD

MAKES 1 loaf (18 slices) • BAKE: 20 minutes

INGREDIENTS

ESSENTIAL EQUIPMENT: *heavy-duty aluminum foil*

1 clove garlic or 1/4 teaspoon garlic powder

1/3 cup margarine or butter at room temperature

1 loaf (1 pound) French bread

DIRECTIONS

1 Heat the oven to 400°.

2 Peel and finely chop the garlic. Mix the garlic and margarine.

3 Cut the bread crosswise into 1-inch slices. Spread margarine mixture over 1 side of each bread slice. Reassemble the loaf, and wrap securely in heavy-duty aluminum foil.

4 Bake 15 to 20 minutes or until hot.

1 SLICE: Calories 95 (Calories from Fat 35); Fat 4g (Saturated 1g); Cholesterol 0mg; Sodium 190mg; Carbohydrate 13g (Dietary Fiber 0g); Protein 2g

HERB-CHEESE BREAD: Omit the garlic. Mix 2 teaspoons chopped fresh parsley, 1/2 teaspoon dried oregano leaves, 2 tablespoons grated Parmesan cheese and 1/8 teaspoon garlic salt with the margarine.

ONION BREAD: Omit the garlic. Mix 2 tablespoons finely chopped onion or chives with the margarine.

SEEDED BREAD: Omit the garlic. Mix 1 teaspoon celery seed, poppy seed, dill seed or sesame seed with the margarine.

TiP TO SAVE TIME, HEAT THE BREAD in your microwave. Do not wrap loaf in foil. Instead, divide loaf in half, and place halves side by side in napkin-lined microwavable basket or on microwavable dinner plate. Cover with napkin and microwave on Medium (50%) 1 1/2 to 3 minutes, rotating basket 1/2 turn after 1 minute, until bread is hot.

TiP IF USING MARGARINE, purchase regular margarine or a spread that contains at least 65 percent vegetable oil and is in a stick form. Spreads with less fat have more water, and the bread may get slightly soggy.

Assembling Loaf of Bread

Spread margarine mixture over 1 side of each bread slice. Reassemble the loaf, and wrap securely in heavy-duty aluminum foil.

Garlic Bread

CAESAR SALAD

MAKES 6 servings

INGREDIENTS

ESSENTIAL EQUIPMENT: *large salad or mixing bowl*

1 large bunch or 2 small bunches romaine

1 clove garlic

8 flat anchovy fillets (from 2-ounce can), if desired

1/3 cup olive or vegetable oil

3 tablespoons lemon juice

1 teaspoon Worcestershire sauce

1/4 teaspoon salt

1/4 teaspoon ground mustard (dry)

Freshly ground pepper

1 cup garlic-flavored croutons

1/3 cup grated Parmesan cheese

DIRECTIONS

1 Remove any limp outer leaves from the romaine, and discard. Break remaining leaves off the core, and rinse with cool water. Shake off excess water, and blot to dry, or roll up the leaves in a clean, kitchen towel or paper towel to dry. Tear the leaves into bite-size pieces. You will need about 10 cups of romaine pieces.

2 Peel the garlic, and cut the clove in half. Rub the inside of the bowl—a wooden salad bowl works best—with the cut sides of the garlic. Allow a few small pieces of garlic to remain in the bowl if desired.

3 Cut up the anchovies, and place in the bowl. Add the oil, lemon juice, Worcestershire sauce, salt, mustard and pepper. Mix well with a fork or wire whisk.

4 Add the romaine, and toss with 2 large spoons or salad tongs until coated with the dressing. Sprinkle with the croutons and cheese. To keep salad crisp, serve immediately.

1 SERVING: Calories 165 (Calories from Fat 125); Fat 14g (Saturated 3g); Cholesterol 10mg; Sodium 430mg; Carbohydrate 7g (Dietary Fiber 2g); Protein 5g

 CAESAR SALAD: For 9 grams of fat and 120 calories per serving, decrease oil to 3 tablespoons, increase lemon juice to 1/4 cup and add 2 tablespoons water to anchovy mixture. Decrease cheese to 3 tablespoons.

✔ **SOME TRADITIONAL** Caesar salad recipes may call for raw egg. Using uncooked eggs may cause certain types of food poisoning, so these recipes should be avoided.

TiP **TO SAVE TIME,** purchase romaine already washed, torn and ready to use. You will need 10 cups, which is about 14 ounces.

TiP **TO DO AHEAD,** wash and dry romaine and seal in a plastic bag or airtight container. It will keep up to a week in the refrigerator.

Drying Romaine

Shake off excess water, and blot to dry, or roll up the leaves in a clean, kitchen towel or paper towel to dry.

Caesar Salad

GREEK SALAD

MAKES 8 servings

INGREDIENTS

DIRECTIONS

ESSENTIAL EQUIPMENT: *large salad or mixing bowl*

Lemon Dressing (below)

1 bunch spinach
(1/2 pound)

1 head Boston or Bibb
lettuce

3 medium green onions
with tops

1 medium cucumber

3 medium tomatoes

24 pitted whole ripe olives
(from a 6-ounce can)

3/4 cup crumbled feta
cheese (3 ounces)

LEMON DRESSING

1/4 cup vegetable oil

2 tablespoons lemon juice

1/2 teaspoon sugar

1 1/2 teaspoons Dijon
mustard

1/4 teaspoon salt

1/8 teaspoon pepper

1 Prepare Lemon Dressing (below).

2 Remove and discard the stems of the spinach. Rinse the leaves in cool water. Shake off excess water, and blot to dry, or roll up the leaves in a clean, dry kitchen towel or paper towel to dry. Tear the leaves into bite-size pieces, and place in the bowl. You will need about 5 cups of spinach pieces.

3 Separate the leaves from the head of lettuce. Rinse the leaves with cool water. Shake off excess water, and blot to dry. Tear the leaves into bite-size pieces, and add to the bowl.

4 Peel and slice the green onions. Slice the cucumber. Cut the tomatoes into wedges. Add these vegetables and the olives to the bowl.

5 Break up any large pieces of the cheese with a fork, and add to the bowl.

6 Pour the dressing over the salad ingredients, and toss with 2 large spoons or salad tongs. To keep salad crisp, serve immediately.

LEMON DRESSING Shake all ingredients in a tightly covered jar or container. Shake again before pouring over salad.

1 SERVING: Calories 135 (Calories from Fat 100); Fat 11g (Saturated 3g); Cholesterol 10mg; Sodium 350mg; Carbohydrate 7g (Dietary Fiber 2g); Protein 4g

TiP **ALTHOUGH THE SPINACH** you purchase may be labeled *washed*, you should wash it again because it may still contain some sand and dirt. Ready-to-eat spinach, available in bags, does not need to be washed.

TiP **IF YOU DO NOT** want to eat the entire salad, save a portion of it in a plastic bag before adding the dressing. Seal tightly and refrigerate up to two days. Add just enough dressing to the salad to be served to coat the leaves lightly, and refrigerate remaining dressing.

Washing Spinach

Remove and discard spinach stems. Place leaves in a sink or bowl filled with cool water. Swish with your hands to rinse off the dirt. Lift the leaves up to drain off excess water. Repeat until no dirt remains.

Preparing Boston Lettuce

Separate the leaves from the head of lettuce. Rinse thoroughly, and blot to dry.

Greek Salad

SPINACH-STRAWBERRY SALAD

MAKES 4 servings

INGREDIENTS

ESSENTIAL EQUIPMENT: *large salad or mixing bowl*

Honey-Dijon Dressing (below)

1 small jicama

2 kiwifruit

1/2 pint (1 cup) strawberries

7 to 8 cups ready-to-eat spinach (from 10-ounce bag)

1 cup alfalfa sprouts

HONEY-DIJON DRESSING

2 tablespoons vegetable oil

2 tablespoons honey

2 tablespoons orange juice

1 tablespoon seasoned rice vinegar or white vinegar

1 teaspoon poppy seed, if desired

2 teaspoons Dijon mustard

DIRECTIONS

1 Prepare Honey-Dijon Dressing (below).

2 Peel the jicama, removing the brown skin and a thin layer of the flesh just under the skin. The skin can sometimes be slightly tough. Cut about half of the jicama into about 1 × 1/4-inch sticks to measure about 3/4 cup. Wrap remaining jicama, and refrigerate for another use.

3 Peel the kiwifruit. Cut lengthwise in half, then cut into slices.

4 Rinse the strawberries with cool water, and pat dry. Remove the leaves, and cut the berries lengthwise into slices.

5 Remove the stems from the spinach leaves, and tear any large leaves into bite-size pieces. Place the spinach, strawberries, alfalfa sprouts, jicama sticks and kiwifruit slices in the bowl. Pour the dressing over the salad ingredients, and toss with 2 large spoons or salad tongs. To keep salad crisp, serve immediately.

HONEY-DIJON DRESSING Shake all ingredients in a tightly covered jar or container. Shake again before pouring over salad.

1 SERVING: Calories 165 (Calories from Fat 90); Fat 8g (Saturated 1g); Cholesterol 0mg; Sodium 45mg; Carbohydrate 28g (Dietary Fiber 8g); Protein 3g

TiP **BESIDES THE SPINACH,** packaged mixed salad greens that are already cleaned and ready to use are available in the produce section of the supermarket. A 10-ounce bag is about 7 cups of greens. The Italian variety is especially pretty.

TiP **LEFTOVER JICAMA** can be cut into sticks and served with other raw vegetables for a snack or appetizer.

Shaking Dressing

Shake all ingredients for the Honey-Dijon Dressing in a tightly covered jar.

Cutting up Jicama

Peel jicama, and cut into 1/4-inch slices. Cut slices into sticks for a salad or raw vegetable platter.

Spinach-Strawberry Salad

CREAMY COLESLAW

MAKES 4 servings • REFRIGERATE: 1 hour

INGREDIENTS

DIRECTIONS

ESSENTIAL EQUIPMENT: *small and medium bowls*

1/4 cup sour cream

2 tablespoons mayonnaise or salad dressing

1 1/2 teaspoons sugar

1 teaspoon lemon juice

1 teaspoon Dijon mustard

1/4 teaspoon celery seed

1/8 teaspoon pepper

1/4 of a medium head of cabbage

1/2 of a small carrot

1/2 of a small onion

1 Mix the sour cream, mayonnaise, sugar, lemon juice, mustard, celery seed and pepper in the small bowl.

2 Place a flat side of the 1/4 head of cabbage on a cutting board, and cut off the core. Cut the cabbage into thin slices with a large sharp knife. Cut the slices several times to make smaller pieces. You should have about 2 cups.

3 Peel and shred the carrot. Peel and chop the onion.

4 Place the cabbage, carrot and onion in the medium bowl. Pour the sour cream mixture over the vegetables, and mix with a large spoon until the vegetables are evenly coated with the dressing.

5 Cover and refrigerate the coleslaw at least 1 hour to blend flavors. Cover and refrigerate any remaining coleslaw.

1 SERVING: Calories 115 (Calories from Fat 80); Fat 9g (Saturated 3g); Cholesterol 15mg; Sodium 75mg; Carbohydrate 7g (Dietary Fiber 1g); Protein 2g

 Lighter **CREAMY COLESLAW:** For 1 gram of fat and 55 calories per serving, use reduced-fat sour cream and fat-free mayonnaise.

TiP **TO SAVE TIME,** purchase a prepackaged coleslaw mixture, washed and ready to use, from the produce section of the supermarket. Substitute it for the cabbage, carrots and onion. You will need about 3 cups of the mixture (6 to 7 ounces).

TiP **YOU CAN PURCHASE** lemon juice that's ready to use in bottles or lemon-shaped plastic containers.

Shredding Cabbage

Place a flat side of the 1/4 head of cabbage on a cutting board. Cut into thin slices with a large sharp knife. Cut slices several times to make smaller pieces.

Creamy Coleslaw

ITALIAN PASTA SALAD

MAKES 6 servings • REFRIGERATE: 30 minutes

INGREDIENTS

DIRECTIONS

ESSENTIAL EQUIPMENT: *Dutch oven (about 4-quart size)*

Garlic Vinaigrette Dressing (below)

2 cups uncooked rotini or rotelle (spiral) pasta (6 ounces)

1 large tomato

1/2 of a medium cucumber

3 or 4 medium green onions with tops

1 small red or green bell pepper

1/4 cup chopped ripe olives, if desired

GARLIC VINAIGRETTE DRESSING

1 clove garlic

1/4 cup rice vinegar or white vinegar

2 tablespoons water

2 tablespoons olive or vegetable oil

1/2 teaspoon salt

1/2 teaspoon sesame or vegetable oil

1 Prepare Garlic Vinaigrette Dressing (below).

2 Fill the Dutch oven about half full of water. Add 1/4 teaspoon salt if desired. Cover and heat over high heat until the water is boiling rapidly. Add the pasta. Heat to boiling again. Boil uncovered, stirring frequently, 8 to 10 minutes for rotini, 9 to 11 minutes for rotelle, until tender.

3 While the water is heating and pasta is cooking, chop the tomato and cucumber, and peel and chop the onions. Place the vegetables in a large bowl.

4 Cut the bell pepper lengthwise in half, and cut out seeds and membrane. Cut bell pepper into pieces, and add to vegetables in bowl.

5 Drain the pasta in a strainer or colander, and rinse thoroughly with cold water. Add pasta to vegetables in bowl. Add the olives.

6 Pour the dressing over the vegetables and pasta, and mix thoroughly. Cover and refrigerate about 30 minutes or until chilled.

GARLIC VINAIGRETTE DRESSING Peel and finely chop the garlic. Shake garlic and remaining ingredients in a tightly covered jar or container. Shake again before pouring over vegetables and pasta.

1 SERVING: Calories 170 (Calories from Fat 55); Fat 6g (Saturated 1g); Cholesterol 0mg; Sodium 200mg; Carbohydrate 26g (Dietary Fiber 1g); Protein 4g

RANCH PASTA SALAD: Use about 1/2 cup ranch dressing from the supermarket instead of the Garlic Vinaigrette Dressing.

TiP **THE WATER BEING HEATED** for cooking the pasta will boil sooner if it is covered with a lid.

TiP **WRAP ANY LEFTOVER** onions and cucumber in plastic wrap and store in the refrigerator.

Cutting up a Bell Pepper

Cut bell pepper lengthwise in half; cut out seeds and membrane.

Italian Pasta Salad

OLD-FASHIONED POTATO SALAD

MAKES 5 servings • REFRIGERATE: 4 hours

INGREDIENTS

DIRECTIONS

ESSENTIAL EQUIPMENT: *large saucepan (about 3-quart size); medium saucepan (about 2-quart size)*

3 medium boiling potatoes (about 1 pound)

2 eggs

1 medium stalk celery

1 medium onion

3/4 cup mayonnaise or salad dressing

1 1/2 teaspoons white vinegar

1 1/2 teaspoons mustard

1/2 teaspoon salt

1/8 teaspoon pepper

1 Peel the potatoes, and cut any large potatoes in half. Add 1 inch of water to the large saucepan. Cover and heat the water to boiling over high heat. Add potatoes. Cover and heat to boiling again. Once water is boiling, reduce heat just enough so water bubbles gently. Cook covered 20 to 25 minutes or until potatoes are tender when pierced with a fork. Drain potatoes in a strainer, and cool slightly. Cut potatoes into cubes.

2 While the potatoes are cooking, place the eggs in the medium saucepan. Cover with at least 1 inch of cold water, and heat to boiling over high heat. Remove the saucepan from the heat. Let stand covered 18 minutes. Immediately pour off the hot water from the eggs, then run cool water over them several seconds to prevent further cooking; drain.

3 Peel and chop the eggs. Chop the celery. Peel the onion, and chop enough of the onion to measure 1/4 cup. Wrap any remaining onion, and refrigerate for another use.

4 Mix the mayonnaise, vinegar, mustard, salt and pepper in a large bowl. Gently stir in the potatoes, celery and onion. Stir in the chopped eggs.

5 Cover and refrigerate at least 4 hours to blend flavors and to chill. Cover and refrigerate any remaining salad.

1 SERVING: Calories 330 (Calories from Fat 250); Fat 28g (Saturated 5g); Cholesterol 105mg; Sodium 470mg; Carbohydrate 17g (Dietary Fiber 1g); Protein 4g

POTATO SALAD: For 1 gram of fat and 100 calories per serving, substitute 1/4 cup fat-free mayonnaise and 1/2 cup plain fat-free yogurt for the 3/4 cup mayonnaise. Use 1 egg.

CELERY IS GROWN AND SOLD as a bunch and can be stored in a plastic bag in the refrigerator for up to 2 weeks. A stalk, or rib, is one stem out of the bunch. Stalks should be left attached to the bunch until used. Be sure to rinse the stalks and cut off the base and the leaves.

TiP **TO DO AHEAD, PEEL POTATOES** 2 or 3 hours before you plan to cook them. Put them in a bowl of cold water to keep them from turning a dark color, then cover and refrigerate.

Choosing Potatoes for Boiling

Choose round red or round white potatoes to boil for potato salad because they will hold their shape when cooked. Russet potatoes do not work as well for potato salad.

Old-Fashioned Potato Salad

FRESH FRUIT WITH HONEY-POPPY SEED DRESSING

MAKES 6 servings

INGREDIENTS

ESSENTIAL EQUIPMENT: *large salad or mixing bowl*

Honey-Poppy Seed Dressing (below)

1 large unpeeled apple or 2 medium apricots or nectarines

1 medium orange

1 medium pineapple

1 small bunch seedless green grapes

HONEY-POPPY SEED DRESSING

1/4 cup vegetable oil

3 tablespoons honey

2 tablespoons lemon juice

1 1/2 teaspoons poppy seed

DIRECTIONS

1 Prepare Honey-Poppy Seed Dressing (below).

2 Cut the unpeeled apple into slices, or peel and slice the apricots or nectarines.

3 Peel the orange, then cut along the membrane of both sides of one orange section. Remove that section, and continue with the rest of the orange.

4 Cut the pineapple lengthwise into fourths. Cut off the rind and the core. Cut the pineapple into chunks, removing any "eyes" or spots left from the rind.

5 Wash the grapes, and cut in half.

6 Mix the fruits and the dressing in a large bowl. Cover and refrigerate until ready to serve. Cover and refrigerate any remaining salad.

HONEY-POPPY SEED DRESSING Shake all ingredients in a tightly covered jar or container. Shake again before pouring over fruit.

1 SERVING: Calories 215 (Calories from Fat 90); Fat 10g (Saturated 2g); Cholesterol 0mg; Sodium 5mg; Carbohydrate 32g (Dietary Fiber 2g); Protein 1g

TiP **IF YOU'RE IN A HURRY,** substitute 1/2 cup frozen whipped topping, thawed, and 1/2 teaspoon grated lemon peel for the Honey-Poppy Seed Dressing. Stir into fruit just before serving.

TiP **TWO CUPS STRAWBERRIES,** cut in half, can be substituted for half of the pineapple.

Cutting an Orange into Sections

Cut along the membrane of both sides of one orange section. Remove that section, and continue with the rest of the orange.

Peeling and Cutting up Pineapple

Cut pineapple lengthwise into fourths. Cut off the rind and the core. Cut pineapple into chunks, removing any "eyes" or spots left from the rind.

Fresh Fruit with Honey-Poppy Seed Dressing

ASPARAGUS

1 1/2 pounds is enough for 4 servings

When Shopping: Look for smooth, firm, medium-size spears with tightly closed tips. Cover stem ends with damp paper towel, wrap airtight and store in the refrigerator up to 3 days.

Preparing for Cooking: Break off and discard the tough ends of the asparagus stalks where they snap easily. Wash asparagus thoroughly, including the tips, to remove any sandy soil. Remove the scales if sandy or tough. If stalk ends are quite large, peel about 2 inches of the end with a vegetable peeler, so they will be more tender after cooking.

Boiling: Add 1 inch of water (and 1/4 teaspoon salt if desired) to a large skillet (about 10-inch size). Cover and heat to boiling over high heat. Add asparagus spears. Cover and heat to boiling again. Once water is boiling, reduce heat just enough so water bubbles gently. Cook covered 8 to 12 minutes or until crisp-tender when pierced with a fork. Thinner, young asparagus will cook more quickly than the more mature, thicker stalks. Lift asparagus from water with tongs, allowing extra water to drip off.

Steaming: Place a steamer basket in 1/2 inch of water in a skillet or saucepan. The water should not touch the bottom of the basket. Place asparagus spears in basket. Cover tightly and heat to boiling over high heat. Once water is boiling, reduce heat to low. Steam covered 6 to 8 minutes or until crisp-tender when pierced with a fork.

Microwaving: Place asparagus spears and 1/4 cup water in an 8-inch square microwavable dish. Cover with plastic wrap, folding back 2-inch edge to vent. Microwave on High 6 to 9 minutes, rotating dish 1/2 turn after 3 minutes, until crisp-tender when pierced with a fork. Let stand covered 1 minute; drain in a strainer.

1 SERVING: Calories 20 (Calories from Fat 0); Fat 0g (Saturated 0g); Cholesterol 0mg; Sodium 5mg; Carbohydrate 4g (Dietary Fiber 1g); Protein 2g

Storing Asparagus

Cover stem ends with damp paper towel, wrap airtight and store in refrigerator up to 4 days.

Preparing Asparagus for Cooking

Break off tough ends of asparagus stalks where they snap easily; discard.

GREEN AND YELLOW WAX BEANS

1 pound is enough for 4 servings

When Shopping: The wax bean is a pale yellow variety of green bean. For green or yellow beans, look for long, smooth, crisp pods with fresh-looking tips and bright green or waxy yellow color. Wrap airtight and store in the refrigerator up to 5 days.

Preparing for Cooking: Wash beans, and cut off ends. Leave whole, or cut crosswise into about 1-inch pieces. To save time when cutting, place 3 to 4 beans side by side on a cutting board, and cut off all the ends at one time.

Boiling: Add 1 inch of water (and 1/4 teaspoon salt if desired) to a medium saucepan (about 2-quart size). Add the beans. Cover and heat to boiling over high heat. Once water is boiling, reduce heat just enough so water bubbles gently. Cook uncovered 5 minutes. Cover and cook 5 to 10 minutes longer or until crisp-tender when pierced with a fork; drain in a strainer.

Steaming: Place a steamer basket in 1/2 inch of water in a skillet or saucepan. The water should not touch the bottom of the basket. Place beans in basket. Cover tightly and heat to boiling over high heat. Once water is boiling, reduce heat to low. Steam covered 10 to 12 minutes or until crisp-tender when pierced with a fork.

Microwaving Pieces: Place beans and 1/2 cup water in a 1 1/2-quart microwavable casserole. Cover with plastic wrap, folding back 2-inch edge to vent. Microwave on High 9 to 12 minutes, stirring every 5 minutes, until crisp-tender when pierced with a fork. Let stand covered 5 minutes; drain in a strainer.

1 SERVING: Calories 20 (Calories from Fat 0); Fat 0g (Saturated 0g); Cholesterol 0mg; Sodium 10mg; Carbohydrate 6g (Dietary Fiber 2g); Protein 1g

Purchasing Beans

Look for long, smooth, crisp pods with fresh-looking tips and bright green or waxy yellow color.

Cutting Beans

Lay 3 or 4 beans side by side on cutting board; cut off all the ends at one time. Cut crosswise into 1-inch pieces.

BROCCOLI

1 1/2 pounds is enough for 4 servings

When Shopping: Look for firm, compact dark green clusters, and avoid thick, tough stems. Wrap broccoli tightly and store in the refrigerator up to 5 days.

Preparing for Cooking: Trim the large leaves, and cut off any tough ends of lower stems. Rinse with cool water. For spears, cut lengthwise into 1/2-inch-wide stalks. For pieces, cut into 1/2-inch-wide stalks, then cut crosswise into 1-inch pieces.

Boiling: Add 1 inch of water (and 1/4 teaspoon salt if desired) to a medium saucepan (about 3-quart size). Add the broccoli spears or pieces. Cover and heat to boiling over high heat. Once water is boiling, reduce heat just enough so water bubbles gently. Cook uncovered 10 to 12 minutes or until crisp-tender when pierced with a fork; drain in a strainer.

Steaming: Place a steamer basket in 1/2 inch of water in a skillet or saucepan. The water should not touch the bottom of the basket. Place broccoli spears or pieces in basket. Cover tightly and heat to boiling over high heat. Once water is boiling, reduce heat to low. Steam covered 10 to 11 minutes or until stems are crisp-tender when pierced with a fork.

Microwaving Spears: Place broccoli in an 8-inch square microwavable dish, arranging in a spoke pattern with flowerets toward the center. Add 1 cup water. Cover with plastic wrap, folding back 2-inch edge to vent. Microwave on High 9 to 11 minutes, rotating dish 1/4 turn every 4 minutes, until crisp-tender when pierced with a fork. Let stand covered 5 minutes; drain in a strainer.

Microwaving Pieces: Place broccoli and 1 cup water in a 2-quart microwavable casserole. Cover with plastic wrap, folding back 2-inch edge to vent. Microwave on High 9 to 11 minutes, stirring every 4 minutes, until crisp-tender when pierced with a fork. Let stand covered 5 minutes; drain.

1 SERVING: Calories 20 (Calories from Fat 0); Fat 0g (Saturated 0g); Cholesterol 0mg; Sodium 30mg; Carbohydrate 5g (Dietary Fiber 3g); Protein 3g

Cutting Broccoli

To make spears, cut lengthwise into 1/2-inch stalks. For pieces, cut the 1/2-inch stalks crosswise into 1-inch pieces.

Arranging Broccoli Spears for Microwaving

Place broccoli in an 8-inch square microwavable dish, arranging in a spoke pattern with flowerets toward the center.

CARROTS

1 pound (6 or 7 medium) is enough for 4 servings

When Shopping: Look for firm, smooth carrots, and avoid carrots with cracks or any that have become soft or limp. Store airtight in the refrigerator up to 2 weeks.

Preparing for Cooking: Peel carrots with a vegetable peeler, and cut off ends. Cut carrots crosswise into 1/4-inch slices.

Boiling: Add 1 inch of water (and 1/4 teaspoon salt if desired) to a medium saucepan (about 2-quart size). Cover and heat to boiling over high heat. Add the carrot slices. Cover and heat to boiling again. Once water is boiling, reduce heat just enough so water bubbles gently. Cook covered 12 to 15 minutes or until tender when pierced with a fork; drain in a strainer.

Steaming: Place a steamer basket in 1/2 inch of water in a skillet or saucepan. The water should not touch the bottom of the basket. Place carrot slices in basket. Cover tightly and heat to boiling over high heat. Once water is boiling, reduce heat to low. Steam covered 9 to 11 minutes or until tender when pierced with a fork.

Microwaving: Place carrot slices and 1/4 cup water in a 1-quart microwavable casserole. Cover with plastic wrap, folding back 2-inch edge to vent. Microwave on High 6 to 8 minutes, stirring after 4 minutes, until tender when pierced with a fork. Let stand covered 1 minute; drain in a strainer.

1 SERVING: Calories 35 (Calories from Fat 0); Fat 0g (Saturated 0g); Cholesterol 0mg; Sodium 40mg; Carbohydrate 11g (Dietary Fiber 3g); Protein 1g

Purchasing Carrots

Look for firm, smooth carrots; avoid carrots with cracks or any that have become soft or limp.

Cutting up Carrots

Peel carrots with a vegetable peeler, and cut off ends. Cut carrots crosswise into 1/4-inch slices.

CAULIFLOWER

1 medium head (2 pounds) is enough for 4 servings

When Shopping: Look for a clean, firm cauliflower with nonspreading flower clusters (the white portion) and green leaves. Some supermarkets sell just the flower clusters, which are already removed from the stalks. Wrap tightly and store in the refrigerator up to 1 week.

Preparing for Cooking: Remove outer leaves, and cut off the core, or stem, close to the head. Cut any discoloration off of the flower clusters. Wash cauliflower. Cut the flower clusters (flowerets) off the core, and discard the core.

Boiling: Add 1 inch of water (and 1/4 teaspoon salt if desired) to a medium saucepan (about 3-quart size). Cover and heat to boiling over high heat. Add the flowerets. Cover and heat to boiling again. Once water is boiling, reduce heat just enough so water bubbles gently. Cook covered 10 to 12 minutes or until tender when pierced with a fork; drain in a strainer.

Steaming: Place a steamer basket in 1/2 inch of water in a skillet or saucepan. The water should not touch the bottom of the basket. Place flowerets in basket. Cover tightly and heat to boiling over high heat. Once water is boiling, reduce heat to low. Steam covered 6 to 8 minutes or until tender when pierced with a fork.

Microwaving: Place flowerets and 1/4 cup water in a 2-quart microwavable casserole. Cover with plastic wrap, folding back 2-inch edge to vent. Microwave on High 12 to 14 minutes, stirring after 6 minutes, until tender when pierced with a fork. Let stand covered 1 minute; drain in a strainer.

1 SERVING: Calories 30 (Calories from Fat 0); Fat 0g (Saturated 0g); Cholesterol 0mg; Sodium 45mg; Carbohydrate 7g (Dietary Fiber 3g); Protein 3g

Cutting off Cauliflower Core

Cut off the core, or stem, close to the head.

Cutting Flower Clusters from Cauliflower Head

Cut flower clusters (flowerets) off the core; discard the core.

CORN

4 ears of corn is enough for 4 servings

When Shopping: Look for bright green, tight-fitting fresh-looking silk and kernels that are plump but not too large. Corn tastes best if it is purchased and cooked the same day that it was picked. If that's not possible, wrap unhusked ears in damp paper towels and refrigerate the corn up to 2 days.

Preparing for Cooking: Pull the green husks off the ears and remove the silk just before cooking. Do not put the corn husks or silk in your garbage disposal. If there are any bad spots on the ears, cut them out. Break off any long stems, so the corn will fit easily into the pan. If any ears are too long for your pan, cut or break them in half.

Boiling: Fill a Dutch oven about half full of water. Do not add any salt because that will make the corn tough. Place the corn in the water. Cover and heat to boiling over high heat. Once water is boiling, continue cooking uncovered 2 minutes. Remove from heat, and let stand uncovered about 10 minutes or until tender when pierced with a fork. Lift corn from water with tongs, allowing extra water to drip off. Serve immediately with margarine or butter, salt and pepper.

Microwaving: Place corn and 1/4 cup water in an 8-inch square microwavable dish. Cover with plastic wrap, folding back 2-inch edge to vent. Microwave on High 9 to 14 minutes, rearranging ears with tongs after 5 minutes, until tender when pierced with a fork. Let stand covered 5 minutes. Lift corn from water with tongs, allowing extra water to drip off.

1 SERVING: Calories 90 (Calories from Fat 10); Fat 1g (Saturated 0g); Cholesterol 0mg; Sodium 15mg; Carbohydrate 19g (Dietary Fiber 2g); Protein 3g

Husking Corn

Pull the green husks off the ears and remove silk just before cooking. Do not put the corn husks or silk in your garbage disposal.

MUSHROOMS

1 pound is enough for 4 servings

When Shopping: Look for creamy white to light brown caps that are tightly closed around the stems. If the caps have started to open and show the underside, or "gills," the mushrooms may not be fresh. To store, do not wash. Wrap in damp paper towels and refrigerate in a plastic bag up to 4 days.

Preparing for Cooking: Rinse mushrooms with cool water, but do not soak them because they will absorb water and become mushy. Dry thoroughly. Do not peel. Cut off and discard the end of each stem. Cut each mushroom lengthwise into 1/4-inch slices.

Sautéing: Heat 2 tablespoons margarine or butter in a large skillet (about 10-inch size) over medium-high heat 1 to 2 minutes or until margarine begins to bubble. Add 1/2 pound mushroom slices (about 3 cups). Cook 6 to 8 minutes, lifting and stirring constantly with a turner or large spoon, until tender when pierced with a fork. If using a nonstick pan, you can use just 1 tablespoon margarine.

Steaming: Place a steamer basket in 1/2 inch of water in a skillet or saucepan. The water should not touch the bottom of the basket. Place mushroom slices in basket. Cover tightly and heat to boiling over high heat. Once water is boiling, reduce heat to low. Steam covered 6 to 8 minutes or until tender when pierced with a fork.

Microwaving: Place mushroom slices and 1/4 cup water in a 1 1/2-quart microwavable casserole. Cover with plastic wrap, folding back 2-inch edge to vent. Microwave on High 5 to 7 minutes or until tender when pierced with a fork; drain in a strainer.

1 SERVING: Calories 130 (Calories from Fat 110); Fat 12g (Saturated 2g); Cholesterol 0mg; Sodium 140mg; Carbohydrate 5g (Dietary Fiber 1g); Protein 2g

Washing Mushrooms

Rinse mushrooms with cool water.

Slicing Mushrooms

Cut mushrooms lengthwise into 1/4-inch slices by placing them on a cutting board with the stems up.

ACORN SQUASH

1 1/2 to 2 pounds is enough for 4 servings

When Shopping: Look for hard, tough rinds with no soft spots. The squash should feel heavy for its size.

Preparing for Cooking: Wash squash. Cut lengthwise in half. You will need to do this on a cutting board and using your biggest knife because the shell is quite tough. Scrape out the seeds and fibers with a soup spoon.

Baking: Heat the oven to 400°. Place squash, cut sides up, in a baking dish. Sprinkle cut sides with salt and pepper. Place small dabs of margarine or butter over cut surface and in cavity, using about 1 tablespoon margarine for each squash. Pour water into baking dish until it is about 1/4 inch deep. Cover with aluminum foil. The squash will probably be taller than the baking dish, so the foil may touch the squash.

Bake 30 to 40 minutes or until tender when pierced with a fork. When removing the foil to test for doneness, open a side of the foil away from you to allow steam to escape. Lift the squash from the baking dish with a large spoon or spatula. Scrape the cooked squash out of the shell and into a serving dish.

Microwaving: Pierce whole squash with knife in several places to allow steam to escape. Place on paper towel. Microwave 4 to 6 minutes or until squash is hot and rind is firm but easy to cut; cool slightly. Carefully cut in half; remove seeds. Arrange halves, cut sides down, on 10-inch plate. Cover and microwave 5 to 8 minutes or until squash is tender when pierced by knife.

1 SERVING: Calories 115 (Calories from Fat 25); Fat 3g (Saturated 1g); Cholesterol 0mg; Sodium 190mg; Carbohydrate 25g (Dietary Fiber 5g); Protein 2g

TiP USE A GLASS BAKING DISH if possible. If you use a metal pan, the water may leave a dark mark on it.

TiP FOR MORE FLAVOR, mash the cooked squash with a fork, then stir in about 1 tablespoon margarine or butter and 1 tablespoon packed brown sugar.

Testing Squash for Doneness

Carefully open a side of the foil farthest away from you, so you will not get burned by the steam that escapes.

Mashed Potatoes

MAKES 4 to 6 servings • COOK: 25 minutes

INGREDIENTS

ESSENTIAL EQUIPMENT: *large saucepan (about 3-quart size); potato masher or electric mixer*

6 medium potatoes (about 2 pounds)

1/4 cup (1/2 stick) margarine or butter

1/4 teaspoon salt, if desired

1/2 cup milk

1/2 teaspoon salt

Dash of pepper

DIRECTIONS

1 Wash and peel the potatoes, and cut into large pieces. Remove the margarine from the refrigerator so it can soften while the potatoes cook.

2 Add 1 inch of water (and the 1/4 teaspoon salt if desired) to the saucepan. Cover and heat to boiling over high heat. Add potato pieces. Cover and heat to boiling again. Once water is boiling, reduce heat just enough so water bubbles gently.

3 Cook covered 20 to 25 minutes or until tender when pierced with a fork. The cooking time will vary, depending on the size of the potato pieces and the type of potato used. Drain potatoes in a strainer.

4 Return the drained potatoes to the saucepan, and cook over low heat about 1 minute to dry them. While cooking, shake the pan often to keep the potatoes from burning, which can happen very easily once the water has been drained off.

5 Place the potatoes in a medium bowl to be mashed. You can mash them in the same saucepan they were cooked in if the saucepan will not be damaged by the potato masher or electric mixer.

6 Mash the potatoes with a potato masher or electric mixer until no lumps remain. Add the milk in small amounts, beating after each addition. You may not use all the milk because the amount needed to make potatoes smooth and fluffy depends on the type of potato used. Add the margarine, 1/2 teaspoon salt and the pepper. Beat vigorously until potatoes are light and fluffy.

1 SERVING: Calories 265 (Calories from Fat 110); Fat 12g (Saturated 3g); Cholesterol 5mg; Sodium 450mg; Carbohydrate 38g (Dietary Fiber 3g); Protein 4g

MASHED POTATOES: For 6 grams of fat and 210 calories per serving, use skim milk and decrease the margarine to 2 tablespoons.

GARLIC MASHED POTATOES: Peel 6 cloves of garlic, and cook them with the potatoes. Mash the garlic cloves with the potatoes.

TiP **MOST TYPES OF POTATOES** can be used for mashed potatoes. Although russets are known as baking potatoes, they also can be boiled and mashed. Look for potatoes that are nicely shaped, smooth and firm with unblemished skin that is free from discoloration.

TiP **PLACE THE MILK** in a microwavable measuring cup and microwave uncovered on High 40 seconds before adding to the mashed potatoes. The potatoes will stay hotter.

Mashing Potatoes

Use a handheld potato masher for the fluffiest mashed potatoes. If using an electric mixer, do not mix too long; overmixing releases more potato starch, and the potatoes can become gummy.

Mashed Potatoes

BAKED POTATOES

MAKES 1 potato for each serving • BAKE: 1 hour 15 minutes

INGREDIENTS

DIRECTIONS

ESSENTIAL EQUIPMENT: *nothing special*

1 Heat the oven to 375°. Scrub the potatoes thoroughly with a vegetable brush, but do not peel.

1 or more medium baking potatoes (russet or Idaho), all about the same size

2 Pierce the potatoes on all sides with a fork to allow steam to escape while the potatoes bake. Place potatoes directly on the oven rack.

Margarine or butter, if desired

3 Bake 1 hour to 1 hour 15 minutes or until potatoes feel tender when squeezed gently. Be sure to use a pot holder because potatoes will be very hot to the touch.

Sour cream or plain yogurt, if desired

4 To serve, cut an X in the top of each potato. Gently squeeze potato from the bottom to force the potato open. Serve with margarine or sour cream.

1 SERVING: Calories 85 (Calories from Fat 0); Fat 0g (Saturated 0g); Cholesterol 0mg; Sodium 5mg; Carbohydrate 20g (Dietary Fiber 1g); Protein 2g

TO MICROWAVE 4 POTATOES: Scrub the potatoes thoroughly with a vegetable brush, but do not peel. Pierce potatoes on all sides with a fork to allow steam to escape while the potatoes cook. Arrange potatoes about 2 inches apart in a circle on a microwavable paper towel in microwave oven. Microwave uncovered on High 11 to 13 minutes, turning potatoes over after 6 minutes, until tender when squeezed gently. Be sure to use a pot holder because potatoes will be very hot to the touch. Let stand uncovered 5 minutes. Continue with step 4

TiP **THE BAKE TIME** and oven temperature for baking potatoes can be adjusted so that other foods can be baking in the oven at the same time. Bake potatoes in a 350° oven 1 hour 15 minutes to 1 hour 30 minutes, in a 325° oven about 1 hour 30 minutes.

TiP **IF POTATOES ARE WRAPPED** in aluminum foil before being baked, the steam cannot escape during baking, so the potatoes will be gummy instead of fluffy.

Cutting X in Baked Potato

Cut an X in the top of each potato, then gently squeeze from the bottom to force the potato open.

Baked Potato

TWICE-BAKED POTATOES

MAKES 4 servings • BAKE: 1 hour 15 minutes for first baking plus 20 minutes for second baking

INGREDIENTS

ESSENTIAL EQUIPMENT: *potato masher or electric mixer; cookie sheet*

2 large baking potatoes (russet or Idaho), 8 to 10 ounces each

2 tablespoons margarine or butter

2 to 4 tablespoons milk

1/8 teaspoon salt

Dash of pepper

1/2 cup shredded Cheddar cheese (2 ounces)

2 teaspoons chopped fresh chives, if desired

DIRECTIONS

1 Heat the oven to 375°. Scrub the potatoes thoroughly with a vegetable brush, but do not peel. Pierce the potatoes on all sides with a fork to allow steam to escape while the potatoes bake. Place potatoes directly on the oven rack. Measure margarine, and let it stand at room temperature to soften.

2 Bake potatoes 1 hour to 1 hour 15 minutes or until potatoes feel tender when squeezed gently. Be sure to use a pot holder because potatoes will be very hot to the touch.

3 When potatoes are cool enough to handle, cut them lengthwise in half. Scoop out the insides into a medium bowl, leaving about a 1/4-inch shell in the potato skin.

4 Increase the temperature of the oven to 400°.

5 Mash the potatoes with a potato masher or electric mixer until no lumps remain. Add the milk in small amounts, beating after each addition. The amount of milk needed to make potatoes smooth and fluffy depends on the type of potato used.

6 Add the margarine, salt and pepper. Beat vigorously until potatoes are light and fluffy. Stir in the cheese and chives. Fill the potato shells with the mashed potato mixture. Place on an ungreased cookie sheet. Bake potatoes uncovered about 20 minutes or until hot.

1 SERVING: Calories 180 (Calories from Fat 100); Fat 11g (Saturated 4g); Cholesterol 15mg; Sodium 230mg; Carbohydrate 16g (Dietary Fiber 1g); Protein 5g

TiP **TO SAVE TIME,** arrange filled potato shells in a circle on a 10-inch microwavable plate. Cover with waxed paper and microwave on High 6 to 8 minutes, rotating plate 1/2 turn after 3 minutes, until hot.

TiP **TO DO AHEAD,** wrap filled potato shells airtight and refrigerate no longer than 24 hours or freeze no longer than 2 months. Unwrap potatoes and place on cookie sheet. Heat in 400° oven about 30 minutes for refrigerated potatoes, about 40 minutes for frozen potatoes, until hot.

Scooping Potato from Shells

Using a soup spoon, carefully scoop out the inside of each potato half, leaving about a 1/4-inch shell.

Twice-Baked Potatoes

BAKED POTATO WEDGES

MAKES 4 servings • **BAKE: 30 minutes**

INGREDIENTS

ESSENTIAL EQUIPMENT: *rectangular pan (about 13×9 inches)*

3/4 teaspoon salt

1/2 teaspoon sugar

1/2 teaspoon paprika

1/4 teaspoon ground mustard (dry)

1/4 teaspoon garlic powder, if desired

3 medium baking potatoes (russet or Idaho), 8 to 10 ounces each

Cooking spray

DIRECTIONS

1 Heat the oven to 425°. Mix the salt, sugar, paprika, mustard and garlic powder in a small bowl or measuring cup.

2 Scrub the potatoes thoroughly with a vegetable brush, but do not peel. Cut each potato lengthwise in half. Turn potatoes cut sides down, and cut each half lengthwise into 4 wedges. Place potato wedges, skin sides down, in the pan.

3 Spray the potato wedges with cooking spray until lightly coated. Sprinkle with the salt mixture.

4 Bake uncovered 25 to 30 minutes or until potatoes are tender when pierced with fork. The baking time will vary, depending on the size and type of the potato used.

1 SERVING: Calories 90 (Calories from Fat 0); Fat 0g (Saturated 0g); Cholesterol 0mg; Sodium 115mg; Carbohydrate 23g (Dietary Fiber 2g); Protein 2g

TiP **FOR RECIPE SUCCESS,** cut up potatoes just before using, or the cut sides will turn brown.

TiP **USE RUSSET OR IDAHO** potatoes because they are best for baking.

Cutting Potato Wedges

Cut each potato lengthwise in half. Turn potatoes cut sides down, and cut each half lengthwise into 4 wedges.

Baked Potato Wedges

PARSLEY POTATOES

MAKES 4 servings • COOK: 25 minutes

INGREDIENTS

ESSENTIAL EQUIPMENT: *Dutch oven (about 4-quart size)*

10 to 12 new potatoes (about 1 1/2 pounds)

2 tablespoons margarine or butter

Parsley sprigs

1/4 teaspoon salt, if desired

1/8 teaspoon pepper, if desired

DIRECTIONS

1 Scrub the potatoes thoroughly with a vegetable brush to remove all the dirt. Peel a narrow strip around the center of each potato with a vegetable peeler. This will make the potatoes look prettier when they are served. If you're in a hurry, you don't need to peel this strip.

2 Add 1 inch of water to the Dutch oven. Cover and heat the water to boiling over high heat. Add potatoes. Cover and heat to boiling again. Once water is boiling, reduce heat just enough so water bubbles gently. Cook covered 20 to 25 minutes or until tender when pierced with a fork; drain in a strainer.

3 While the potatoes are cooking, place the margarine in a small microwavable bowl or measuring cup. Microwave uncovered on High 15 to 30 seconds or until melted.

4 Rinse a few sprigs of the parsley with cool water, and pat dry with a paper towel. Chop enough parsley leaves into small pieces on a cutting board using a chef's knife to measure 1 tablespoon, or place the leafy portion of the parsley in a small bowl or cup and snip into very small pieces with kitchen scissors. Discard the stems.

5 After draining the potatoes, return them to the Dutch oven. Drizzle the melted margarine over the potatoes, and sprinkle with the chopped parsley, salt and pepper. Stir gently to coat the potatoes.

TO MICROWAVE 4 POTATOES: Choose potatoes of similar size. Pierce potatoes with a fork to allow steam to escape. Place potatoes and 1/4 cup water in a 2-quart microwavable casserole, arranging larger potatoes to the outside edge. Cover with plastic wrap, folding back 2-inch edge to vent. Microwave on High 10 to 12 minutes, stirring after 5 minutes, until tender when pierced with a fork. Let stand covered 1 minute; drain in a strainer. Melt margarine as directed in step 3, and continue with the recipe.

1 SERVING: Calories 270 (Calories from Fat 55); Fat 6g (Saturated 1g); Cholesterol 0mg; Sodium 85mg; Carbohydrate 54g (Dietary Fiber 5g); Protein 5g

TiP **WHEN SHOPPING,** look for nicely shaped, smooth, firm potatoes with unblemished skins that are free from discoloration. Store in a cool, dark place, and use within 3 days.

TiP **FOR EASY PREPARATION,** purchase potatoes that are all about the same size so they will cook in the same length of time.

Scrubbing New Potatoes

Scrub potatoes thoroughly with a vegetable brush to remove all the dirt.

Chopping Fresh Parsley

Place parsley leaves in a small bowl or cup and snip into very small pieces with kitchen scissors. Discard the stems.

Parsley Potatoes

ROASTED RED POTATOES

MAKES 4 servings • BAKE: 1 hour 15 minutes

INGREDIENTS

DIRECTIONS

ESSENTIAL EQUIPMENT: *baking pan, such as 8- or 9-inch square or 13×9-inch rectangle*

12 small red potatoes (about 1 1/2 pounds)

2 medium green onions with tops

2 tablespoons olive or vegetable oil

2 tablespoons chopped fresh or 2 teaspoons dried rosemary leaves, crumbled

1 Heat the oven to 350°.

2 Scrub the potatoes thoroughly with a vegetable brush to remove all the dirt.

3 Peel and slice the green onions.

4 Place the potatoes in the ungreased pan. Drizzle the oil over the potatoes, and turn potatoes so all sides are coated.

5 Sprinkle the onions and rosemary over the potatoes, and stir the potatoes.

6 Bake uncovered about 1 hour 15 minutes, stirring occasionally, until potatoes are tender when pierced with a fork.

1 SERVING: Calories 325 (Calories from Fat 65); Fat 7g (Saturated 1g); Cholesterol 0mg; Sodium 20mg; Carbohydrate 66g (Dietary Fiber 6g); Protein 6g

TiP **MOST SMALL RED POTATOES** are about 2 inches in diameter. If they are much bigger, cut them in half so they will roast more quickly.

TiP **LEFTOVER ROASTED POTATOES** can be cut into pieces and panfried for quick fried potatoes. To pan-fry, cook potato pieces in a small amount of oil over medium heat, stirring occasionally, until hot.

Drizzling Oil over Potatoes

Place potatoes in pan. Drizzle the oil over the potatoes, and turn potatoes so all sides are coated.

Roasted Red Potatoes

AU GRATIN POTATOES

MAKES 6 servings • **BAKE: 1 hour 10 minutes** • **LET STAND: 5 minutes**

INGREDIENTS

ESSENTIAL EQUIPMENT: *shallow 2-quart casserole or 8-inch square baking dish; medium saucepan (about 2-quart size)*

Cooking spray

6 medium potatoes (about 2 pounds)

1 small onion

2 tablespoons margarine or butter

1 tablespoon all-purpose flour

1/2 teaspoon salt

1/4 teaspoon pepper

2 cups milk

2 cups shredded natural sharp Cheddar cheese (8 ounces)

1/4 cup dry bread crumbs

DIRECTIONS

1 Heat the oven to 375°. Spray the casserole with cooking spray. Scrub the potatoes thoroughly with a vegetable brush. Peel the onion, and chop into very small pieces.

2 Melt the margarine in the saucepan over medium heat. Cook the onion in the margarine about 2 minutes, stirring occasionally, until softened.

3 Stir in the flour, salt and pepper. Cook 1 to 2 minutes, stirring constantly, until smooth and bubbly. Remove the saucepan from the heat.

4 Stir in the milk. Heat to boiling over medium heat, stirring constantly. Continue boiling 1 minute, stirring constantly. Remove the saucepan from the heat. Stir in 1 1/2 cups of the cheese until it is melted.

5 Peel the potatoes if you like, but peeling is not necessary. Cut the potatoes into enough thin slices to measure about 6 cups. Spread half the slices in the sprayed casserole. Pour half the sauce over the potatoes. Repeat with the remaining potatoes and sauce.

6 Bake uncovered 1 hour. Remove the casserole from the oven. Sprinkle with the bread crumbs and remaining 1/2 cup cheese. Bake uncovered about 10 minutes longer or until cheese is melted and potatoes are tender when pierced with a fork. Let stand 5 minutes before serving.

1 SERVING. Calories 370 (Calories from Fat 160); Fat 18g (Saturated 10g); Cholesterol 45mg; Sodium 50mg; Carbohydrate 39g (Dietary Fiber 3g); Protein 16g

TiP **THE SAUCE MAY SEPARATE** a bit after the potatoes bake. Cool, and the flavor will be just as good.

TiP **TO MEASURE THE CAPACITY** of your casserole dish, fill it with water using a measuring cup. A 2-quart casserole will hold 8 cups of water.

Making Cheese Sauce

Stir the flour, salt and pepper into the cooked onions. Cook, stirring constantly, until the mixture is smooth and bubbly.

Au Gratin Potatoes

STIR-FRIED GREEN BEANS AND PEPPER

MAKES 4 servings • COOK: 8 minutes

INGREDIENTS

ESSENTIAL EQUIPMENT: *10-inch skillet*

1/2 pound green beans

1 medium yellow or red bell pepper

1/4 cup water

1 tablespoon vegetable oil

2 teaspoons chopped fresh or 1/2 teaspoon dried marjoram leaves

DIRECTIONS

1 Cut off ends of green beans and discard. Cut beans crosswise in half.

2 Cut the bell pepper lengthwise in half, and cut out seeds and membrane. Cut bell pepper into 1/2-inch pieces.

3 Heat the water and beans to boiling in the skillet over high heat. Reduce heat just enough so water bubbles gently. Cover and cook about 5 minutes or until beans are crisp-tender when pierced with a fork. Larger, more mature beans will need to cook longer than young, small beans. If necessary, drain off any excess water.

4 Add the bell pepper and oil to the beans in the skillet. Increase heat to medium-high. Stir-fry with a turner or large spoon about 2 minutes, lifting and stirring constantly, until bell pepper is crisp-tender when pierced with a fork. Stir in marjoram.

1 SERVING. Calories 50 (Calories from Fat 35); Fat 4g (Saturated 1g); Cholesterol 0mg; Sodium 5mg; Carbohydrate 4g (Dietary Fiber 1g); Protein 1g

TiP **TO DO AHEAD,** wash and cut up green beans and bell pepper. Store airtight in refrigerator until needed.

TiP **DRAIN ANY REMAINING** water from the beans by pouring them into a strainer or colander. Then return them to the skillet.

Cutting a Bell Pepper

Cut the bell pepper lengthwise in half, and cut out seeds and membrane. Cut bell pepper into 1/2-inch pieces.

Stir-Fried Green Beans and Pepper

DILLED CARROTS AND PEA PODS

MAKES 4 servings • **COOK: 7 minutes**

INGREDIENTS

ESSENTIAL EQUIPMENT: *medium saucepan (about 2-quart size)*

1 1/2 cups snow (Chinese) pea pods (about 5 ounces)

1 1/2 cups baby-cut carrots

1 tablespoon margarine or butter

2 teaspoons chopped fresh or 1/2 teaspoon dried dill weed

1/8 teaspoon salt

DIRECTIONS

1 Snap off the stem end of each pea pod, and pull the string across the pea pod to remove it.

2 Add 1 inch of water to the saucepan. Cover and heat the water to boiling over high heat. Add carrots. Cover and heat to boiling again. Once water is boiling, reduce heat just enough so water bubbles gently. Cook covered about 4 minutes or until carrots are crisp-tender when pierced with a fork. Do not drain water.

3 Add pea pods to carrots in saucepan. Heat uncovered until water is boiling again; continue boiling uncovered 2 to 3 minutes, stirring occasionally, until pea pods are crisp-tender. Pea pods cook very quickly, so be careful not to overcook them. Drain carrots and pea pods in a strainer, then return to saucepan.

4 Stir margarine, dill weed and salt into carrots and pea pods until margarine is melted.

1 SERVING. Calories 45 (Calories from Fat 25); Fat 3g (Saturated 1g); Cholesterol 0mg; Sodium 130mg; Carbohydrate 6g (Dietary Fiber 2g); Protein 1g

TiP **SNOW PEA PODS** are very similar to snap pea pods, and they can be used interchangeably. Both are edible pea pods with tender, sweet peas inside.

TiP **ONE 6-OUNCE PACKAGE** of frozen snow (Chinese) pea pods can be substituted for the fresh pea pods. Thaw them before cooking in step 3

Removing Tips and Strings from Pea Pods

Snap off the stem end of pea pod, and pull the string across the pea pod to remove it.

Dilled Carrots and Pea Pods

ROASTED VEGETABLES

MAKES 4 servings • BAKE: 25 minutes

INGREDIENTS

ESSENTIAL EQUIPMENT: *rectangular pan (about 13×9 inches)*

1 medium red or green bell pepper

1 medium onion

1 medium zucchini

1/4 pound mushrooms

Olive oil-flavored or regular cooking spray

1/4 teaspoon salt

1/8 teaspoon pepper

2 tablespoons chopped fresh or 2 teaspoons dried basil leaves, if desired

DIRECTIONS

1 Cut the bell pepper lengthwise in half, and cut out seeds and membrane. Cut each half lengthwise into 4 strips.

2 Peel the onion, and cut in half. Wrap one half of onion, and refrigerate for another use. Cut remaining half into 4 wedges, then separate into pieces.

3 Cut the zucchini crosswise into 1-inch pieces. Cut off and discard the end of each mushroom stem, and leave the mushrooms whole.

4 Heat the oven to 425°. Spray the bottom of the pan with cooking spray. Arrange the vegetables in a single layer in the sprayed pan. Spray the vegetables with cooking spray until lightly coated. Sprinkle with salt, pepper and basil.

5 Bake uncovered 15 minutes. Remove the pan from the oven. Turn vegetables over. Bake uncovered about 10 minutes longer or until vegetables are crisp-tender when pierced with a fork.

1 SERVING. Calories 30 (Calories from Fat 0); Fat 0g (Saturated 0g); Cholesterol 0mg; Sodium 150mg; Carbohydrate 6g (Dietary Fiber 1g); Protein 2g

TiP **IN MANY SUPERMARKETS,** you can buy mushrooms that have not been prepackaged. Just buy as many as you need.

TiP **REMOVE THE PAN** of vegetables from the oven when it's time to turn them over. Place pan on a heatproof surface such as the burners of your range, and close the oven door to retain the heat.

Cutting an Onion

Cut the onion half into 4 wedges, then separate into pieces.

Roasted Vegetables

SNACKS AND DESSERTS

Quick Guacamole

MAKES about 2 cups dip

INGREDIENTS

ESSENTIAL EQUIPMENT: *large knife, such as a chef's knife*

2 large ripe avocados

1 tablespoon lime juice

1/3 cup chunky-style salsa

Tortilla chips, if desired

DIRECTIONS

1 Cut the avocado lengthwise in half around the pit, and pull apart the halves. The pit will stay in one of the halves. Firmly and carefully strike the exposed pit with the sharp edge of the large knife. While grasping the avocado, twist the knife to loosen and remove the pit.

2 Scoop out the avocado pulp into a medium bowl, using a spoon. Add the lime juice, and mash the avocado with a fork.

3 Stir in the salsa. Serve with tortilla chips. Cover and refrigerate any remaining dip.

1 TABLESPOON: Calories 20 (Calories from Fat 20); Fat 2g (Saturated 0g); Cholesterol 0mg; Sodium 10mg; Carbohydrate 1g (Dietary Fiber 0g); Protein 0g

TiP **FIRM, UNRIPE AVOCADOS** are usually what are available in the supermarket. Let the avocado ripen at room temperature until it yields to gentle pressure but is still firm.

TiP **THE LIME JUICE** keeps the color of the mashed avocado from darkening. Add it to the avocado pulp as soon as possible.

Removing Avocado Pit

Firmly and carefully strike the exposed pit with the sharp edge of a knife. While grasping the avocado, twist the knife to loosen and remove the pit.

Quick Guacamole

HOT ARTICHOKE DIP

MAKES about 1 1/2 cups dip • **BAKE: 20 to 25 minutes**

INGREDIENTS

DIRECTIONS

ESSENTIAL EQUIPMENT: *1-quart casserole*

4 medium green onions with tops

1 can (16 ounces) artichoke hearts

1/2 cup mayonnaise or salad dressing

1/2 cup grated Parmesan cheese

Crackers or cocktail rye bread, if desired

1 Heat the oven to 350°.

2 Peel and chop the green onions.

3 Drain the artichoke hearts in a strainer. Chop the artichoke hearts into small pieces.

4 Mix the green onions, artichoke hearts, mayonnaise and cheese in the ungreased casserole.

5 Cover with lid or aluminum foil and bake 20 to 25 minutes or until hot. Serve with crackers.

1 TABLESPOON: Calories 45 (Calories from Fat 35); Fat 4g (Saturated 1g); Cholesterol 5mg; Sodium 105mg; Carbohydrate 2g (Dietary Fiber 1g); Protein 1g

ARTICHOKE DIP: For 1 gram of fat and 20 calories per serving, use 1/3 cup plain fat-free yogurt and 3 tablespoons reduced-fat mayonnaise for the 1/2 cup mayonnaise.

TiP **TO SAVE TIME,** mix ingredients in a microwavable casserole. Cover with plastic wrap, folding back 2-inch edge to vent. Microwave on Medium-High (70%) 4 to 5 minutes, stirring after 2 minutes.

TiP **PREPARE THIS DIP** ahead of time, and refrigerate up to 24 hours. Heat when you are ready to serve it. Increase bake time about 5 minutes.

Chopping Artichoke Hearts

Chop the artichoke hearts into small pieces.

Hot Artichoke Dip

SPINACH DIP IN BREAD BOWL

MAKES 4 1/2 cups • REFRIGERATE: 1 hour

INGREDIENTS

ESSENTIAL EQUIPMENT:
serving plate

2 packages (10 ounces each) frozen chopped spinach, thawed

1 can (8 ounces) sliced water chestnuts

9 medium green onions with tops

1 clove garlic

1 cup sour cream

1 cup plain yogurt

2 teaspoons chopped fresh or 1/2 teaspoon dried tarragon leaves

1/2 teaspoon salt

1/2 teaspoon ground mustard (dry)

1/4 teaspoon pepper

1-pound unsliced round bread loaf

DIRECTIONS

1 Drain the thawed spinach in a strainer, then squeeze out the excess moisture from the spinach, using paper towels or a clean kitchen towel, until the spinach is dry. Place in a large bowl.

2 Drain the water chestnuts in a strainer. Chop them into small pieces, and add to the bowl.

3 Peel and chop the green onions. You will need about 1 cup. Add the onions to the bowl. Peel and crush the garlic, and add to the bowl.

4 Add the sour cream, yogurt, tarragon, salt, mustard and pepper to the bowl. Mix all ingredients thoroughly. Cover and refrigerate at least 1 hour to blend flavors.

5 Just before serving, cut a 1- to 2-inch slice from the top of the loaf of bread. Hollow out the loaf by cutting along the edge with a serrated knife, leaving about a 1-inch shell, and pulling out large chunks of bread. Cut or tear the top slice and the hollowed-out bread into bite-size pieces.

6 Fill the bread loaf with the spinach dip, and place on the serving plate. Arrange the bread pieces around the loaf to use for dipping.

1 TABLESPOON: Calories 30 (Calories from Fat 10); Fat 1g (Saturated 1g); Cholesterol 5mg; Sodium 60mg; Carbohydrate 4g (Dietary Fiber 0g); Protein 1g

 SPINACH DIP: For 0 grams of fat and 25 calories per serving, substitute 1/2 cup reduced-fat sour cream for the 1 cup sour cream and 1 1/2 cups plain fat-free yogurt for the 1 cup yogurt.

TiP **A LOAF OF RYE BREAD** looks nice filled with the Spinach Dip, but white, whole wheat and multigrain breads also taste delicious with this snack.

TiP **PLACE THE FROZEN SPINACH** in the refrigerator the day before you need it so it can thaw, or thaw it in the microwave.

Draining Frozen Spinach

Squeeze excess moisture from spinach, using paper towels or a clean kitchen towel, until the spinach is dry.

Making a Bread Bowl

Cut a 1- to 2-inch slice from top of loaf. Hollow out the loaf by cutting along the edge with a serrated knife, leaving about a 1-inch shell, and pulling out large chunks of bread. Cut or tear the top slice and the hollowed-out bread into bite-size pieces for dipping.

Spinach Dip in Bread Bowl

MEXICAN SNACK PLATTER

MAKES about 16 servings

INGREDIENTS | DIRECTIONS

ESSENTIAL EQUIPMENT: *12- or 13-inch round serving plate or pizza pan*

1 can (15 ounces) refried beans

2 tablespoons salsa, chili sauce or ketchup

1 1/2 cups sour cream

1 cup purchased guacamole

1 cup shredded Cheddar cheese (4 ounces)

2 medium green onions with tops

Tortilla chips, if desired

1 Mix the refried beans and salsa in a small bowl. Spread in a thin layer over the serving plate.

2 Spread the sour cream over the beans, leaving about a 1-inch border of beans around the edge. Spread the guacamole over the sour cream, leaving a border of sour cream showing.

3 Sprinkle the cheese over the guacamole. Peel and chop the green onions; sprinkle over the cheese. Cover with plastic wrap and refrigerate until serving time.

4 Serve the dip with tortilla chips for dipping.

1 SERVING. Calories 115 (Calories from Fat 80); Fat 9g (Saturated 5g); Cholesterol 25mg; Sodium 210mg; Carbohydrate 7g (Dietary Fiber 2g); Protein 4g

TIP **PURCHASE GUACAMOLE** in the dairy section of the supermarket. It may be called "avocado dip" instead of "guacamole."

TIP **FOR A HOTTER FLAVOR,** use a flavored shredded cheese, such as pizza or nacho, instead of plain Cheddar.

Spreading Guacamole over Sour Cream

Spread guacamole over sour cream, leaving a border of sour cream showing.

Mexican Snack Platter

VEGETABLE TRAY WITH TANGY YOGURT DIP

MAKES about 1 cup • REFRIGERATE: 1 hour

INGREDIENTS

ESSENTIAL EQUIPMENT:
serving plate

1 cup plain fat-free yogurt

2 tablespoons chili sauce

1 teaspoon prepared horseradish

Assorted Fresh Vegetables (below)

ASSORTED FRESH VEGETABLES

Bell pepper strips

Broccoli flowerets

Carrot slices or sticks or baby-cut carrots

Cauliflowerets

Celery sticks

Cherry tomatoes

Cucumber slices

Jicama sticks

Snow (Chinese) pea pods or snap pea pods

Zucchini sticks

DIRECTIONS

1 Mix the yogurt, chili sauce and horseradish in a medium bowl. Cover and refrigerate at least 1 hour to blend flavors.

2 Arrange at least 4 or 5 different raw Assorted Fresh Vegetables on the serving plate. Serve with the dip.

1 TABLESPOON: Calories 10 (Calories from Fat 0); Fat 0g (Saturated 0g); Cholesterol 0mg; Sodium 35mg; Carbohydrate 2g (Dietary Fiber 0g); Protein 1g

TiP **TASTE THE DIP** before serving it, and add another teaspoon of horse-radish if you want a stronger flavor.

TiP **YOU CAN PURCHASE** whole baby-cut carrots, broccoli flowerets and cauliflowerets cleaned and ready to eat in the produce section of the supermarket.

Cutting Carrots into Diagonal Slices

Cut carrots diagonally to make large slices that are easy to dip.

Removing Strings from Pea Pods

Snap off the stem end of pea pod, and pull the string across the pea pod to remove it.

Vegetable Tray with Tangy Yogurt Dip

FRESH TOMATO SALSA

MAKES about 3 1/2 cups • **REFRIGERATE: 1 hour**

INGREDIENTS

ESSENTIAL EQUIPMENT:
large bowl

3 medium tomatoes

1 small green bell pepper

6 medium green onions
with tops

3 cloves garlic

1 medium jalapeño chili

2 tablespoons chopped
fresh cilantro

2 tablespoons lime juice

1/2 teaspoon salt

Flour tortillas or tortilla
chips, if desired

DIRECTIONS

1 Place the bowl near your cutting board. After cutting or chopping each ingredient, add each one to the bowl. Cut the tomato crosswise in half. Gently squeeze each half, cut side down, to remove the seeds. Chop the tomatoes.

2 Cut the bell pepper lengthwise in half, and cut out seeds and membrane. Chop the bell pepper.

3 Peel and slice the green onions. Peel and finely chop the garlic.

4 Cut the stem off the jalapeño chili, cut the chili lengthwise in half and scrape out the seeds. Cut the chili into strips, and then finely chop.

5 Add the cilantro, lime juice and salt. Mix all the ingredients. Cover and refrigerate at least 1 hour to blend flavors but no longer than 7 days.

6 Serve salsa with flour tortillas or tortilla chips or as an accompaniment to chicken, fish and other main dishes.

1 TABLESPOON: Calories 5 (Calories from Fat 0); Fat 0g (Saturated 0g); Cholesterol 0mg; Sodium 20mg; Carbohydrate 1g (Dietary Fiber 0g); Protein 0g

TiP **IF YOU DESIRE** a hotter salsa, leave some of the seeds in the jalapeño chili.

✔ **THE FLESH, RIBS AND SEEDS** of chilies contain irritating, burning oils. Wash hands and utensils in soapy water, and be especially careful not to rub your face or eyes until the oils have been washed away.

Seeding a Jalapeño Chili

Cut the stem off the jalapeño chili, cut the chili lengthwise in half and scrape out the seeds.

Fresh Tomato Salsa

CREAM CHEESE FIESTA SPREAD

MAKES 8 servings

INGREDIENTS

ESSENTIAL EQUIPMENT: *serving plate or dinner plate*

1 package (8 ounces) cream cheese

1/4 cup salsa

1/4 cup apricot preserves or orange marmalade

1 tablespoon chopped fresh cilantro or parsley

1 tablespoon finely shredded Cheddar or Monterey Jack cheese

1 tablespoon chopped ripe olives

Assorted crackers, if desired

DIRECTIONS

1 Place block of cream cheese on the plate, and let stand at room temperature about 30 minutes to soften it slightly before serving. Or to soften in the microwave, remove foil wrapper and place cream cheese on microwavable plate; microwave on medium (50%) 1/2 to 1 minute.

2 Mix the salsa and preserves, and spread over cream cheese. Sprinkle with the cilantro, cheese and olives. Serve with crackers.

1 SERVING. Calories 135 (Calories from Fat 90); Fat 10g (Saturated 6g); Cholesterol 30mg; Sodium 125mg; Carbohydrate 8g (Dietary Fiber 0g); Protein 3g

CRUNCHY CREAM CHEESE-RASPBERRY SPREAD: Omit salsa, preserves, cilantro, cheese and olives. Spread 1/3 cup raspberry spreadable fruit over the cream cheese. Sprinkle with 2 tablespoons each of finely chopped toasted almonds, miniature semisweet chocolate chips and flaked coconut.

CURRIED CREAM CHEESE-CHUTNEY SPREAD: Omit salsa, preserves, cilantro, cheese and olives. Spread 1/3 cup chopped chutney over the cream cheese. Sprinkle generously with curry powder. Sprinkle with 1 tablespoon each of chopped peanuts, chopped green onions, raisins and chopped cooked egg yolk.

CREAM CHEESE FIESTA SPREAD: For 1 gram of fat and 55 calories per serving, use fat-free cream cheese.

TiP **IF THE PRESERVES** or marmalade contain large pieces of fruit, snip them into smaller pieces with a kitchen scissors.

TiP **A WIDE SELECTION** of salsas is available in the supermarket, including fresh salsa in the refrigerated section. Some are mild, some quite spicy. Choose the one you prefer.

Spreading Salsa Mixture over Cream Cheese

Mix salsa and preserves; spread over cream cheese.

Cream Cheese Fiesta Spread

ROASTED GARLIC

MAKES 2 to 8 servings • **BAKE: 50 minutes**

INGREDIENTS

ESSENTIAL EQUIPMENT:
aluminum foil; baking pan or pie plate

1 to 4 garlic bulbs

2 teaspoons olive or vegetable oil for each garlic bulb

Salt and pepper to taste

Sliced French bread, if desired

TiP GARLIC BECOMES rich and mellow when roasted.

DIRECTIONS

1 Heat the oven to 350°.

2 Carefully peel the paperlike skin from around each bulb of garlic, leaving just enough to hold the cloves together. Cut a 1/4- to 1/2-inch slice from the top of each bulb to expose the cloves. Place bulb, cut side up, on a 12-inch square of aluminum foil.

3 Drizzle 2 teaspoons oil over each bulb. Sprinkle with salt and pepper. Wrap foil securely around the bulb. Place in the baking pan or pie plate.

4 Bake 45 to 50 minutes or until garlic is tender when pierced with a toothpick or fork. Cool slightly. To serve, gently squeeze one end of each clove to release the roasted garlic. Spread on slices of bread.

1 SERVING. Calories 75 (Calories from Fat 45); Fat 5g (Saturated 1g); Cholesterol 0mg; Sodium 75mg; Carbohydrate 6g (Dietary Fiber 0g); Protein 1g

TiP GARLIC BULBS, sometimes called "heads" of garlic, are made up of as many as fifteen sections called "cloves," each of which is covered with a thin skin. You can find garlic bulbs in the produce section of the supermarket.

Preparing Garlic for Roasting

Carefully peel paperlike skin from around each garlic bulb, leaving just enough to hold the cloves together. Cut a 1/4- to 1/2-inch slice from top of each bulb to expose cloves.

Wrapping Garlic for Roasting

Place bulb, cut side up, on 12-inch square of aluminum foil. Drizzle 2 teaspoons oil over each bulb. Sprinkle with salt and pepper. Wrap foil securely.

Roasted Garlic

STRAWBERRY SMOOTHIE

MAKES 4 servings (about 1 cup each)

INGREDIENTS

ESSENTIAL EQUIPMENT: *blender*

2 cups (1 pint) strawberries

1 cup milk

2 containers (6 ounces each) strawberry yogurt (2/3 cup)

DIRECTIONS

1 Reserve 4 strawberries for the garnish. Cut out the hull, or "cap," from the remaining strawberries with the point of a paring knife (see page 215).

2 Place strawberries, milk and yogurt in a blender. Cover and blend on high speed about 30 seconds or until smooth.

3 Pour mixture into 4 glasses. Garnish each with a strawberry.

1 SERVING. Calories 150 (Calories from Fat 35); Fat 4g (Saturated 3g); Cholesterol 15mg; Sodium 80mg; Carbohydrate 24g (Dietary Fiber 1g); Protein 6g

ORANGE SMOOTHIE

MAKES 4 servings (about 1 cup each)

INGREDIENTS

ESSENTIAL EQUIPMENT: *blender*

1 quart vanilla frozen yogurt or ice cream, slightly softened

1/2 cup frozen (thawed) orange juice concentrate

1/4 cup milk

Fresh orange slices, if desired

DIRECTIONS

1 Place the yogurt, orange juice concentrate and milk in a blender. Cover and blend on medium speed about 45 seconds, stopping blender occasionally to scrape sides, until thick and smooth.

2 Pour mixture into 4 glasses. Garnish with orange slices.

1 SERVING. Calories 280 (Calories from Fat 55); Fat 6g (Saturated 4g); Cholesterol 20mg; Sodium 110mg; Carbohydrate 47g (Dietary Fiber 0g); Protein 9g

TiP **SERVE THESE** special drinks in your prettiest clear glasses for a quick, freshly made dessert.

TiP **LEAVE THE GREEN LEAVES** on the strawberries that will be used to garnish the Strawberry Smoothie.

Smoothies

Making a Strawberry Smoothie

Place strawberries, milk and yogurt in a blender. Cover and blend on high speed about 30 seconds or until smooth.

FROZEN CHOCOLATE MOUSSE

MAKES 8 servings • FREEZE: 4 hours

INGREDIENTS

DIRECTIONS

ESSENTIAL EQUIPMENT: *electric mixer or hand beater; 9-inch square pan*

2 cups whipping (heavy) cream

1/4 cup almond-, chocolate- or coffee-flavored liqueur

1/2 cup chocolate-flavored syrup

Crushed cookies or chopped nuts, if desired

1 Beat the whipping cream in a chilled large bowl with the electric mixer on high speed until stiff peaks form.

2 Gently pour the liqueur and chocolate syrup over the whipped cream. To fold ingredients together, use a rubber spatula to cut down vertically through the whipped cream, then slide the spatula across the bottom of the bowl and up the side, turning the whipped cream over. Rotate the bowl one-fourth turn, and repeat this down-across-up motion. Continue mixing in this way just until ingredients are blended.

3 Spread whipped cream mixture into the ungreased pan.

4 Cover and freeze at least 4 hours but no longer than 2 months. Cut mousse into squares. Garnish with crushed cookies. Serve immediately. Cover and freeze any remaining mousse.

1 SERVING. Calories 245 (Calories from Fat 170); Fat 19g (Saturated 12g); Cholesterol 65mg; Sodium 40mg; Carbohydrate 17g (Dietary Fiber 0g); Protein 2g

TiP **THE WHIPPING CREAM** will beat up more easily if the bowl and mixer beaters are chilled in the refrigerator for about 20 minutes before beating.

TiP **THE LIQUEUR KEEPS** this dessert from freezing totally solid. That's why the mousse can be served immediately after taking it from the freezer.

Folding Liqueur and Chocolate Syrup into Whipped Cream

To fold ingredients together, use a rubber spatula to cut down vertically through the whipped cream, then slide the spatula across the bottom of the bowl and up the side, turning the whipped cream over. Rotate the bowl one-fourth turn, and repeat this down-across-up motion. Continue mixing in this way just until ingredients are blended.

Frozen Chocolate Mousse

FUDGY BROWNIE CAKE WITH RASPBERRY SAUCE

MAKES 8 servings • BAKE: 40 minutes

INGREDIENTS

ESSENTIAL EQUIPMENT: *9-inch round pan or 8-inch square pan; small saucepan (about 1-quart size)*

Shortening to grease pan

1 1/2 cups sugar

3/4 cup all-purpose flour

3/4 cup (1 1/2 sticks) margarine or butter, melted

1/2 cup baking cocoa

1 1/2 teaspoons vanilla

1/4 teaspoon salt

3 eggs

Raspberry Sauce (below)

Fresh raspberries for garnish, if desired

RASPBERRY SAUCE

3 tablespoons sugar

2 teaspoons cornstarch

1/3 cup water

1 package (10 ounces) frozen raspberries in syrup, thawed and undrained

DIRECTIONS

1 Heat the oven to 350°. Grease the bottom and side of the pan with shortening. Sprinkle a small amount of flour over the greased surface, shake the pan to distribute the flour evenly, then turn the pan upside down and tap the bottom to remove excess flour.

2 Mix the sugar, flour, margarine, cocoa, vanilla, salt and eggs in a medium bowl with a spoon or wire whisk. Pour into the greased and floured pan.

3 Bake 40 to 45 minutes or until the top appears dry. While the cake is baking, prepare Raspberry Sauce (below).

4 Cool the cake 10 minutes, then remove it from the pan and place on a wire cooling rack. Or you can leave the cake in the pan. Cool cake, and serve with the sauce. Garnish with fresh raspberries.

RASPBERRY SAUCE Mix the sugar and cornstarch in the saucepan. Stir in water and raspberries. Cook over medium heat, stirring constantly, until the mixture thickens and boils. Continue boiling 1 minute, stirring constantly. Remove the saucepan from the heat. Strain the sauce through a strainer to the remove the raspberry seeds if desired. Serve sauce slightly warm or cool.

1 SERVING. Calories 420 (Calories from Fat 180); Fat 20g (Saturated 5g); Cholesterol 80mg; Sodium 300mg; Carbohydrate 59g (Dietary Fiber 4g); Protein 5g

TiP **IF USING A MARGARINE** or spread, make sure it contains at least 65 percent vegetable oil. Spreads with less fat are not recommended for baking.

TiP **FOR EASIER CLEANUP,** heat the margarine in a microwavable mixing bowl on High for 30 to 45 seconds until melted, then add the remaining ingredients for the cake.

Straining Raspberry Sauce

Strain sauce through a strainer to remove the raspberry seeds.

Fudgy Brownie Cake with Raspberry Sauce

TIRAMISU

MAKES 9 servings • REFRIGERATE: 4 hours

INGREDIENTS

DIRECTIONS

ESSENTIAL EQUIPMENT: *electric mixer or hand beater; 8-inch square pan or 9-inch round pan*

1 cup whipping (heavy) cream

1 package (8 ounces) cream cheese at room temperature

1/2 cup powdered sugar

2 tablespoons light rum or 1/2 teaspoon rum extract

1 package (3 ounces) ladyfingers (12 ladyfingers)

1/2 cup cold prepared espresso or strong coffee

2 teaspoons baking cocoa

Maraschino cherries with stems for garnish, if desired

1 Pour the whipping cream into a medium bowl, and place in the refrigerator to chill. The cream will whip better in a cold bowl.

2 Beat the cream cheese and powdered sugar in another medium bowl with the electric mixer on medium speed until smooth. Beat in the rum on low speed, and set aside.

3 Beat the whipping cream on high speed until stiff peaks form. Gently spoon the whipped cream onto the cream cheese mixture. To fold together, use a rubber spatula to cut down vertically through the mixtures, then slide the spatula across the bottom of the bowl and up the side, turning the mixtures over. Rotate the bowl one-fourth turn, and repeat this down-across-up motion. Continue mixing in this way just until ingredients are blended.

4 Split each ladyfinger horizontally in half. Arrange half of them, cut sides up, over the bottom of the ungreased pan. Drizzle 1/4 cup of the cold espresso over the ladyfingers. Spread half of the cream cheese mixture over ladyfingers.

5 Arrange the remaining ladyfingers, cut sides up, over the cream cheese mixture. Drizzle with the remaining 1/4 cup cold espresso, and spread with the remaining cream cheese mixture.

6 Sprinkle the cocoa over the top of the dessert. If you have a small strainer, place the cocoa in the strainer and shake it over the dessert. Otherwise, shake the cocoa from a spoon. Cover and refrigerate about 4 hours or until the filling is firm. Garnish each serving with a cherry.

1 SERVING. Calories 240 (Calories from Fat 160); Fat 18g (Saturated 11g); Cholesterol 60mg; Sodium 115mg; Carbohydrate 17g (Dietary Fiber 0g); Protein 3g

 TIRAMISU: For 8 grams of fat and 165 calories per serving, use reduced-fat cream cheese (Neufchâtel) instead of regular cream cheese. Use 2 cups frozen (thawed) reduced-fat whipped topping for the whipping cream.

TiP **LADYFINGERS** are small, oval-shaped cakes usually found in the bakery department or freezer section of the supermarket.

TiP **TIRAMISU MAY BE FROZEN;** be sure to cover tightly. Allow to thaw several hours in the refrigerator before serving.

Arranging Ladyfingers in Pan

Split ladyfingers horizontally in half. Arrange half of them, cut sides up, over bottom of pan. Drizzle with 1/4 cup of the cold espresso.

Sprinkling with Cocoa

Place cocoa in a small strainer, and shake it over the dessert.

Tiramisu

APPLE CRISP

MAKES 6 servings • **BAKE: 30 minutes**

INGREDIENTS

ESSENTIAL EQUIPMENT: *8-inch square pan or 9-inch round pan*

Shortening to grease pan

4 medium tart cooking apples, such as Granny Smith, Wealthy or Rome Beauty

2/3 cup packed brown sugar

1/2 cup all-purpose flour

1/2 cup quick-cooking or old-fashioned oats

1/3 cup margarine or butter at room temperature

3/4 teaspoon ground cinnamon

3/4 teaspoon ground nutmeg

Half-and-half or ice cream, if desired

DIRECTIONS

1 Heat the oven to 375°. Grease the bottom and sides of the pan with the shortening.

2 Peel the apples if desired. Cut the apple into fourths, and remove seeds. Cut each fourth into slices. You will need about 4 cups of apple slices. Spread the slices in the greased pan.

3 Mix the brown sugar, flour, oats, margarine, cinnamon and nutmeg with a fork. The mixture will be crumbly. Sprinkle this mixture evenly over the apples.

4 Bake about 30 minutes or until the topping is golden brown and the apples are tender when pierced with a fork. Serve warm with half-or-half or ice cream.

1 SERVING. Calories 300 (Calories from Fat 100); Fat 11g (Saturated 2g); Cholesterol 0mg; Sodium 130mg; Carbohydrate 51g (Dietary Fiber 3g); Protein 2g

BLUEBERRY CRISP: Substitute 4 cups fresh or frozen blueberries for the apples. If using frozen blueberries, thaw and drain them first.

CHERRY CRISP: Substitute a 21-ounce can cherry pie filling for the apples.

Slicing Apples

Peel apples if desired. Cut the apple into fourths and remove seeds. Cut each fourth into slices.

Sprinkling Brown Sugar Mixture over Apples

Mix brown sugar, flour, oats, margarine, cinnamon and nutmeg with a fork. The mixture will be crumbly. Sprinkle evenly over apples.

Apple Crisp

STRAWBERRY SHORTCAKES

MAKES 6 servings • **LET STAND: 1 hour** • **BAKE: 12 minutes**

INGREDIENTS

ESSENTIAL EQUIPMENT: *cookie sheet; electric mixer or hand beater*

1 quart (4 cups) strawberries

1/2 cup sugar

2 cups all-purpose flour

2 tablespoons sugar

3 teaspoons baking powder

1 teaspoon salt

1/3 cup shortening

3/4 cup milk

**Sweetened Whipped Cream (below) or
1 1/2 cups frozen (thawed) whipped topping, if desired**

SWEETENED WHIPPED CREAM

3/4 cup whipping (heavy) cream

2 tablespoons granulated or powdered sugar

DIRECTIONS

1 Wash strawberries, and dry on paper towels. Cut out the hull, or "cap," with the point of a paring knife. Cut the strawberries lengthwise into slices. Mix sliced strawberries and 1/2 cup sugar in a large bowl. Let stand 1 hour.

2 Heat the oven to 450°.

3 Mix the flour, 2 tablespoons sugar, the baking powder and salt in a medium bowl. Cut the shortening into the flour mixture, using a pastry blender or crisscrossing 2 knives, until the mixture looks like fine crumbs.

4 Stir the milk into the crumb mixture just until blended and a dough forms. If the crumb mixture is not completely moistened, stir in an additional 1 to 3 teaspoons milk. Drop the dough by 6 spoonfuls onto the ungreased cookie sheet.

5 Bake 10 to 12 minutes or until golden brown.

6 Just before serving, prepare Sweetened Whipped Cream (below). Split warm or cool shortcakes horizontally. Spoon whipped cream and strawberries over bottoms of shortcakes. Top with tops of shortcakes and additional whipped cream and strawberries.

SWEETENED WHIPPED CREAM Beat the whipping cream and sugar in a chilled medium bowl with the electric mixer on high speed until stiff peaks form. Serve immediately.

1 SERVING. Calories 375 (Calories from Fat 115); Fat 13g (Saturated 3g); Cholesterol 5mg; Sodium 650mg; Carbohydrate 62g (Dietary Fiber 3g); Protein 6g

TiP **WASH STRAWBERRIES** just before you plan to use them.

TiP **THE WHIPPING CREAM** will beat up more easily if the bowl and beaters for the mixer are chilled in the refrigerator for about 20 minutes before beating.

Removing Hull from Strawberry

Cut out the hull, or "cap," with the point of a paring knife.

Dropping Shortcake Dough onto Cookie Sheet

Drop dough by 6 spoonfuls onto ungreased cookie sheet.

Strawberry Shortcakes

CREAMY LEMON DESSERT

MAKES 9 servings • **REFRIGERATE: 2 hours**

INGREDIENTS

DIRECTIONS

ESSENTIAL EQUIPMENT: *9-inch square pan or 9-inch pie pan; electric mixer or hand beater*

2 cups whipping (heavy) cream

Graham Cracker Crust (below)

1 can (14 ounces) sweetened condensed milk

1/2 cup lemon juice

2 teaspoons grated lemon peel, if desired

Few drops of yellow food color, if desired

Whole strawberries for garnish, if desired

GRAHAM CRACKER CRUST

16 graham cracker squares

2 tablespoons sugar

1/4 cup (1/2 stick) margarine or butter, melted

1 Pour the whipping cream into a large bowl, and place in the refrigerator to chill. The whipping cream will whip better in a cold bowl.

2 Prepare Graham Cracker Crust (below). While crust is cooling, continue with recipe.

3 Mix milk, lemon juice and lemon peel in a small bowl, and set aside.

4 Add the food color to the whipping cream. Beat the whipping cream with the electric mixer on high speed until stiff peaks form.

5 Gently pour the lemon mixture over the whipped cream. To fold together, use a rubber spatula to cut down vertically through the whipped cream, then slide the spatula across the bottom of the bowl and up the side, turning the whipped cream over. Rotate the bowl one-fourth turn, and repeat this down-across-up motion. Continue mixing in this way just until ingredients are blended.

6 Pour the folded mixture over the crust. Cover and refrigerate at least 2 hours but no longer than 48 hours.

7 Cut dessert into 3-inch squares. Garnish each serving with a strawberry. Cover and refrigerate any remaining dessert.

GRAHAM CRACKER CRUST Heat the oven to 350°. Place a few crackers at a time in a plastic bag. Seal the bag, and crush crackers into fine crumbs with a rolling pin or bottle. Mix the crumbs, sugar and margarine in a medium bowl. Press firmly and evenly on the bottom of the square pan. If using a pie pan, press crumb mixture against bottom and side of pan. Bake 10 minutes; cool.

1 SERVING. Calories 420 (Calories from Fat 245); Fat 27g (Saturated 14g); Cholesterol 75mg; Sodium 210mg; Carbohydrate 39g (Dietary Fiber 0g); Protein 5g

TiP **BE SURE TO PURCHASE** sweetened condensed milk, not evaporated milk. They are used very differently in recipes.

TiP **INSTEAD OF USING** graham crackers, purchase packaged graham cracker crumbs at the supermarket, and use 1 1/4 cups of them in the crust.

Crushing Graham Crackers

Place a few crackers at a time in a plastic bag. Seal bag, and crush crackers into fine crumbs with a rolling pin or bottle.

Creamy Lemon Dessert

PUMPKIN PIE

MAKES 8 servings • **BAKE: 1 hour**

INGREDIENTS

DIRECTIONS

ESSENTIAL EQUIPMENT: *9-inch pie pan; electric mixer or hand beater*

Pat-in-the-Pan Pastry (below)

2 eggs

1/2 cup sugar

1 teaspoon ground cinnamon

1/2 teaspoon salt

1/2 teaspoon ground ginger

1/8 teaspoon ground cloves

1 can (16 ounces) pumpkin

1 can (12 ounces) evaporated milk

Sweetened Whipped Cream (below) or 1 cup frozen (thawed) whipped topping

PAT-IN-THE-PAN PASTRY

1 1/3 cups all-purpose flour

1/3 cup vegetable oil

1/2 teaspoon salt

2 tablespoons cold water

SWEETENED WHIPPED CREAM

1/2 cup whipping (heavy) cream

1 tablespoon granulated or powdered sugar

1 Heat the oven to 425°. Prepare Pat-in-the-Pan Pastry (below).

2 Beat the eggs slightly in a large bowl with a wire whisk or hand beater. Beat in the sugar, cinnamon, salt, ginger, cloves, pumpkin and milk.

3 To prevent spilling, place pastry-lined pie plate on oven rack before adding filling. Carefully pour the pumpkin filling into the pie plate. Bake 15 minutes.

4 Reduce the oven temperature to 350°. Bake about 45 minutes longer or until a knife inserted in the center comes out clean. Place pie on a wire cooling rack after baking. If after 4 to 6 hours the pie has not been served, cover and refrigerate it.

5 Serve pie with Sweetened Whipped Cream (below). Cover and refrigerate any remaining pie up to 3 days.

PAT-IN-THE-PAN PASTRY Mix the flour, oil and salt with a fork in a medium bowl until all flour is moistened. Sprinkle with cold water, 1 tablespoon at a time, tossing with fork until all water is absorbed. Shape pastry into a ball, using your hands. Press pastry in bottom and up side of pie pan.

SWEETENED WHIPPED CREAM Beat the whipping cream and sugar in a chilled medium bowl with the electric mixer on high speed until stiff peaks form. Serve immediately, or continue with recipe to freeze and use later. Place waxed paper on cookie sheet. Drop whipped cream by 8 spoonfuls onto waxed paper. Freeze uncovered at least 2 hours. Place frozen mounds of whipped cream in a freezer container. Cover tightly and freeze no longer than 2 months.

1 SERVING. Calories 345 (Calories from Fat 160); Fat 18g (Saturated 7g); Cholesterol 85mg; Sodium 360mg; Carbohydrate 40g (Dietary Fiber 2g); Protein 8g

Lighter

PUMPKIN PIE: For 2 grams of fat and 120 calories per serving, omit Pat-in-the-Pan Pastry. Heat the oven to 350°. Spray 9-inch pie pan with cooking spray. Use evaporated skimmed milk. Prepare filling as directed; pour into sprayed pie pan. Bake about 45 minutes or until knife inserted in center comes out clean.

TiP **BE SURE TO PURCHASE** canned pumpkin, not pumpkin pie mix, for this recipe. The pumpkin pie mix would require a different recipe.

TiP **THE WHIPPING CREAM** will beat up more easily if the bowl and beaters for the mixer are chilled in the refrigerator for about 20 minutes before beating.

Patting Pastry into pan

Press pastry in bottom and up side of pie pan.

Freezing Mounds of Whipped Cream

Drop whipped cream by 8 spoonfuls onto waxed paper. Freeze uncovered at least 2 hours.

Pumpkin Pie

BEYOND THE BASICS

COMMON PREPARATION TECHNIQUES

CHOP: Cut into pieces of irregular sizes.

GRATE: Cut into tiny particles by rubbing food across the small rough holes of a grater.

CRUSH: Press with side of knife, mallet or rolling pin to break into small pieces.

JULIENNE: Stack thin slices; cut into matchlike sticks.

CUBE: Cut into 1/2-inch or wider strips; cut across strips into cubes.

PEEL: Cut off outer covering with a knife or vegetable peeler, or strip off outer covering with fingers.

CUT UP: Cut into small irregular pieces with kitchen scissors or knife.

SHRED: Cut into long thin pieces by rubbing food across the large holes of a shredder or by using a knife to slice very thinly.

DICE: Cut into 1/2-inch or narrower strips; cut across strips into cubes.

SLICE: Cut into pieces of the same width.

SLICE DIAGONALLY: Cut with knife at 45-degree angle into pieces of the same width.

SNIP: Cut into very small pieces with kitchen scissors.

SLICING AN APPLE: Cut apple into fourths, and remove seeds. Cut each fourth into wedges.

SEEDING AN AVOCADO: Cut avocado lengthwise in half. Hit the seed of the avocado with the sharp edge of a knife. Grasp the avocado half, then twist the knife to loosen and remove the seed.

CUTTING A BELL PEPPER: Cut bell pepper lengthwise in half. Cut out seeds and membrane.

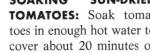

SOAKING SUN-DRIED TOMATOES: Soak tomatoes in enough hot water to cover about 20 minutes or until tender; drain. Chop or cut up tomatoes.

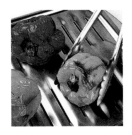

ROASTING BELL PEPPERS OR CHILIES: Broil whole peppers with tops 5 inches from heat, turning occasionally, until skin is blistered and evenly browned but not burned. Place peppers in a plastic bag and let stand 20 minutes. Peel skin from peppers.

MAKING BREAD CRUMBS (DRY): Place bread on cookie sheet and heat in 200° oven about 20 minutes or until dry; cool. Place in heavy plastic bag; crush with rolling pin into very small pieces. Or blend in blender or food processor to make fine bread crumbs.

MAKING BREAD CRUMBS (SOFT): Tear soft bread with fingers into small pieces.

SHREDDING CABBAGE: Place a flat side of one fourth of a head of cabbage on a cutting board; cut off core. Cut cabbage into thin slices with a large knife. Cut slices several times to make smaller pieces.

COATING CHICKEN OR FISH: Place seasonings and bread crumbs or flour in a paper or plastic bag. Add a few pieces of chicken or fish at a time; seal bag and shake until each piece is evenly coated. If chicken or fish is dipped into milk or egg mixture before coating with crumbs, use one hand for handling the wet food and the other for handling the dry food.

MELTING CHOCOLATE:
Heat chocolate in small saucepan over low heat, stirring frequently, until melted. Or place 1 to 2 ounces chocolate in microwavable bowl. Microwave uncovered on Medium 3 to 4 minutes, stirring after 2 minutes.

TOASTING COCONUT OR NUTS: Bake coconut or nuts in shallow pan in 350° oven about 10 minutes, stirring occasionally, until golden brown. Or sprinkle 1/2 cup coconut or nuts in ungreased heavy skillet. Cook over medium-low heat 6 to 14 minutes for coconut or 5 to 7 minutes for nuts, stirring frequently until browning begins, then stirring constantly until golden brown. (Watch carefully; time varies greatly between gas and electric ranges.)

MAKING CROUTONS: Cut bread into 1/2-inch slices; spread one side with softened margarine or butter. Cut into 1/2-inch cubes. Sprinkle with chopped herbs, grated Parmesan cheese or spices if desired. Cook in ungreased heavy skillet over medium heat 4 to 7 minutes, stirring frequently, until golden brown.

SEPARATING EGGS: Eggs are easiest to separate when cold. Purchase an inexpensive egg separator. Place separator over a small bowl. Crack egg; open shell, allowing egg yolk to fall into center of separator.

The egg white will slip through the slots of the separator into the bowl. Do not pass the egg yolk back and forth from shell half to shell half; bacteria may be present in the pores of the shell, which could contaminate the yolk or white.

SKIMMING FAT: Remove fat floating on top of broth or soup by dipping large spoon or fat skimmer into broth. Remove fat, leaving as much of the broth as possible.

CHOPPING GARLIC: Hit garlic clove with flat side of heavy knife to crack the skin, which will then slip off easily. Finely chop garlic with knife.

PREPARING AND CHOPPING GINGERROOT: Peel gingerroot with a paring knife. Cut into thin slices, then chop finely or grate finely.

CRUSHING GRAHAM CRACKERS: Place a few crackers at a time in a plastic bag. Seal bag, and crush crackers into fine crumbs with a rolling pin. Use the same technique for crushing cookies and chips. Or blend in blender or food processor to make fine crumbs.

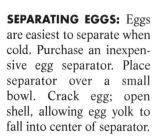

CUTTING GREEN ONIONS:
Cut green onions into thin slices, using some of the green part. Discard the tip with the stringy end.

PREPARING MUSHROOMS:
Rinse mushrooms, and cut off stem ends. Leave mushrooms whole, or cut into slices.

SEEDING A JALAPEÑO CHILI:
Cut the stem off the jalapeño chili, cut the chili lengthwise in half and scrape out the seeds.

SOAKING DRIED MUSHROOMS:
Soak mushrooms in enough warm water to cover about 30 minutes. Rinse well and squeeze out moisture. Cut off and discard the tough stems.

PEELING A KIWIFRUIT:
Cut the fuzzy brown skin from the fruit with a paring knife. Cut fruit into slices or wedges.

CUTTING PINEAPPLE:
Twist top from pineapple. Cut pineapple into fourths. Holding pineapple securely, cut fruit from rind. Cut off pineapple core and remove "eyes." Cut pineapple crosswise or lengthwise into chunks or spears.

MELTING MARGARINE OR BUTTER:
To microwave 3 to 4 tablespoons margarine, remove foil wrapper and place margarine in microwavable bowl. Microwave uncovered on High 30 to 45 seconds. Or melt margarine in small saucepan over very low heat about 1 minute.

HULLING STRAWBERRIES (REMOVING THE CAPS):
Use the tip of a paring knife to remove the hull, or use an inexpensive strawberry huller (very short, fat tweezers). Or push one end of a plastic drinking straw into the point of the berry and push it through to pop off the cap.

CUTTING GRAIN OF MEAT:
The "grain" of the meat refers to the muscle fibers that run the length of a cut of meat. Cut with the grain into strips, then cut across the grain into slices.

SOFTENING TORTILLAS:
Place 2 tortillas between dampened microwavable paper towels or microwavable plastic wrap. Microwave on High 15 to 20 seconds to soften.

Twelve Terrific Herbs to Add Aroma and Flavor

Herbs can add great flavor and variety to your favorite dishes. Most herbs are available fresh, dried or ground. If you have the space, you can even grow your own.

Too much of any herb can overwhelm a food or become bitter, so use small amounts of herbs, then taste the dish before adding more. Dried herbs are more concentrated than fresh; if a recipe calls for 1 tablespoon chopped fresh herbs, substitute 1 teaspoon dried herbs. For the best flavor when using dried herbs, crumble the herbs in the palm of your hand after measuring them to release more flavor. To chop fresh herbs, see page 71.

To store fresh herbs such as basil, chives, cilantro, parsley and rosemary, snip off the stem ends, and place the herbs in a glass or jar with the stems in about 1 inch of water. Seal the glass or jar in a plastic bag, and refrigerate for up to a week. For other herbs, such as oregano, tarragon and thyme, store dry in a dry plastic bag in the refrigerator; they should last four to six days.

Dried and ground herbs begin to lose their flavor after six months on the shelf and should be replaced after one year. When you buy dried herbs, write the date on the box or jar, so you will know when to replace them. Because herbs are perishable, buy them in the smallest quantity; this is one time when buying the large economy size is not a good idea.

BASIL: Fresh and dried leaves; ground
Flavor: Sweet with pungent tang
Uses: Eggs, pesto, spaghetti sauce, tomatoes

BAY LEAF: Fresh and dried leaves
Flavor: Pungent and aromatic
Uses: Meats, sauces, soups, stews

CHIVES: Fresh and freeze-dried
Flavor: Onion-like
Uses: Appetizers, cream soups, eggs, salads

CILANTRO: Fresh and dried leaves
Flavor: Aromatic and parsleylike
Uses: Chinese, Italian and Mexican dishes, pesto

DILL WEED: Fresh and dried
Flavor: Pungent and tangy
Uses: Dips, fish, soups, stews

MARJORAM: Fresh and dried leaves; ground
Flavor: Aromatic with bitter overtone
Uses: Fish, poultry, soups, stews

OREGANO: Fresh and dried leaves; ground
Flavor: Aromatic with pleasant bitter overtone
Uses: Eggs, Italian dishes, meats, sauces

PARSLEY: Fresh and dried leaves
Flavor: Slightly peppery
Uses: Garnishes, herb mixtures, sauces, soups

ROSEMARY: Fresh and dried leaves
Flavor: Fresh, sweet flavor
Uses: Breads, casseroles, pork, vegetables

SAGE: Fresh and dried leaves; rubbed; ground
Flavor: Aromatic, slightly bitter
Uses: Fish, meats, poultry, stuffing

TARRAGON: Fresh and dried leaves
Flavor: Piquant, aniselike
Uses: Eggs, meats, salads, sauces

THYME: Fresh and dried leaves; ground
Flavor: Aromatic, pungent
Uses: Fish, meats, poultry, stews

TOP FIVE SPICES FOR FLAVOR

The seeds, buds, fruit, bark or roots of plants, spices have added zest and a flavor boost to foods for hundreds of years. Store spices in a cool, dry place. Ground spices loose some of their flavor after six months and whole spices after one year. When you purchase spices, write the date on the box or jar, so you will know when to replace them.

CHILI POWDER: Ground
Flavor: Blend of chili peppers and spices; hot and spicy
Uses: Casseroles, Mexican dishes, soups, stews

CINNAMON: Stick and ground
Flavor: Aromatic, sweet and pungent
Uses: Cakes, cookies, desserts, pies

GINGER: Fresh and ground
Flavor: Pungent and spicy
Uses: Cookies, cakes, desserts, pies

NUTMEG: Whole and ground
Flavor: Fragrant, sweet and spicy
Uses: Beverages, cakes, cookies, desserts

PAPRIKA: Ground
Flavor: Slightly bitter; ranges from sweet to hot
Uses: Casseroles, eggs, garnishes, meats

ABOUT PASTA

The versatility of pasta makes it popular and convenient for today's meals. Pasta is available in three forms—dried, fresh and frozen—and in many shapes and sizes. Here are some of the most popular dried varieties; many are shown in the photo to the right.

ACINI DE PEPE (OR DOT SHAPE): Peppercorn-size pieces of cut spaghetti.

CAPELLINI (OR ANGEL HAIR): The thinnest of the long spaghettis.

CONCHIGLE: Medium to small shapes with or without grooves.

COUSCOUS: The tiniest form of pasta made from granular semolina.

EGG NOODLES: Flat or curly, short pasta strips usually made with eggs or egg yolks.

ELBOW MACARONI: Short, curved, tubular-shaped pasta.

FARFALLE (OR BOW-TIES): Shaped like bow-ties. Miniature bow-ties are known as tripolini.

FETTUCCINE: Long, flat noodles, usually 1/4 inch wide.

FUSILLI: Long or short spring-shaped pasta.

JAPANESE CURLY NOODLES: Wavy, thin, long noodles in thin "bricks."

LASAGNA: Flat noodle about 2 inches wide with either ruffled or straight edges.

LINGUINE: Long, flat, thin noodle usually 1/8 inch wide.

MANICOTTI (OR CANNELLONI): Large 4-inch hollow pasta tubes that are usually stuffed and baked.

NOVELTY SHAPES: Seasonal or other pasta shapes, such as trees, rabbits, hearts, etc., sometimes flavored.

PENNE: Narrow, short, diagonal-cut pasta about 1 1/4 inches long, smooth or with grooves.

RAMEN: Quick-cooking, deep-fried noodles used dry or cooked.

RAVIOLI: Filled pillow-shaped pasta usually stuffed with cheese or spinach.

RICE NOODLES: Translucent, thin strands made from rice flour and water.

RIGATONI: Short-cut, wide tubular pasta about 1 inch long with grooves.

ROSAMARINA (OR ORZO): Resembles rice but is slightly larger and longer.

ROTINI: Short-cut corkscrew-shaped pasta. Wider version is called rotelle.

SPAGHETTI: Long, thin, solid strands.

TORTELLINI: Filled, slightly irregularly shaped little rings.

WAGON WHEEL: Small, round pasta resembling a wheel with spokes.

ZITI: Short-cut, 2-inch tubular noodle with smooth surface.

STORING AND REHEATING COOKED PASTA

You can refrigerate or freeze leftover pasta for a future meal. Store in tightly sealed containers or plastic bags in the refrigerator up to five days, or freeze up to two months. To reheat pasta, choose one of these three quick and easy methods:

- Place pasta in rapidly boiling water for up to 2 minutes. Drain and serve immediately.

- Place pasta in colander and pour boiling water over it until heated through. Drain and serve immediately.

- Place pasta in microwavable dish or container. Cover and microwave on High for 1 to 3 minutes per 2 cups or until heated through. Serve immediately.

Capellini

Spaghetti

Fettuccine

Lasagna Noodles

Linguine

Japanese Curly Noodles

Rotini

Rosomarina (orzo)

Fusilli

Rigatoni

Rice Noodles

Manicotti

Egg Noodles

Wagon Wheels

Farfelle (bow ties)

Tortellini

Acini de Pepe

Couscous

Penne

Macaroni

Novelty Pasta Shapes

Conchigle

ABOUT SALAD GREENS

Once you know the different types of greens available, your salads can have more variety. Some greens tend to be bitter, and others are mild. You can have fun experimenting to find those you like best. Be sure to purchase fresh, crisp greens. Avoid limp or bruised greens and those with rust spots. Here are some of the more popular varieties, shown in the photo to the right.

ARUGULA (OR ROCKET) has small, slender, dark green leaves similar to radish leaves with a slightly bitter peppery mustard flavor. Choose smaller leaves for a less distinctive flavor.

BELGIAN (OR FRENCH) ENDIVE has closed, narrow, pale leaves with a distinct bitter flavor.

BIBB LETTUCE (OR LIMESTONE) has tender, pliable leaves similar to Boston lettuce leaves but smaller; it has a delicate, mild flavor.

BOSTON LETTUCE (OR BUTTERHEAD) has small rounded heads of soft, buttery leaves with the same delicate flavor of Bibb lettuce.

CABBAGE comes in a variety of types; the most familiar are green and red. Look for compact heads. Green cabbage also is available already shredded. Savoy cabbage has crinkled leaves, and Chinese (or napa) cabbage has long, crisp leaves. The flavor of cabbage can range from strong to slightly sweet.

CURLY ENDIVE has frilly narrow leaves with a slightly bitter taste.

ESCAROLE, also part of the endive family, has broad dark green leaves and a mild flavor.

GREENS (BEET, DANDELION, MUSTARD) all have a strong, biting flavor. When young, they are tender and milder in flavor and make a nice addition to tossed salads.

ICEBERG LETTUCE (OR CRISPHEAD) has a bland, mild flavor, making it the most popular and versatile green. Look for solid, compact heads with tight leaves that range from medium green on the outside to pale green inside.

LEAF LETTUCE, either red or green, has tender leaves that do not form heads. These leafy bunches have a mild, bland flavor.

MIXED SALAD GREENS, which you can find in bags in the produce section of most supermarkets, are already cleaned and ready to use. The package can include one type of green or a mixture of several varieties, which can add color, flavor and texture to your salads.

RADICCHIO, another member of the endive family, resembles a small, loose-leaf cabbage with smooth, tender leaves. The most familiar variety is usually rose-colored and may have a slightly bitter taste.

ROMAINE (OR COS) has narrow, elongated dark leaves with a crisp texture. This mild-flavored green is used in the traditional Caesar salad.

SPINACH has smooth, tapered, dark green leaves, sometimes with crumpling at the edges. Larger leaves may be tougher and stronger in flavor.

WATERCRESS has large, dark green leaves with a strong peppery flavor.

STORING AND HANDLING SALAD GREENS

Store greens in the crisper section of your refrigerator. You can keep them in the original wrap or place them in a plastic bag. Romaine and iceberg lettuce will keep up to one week. Most other greens will wilt within a few days.

Before using, be sure to wash greens thoroughly in several changes of cold water and then shake off excess moisture. For greens that may be sandy, such as spinach, after washing separate the leaves with your fingers to remove all grit. Toss them in a cloth towel and gently blot dry, or use a salad spinner to remove excess moisture. You can refrigerate unused washed greens in a sealed plastic bag or bowl with an airtight lid for three to four days.

Curly Endive

Romaine

Cabbage

Turnip Greens

Escarole

Iceberg Lettuce

Boston Lettuce

Spinach

Leaf Lettuce

Belgian Endive

Radicchio

Mustard Greens

Watercress

Mixed Salad Greens

Arugula

Beyond the Basics—Equipment

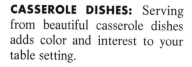

Special utensils and equipment will broaden the range of recipes you can prepare and will make some common tasks easier. If you enjoy cooking, plan to add some of these special things to your kitchen.

CASSEROLE DISHES: Serving from beautiful casserole dishes adds color and interest to your table setting.

CUSTARD CUPS: Small glass cups that can be used in many ways, including combining ingredients or snipping fresh herbs.

EGG SEPARATOR: A tool for separating the egg white from the yolk.

FUNNEL: Helps when transferring liquids to a smaller container.

GARLIC PRESS: Pressing cloves of garlic is faster than chopping them and imparts more garlic flavor.

ICE-CREAM SCOOP: Choose a sturdy scoop that will work well in solidly frozen ice cream and yogurt.

KNIVES: Once you have the basic 3 knives—paring, chef's and all-purpose serrated, you may find that adding a utility knife, boning knife, carving knife and slicing knife would be helpful. Or simply add more sizes of the types of knives you use most often.

PANS

Having the pans shown below adds variety to your baking.

BUNDT CAKE PAN

ANGEL FOOD CAKE PAN

JELLY ROLL PAN

LOAF PAN

OMELET PAN

MUFFIN PAN

PASTRY BRUSH: Perfect for greasing baking pans, brushing meats and poultry with oil or a marinade and for use in making special pastries.

PEPPER MILL: Makes freshly ground pepper from peppercorns.

ROASTING PAN WITH A RACK: A large shallow pan for roasting meat and poultry. The rack suspends the meat so it doesn't cook in its own juices or fat.

ROLLING PIN: The best piece of equipment for rolling out cookie dough or pastry.

SALAD SPINNER: After rinsing greens, this is a quick and easy way to dry them.

SPAGHETTI SERVER: Separates long pasta strands for easy serving.

STOCKPOT: A large pot, usually 5-quart size or larger, used to simmer soups and stews and for cooking pasta.

WIRE COOLING RACKS: These allow air to circulate around freshly baked breads, cookies and desserts as they cool.

ZESTER: A special tool for removing the thin, flavorful colored layer, called the zest, from the peel of lemons, limes and oranges.

SMALL ELECTRICAL APPLIANCES

GRIDDLE

FOOD PROCESSOR

WAFFLE IRON

WOK

BASICS FOR GREAT GRILLING

Grilled food tastes delicious! Plus it's so easy to prepare and convenient, with little cleanup required. Outdoor grilling not only puts great-tasting food on the table, but also turns a meal into a special event.

SELECTING A GRILL

The variety of styles and sizes of grills can seem endless. To decide what model best fits your needs, consider how often you grill, where you grill, which technique you prefer, how many people you feed and how much money you're planning to spend.

Here are some features to look at: cooking grill racks that resist corrosion (such as those made of stainless steel), nonstick racks for easier cleanup, handles designed to be gripped easily and comfortably that are not too close to the heat source. On gas grills, look for an easy-to-replace gas tank with a fuel gauge, so you won't be caught on empty.

STYLES OF OUTDOOR GRILLS

Open

OPEN GRILLS OR BRAZIERS

This simplest form of a grill consists of a shallow firebox to hold the charcoal and a metal cooking grill rack for the food. The grill rack is usually just a few inches from the coals, so these grills are best for direct-heat grilling (grilling foods directly over charcoal) of burgers, chops, steaks and chicken. Braziers have a crank-type handle so you can raise and lower the cooking grill rack. They may be partially hooded for protection from the wind and for heat retention.

Covered

KETTLES AND COVERED COOKERS

"Kettle" describes the round version, whereas "covered cooker" describes the square and rectangular models. Because of their deep, rounded bottoms and generous lids, these grills are great for a wide range of cooking methods—grilling, roasting, steaming and smoking. Without their covers, they are used for direct-heat grilling. Covered, foods can be grilled and lightly smoked at the same time. Draft vents in the bottom and the cover help control the temperature.

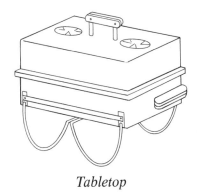

Tabletop

PORTABLE OR TABLETOP GRILLS

These grills are lightweight for transporting, are easy to clean and take up little storage space. They range from uncovered simple cast-metal hibachis of Japanese origin to miniature versions of kettles and covered cookers. They're great for direct-heat cooking for two, beach cookouts, tailgating parties and picnics. Because the cooking surface is much smaller than that of standard grills, portable grills are not designed for indirect-heat cooking of roasts or whole poultry, feeding crowds or long cooking times. Use them outdoors only.

TYPES OF GRILLS BY FUEL SOURCE

CHARCOAL GRILLS

If there is a tradition in grilling, charcoal is it. Available in all types and sizes, the simplest charcoal grill consists of a firebox with a grate to hold the charcoal, a grill rack for the food and sometimes a cover or lid.

ELECTRIC GRILLS

If you live in an apartment or condominium building where charcoal or gas grills are prohibited, an electric outdoor grill may be your obvious choice. Mobility can be limited because these grills require a separate 110/120-volt grounded outlet with 1,600 to 1,800 watts of cooking power. Most electric grills include a smoking element, such as lava rock, which will give food a grilled flavor similar to that produced by charcoal and gas grills.

GAS GRILLS

Convenience is the key to the popularity of gas grills. They're quick and easy to start with no charcoal required. Heat controls let you cook food more evenly and accurately. Gas is used to heat semipermanent ceramic briquettes, or lava rock, made from natural volcanic stone. Most models are fueled by refillable liquid propane (LP) gas tanks; others are directly hooked up to a natural gas line.

STARTING THE FIRE

CHARCOAL GRILLS

For greatest success, follow manufacturer's directions for lighting coals well before cooking. Most coals take between 30 and 45 minutes to reach proper temperature.

Arrange the desired number of charcoal briquettes in a pyramid shape in the firebox. This shape allows air to circulate, heating the briquettes faster. An electric coil starter or liquid fire starter will make starting the fire easier; follow manufacturer's directions.

In daylight, you can tell the coals are ready for grilling when they are about 80 percent ashy gray. If it's dark outside, coals should have an even red glow. Bright red coals are too hot, black coals are too cool and a mix of red and black coals gives off uneven heat.

Check the temperature of the coals by placing your hand, palm side down, near but not touching the cooking grill rack. If you can keep your hand there for two seconds (count: one thousand one, one thousand two), the temperature is high; three seconds is medium-high, four seconds is medium and five seconds is low.

GAS GRILLS

Follow manufacturer's directions, or heat 5 to 10 minutes before cooking.

The recipes in this book call for direct-heat cooking, where you cook the food directly over the heat. If you're using indirect heat for longer-cooking foods such as whole poultry and whole turkey breasts, arrange the coals around the edge of the firebox and place a drip pan under the grilling area.

SUCCESS TIPS FOR GRILLING

- Before lighting coals or turning on gas, grease or oil the rack or spray it with cooking spray.

- Place the grill rack 4 to 6 inches above the coals or gas burners.

- For even cooking, place thicker foods in the center of the grill rack and smaller pieces on the edges; turn pieces frequently.

- Keep the heat as even as possible throughout the grilling period.

- If you're not getting a sizzle, the fire may be too cool. Regulate the heat by spreading the coals or raking them together, opening or closing the vents or adjusting the control on a gas or electric grill. Raising or lowering the cooking grill or covering it will also help control the heat.

- Use long-handled barbecue tools to allow for a safe distance between you and the intense heat of the grill.

SETTING THE TABLE AND SERVING THE MEAL

How the dinner table looks and how you present the food are part of the overall dining experience. But setting the table with multiple pieces of flatware and glassware can be baffling. You can do it easily with the suggestions that follow.

• Place the flatware 1 inch from the edge of the table, arranging the pieces used first the farthest from the plate, so you can use the flatware from the outside toward the plate. The forks are typically to the left, and the knife (with the blade toward the plate), then the spoons, to the right.

• If a butter plate is used, place it above the forks.

• If salad is to be served with the main course, place the salad plate to the left of the forks. The salad fork may be placed at either side of the dinner fork.

• Arrange glasses above the knife. The water glass is usually at the tip of the knife, with beverage and wine glasses to the right of the water glass.

• If coffee or tea is served at the table, place the cup slightly above and to the right of the spoons.

• Place the napkin either in the center of the dinner plate or to the left of the forks at each place setting. There are many creative ways of folding napkins to make any meal festive.

• Before offering dessert, clear the table of all serving dishes, plates, salt and pepper shakers and any flatware that won't be used for the dessert course.

SERVING BUFFET STYLE

Buffet service is a convenient way for you to serve small or large groups. It works well for both casual and formal occasions. If you have limited seated or serving space, a buffet makes entertaining much easier. When the meal is served from a buffet, guests select food, beverage and flatware from the buffet table, then move to sit wherever they're comfortable. It's important to serve foods that do not need to be cut with a knife, because your guests will usually have to balance plates on their laps. Serve rolls or bread already buttered, and provide small tables on which your guests can place their beverages. You can go around to guests with any accompaniments such as sauce, gravy or salsa.

You can set up the buffet wherever it's most convenient—on the dining-room table, a picnic table, two card tables placed together, a kitchen counter or a desk.

The key to success is to create a buffet table setting so the traffic flows smoothly and easily. Place the buffet table in the center of the room, so guests can help themselves from all sides of the table. Or push it against a wall to save space.

Place the food in order so guests can serve themselves without backtracking. Plates first, main course and vegetables next, then salad, condiments, bread and flatware and napkins last. Placing flatware and napkins at the end of the line allows guests to have a hand free to serve themselves.

While guests finish the main course, you can clear the buffet table and arrange the dessert, dessert plates and flatware on the buffet table or on a side table.

Classy Centerpieces in Minutes

Centerpieces needn't be expensive or time-consuming to make. One of these easy ideas is sure to be a hit at your next dinner.

• Pile an assortment of lemons and limes in a rustic wooden bowl or basket. Accent with feathery greens from the florist, or tuck a trailing ivy plant among the fruit.

• Wrap the pot of your healthiest houseplant with a bright and colorful paper napkin or scarf, and hold the napkin in place with a raffia bow.

• Fill a favorite basket with a collection of fresh and aromatic garden herbs. The herbs can be potted or cut fresh and placed in small bottles or juice glasses filled with water.

• Fill a glass bowl with bright red apples and green pears. Tie yarn or a narrow ribbon around the stem of each piece of fruit.

• Arrange an assortment of fruits and vegetables in a large basket. Be creative with grapes, broccoli, savoy cabbage, radicchio, carrots with the green tops left on, oranges, miniature pumpkins, squash and leaf lettuce.

STOCKING THE PANTRY

You can prepare quick meals or make an easy snack or dessert without planning ahead if you keep the essential ingredients on hand in your kitchen. Check the lists below for the foods you like to serve, and add them to your cupboard, refrigerator or freezer. Then keep a running shopping list, and add items as your supply runs low. See our food-storage guide (pages 243–245) for information on how long you can plan to store some of these items.

Cupboard

Breads (buns, loaves, pitas, tortillas)
Canned
 Beans (black, kidney, navy)
 Broth (beef, chicken, vegetable)
 Meats (chicken, salmon, tuna)
 Tomatoes (diced or peeled whole)
Cereals
Coffee and tea
Cookies and crackers
Herbs and spices (see page 226)
Jams and jellies
Ketchup
Main-dish mixes
Mayonnaise
Mustard
Olives
Pasta (fettuccine, macaroni, spaghetti)
Pasta sauces (Alfredo, pesto, spaghetti)
Peanut butter
Pickles
Rice and rice mixtures
Salsa
Salt and pepper
Soft drinks
Soups (canned or dried)
Soy sauce and marinating sauces
Syrups (butterscotch, chocolate, maple)
Tomato sauce and tomato paste
Vegetable oil
Vinegar

Refrigerator

Cheeses (Cheddar, cottage, Parmesan)
Eggs
Fruit juice
Margarine or butter
Milk
Packaged salad greens
Sour cream
Yogurt

Freezer

Chicken (skinless, boneless breasts)
Fruit juice concentrate
Ground beef or turkey
Ice cream or frozen yogurt
Vegetables (packaged)

Baking

Baking cocoa
Baking mix (Bisquick®)
Baking powder and baking soda
Brownie mix
Cake mix and canned frosting
Flour
Sugars (brown, granulated, powdered)
Vanilla and almond extract

Nonfood Supplies

All-purpose spray cleanser
Aluminum foil
Dishwasher detergent
Food-storage bags
Liquid detergent
Napkins
Nonabrasive scrubbing pads
Paper towels
Plastic wrap
Sponges
Storage containers
Toothpicks
Waxed paper

THREE WAYS TO KEEP FOODS SAFE

Keeping the food you buy safe to eat is very easy and involves just three things: keep everything in the kitchen clean, keep hot foods hot and keep cold foods cold. Occasionally, a food will look or smell bad and should obviously be thrown away. Some foods, though, may look, smell and taste good but actually be harmful. If in doubt, don't taste it; just throw it out.

1 Keep everything in the kitchen clean

- Use hard plastic cutting boards for raw meat, poultry and fish. They are less porous than wooden cutting boards and can be cleaned easily with hot soapy water or washed in the dishwasher. Wash the board, as well as your knives, before using it for cutting any other foods.

- After using a plate for raw meat, poultry or fish, do not serve the cooked meat on the same unwashed plate. Either wash it in hot soapy water or use a clean plate for serving the cooked food.

- After working with raw foods, especially meat, poultry and fish, use disposable paper towels to wipe any spills from the counter. Then, wipe again with hot, soapy water.

- Always keep countertops, appliances, utensils and dishes clean. Remember to occasionally wipe all the special drawers or bins in the refrigerator for clean, safe food storage.

- Wash hands thoroughly before preparing food, and cover any cuts or infection with a bandage or wear rubber gloves.

- Keep kitchen towels and sponges clean.

2 Keep hot foods hot

- Hot foods can remain lukewarm or at room temperature for only two hours or less before they become unsafe to eat. Foods spoil easily and rapidly at lukewarm temperatures. If they need to stand out longer, be sure they are kept hot in an electric skillet or a chafing dish or on a hot tray. Warming units heated with a candle will not keep them hot enough to be safe.

- Lower temperatures can cause the meat to spoil before cooking is complete.

- Once food has been cooked, keep it hot until serving, or refrigerate it as soon as possible.

3 Keep cold foods cold

- Cold foods can remain lukewarm or at room temperature for only two hours or less before they become unsafe to eat. Foods spoil easily and rapidly at lukewarm temperatures.

- When shopping, purchase cold foods such as meats and dairy products last so they will stay cold until you can refrigerate them when you get home. Try to refrigerate them within 30 minutes after purchasing. Even short stops during hot weather can cause perishable groceries in a hot car to reach unsafe temperatures.

- When shopping, wrap foods from the meat department in plastic bags to prevent meat juices from dripping onto other foods in your shopping cart. These bags usually are available near the meat counter.

- Frozen foods should not be thawed at room temperature. Thaw them in the refrigerator or the microwave. If foods are thawed in the microwave, finish cooking them immediately because some cooking may have started during the thawing process.

FOOD SAFETY TIPS

1 CANNED FOODS: Do not buy or use food in a can that is leaking, bulging or dented. Jars of food should not have cracks or loose or bulging lids.

2 UNCOOKED EGGS:

● Store in refrigerator in the carton for as long as the date on the carton indicates.

● "Do-ahead" recipes that contain raw eggs should be refrigerated only 24 hours or less before they are baked.

● Do not eat cookie dough or cake batter containing raw eggs.

● Do not use uncooked eggs in recipes that will not be baked, such as Caesar salad, frostings or desserts unless you purchase eggs marked pasteurized or use egg substitutes.

3 FRUITS AND VEGETABLES: Wash with cool water, using a vegetable brush if necessary.

4 GROUND BEEF: Ground meats should be cooked at least until they are brownish pink in the center. Cooking them until well done is even safer. Any contamination that may have been on the outside of a piece of meat becomes mixed into the meat as it is ground up.

5 HAM: Most hams are already fully cooked and need only to be reheated. But check the label to be sure it does not need to be cooked. If you are uncertain, cook it until a meat thermometer reaches 165°.

6 MARINADES: Place foods to be marinated in a heavy plastic food-storage bag or non-metal utensil. Always refrigerate when marinating; do not leave at room temperature.

Discard leftover marinade or sauces that touched raw meat, fish or poultry, or heat the marinade or sauce to a full boil and boil for 1 minute before serving.

7 POULTRY: Cook all poultry until the juices are no longer pink when you cut into the centers of thickest pieces.

STORING FOODS

Many foods are labeled with a "sell by," "use by" or expiration date that will tell you how long they can be stored either in your cupboard at room temperature or in the refrigerator. This is helpful information you should check before purchasing to make sure all foods are fresh. Foods stored at room temperature should be kept in a cool, dry place to prolong their freshness. Avoid cupboards in areas over the stove or microwave, near the dishwasher or above the refrigerator because they tend to be warm.

The temperature in your refrigerator should be between 34° and 40°, and your freezer should be at 0° or below. Having a refrigerator thermometer and a freezer thermometer is helpful, so you know that your foods are being properly chilled or frozen. Allow space between foods when you place them in the refrigerator and freezer, so air can circulate and chill or freeze the food more quickly.

Refrigerated foods stay colder near the back of the refrigerator rather than in the door. Wrap foods that will be frozen tightly in aluminum foil or plastic food-storage bags. The storage times shown here are just a guide because the conditions under which foods are stored will affect the quality.

Room Temperature Storage

Foods	Length of Time	Storage Tips
Bread crumbs, dry	6 months	After opening, close tightly.
Breads and rolls	5 to 7 days	Store in tightly closed original package; refrigerate in hot humid weather.
Canned foods	1 year	Date the cans; use oldest first.
Cereals Ready-to-cook Ready-to-eat	4 to 6 months Check package label	Refold inner lining after opening to keep crisp.
Chocolate syrup	Use within 2 years*	Refrigerate after opening.
Cookies, packaged and unopened	2 months	After opening, close tightly.
Crackers	8 months	After opening, close tightly.
Dressings, bottled	Check date on bottle.	Refrigerate after opening.
Flour All-purpose Whole wheat	15 months 6 to 8 months	Store in airtight container; may be refrigerated or frozen. Bring to room temperature before using. Same as for all-purpose flour.
Honey	1 year	
Jams and Jellies	1 year*	Refrigerate after opening.
Main-dish mixes	1 year	
Olives	Use within 1 year*	Refrigerate after opening.
Pasta, dried	1 year	Store in original packaging or in airtight glass or plastic containers.
Peanut butter Unopened Opened	Use within 9 months* 2 to 3 months	
Pickles	Use within 1 year*	Refrigerate after opening.
Rice Brown or wild White	6 months 1 year	Use seasoned mixes within 6 months.
Sugar Brown or powdered White (granulated)	4 months 2 years	Store airtight.
Syrups	1 year	Store in cool, dark place.
Vegetable oil Unopened Opened	Use within 6 months* 1 to 3 months	Store in cool, dark place.

This is total storage time, including the time after it has been opened.

REFRIGERATOR AND FREEZER STORAGE

Foods	Refrigerator (34° to 40°)	Freezer (0° or below)
Breads, coffee cakes, muffins	5 to 7 days	2 to 3 months
Butter	Up to 2 weeks, if opened	Up to 2 months
Cakes	3 to 5 days	3 to 4 months unfrosted, 2 to 3 months, frosted
Cheesecakes, baked	3 to 5 days	4 to 5 months
Chocolate syrup	3 months, after opening	
Dairy foods (milk, yogurt, cheese)	Check package labels	
Eggs Raw and in the shell	3 weeks	Not recommended
Cooked	1 week	Not recommended
Ice cream, sorbet and frozen yogurt	Freeze only	2 to 4 months
Jams and jellies	1 year	
Margarine or spread	Up to 1 month, if opened	Up to 2 months
Meats, cooked, including meats purchased at the deli	3 to 5 days	2 to 3 months
Meats, processed Cold cuts	Check date on package, 3 to 5 days after opening	Not recommended
Cured bacon	5 to 7 days after opening	Up to 1 month
Hot dogs	Check date on package, 2 weeks after opening	1 to 2 months
Ham, canned, unopened	Check date on can	Not recommended
Ham, whole or half, cooked	5 to 7 days	1 to 2 months
Ham, slices fully cooked,	3 to 4 days	1 to 2 months

Foods		Refrigerator (34° to 40°)	Freezer (0° or below)
Meats, uncooked	Chops	3 to 5 days	4 to 6 months
	Ground	1 to 2 days	3 to 4 months
	Roasts and steaks	3 to 5 days	6 to 12 months
Olives		2 months after opening	
Pasta, fresh		Check date on package	9 months, unopened; 3 months if opened
Pickles		2 months after opening	
Poultry	Cooked, including poultry purchased at the deli	3 to 4 days	4 months
	Uncooked, cut up	1 to 2 days	Up to 9 months
	Uncooked, whole (including game birds, ducks and geese)	1 to 2 days	Up to 12 months
Seafood	Fish, uncooked	1 to 2 days	2 to 3 months
	Shellfish, cooked	3 to 4 days	1 to 2 months
	Shellfish, uncooked	1 to 2 days	3 to 4 months

Yields and Equivalents

Knowing how many apples or carrots you may need for a recipe can be difficult, so here's a guide of common ingredients to help you when shopping for groceries and preparing recipes.

Food		If Your Recipe States	You Will Need Approximately
Apples		1 cup chopped	1 medium
		1 medium apple, thinly sliced	1 1/3 cups
Asparagus		16 to 20 stalks	1 pound
Bacon		1/2 cup crumbled	8 slices, crisply cooked
Beans, dried	Black, kidney, lima, pinto, red	5 to 6 cups cooked	1 pound dried (2 1/4 cups)
	Green or wax	3 cups 1-inch pieces	1 pound
Bread, white		12 slices (1/2 inch)	1-pound loaf
		1 cup soft crumbs	1 1/2 slices
		1 cup dry crumbs	4 to 5 slices, oven-dried
Broccoli		1 bunch	1 1/2 pounds
		2 cups flowerets, 1-inch pieces or chopped	6 ounces
Cabbage	Green	1 medium head	1 1/2 pounds
		4 cups shredded	1 pound
	Slaw (bag)	7 cups	16 ounces
Carrots		1 medium	7 inches
		1 cup shredded	1 1/2 medium
		1 cup 1/4-inch slices	2 medium
Cauliflower		1 medium head	2 pounds (with leaves)
		3 cups flowerets	1 pound
Celery		1 medium bunch	2 pounds (11 inches)
		1 cup thinly sliced or chopped	2 medium stalks

Food		If Your Recipe States	You Will Need Approximately
Cheese	Hard (blue, Cheddar, feta, mozzarella, Swiss), shredded or crumbled	1 cup	4 ounces
	Cottage	2 cups	16 ounces
	Cream	1 cup	8 ounces
Chocolate	Chips	1 cup	6 ounces
	Unsweetened or semisweet baking	1 square or bar	1 ounce
Corn, sweet		1 medium ear	8 ounces
		1 cup kernels	2 medium ears
Cream	Sour	1 cup	8 ounces
	Whipping (heavy)	1 cup (2 cups whipped)	1/2 pint
Crumbs, finely crushed	Chocolate wafer cookie	1 1/2 cups	27 cookies
	Graham cracker	1 1/2 cups	21 squares
	Saltine cracker	1 cup	29 squares
	Vanilla wafer cookie	1 1/2 cups	38 cookies
Eggs, large	Whole	1 cup	4 large eggs
		1 egg	1/4 cup fat-free cholesterol-free egg product
Flour		3 1/2 cups	1 pound
Garlic		1/2 teaspoon finely chopped	1 medium clove
Jalapeño chili		1 tablespoon	1 medium, seeded and chopped
Lemon or lime		1 1/2 to 3 teaspoons grated peel	1 medium
		2 to 3 tablespoons juice	1 medium
Lettuce	Iceberg or romaine	1 medium head	1 1/2 pounds
		2 cups shredded	5 ounces
		6 cups bite-size pieces	1 pound

(CONTINUED)

Food	If Your Recipe States	You Will Need Approximately
Margarine, butter or spread	2 cups 1/2 cup	1 pound 1 stick
Marshmallows	1 large	10 miniature
Meat, cooked Beef, pork and poultry	bite-size pieces	1 cup chopped or 6 ounces
Mushrooms Fresh Canned	6 cups sliced 2 1/2 cups chopped 4-ounce can sliced, drained	1 pound 8 ounces 2/3 cup fresh, sliced and cooked (5 ounces uncooked)
Nuts (without shells) Chopped, sliced or slivered Whole or halves	1 cup 3 to 4 cups	4 ounces 1 pound
Olives Pimiento-stuffed Ripe, pitted	1 cup sliced 1 cup sliced	24 large or 36 small 32 medium
Onions Green, with tops Yellow or white	1 medium 2 tablespoons chopped 1/4 cup sliced 1 medium 1/2 cup chopped	1/2 ounce 2 medium 3 or 4 medium 3 ounces 1 medium
Orange	1 to 2 tablespoons grated peel 1/3 to 1/2 cup juice	1 medium 1 medium
Pasta Macaroni Noodles, egg Spaghetti	4 cups cooked 4 cups cooked 4 cups cooked	6 to 7 ounces uncooked (2 cups) 7 ounces uncooked (4 to 5 cups) 7 to 8 ounces uncooked
Peppers, bell	1/2 cup chopped 1 cup chopped 1 1/2 cups chopped	1 small 1 medium 1 large

Food		If Your Recipe States	You Will Need Approximately
Potatoes	New Red, white, sweet or yams Red or white	10 to 12 small 1 medium 1 cup 1/2-inch pieces	1 1/2 pounds 5 to 6 ounces 1 medium
Rice	Brown Parboiled(converted) Precooked (white) instant Regular long grain Wild	4 cups cooked 3 to 4 cups cooked 2 cups cooked 3 cups cooked 3 cups cooked	1 cup uncooked 1 cup uncooked 1 cup uncooked 1 cup uncooked 1 cup uncooked
Shrimp, uncooked, with shells	Jumbo Large Medium Small	1 pound 1 pound 1 pound 1 pound	10 to 12 count 15 to 20 count 26 to 30 count 40 to 50 count
Shrimp, cooked without shells		1 pound	1 1/3 pounds uncooked (with shells)
Sugar	Brown Granulated Powdered	2 1/4 cups packed 2 1/4 cups 4 cups	1 pound 1 pound 1 pound
Tomatoes		3/4 cup chopped (1 medium) 1 cup chopped 1/2 cup chopped	5 ounces 1 large 1 small

SUBSTITUTIONS

Using the ingredients recommended in a recipe is best. Sometimes, no practical alternatives or substitutions exist. If you must substitute, try the following:

Food	Instead of: Amount	Use
Arborio rice	1 cup uncooked	1 cup uncooked short grain white rice, regular long-grain rice or brown rice
Balsamic vinegar	1 tablespoon	1 tablespoon sherry or cider vinegar
Bread crumbs, dry	1/4 cup	1/4 cup finely crushed cracker crumbs, cornflakes or quick-cooking or old-fashioned oats
Broth, chicken, beef or vegetable	1 cup	1 teaspoon chicken, beef or vegetable bouillon granules (or 1 cube) dissolved in 1 cup boiling water
Buttermilk or sour milk	1 cup	1 tablespoon lemon juice or white vinegar plus enough milk to measure 1 cup. Let stand a few minutes. Or use 1 cup plain yogurt.
Chocolate Semisweet baking	1 ounce	1 ounce unsweetened baking Chocolate plus 1 tablespoon sugar
Semisweet chips	1 cup	6 ounces semisweet baking chocolate, chopped
Unsweetened baking	1 ounce	3 tablespoons baking cocoa plus 1 tablespoon shortening or margarine
Cornstarch	1 tablespoon	2 tablespoons all-purpose flour
Eggs	1 large	2 egg whites or 1/4 cup fat-free cholesterol-free egg product
Flour All-purpose	1 cup	1 cup plus 2 tablespoons cake flour
Cake	1 cup	1 cup minus 2 tablespoons all-purpose flour
Garlic, finely chopped	1 medium clove	1/8 teaspoon garlic powder or 1/4 teaspoon instant minced garlic
Gingerroot, grated or finely chopped	1 teaspoon	3/4 teaspoon ground ginger

Food	Instead of: Amount	Use
Herbs, chopped fresh	1 tablespoon	3/4 to 1 teaspoon dried herbs
Honey	1 cup	1 1/4 cups sugar plus 1/4 cup water or apple juice
Lemon juice, fresh	1 tablespoon	1 tablespoon bottled lemon juice or white vinegar
Lemon peel, grated	1 teaspoon	1 teaspoon dried lemon peel
Mushrooms, fresh	2/3 cup sliced and cooked	1 can (4 ounces) mushroom stems and pieces, drained
Mustard	1 tablespoon	1 teaspoon ground mustard (dry)
Orange peel, grated	1 teaspoon	1 teaspoon dried orange peel
Raisins	1/2 cup	1/2 cup currants, dried cherries, dried cranberries or chopped dates
Red pepper sauce	3 or 4 drops	1/8 teaspoon ground red pepper (cayenne)
Sugar Brown, packed	1 cup	1 cup granulated sugar plus 2 tablespoons molasses or dark corn syrup
White, granulated	1 cup	1 cup light brown sugar (packed) or 2 cups powdered sugar
Tomato paste	1/2 cup	1 cup tomato sauce cooked uncovered until reduced to 1/2 cup
Tomato sauce	2 cups	3/4 cup tomato paste plus 1 cup water
Tomatoes, canned	1 cup	About 1 1/3 cups cut-up fresh tomatoes, simmered 10 minutes
Whipping cream, whipped	1 cup	1 cup frozen (thawed) whipped topping or prepared whipped topping mix
Wine Red	1 cup	1 cup apple cider or beef broth
White	1 cup	1 cup apple juice, apple cider or chicken broth
Yogurt, plain	1 cup	1 cup sour cream

GLOSSARY OF INGREDIENTS

Using the right ingredient helps you to be successful when you cook. This glossary lists the ingredients used in this cookbook, as well as other ingredients you might find in your supermarket.

BAKING POWDER: Leavening mixture made from baking soda, an acid and a moisture absorber. Double-acting baking powder forms carbon dioxide twice: once when mixed with moist ingredients and once during baking. Do not substitute baking powder for baking soda because acid proportions in the recipe may be unbalanced.

BAKING SODA: Leavening known as bicarbonate of soda. Must be mixed with an acid ingredient (such as lemon juice, buttermilk or molasses) to release carbon dioxide gas bubbles.

BALSAMIC VINEGAR: Italian vinegar that has been aged in barrels, resulting in darker color and sweeter flavor. May contain sulfites, which can cause allergic reactions.

BISQUICK® ORIGINAL BAKING MIX: A convenience baking mix made from flour, shortening, baking powder and salt. Used for biscuits, muffins, other quick breads, cakes, cookies and some main dishes.

BOUILLON/BROTH/STOCK: Strained liquid made from cooking vegetables, meat, poultry or fish. Used for making soups and sauces. Beef, chicken and vegetable broths are available canned; dehydrated bouillon is available in granules or cubes.

CAPERS: Unopened flower buds of a Mediterranean plant that are usually pickled in vinegar brine. Used to flavor salad dressings, sauces and condiments.

CHILIES: A family of more than 200 varieties, chilies are used in cooking around the world. Available fresh and dried in red, green, yellow and purple. Length ranges from 1/4 inch to 12 inches. The seeds of chilies are hotter than the flesh. Chilies contain oils that can irritate. To avoid transferring these oils to your eyes or skin, wash hands thoroughly after seeding or wear rubber gloves when handling.

- **Anaheim chilies:** Slim and various shades of green, between 5 and 8 inches long, mildly hot. They are occasionally stuffed and can be purchased in cans as "mild green chilies."

- **Ancho chilies:** Are dried ripened poblano chilies.

- **Cascabel chilies:** Hot, with a distinctive flavor. Round, 1 1/2 inches in diameter.

- **Chipotle chilies:** Smoked, dried jalapeño chilies. Can be purchased loose (dry) or canned in adobo sauce. Often used in sauces.

- **Jalapeño chilies:** Very hot, jade green or red chilies, 2 to 3 inches long. Smallest ones are the hottest. Favorite for nachos, salsas and other sauces. Available fresh and pickled.

- **Poblano chilies:** Chilies most frequently used for *chiles rellenos.* Dark green; range from mild to hot.

- **Serrano chilies:** Short, thin chilies that start out green then develop to brilliant red when ripe. Among the hottest of chilies.

CHEESE: There are four categories of identification for all cheeses: natural cheese, pasteurized process cheese, cheese food and pasteurized cheese spread.

- **Natural cheese:** Made from the milk or cream of cows, sheep or goats that has been solidified by the process of curdling and the liquid (whey) removed. These cheeses range from soft to hard and from mild to sharp flavor. They may or may not be aged or ripened. Examples of soft cheeses are Boursin, Brie, cottage cheese, cream cheese and ricotta. Semisoft varieties are Colby, feta, Monterey Jack and mozzarella. Examples of hard cheeses are Cheddar, Edam, Swiss and Gruyère. Very hard cheeses, such as Parmesan and Romano, tend to be sharp in flavor; hard and semisoft cheeses range from sharp to mild. Many soft cheeses, such as Brie and Camembert vary from mild to pungent.

- **Cheese food:** Cheese made from one or more varieties of natural cheese that are blended, then combined with cream, milk, skim milk or whey. This results in a higher moisture content than in other cheeses. Cheese food usually is sold in tubs or jars and is sometimes flavored.

- **Pasteurized cheese spread:** This cheese is similar to pasteurized process cheese except it is easily spreadable at room temperature. Cheeses in aerosol cans are examples of pasteurized cheese spread.

- **Pasteurized process cheese:** Usually a blend of one or more varieties of natural cheese that are ground, blended and heated. This process stops the aging, or ripening, of the cheese. The very popular American cheese is a good example of this type of cheese.

CHOCOLATE: Made from cocoa beans that are shelled, roasted, ground and liquefied. Chocolate liquor is the product of cocoa beans that have been shelled, roasted and ground; hardened chocolate liquor becomes unsweetened baking chocolate. Cocoa butter is the fat or oil of the cocoa bean. Chocolate is processed in various ways:

- **Baking cocoa:** Dried chocolate liquor (cocoa butter removed) is ground into unsweetened cocoa. Does not substitute directly for cocoa drink mixes, which contain added milk powder and sugar.

- **Semisweet, bittersweet, sweet and milk chocolates:** Contain from 10 to 35 percent chocolate liquor, varying amounts of cocoa butter, sugar and, for some, milk and flavorings. Available in bars and chips; use for baking or eating. Quality varies, so follow package directions when melting.

- **"White" chocolate:** Not a true chocolate. Contains some cocoa butter but no cocoa or chocolate liquor. Often called vanilla milk chips or vanilla baking bar.

COCONUT: From the meat of the coconut fruit. Available shredded or flaked, either sweetened or unsweetened, in cans or plastic bags.

CONDIMENT: Term for an accompaniment to food. Examples are ketchup, mustard, salsa and relish.

CORN SYRUP: Clear, thick liquid (dark and light are interchangeable in recipes) made from corn sugar mixed with acid. It's one sweetener that doesn't crystallize and is especially good for pecan pie, frostings, fruit sauces and jams.

CORNSTARCH: A thickener for soups, sauces and desserts that comes from a portion of the corn kernel. This finely ground flour keeps sauces clear, not opaque as are sauces thickened with wheat flour. To substitute for all-purpose flour, use half as much cornstarch.

CREAM: Smooth, rich product made by separating butterfat from the liquid in whole milk. Pasteurized and processed into several forms:

- **Half-and-half:** Milk and cream are mixed; contains 10 to 12 percent butterfat. It won't whip, but it can be used in place of whipping (heavy) cream in many recipes.

- **Sour cream:** Commercially cultured with lactic acid to give a tangy flavor. Regular sour cream is 18 to 20 percent butterfat. Reduced-fat sour cream is made from half-and-half and can be substituted for regular sour cream in most recipes. Fat-free sour cream has all the fat removed and may not be successful in all recipes that call for regular sour cream.

- **Whipping (heavy) cream:** The richest cream available in the United States, it has 36 to 40 percent butterfat. It doubles in volume when whipped.

CREAM OF TARTAR: After wine is made, the acid left in wine barrels is processed into cream of tartar. When cream of tartar is added to egg whites in beginning beating stages, the egg whites are more stable and have more volume. Also contributes to creamier frostings and candy.

CRÈME FRAÎCHE: Very thick cream often served with soup, fresh fruit and cobblers. Unlike sour cream, it does not curdle when heated.

CRUDITÉS: Fresh, raw vegetables, usually served with a dip.

EGGS: For preparation, see page 132; for food safety, see page 242.

FATS AND OILS: In cooking, fats and oils add richness and flavor to food, aid in browning, help bind ingredients together, tenderize baked goods and are used for frying. But not all fats are created equal in texture and flavor. In our recipes, ingredient listings for fats vary because of their cooking and baking characteristics. See specific examples that follow.

● **Butter:** A saturated fat made from cream that must be at least 80 percent butterfat by USDA standards. It is high in flavor and has a melt-in-your-mouth texture. Butter is sold in sticks, whipped in tubs and as butter-flavored granules. For baking, use only the sticks; whipped butter will give a different texture because of the air beaten into it.

● **Margarine:** An unsaturated butter substitute made with no less than 80 percent fat (most use vegetable oils made from soybeans, cottonseed and corn) by weight and flavoring from dairy products. Textures and flavors vary. Use as a table spread and for cooking and baking. Sold in sticks and as soft spreads in tubs.

● **Oils for cooking:** Low in saturated fats and containing no cholesterol, these liquid fats are delicate to blend in flavor and are treated to withstand high-temperature cooking and long storage. In our recipes, they are listed as follows:

● **Cooking spray:** Used to spray cookware and bakeware before using to prevent food from sticking during cooking and baking. Sometimes used directly on foods in low-fat cooking.

● **Olive oil:** Pressed from pitted ripe (black) olives. Olive oil is graded based on its acidity. The lower the acidity, the stronger the olive flavor. Cold-pressed (processed without heat) oil is called extra virgin and is the result of the first pressing of the olives. For the second olive pressing, solvents are used, and this yields "virgin olive oil." Successive pressings yield less-delicate oils. Use olive oil for marinades, salad dressings and cooking.

● **Vegetable oil:** An economical blend of oils from various vegetables, such as corn, cottonseed, peanut, safflower and soybean. Use for all cooking and baking.

● **Reduced-calorie or low-fat butter or margarine:** These products have water and air added and contain at least 20 percent less fat than regular butter or margarine. Do not use for baking.

● **Shortening:** Vegetable oils that are hydrogenated to change them from liquid to solid at room temperature. Shortening is used especially for flaky, tender pastry and to grease baking pans. Sold in cans and in stick form.

● **Vegetable-Oil Spreads:** Margarine products with less than 80 percent fat (vegetable oil) by weight usually are labeled as vegetable-oil spreads. These products, like margarine, can be used for a variety of purposes, from spreading to cooking to baking. Vegetable-oil spreads are sold in sticks (for all-purpose use, including some baking if more than 65 percent fat), in tubs (to use as a table spread—do not use for baking) and as liquid squeeze spreads (to use for topping vegetables and popcorn or for basting—do not use for baking).

FLOUR: The primary ingredient in breads, cakes, cookies and quick breads.

● **All-purpose flour:** Selected wheats blended to be used for all kinds of baking. Available both bleached and unbleached.

● **Bread flour:** Wheats higher in gluten-forming protein, which gives more structure to bread, than all-purpose flour. For other bakings, bread flour can make some recipes too tough.

● **Cake flour:** Milled from soft wheats. Cake flour results in tender, fine-textured cakes.

● **Self-rising flour:** A convenience flour made from a blend of hard and soft wheats that includes leavening and salt. For best results, don't substitute self-rising flour for other kinds of flour, unless directed in a recipe, because leavening and salt proportions won't be accurate.

● **Whole wheat flour:** Ground from the complete wheat kernel, whole wheat flour gives a nutty flavor and dense texture to breads and other baked goods. Baked goods made with whole wheat flour rise less than those made with all-purpose flour.

GELATIN: An odorless and colorless powder; its thickening power is released when it is mixed with hot liquid. Gelatin is pure protein, processed from beef and veal bones and cartilage or pig skin. Available flavored and sweetened.

GINGERROOT: Plump tubers with knobby branches. Side branches have a milder tangy ginger flavor than the main root. Grate unpeeled gingerroot, or peel and chop or slice it, to add flavor to foods such as stir-fries, sauces and baked goods.

HERBS: Available fresh and dried. Before using fresh herbs, chop them finely. Crumble dried herb leaves between fingers before using. (See also "Twelve Terrific Herbs" and "Top Five Spices," pages 226–227.)

LEGUMES: A term for beans, peas and lentils, which are the nutritious seeds of leguminous plants. They can be purchased dried, canned or frozen. Legumes are rich with soluble fiber and are virtually fat-free. Legumes are a staple part of the diet all around the world.

Top: great northern beans, kidney beans, black beans, baby lima beans

Middle: navy beans, pinto beans, lima beans

Bottom: yellow split peas, green split beans, garbanzo beans

LEAVENING: Ingredients that cause baked goods to rise and develop lighter textures. (*See also* Baking Powder, Baking Soda, Yeast.)

MAYONNAISE: Smooth, rich mixture made from egg yolks, vinegar and seasonings. Beaten to make a permanent emulsion that retains its creamy texture through storage. Available in jars. The product "salad dressing" is similarly prepared but is lower in fat because it's made with a starch thickener, vinegar, eggs and sweetener.

MERINGUE: A soft topping for desserts such as pies or a hardened baked shell for fruit.

● A mixture of stiffly beaten egg whites and sugar spread over pie or other desserts and baked at high temperature until lightly browned.

● Egg white and sugar mixture spooned onto cookie sheet and baked several hours at low

temperature until dry and set. Can be used as individual shells or as single large shell to hold fruit, ice cream or pudding.

MILK: Refers to cow's milk throughout this cookbook.

● **Buttermilk:** Thick, smooth liquid that results when skim or part-skim milk is cultured with lactic acid bacteria. Used in baking for tangy flavor.

● **Evaporated milk:** Whole milk with more than half the water removed before mixture is homogenized. Mixture is slightly thicker than whole milk. Use in recipes calling for evaporated milk, or mix with equal amount of water to substitute for whole milk in recipes.

● **Low-fat milk:** Milk with 0.5 to 2 percent of milk fat removed.

● **Skim milk:** Contains less than 0.5 percent fat.

● **Sweetened condensed milk:** Made when about half of the water is removed from whole milk and sweetener is added. Use for such desserts as Creamy Lemon Dessert (page 216).

● **Whole milk:** Contains at least 3.25 percent butterfat.

MOCHA: A hot drink combining coffee and chocolate. Also used to describe coffee/chocolate combination in food.

MUSHROOMS: Available fresh, canned or dried. To prepare fresh mushrooms, cut thin slice from bottom end of stem if necessary. Rinse carefully in cool water just before using. Blot dry with towel.

MUSTARD: From plants grown for sharp-tasting seeds and calcium-rich leaves (mustard greens). Use to add pungent flavor to foods.

● **Ground mustard:** Dried mustard seed that has been finely ground.

● **Mustard:** Yellow mustard (also called American mustard) is prepared from mild white mustard seeds and mixed with sugar, vinegar and seasonings. Dijon mustard, originating in Dijon, France, is prepared from brown mustard seeds mixed with wine, unfermented grape juice and seasonings. Many other flavors of mustards are available.

● **Mustard seed:** Whole seeds used for pickling and to season savory dishes.

ORGANIC: Term used for food or drink that has been produced or grown without chemicals such as fertilizers, additives or pesticides and that has been grown according to federal organic standards.

PASTA: See page 228.

PEPPERCORNS: The spice berry that is ground to produce black and white peppers. Available as whole berries to use in soups and main dishes. Green peppercorns are underripe berries that are packed in brine; they are available in bottles and cans.

PESTO: A sauce traditionally made from fresh basil, pine nuts, Parmesan cheese and garlic. The mixture can be ground or blended until smooth. Most often served with pasta.

PHYLLO (FILO): Paper-thin pastry sheets whose name comes from the Greek word for "leaf"; is the basis of many Greek and Middle Eastern main dishes and sweets. Available frozen or refrigerated. Sheets dry out quickly, so when working with phyllo, cover unused sheets with waxed paper and a damp kitchen towel.

PILAF: Near Eastern dish made by browning rice or bulgur in butter or oil, then cooking in broth or water. Chopped vegetables, meat or poultry can be stirred into cooked mixture.

PINE NUTS: Small white nuts from several varieties of pine trees. Often used in Mediterranean and Mexican dishes. These nuts turn rancid quickly, so refrigerate or freeze to slow the rancidity process.

PUFF PASTRY: Dozens of layers of chilled butter rolled between sheets of pastry dough. Is the basis of croissants, puff pastry shells for creamed poultry or seafood and such desserts as Napoleons and fruit pastries.

RED PEPPER SAUCE: Condiment made from hot chili peppers and cured in either salt or vinegar brine. Many varieties and levels of hotness are available.

RICE: Grain that is a staple in cuisines around the world.

Top: Short grain rice, medium grain rice, long grain rice
Middle: Instant (precooked), parboiled (converted)
Bottom: Brown rice, wild rice

ROASTED BELL PEPPERS: Sweet red or other color bell peppers that have been roasted and packed in jars. Use for appetizers, soups and main dishes.

ROUX: Mixture of flour and fat used to thicken soups, sauces and gravy.

SALAD DRESSING: *See* Mayonnaise.

SALSA: Mexican sauce of tomatoes, onions, green chilies and cilantro. Available fresh, canned and bottled. Green salsa, or "salsa verde," is made with tomatillos.

SCALLION: A vegetable with a white base and green top that's a member of the onion family. Green onions and scallions are used interchangeably in cooking.

SHALLOT: An onion with multiple cloves that looks like garlic. The papery skin that covers the bulbs ranges in color from beige to purple and should be removed before using the shallot. Shallots and onions are used interchangeably.

SOUFFLÉ: A mixture of beaten egg whites and flavored sauce that expands during baking to produce a puffy, light dish. Soufflés can be savory with cheese, seafood or vegetables or sweet with chocolate or lemon flavor. There are also chilled or frozen dessert soufflés.

SOY SAUCE: Chinese and Japanese specialty. A brown sauce made from soybeans, wheat, yeast and salt used for main dishes and vegetables and as a condiment.

SUGAR: Sweetener that may come from sugar beets or cane sugar. Available in several forms:

● **Artificial sweeteners:** A variety of products are available. Best if used in nonbaked items because flavor of some sweeteners may break down during baking.

● **Brown (packed):** Either is produced after refined white sugar is removed from beets or cane or is the result of mixing refined molasses syrup with white sugar crystals. Dark brown sugar has a more intense flavor. If brown sugar hardens, store in a closed container with a slice of apple or a moist slice of bread.

● **Granulated:** Standard white sugar available in sizes from 1-pound boxes to 100-pound bags, as well as in cubes and 1-teaspoon packets.

● **Powdered:** Crushed granulated sugar used for frostings and for dusting pastries and cakes.

SUN-DRIED TOMATOES: Tomatoes dried for use in appetizers, sauces, main dishes and other foods. Available packed in oil or dry; rehydrate the dry form by soaking in hot water until plump, then draining before using.

TOMATILLO: A fruit that resembles a small green tomato. It is covered with a paperlike husk, which is removed before use. Tomatillos have a citrus flavor and are used in salsas and Mexican sauces.

TRUFFLE: A European fungus that is one of the world's most expensive foods. It grows near roots of trees and is hand-harvested, resulting in the high cost. Used in sauces, omelets and as an accompaniment. Available fresh, frozen, canned and in paste form. *Truffle* is also the term for a rich confection of cream, sugar and various flavorings such as chocolate, liqueur, nuts and spices; usually dipped in chocolate.

VINAIGRETTE: A dressing of oil, vinegar, salt and pepper that can be flavored with mustard and a little Worcestershire sauce.

WORCESTERSHIRE SAUCE: Common condiment made from exotic blend of ingredients: garlic, soy sauce, tamarind, onions, molasses, lime, anchovies, vinegar and other seasonings. Named for Worcester, England, where it was first bottled, but it was developed in India by the English.

YEAST: Leavening whose fermentation is the essence of yeast bread. The combination of warmth, food (sugar) and liquid causes yeast to release carbon dioxide bubbles that cause dough to rise. Always use yeast before its expiration date.

● **Bread machine yeast:** A strain of yeast that is finely granulated and works exceptionally well in bread machines.

● **Quick active dry yeast:** Dehydrated yeast that allows bread to rise in less time than regular yeast. Quick active dry yeast can be substituted directly for bread machine yeast.

● **Regular active dry yeast:** Dehydrated yeast that can be substituted directly for quick active dry yeast. When using in bread machines, you may need to increase regular yeast by 1/4 to 1/2 teaspoon, depending on the recipe.

GLOSSARY OF COOKING TERMS AND TECHNIQUES

Cooking has its own vocabulary, just as does any other activity. Although not all-inclusive, this glossary is a handy reference as you select recipes and begin to cook. We've included examples of foods, in some cases, to help familiarize you with the terms. For other food or cooking definitions, see "Glossary of Ingredients" (page 252), "Basics for Great Grilling" (page 234) and "Common Preparation Techniques" (page 222).

AL DENTE: Doneness description for pasta cooked until tender but firm to the bite.

BAKE: Cook in oven surrounded by dry heat. Bake uncovered for dry, crisp surfaces (breads, cakes, cookies, chicken) or covered for moistness (casseroles, chicken, vegetables).

BASTE: Spoon liquid over food (pan drippings over turkey) during cooking to keep it moist.

BATTER: An uncooked mixture of flour, eggs and liquid in combination with other ingredients; thin enough to be spooned or poured (muffins, pancakes).

BEAT: Combine ingredients vigorously with spoon, fork, wire whisk, hand beater or electric mixer until mixture is smooth and uniform.

BLANCH: Plunge food into boiling water for a brief time to preserve color, texture and nutritional value or to remove skin (vegetables, fruits, nuts).

BLEND: Combine ingredients with spoon, wire whisk or rubber scraper until mixture is very smooth and uniform. A blender or food processor also may be used.

BOIL: Heat liquid until bubbles rise continuously and break on the surface and steam is given off. For rolling boil, the bubbles form rapidly.

BREAD: Coat a food (fish, meat, vegetables) by usually first dipping into a liquid (beaten egg or milk) then into bread or cracker crumbs or cornmeal before frying or baking. *See also* Coat.

BROIL: Cook directly under or above a red-hot heating unit.

BROWN: Cook quickly over high heat, causing food surface to turn brown.

CARAMELIZE: Melt sugar slowly over low heat until it becomes a golden brown, caramel-flavored syrup. Or sprinkle granulated, powdered or brown sugar on top of a food, then place under a broiler until the sugar is melted and caramelized. Also a technique for cooking vegetables, especially onions, until golden brown.

CASSEROLE: A deep, usually round, ovenproof baking dish made of glass or ceramic with handles and a cover that's also suitable for serving. Also a mixture that usually contains meat, vegetables, a starch such as pasta or rice and a sauce; in some parts of the country is called a *hot dish*.

CHILL: Place food in the refrigerator until it becomes thoroughly cold.

CHOP: Cut into coarse or fine irregular pieces, using knife, food chopper, blender or food processor.

COAT: Cover food evenly with crumbs or sauce. *See also* Bread.

COOL: Allow hot food to stand at room temperature for a specified amount of time. Placing hot food on a wire rack will help it cool more quickly. Stirring mixture occasionally also will help it cool more quickly and evenly.

CORE: Remove the center of a fruit (apple, pear, pineapple). Cores contain small seeds (apple, pear) or have a woody texture (pineapple).

COVER: Place lid, plastic wrap or aluminum foil over a container of food.

CUT IN: Distribute solid fat in dry ingredients until particles are desired size by crisscrossing two knives, using the side of a table fork, using a wire whisk or cutting with a pastry blender in a rolling motion.

CRISP-TENDER: Doneness description of vegetables cooked until they retain some of the crisp texture of the raw food.

CRUSH: Press into very fine particles (crushing a clove of garlic, using side of chef's knife or a garlic press).

CUBE: Cut food into squares 1/2 inch or larger, using knife.

CUT UP: Cut into small irregular pieces with kitchen scissors or knife. Or cut into smaller pieces (broiler-fryer chicken).

DASH: Less than 1/8 teaspoon of an ingredient.

DEEP-FRY OR FRENCH-FRY: Cook in hot fat that's deep enough to float the food. *See also* Fry, Panfry, Sauté.

DEGLAZE: Remove excess fat from skillet after food has been panfried, add small amount of liquid (broth, water, wine) and stir to loosen browned bits of food in skillet. This mixture is used as base for sauce.

DICE: Cut food into squares smaller than 1/2 inch, using knife.

DISSOLVE: Stir a dry ingredient (flavored gelatin) into a liquid ingredient (boiling water) until the dry ingredient disappears.

DIP: Moisten or coat by plunging below the surface of a liquid, covering all sides (dipping onion ring into batter, dipping bread into egg mixture for French toast).

DOT: Drop small pieces of an ingredient (margarine, butter) randomly over food (sliced apples in an apple pie).

DOUGH: Mixture of flour and liquid in combination with other ingredients (often including a leavening) that is stiff but pliable. Dough can be dropped from a spoon (for cookies), rolled (for pie crust) or kneaded (for bread).

DRAIN: Pour off liquid by putting a food into a strainer or colander that has been set in the sink or over another container. When draining fat from meat, place strainer in disposable container to discard. When liquid is to be saved, place the strainer in a bowl or other container.

DRIZZLE: Pour topping in thin lines from a spoon or liquid measuring cup in an uneven pattern over food (glaze over cake or cookies).

DUST: Sprinkle lightly with flour, granulated sugar, powdered sugar or baking cocoa (dusting coffee cake with powdered sugar).

FLAKE: Break lightly into small pieces, using fork (cooked fish).

FLUTE: Squeeze pastry edge with fingers to make a finished, ornamental edge.

FOLD: Combine mixtures lightly while preventing loss of air. Gently spoon or pour one mixture over another mixture in a bowl. Using a rubber spatula, first cut down vertically through mixtures. Next, slide spatula across bottom of bowl and up the side, turning the bottom mixture over the top mixture. Rotate bowl one-fourth turn, and repeat this down-across-up motion. Continue mixing in this way *just* until mixtures are blended (folding beaten egg yolks into beaten egg whites for soufflé, folding liqueur into whipped cream).

FRY: Cook in hot fat over moderate or high heat. *See also* Deep-fry, Panfry, Sauté.

GARNISH: Decorate food with small amounts of other foods that have distinctive color or texture (parsley, fresh berries, carrot curls) to enhance appearance.

GLAZE: Brush, spread or drizzle an ingredient or mixture of ingredients (meat stock, heated jam, melted chocolate) on hot or cold foods to give a glossy appearance or hard finish.

GRATE: Rub a hard-textured food (chocolate, citrus peel, Parmesan cheese) against the small, rough, sharp-edged holes of a grater to reduce it to tiny particles. For citrus peel, grate only the skin, not the bitter white membrane.

GREASE: Rub the bottom and sides of a pan with shortening, using pastry brush, waxed paper or paper towel, to prevent food from sticking during baking (muffins, some casseroles). Also may use cooking spray. Margarine and butter usually contain salt and may cause hot foods to stick, so they should not be used for greasing unless specified in recipe.

GREASE AND FLOUR: After greasing a pan with shortening, sprinkle a small amount of flour over greased surface and shake the pan to distribute the flour evenly, then turn the pan upside down and tap the bottom to remove excess flour. Is done to prevent food from sticking during baking.

GRILL: See Basics for Great Grilling (page 234).

HEAT OVEN: Turn the oven control(s) to the desired temperature, allowing the oven to heat thoroughly before adding food. Heating takes about ten minutes for most ovens. Also called *preheat.*

HULL: Remove the stem and leaves, using knife or huller (strawberries).

HUSK: Remove the leaves and outer shell (corn on the cob).

JULIENNE: Cut into thin, match-like strips, using knife or food processor (fruits, vegetables, meats).

KNEAD: Work dough on a floured surface, using hands or an electric mixer with dough hooks, into a smooth, elastic mass. Kneading develops the gluten in flour and results in breads, biscuits and other baked goods with an even texture and a smooth, rounded top. Kneading by hand can take up to about 15 minutes.

MARINATE: Let food stand usually in refrigerator in a savory, usually acidic, liquid in a glass or plastic container to add flavor or to tenderize. *Marinade* is the savory liquid in which the food is marinated.

MELT: Turn a solid (chocolate, margarine) into liquid by heating.

MICROWAVE: Cook, reheat or thaw food in a microwave oven.

MINCE: Cut food into very fine pieces; smaller than chopped food.

MIX: Combine ingredients in any way that distributes them evenly.

PANFRY: Fry meat or other food starting with a cold skillet, using little or no fat and usually pouring off fat from meat as it accumulates during cooking. *See also* Deep-fry, Fry, Sauté.

PEEL: Cut off outer covering, using knife or vegetable peeler (apples, potatoes). Also, strip off outer covering, using fingers (bananas, oranges).

POACH: Cook in simmering liquid just below the boiling point (eggs, fish).

POUND: Flatten boneless cuts of chicken and meat to uniform thickness, using mallet or flat side of meat pounder.

PUREE: Mash or blend food until smooth and uniform consistency, using a blender or food processor or by forcing food through a sieve.

REDUCE: Boil liquid uncovered to evaporate some of the liquid and intensify flavor of remaining liquid.

REDUCE HEAT: Lower heat on range top to allow mixture to continue cooking slowly and evenly without scorching pan.

REFRIGERATE: Place food in refrigerator until it becomes thoroughly cold or to store it.

ROAST: Cook meat uncovered on rack in shallow pan in oven without adding liquid.

ROLL: Flatten dough into a thin, even layer, using a rolling pin (cookies, pie crust).

ROLL UP: Roll a flat food covered with a filling (or with filling placed at one end) from one end until it is tube shaped (enchilada, jelly roll).

SAUTÉ: Cook in hot fat over medium-high heat with frequent tossing or turning motion. *See also* Deep-fry, Fry, Panfry.

SCALD: Heat liquid to just below the boiling point. Tiny bubbles form at the edge. A thin skin will form on the top of scalded milk.

SCORE: Cut surface of food about 1/4 inch deep, using knife, to aid in cooking, flavoring or tenderizing or for appearance (meat, yeast bread).

SEAR: Brown meat quickly over high heat to seal in juices.

SEASON: Add flavor, usually with salt, pepper, herbs or spices.

SHRED: Cut into long, thin pieces, using round, smooth holes of shredder, a knife or a food processor (cabbage, carrots, cheese).

SIMMER: Cook in liquid on range top at just below the boiling point. Usually done after reducing heat from a boil. Bubbles will rise slowly and break just below the surface.

SKIM: Remove fat or foam from a soup, broth, stock or stew, using a skimmer (a flat utensil with holes in it), spoon or ladle.

SLICE: Cut into uniform-size flat pieces (bread, meat).

SNIP: Cut into very small pieces, using kitchen scissors.

SOFT PEAKS: Egg whites beaten until peaks are rounded or curl when beaters are lifted from bowl, while still moist and glossy. *See also* Stiff peaks.

SOFTEN: Let cold food stand at room temperature, or microwave at low power setting, until no longer hard (margarine, butter, cream cheese).

STEAM: Cook food by placing on a rack or special steamer basket over a small amount of boiling or simmering water in a covered pan. Also see Vegetables (pages 158–165). Steaming helps retain flavor, shape, color, texture and nutritional value.

STEW: Cook slowly in a small amount of liquid for a long time (stewed fruit, beef stew).

STIFF PEAKS: Egg whites beaten until peaks stand up straight when beaters are lifted from bowl, while still moist and glossy. *See also* Soft Peaks.

STIR: Combine ingredients with circular or figure-eight motion until uniform consistency. Stir once in a while for "stirring occasionally," stir often for "stirring frequently" and stir continuously for "stirring constantly."

STIR-FRY: A Chinese method of cooking uniform pieces of food in small amount of hot oil over high heat, lifting and stirring constantly with a turner or large spoon.

STRAIN: To pour mixture or liquid through a fine sieve or strainer to remove larger particles.

TEAR: Break into pieces, using fingers (lettuce for a salad, bread slices for soft bread crumbs).

TOAST: Brown lightly, using toaster, oven, broiler or skillet (bread, coconut, nuts).

TOSS: Tumble ingredients lightly with a lifting motion (salads).

WHIP: Beat ingredients to add air and increase volume until ingredients are light and fluffy (whipping cream, egg whites).

ZEST: Outside colored layer of citrus fruit (oranges, lemons) that contains aromatic oils and flavor. Also, to remove outside colored layer of citrus fruit in fine strips, using knife, citrus zester or vegetable peeler.

UNDERSTANDING RESTAURANT MENUS

If you've ever been too embarrassed or intimidated to ask what an item on a menu is or have refrained from trying unfamiliar food at a restaurant because you don't know how to pronounce it, this section can help you. Terms used on restaurant menus can be confusing. Many are foreign words that describe a specific cuisine or dish; others describe ingredients or techniques. Here's a list of the most commonly used terms to guide you when you're eating out.

AIOLI (ay-OH-le): Garlic mayonnaise, often served with fish, meat or vegetables; from southern France.

ALFREDO (al-FRAY-doh): Rich Parmesan cheese sauce with butter and cream, usually served over fettuccine with fresh ground pepper; from Italy.

AU GRATIN (oh-GRAH-tihn): Any dish topped with bread crumbs or cheese then baked or broiled.

AU LAIT (oh-LAY): Food or beverages served or prepared with milk.

BEEF TARTARE (tar-TAR): Finely chopped raw lean beef, sometimes served with capers, chopped parsley and onions.

BORDELAISE (bor-dl-AYZ): Sauce made with red or white wine, beef stock or broth, shallots, parsley and herbs; usually served with beef.

BRIOCHE (BREE-osh): A rich yeast bread made with butter and eggs; from France. It can be baked in a large round loaf or individual rolls; each usually has a "topknot."

BRUSHCETTA (brew-SHEH-tah): An appetizer of bread rubbed with garlic, drizzled with olive oil, heated and served warm.

CALAMARI (kal-a-MAHR-ee): Squid, known for chewy texture and mild flavor, often served as an appetizer.

CAPPUCCINO (kap-poo-CHEE-no): Italian coffee topped with foam from steamed milk. Sometimes sprinkled with sweetened cocoa powder or cinnamon.

CARBONNARA (kar-bo-NAH-rah): Dish of spaghetti, cream, eggs, Parmesan cheese and bacon.

CHILES RELLENOS (CHEE-lehs reh-YEH-nohs): Mexican dish of cheese-stuffed chilies that have been dipped in batter and deep-fried.

CROSTINI (kro-STEE-nee): An appetizer of thin slices of toasted bread, brushed with olive oil. Can also be topped with cheese, tomatoes and herbs.

FLAMBÉ (flahm-BAY): Food presentation created by sprinkling dish with liquor and igniting just before serving.

FRITTATA (frih-TAH-ta): Egg dish with ingredients such as cheese and vegetables, cooked over low heat on top of the stove.

GAZPACHO (gahz-PAH-cho): Spanish cold soup usually made from pureed tomatoes, peppers, onions, celery, cucumbers, olive oil, garlic, bread crumbs and vinegar.

HOLLANDAISE (HOL-un-dayz): Creamy, buttery sauce with a touch of lemon, usually served with fish and eggs.

LATTE (LAH-tay): Espresso with lots of foamy steamed milk, usually served in a tall glass mug.

MARINARA (Mah-ree-NAHR-a): Italian sauce for pasta and meat, made from tomatoes, onion, garlic and oregano.

NIÇOISE (nee-SWAHS): Dish that usually includes tomatoes, garlic, anchovies and black olives. A salad niçoise is made with green beans, onions, tuna, eggs and herbs.

PAELLA (pi-AY-yuh): Spanish dish of rice, saffron, seafood, meat, garlic, onion, peas, tomatoes and artichoke hearts, usually served in a wide, shallow pan.

POLENTA (poh-LEN-ta): A cornmeal porridge from northern Italy. Made from cornmeal that is heated with water, then cooled and cut into squares, and fried or baked. It is often mixed with Parmesan cheese and butter and served with a sauce.

PRAWN: Large shrimp; also the name of a seafood species that is more slender than shrimp and has longer legs.

PRIMAVERA (pree-ma-VEHR-ah): Dish that includes fresh vegetables; most well known is pasta primavera.

RAGOUT (ra-GOO): French stew of meat, poultry or fish.

RISOTTO (rih-SAW-to): Italian dish prepared with arborio rice and hot stock or broth. Unlike other rice recipes, stock is added to rice gradually and cooked and stirred constantly to produce a creamy mixture.

SATAY (say-TAY): Marinated cubes of meat, fish or poultry grilled on skewers and served with spicy peanut sauce, from Indonesia.

SCAMPI: Description of shrimp that have been split, brushed with butter and garlic, then broiled.

STRATA: Dish layered with bread and mixtures of cheese, poultry or seafood topped with an egg-milk mixture, which puffs when baked.

SUSHI (sue-SHEE): Japanese finger food consisting of slices of raw fish, rice, chopped vegetables, pickles and tofu all wrapped in sheets of seaweed.

TETRAZZINI (the-trah-ZEE-nee): Italian dish of cooked spaghetti, Parmesan cheese, cream sauce and chicken. Turkey or tuna is sometimes substituted for chicken.

HELPFUL NUTRITION INFORMATION

NUTRITION GUIDELINES:

We provide nutrition information for each recipe that includes calories, fat, cholesterol, sodium, carbohydrate, fiber and protein. Individual food choices can be based on this information

Recommended intake for a daily diet of 2,000 calories as set by the Food and Drug Administration

Total Fat	Less than 65g
Saturated Fat	Less than 20g
Cholesterol	Less than 300mg
Sodium	Less than 2,400mg
Total Carbohydrate	300g
Dietary Fiber	25g

CRITERIA USED FOR CALCULATING NUTRITION INFORMATION:

- The first ingredient is used wherever a choice is given (such as 1/3 cup sour cream or plain yogurt).

- The first ingredient amount is used wherever a range is given (such as 2 to 3 teaspoons milk).

- The first serving number is used wherever a range is given (such as 4 to 6 servings).

- "If desired" ingredients (such as "sprinkle with brown sugar if desired") and recipe variations are *not* included.

- Only the amount of a marinade or frying oil that is estimated to be absorbed by the food during preparation or cooking is calculated.

METRIC CONVERSION GUIDE

VOLUME

U.S. Units	Canadian Metric	Australian Metric
1/4 teaspoon	1 mL	1 ml
1/2 teaspoon	2 mL	2 ml
1 teaspoon	5 mL	5 ml
1 tablespoon	15 mL	20 ml
1/4 cup	50 mL	60 ml
1/3 cup	75 mL	80 ml
1/2 cup	125 mL	125 ml
2/3 cup	150 mL	170 ml
3/4 cup	175 mL	190 ml
1 cup	250 mL	250 ml
1 quart	1 liter	1 liter
1 1/2 quarts	1.5 liters	1.5 liters
2 quarts	2 liters	2 liters
2 1/2 quarts	2.5 liters	2.5 liters
3 quarts	3 liters	3 liters
4 quarts	4 liters	4 liters

WEIGHT

U.S. Units	Canadian Metric	Australian Metric
1 ounce	30 grams	30 grams
2 ounces	55 grams	60 grams
3 ounces	85 grams	90 grams
4 ounces (1/4 pound)	115 grams	125 grams
8 ounces (1/2 pound)	225 grams	225 grams
16 ounces (1 pound)	455 grams	500 grams
1 pound	455 grams	1/2 kilogram

Note: The recipes in this cookbook have not been developed or tested using metric measures. When converting recipes to metric, some variations in quality may be noted.

MEASUREMENTS

Inches	Centimeters
1	2.5
2	5.0
3	7.5
4	10.0
5	12.5
6	15.0
7	17.5
8	20.5
9	23.0
10	25.5
11	28.0
12	30.5
13	33.0
14	35.5
15	38.0

TEMPERATURES

Fahrenheit	Celsius
32°	0°
212°	100°
250°	120°
275°	140°
300°	150°
325°	160°
350°	180°
375°	190°
400°	200°
425°	220°
450°	230°
475°	240°
500°	260°

INDEX

Numbers in *italics* refer to photographs.

Q

How-Tos

LIGHTER RECIPES

Betty Crocker's

ENTERTAINING
BASICS

Betty Crocker's

ENTERTAINING

BASICS

*Learning to Entertain
with Confidence*

WILEY

Wiley Publishing, Inc.

Library of Congress Cataloging-in-Publication Data

Crocker, Betty.
   Betty Crocker's entertaining basics.
      p. cm.
   Includes index.
   ISBN 0-7645-6425-0 (hardcover)
      1. Cookery. 2. Entertaining. I. Title: Entertaining basics. II. Title.
   TX715.C921524 2001
   642'.4—dc21   2001024862

GENERAL MILLS, INC.

Betty Crocker Kitchens

> Manager, Publishing: Lois L. Tlusty
>
> Editor: Kelly Kilen
>
> Recipe Development: Betty Crocker Kitchens
>
> Food Stylists: Mary H. Johnson, Carol Grones and Cindy Ojczyk

Photographic Services

> Photographer: Valerie J. Bourassa

WILEY PUBLISHING, INC.

> Cover and Book Design: Michele Laseau
>
> Photography Art Direction: John and Jeanette Monte
>
> Junior Designer: Holly Wittenberg
>
> Illustrations: Ray Skibinski

For consistent baking results, the Betty Crocker Kitchens recommend Gold Medal Flour.

For more great ideas visit **BettyCrocker.com**

Dear Friends,

Wouldn't it be great to call up your pals on the spur of the moment and invite them over for dinner? Or, around the holidays, to welcome the whole family to your house for a meal with all the trimmings? Inviting guests over for a meal can be fun and enjoyable. Whether you're new to entertaining, or just looking for some fresh and simple new ideas, *Betty Crocker's Entertaining Basics* makes it easy.

If you've ever wanted to learn how to entertain with more confidence, then this is the book for you. Cooking can be a challenge—but also the most fun part of planning a party. Relax! With tried-and-true Betty Crocker recipes, the food is always a winner. And you get planning schedules that make parties a breeze. With a gameplan in hand, you can concentrate on getting it all done—with time to spare. To show how meals can look their best, every recipe in this book is photographed. Plus, there are special presentation and how-to tips that help you make all the food look just as good as it tastes.

Entertaining isn't just about the food, it's about setting the scene and making sure the table looks great. I've come up with fun and easy decorating ideas that will make your home inviting without spending lots of time or money on exotic flowers or elaborate centerpieces. You can use what you already have—whether it's your Grandmother's heirloom china or just some of this and a few pieces of that.

So go ahead and take the plunge! Find some recipes you want to make and invite your friends or family over for dinner—you'll be glad you did.

Betty Crocker

P.S. Have a fun-tastic time at your next party!

Contents

Basics of Entertaining

Entertaining Equation

How do you take four basics—people, food, setting and planning—and turn them into a party? Use the Entertaining Equation! No, we're not talking math here, just a simple formula to help you feel relaxed and confident about entertaining:

Good Company + Good Food + Good Setting + Good Planning = Great Time!

Basically, if you make your guests feel welcome and comfortable in your home and serve them yummy food, they'll enjoy themselves. That's what entertaining is all about. And you can do it, whether you're on a casserole or a caviar budget.

Of course, you've gotten your get-together off to a good start by picking up this book. Here you'll find all kinds of ideas and recipes (for as few as four guests and up to twelve), plus tips for making entertaining fun, enjoyable and stress-free.

Before you do anything else, repeat to yourself, "Good Company + Good Food + Good Setting + Good Planning = Great Time!" Take a deep breath and let it out slowly. You're going to do just fine.

As you get started, remember: the recipe is your friend! Not only is it your step-by-step guide to fixing good food, it also gives you great ideas and helpful information. You'll feel confident, organized and well prepared when trying a recipe for the first time if you read through the entire recipe before beginning to cook. This will give you the opportunity to make sure you have all the ingredients, utensils and pans needed to prepare the recipe. You'll know if the recipe makes as many servings as you need and how much time the food needs to cook or bake. After reviewing the recipe you'll be ready to cook with confidence.

On the next page, you'll see all the other features that are in this book. If you need a little extra help, don't forget, you can always contact me at **www.bettycrocker.com**.

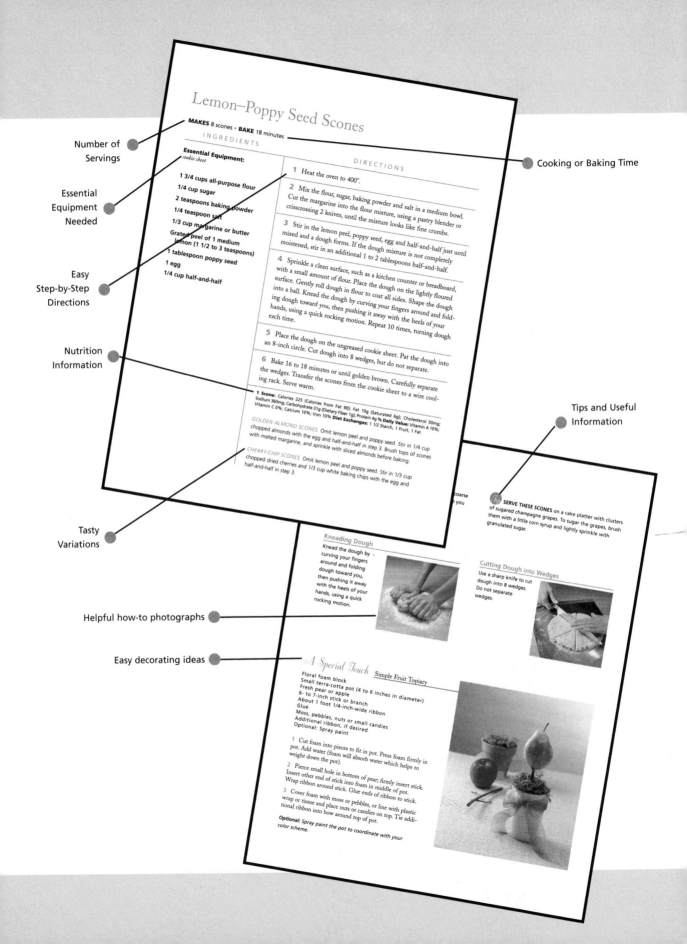

Number of Servings

Essential Equipment Needed

Easy Step-by-Step Directions

Nutrition Information

Tasty Variations

Helpful how-to photographs

Easy decorating ideas

Cooking or Baking Time

Tips and Useful Information

Lemon–Poppy Seed Scones

MAKES 8 scones • **BAKE** 18 minutes

INGREDIENTS

Essential Equipment:
cookie sheet

1 3/4 cups all-purpose flour
1/4 cup sugar
2 teaspoons baking powder
1/4 teaspoon salt
1/3 cup margarine or butter
Grated peel of 1 medium lemon (1 1/2 to 3 teaspoons)
1 tablespoon poppy seed
1 egg
1/4 cup half-and-half

DIRECTIONS

1 Heat the oven to 400°.

2 Mix the flour, sugar, baking powder and salt in a medium bowl. Cut the margarine into the flour mixture, using a pastry blender or crisscrossing 2 knives, until the mixture looks like fine crumbs.

3 Stir in the lemon peel, poppy seed, egg and half-and-half just until mixed and a dough forms. If the dough mixture is not completely moistened, stir in an additional 1 to 2 tablespoons half-and-half.

4 Sprinkle a clean surface, such as a kitchen counter or breadboard, with a small amount of flour. Place the dough on the lightly floured surface. Gently roll dough in flour to coat all sides. Shape the dough into a ball. Knead the dough by curving your fingers around and folding dough toward you, then pushing it away with the heels of your hands, using a quick rocking motion. Repeat 10 times, turning dough each time.

5 Place the dough on the ungreased cookie sheet. Pat the dough into an 8-inch circle. Cut dough into 8 wedges, but do not separate.

6 Bake 16 to 18 minutes or until golden brown. Carefully separate the wedges. Transfer the scones from the cookie sheet to a wire cooling rack. Serve warm.

1 Scone: Calories 225 (Calories from Fat 90); Fat 10g (Saturated 6g); Cholesterol 50mg; Sodium 360mg; Carbohydrate 31g (Dietary Fiber 1g); Protein 4g **% Daily Value:** Vitamin A 10%; Vitamin C 0%; Calcium 10%; Iron 10% **Diet Exchanges:** 1 1/2 Starch, 1 Fruit, 1 Fat

GOLDEN ALMOND SCONES Omit lemon peel and poppy seed. Stir in 1/4 cup chopped almonds with the egg and half-and-half in step 3. Brush tops of scones with melted margarine, and sprinkle with sliced almonds before baking.

CHERRY-CHIP SCONES Omit lemon peel and poppy seed. Stir in 1/3 cup chopped dried cherries and 1/3 cup white baking chips with the egg and half-and-half in step 3.

Tip **SERVE THESE SCONES** on a cake platter with clusters of sugared champagne grapes. To sugar the grapes, brush them with a little corn syrup and lightly sprinkle with granulated sugar.

Kneading Dough

Knead the dough by curving your fingers around and folding dough toward you, then pushing it away with the heels of your hands, using a quick rocking motion.

Cutting Dough into Wedges

Use a sharp knife to cut dough into 8 wedges. Do not separate wedges.

A Special Touch
Simple Fruit Topiary

Floral foam block
Small terra-cotta pot (4 to 6 inches in diameter)
Fresh pear or apple
6- to 7-inch stick or branch
About 1 foot 1/4-inch-wide ribbon
Glue
Moss, pebbles, nuts or small candies
Additional ribbon, if desired
Optional: Spray paint

1 Cut foam into pieces to fit in pot. Press foam firmly in pot. Add water (foam will absorb water which helps to weight down the pot).

2 Pierce small hole in bottom of pear; firmly insert stick. Insert other end of stick into foam in middle of pot. Wrap ribbon around stick. Glue ends of ribbon to stick.

3 Cover foam with moss or pebbles, or line with plastic wrap or tissue and place nuts or candies on top. Tie additional ribbon into bow around top of pot.

Optional: Spray paint the pot to coordinate with your color scheme.

Good Company

So you've decided to have some guests over—that's wonderful! They're the first part of the Entertaining Equation: Good Company.

Remember, your guests are the heart of your get-together, whether you've invited them for a casual afternoon to watch the play-offs, or for something more special like christening your new apartment or celebrating your child's first birthday. Don't forget, these people are friends and family—they're a pretty forgiving bunch. If you're calm and confident about entertaining, they'll relax and enjoy themselves, too.

Now that you've made the "I'll do it" decision, it's time to start planning your gathering. If entertaining is all new territory to you, don't begin by throwing a huge bash. It's perfectly all right to start small. A great get-together can be as simple as inviting a friend or two over for a glass of wine. As your comfort level increases, so will the number of guests you will feel comfortable about inviting. So grab a notepad and start jotting down some ideas. Here are some helpful questions to ask yourself:

What's the Occasion?

A casual gathering of friends and family? Or a special celebration that you'll remember for years to come? New neighbors, reconnecting with old friends, family that's come to visit? Or a traditional holiday such as your first Thanksgiving dinner for the family, an important anniversary, or a new baby on the way? Tied to a theme such as the Super Bowl, a Mexican fiesta or Chinese New Year? What about a wine tasting, pre-concert drinks or a holiday cookie exchange? Will it be casual or fancy? The occasion itself will help you create the rest of your get-together.

Who's Coming?

Your three best friends from college, six of your in-laws, a dozen of your neighbors? Narrowing down who and how many are coming will help you decide the kind of gathering to have—a cocktail party, a sit-down dinner, a backyard barbecue. Who's coming will also affect what you serve. Are your guests food adventurers, or are they more conservative? Are they health conscious, or does counting fat grams make them cringe? Do you have a mix of ages from your six-year-old niece to your eighty-year-old grandparents? Are there vegetarians in the bunch or anyone with food allergies? You'll be prepared if you know ahead of time.

Where and When Will It Be?

Your house or apartment, a party room, your backyard or at a park? The location will help you decide who and how many to invite. If the get-together's in your tiny apartment, you may want to keep your guest list small. If it's at the park, invite the whole crowd—kids and all. Think about the time of day—and time of year, too. Will your guests arrive for a spring brunch, a tailgate party before a football game or dessert after the theater on a frosty winter night?

What's the Budget?

A potluck picnic supper, or a multicourse menu with matching wine choices? The amount of money you plan to spend on your party will help you decide how many people to invite and what to serve. For instance, having friends over for brunch, for coffee and dessert, or for snacks and drinks may fit your budget better than a five-course sit-down dinner.

Good Food

Yes, you could have a party and not serve food. But why? Serving tasty food turns a good party into a great one! This second element of the Entertaining Equation can be the most challenging but also the most fun part of your get-together. In this section, you'll find tips for deciding what and how much to serve, along with some extra ideas on how to serve that good food and make it look its best. (And you thought "Good Food" meant just planning the menu and choosing the recipes!)

What Should I Serve?

All those "Good Company" questions you answered earlier should make planning your menu a little easier. A video night with your college buddies lends itself to drinks and munchies. Dinner for your in-laws? Perhaps start off with an appetizer, followed by the main course and dessert. The neighborhood block party? That's when you fire up the grill. Here are some pointers to help you dream up the perfect menu. (Or check out pages 246 to 252 for some complete menu ideas.)

Plan the main course first. It could be meat-based, such as Beef Kabobs with Chilied Plum Sauce (page 70); a blend of meat, vegetables and starch such as Chicken Stir-Fry with Broccoli (page 98); or meatless, such as Lasagna Primavera (page 112). Then plan the other foods to complement your main course.

Consider where you'll serve the food. At the dining room table or on a picnic blanket at the park? How you plan to serve the food will help you decide what type of food to have. Your guests can "lap it" with sandwiches, but if steak and potatoes are on the menu, a sit-down meal would be a better bet.

Make sure flavors go together. A strongly flavored main dish needs a milder-flavored side dish for balance; a subtle main dish works well with a boldly flavored side dish. If the meal has been on the heavier side,

choose a light dessert; if the meal was a bit lighter, why not finish with something indulgent and rich?

Involve all of your senses—sight, taste, smell, touch. Keep flavors, colors, shapes, textures and temperatures in mind. For example, serve spicy with mild; white or brown with red, yellow or green; tiny pieces with big chunks; creamy with crispy; and hot dishes with cold.

Mix up the temperatures. Planning a combination of temperatures will not only free up space in your oven and on your stove-top, it will also add variety to your menu. Choose some foods than can be served cold (like salad or a chilled soup), some that should be served piping hot (like roast chicken or hot apple crisp) and some that are best at room temperature (like cake or cookies).

Check oven temperatures. If four of your recipes call for four different oven settings and you want to serve them all at the same time, you may want to reconsider your selections or check to see if some if them can be made ahead.

Think about the time of day and time of year. People usually expect a lighter meal at lunch and more hearty dinners. If you're planning a late-night dinner, you may want to consider smaller portions than you would serve at 5:00 or 6:00. The season and the weather also make a difference. You wouldn't want to serve chili on a sweltering evening in July or a frozen ice-cream pie when it's cold and snowing in January. And don't forget to take advantage of seasonal, fresh produce. A quick trip to your supermarket and you'll soon find out what foods are at their best.

Serve what you love to cook and eat! There's no need to astound your guests with exotic kitchen concoctions. If you serve good food that you like to make, your friends and family are sure to enjoy it, too.

How Much Food Do I Need?

Nothing is worse than realizing the main dish is almost gone and the platter hasn't made it all the way around the table. But having mountains of leftovers after the party isn't much better. How do you strike that happy balance between enough but not too much?

It's better to err on the side of having too much. But you know your guests, too. Are they hearty eaters, or do they have smaller appetites? Taking your guests' preferences into consideration, use these guidelines for how much to serve grown-ups (for kids, serve about two-thirds of these amounts):

How Much Food Should I Make?

per person:

Appetizers	4 to 5 per hour
Fruit/vegetables	1/2 to 2/3 cup
Meat, poultry, fish	
Boneless	4 to 6 ounces, uncooked
Bone-in	6 to 8 ounces, uncooked
Pasta/rice/grains	
Main dish	1 cup
Side dish	1/2 cup
Salad	
Tossed	1 to 1 1/2 cups
Vegetable/fruit	1/2 cup
Sauces/dips/dressings	2 to 3 tablespoons
Soups	3/4 cup to 1 cup

Check the number of servings. The recipes you choose will help by telling how many servings (and sometimes what size) they make. For example, 6 servings, 40 bars, 3 cups snack mix, 8 slices. Keep in mind that serving sizes are just guidelines. For instance, a 4-serving main-course recipe might feed only two hearty eaters if it's served alone; but add an appetizer and several sides and it can serve six.

Consider takeout portions. If you're ordering takeout to round out your meal, be familiar with the serving sizes from that restaurant. One serving may be enough to feed two or three.

Plan for the unexpected guest. Just to be on the safe side, make or buy enough food for at least two "invisible" guests. Then you're covered if your guests are extra hungry or if someone shows up unexpectedly.

Let friends bring something. If friends or family offer to bring something, don't hesitate to say yes—but make sure to specify what *you* want or need. If a salad, an appetizer or a dessert would help you out, let them know the other types of food you are serving. If your friend offers to bring something that just doesn't fit your menu, you can always suggest a bottle of wine or a loaf of bread from the bakery instead!

Presenting the Food

The way food looks really does affect how it tastes. With just a smidgen of effort, your food will make a fabulous first impression. Remember, the garnish is the finishing touch, so add it right before serving. Here are a few ideas (photographed opposite) to get you started:

Place sprigs of mint *(1)* in a pitcher of fruit punch.

Float slices of lemons, limes, oranges or maraschino cherries *(2)* in a glass of lemonade or iced tea.

Sprinkle ground cinnamon on baked squash *(3)*, paprika on mashed potatoes or freshly ground pepper on roasted veggies.

Arrange sprigs of fresh herbs *(4)* on serving platters or trays.

Decorate a serving plate with frosted fruit *(5)*. Brush clusters of grapes or cranberries with a little corn syrup, and sprinkle with sugar.

Drizzle melted white baking chips *(6)* in a simple pattern over a frosted chocolate cake.

More Great Ideas

What Is a Multicourse Meal?

You may be serving only one or two courses, and that's just fine. But if you're wondering what a multicourse meal involves, it generally follows this order:

Appetizer or Soup

Salad and bread (sometimes salad is served European-style, which means it follows the main dish)

Main dish and side dishes (such as pasta, rice, potato or vegetables)

Dessert (that's usually when coffee is offered)

Good Setting

You've planned a great menu with food you just know your guests will love. Now show off that good food to its best advantage. That's what setting the table is all about—providing a showcase for the food (as well as something to eat it off of)!

You don't have to own a 12-place-setting service of bone china with matching crystal goblets to throw a fabulous party. What you have on hand will work just fine. Even if all you own are bits and pieces, you can make it work and we'll show you how. And the good news is, mix and match is in! So get out your dishes, flatware and glasses and have fun.

There's also a time and place for paper and plastic, such as a cocktail, picnic or pool party. We'll show you how to set the table with extra-special touches to make it all look terrific.

Here are some dishes, flatware and glasses that are nice to have when entertaining. Of course, you don't have to have all of these items, but you may want to begin adding some of these pieces to your collection.

Plates and Dishes

Soup/fruit bowl
Salad/dessert plate
Dinner plate
Cup and saucer
Charger plate
Bread and butter plate, optional (not pictured)

Flatware

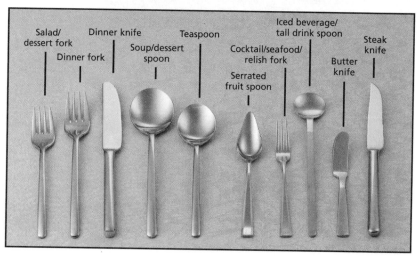

Salad/dessert fork
Dinner knife
Teaspoon
Iced beverage/tall drink spoon
Steak knife
Dinner fork
Soup/dessert spoon
Cocktail/seafood/relish fork
Butter knife
Serrated fruit spoon

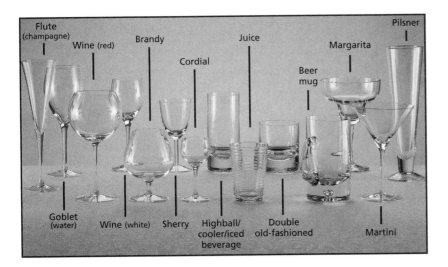

Flute (champagne) · Wine (red) · Brandy · Cordial · Juice · Margarita · Pilsner · Beer mug

Goblet (water) · Wine (white) · Sherry · Highball/cooler/iced beverage · Double old-fashioned · Martini

Glasses and Specialty Glasses for Cocktails and Mixed Drinks

Deciding on a Serving Style

You've picked your menu and figured out how much food to buy, but how do you actually serve the meal? The type of food you're serving, your guests and the type of party you're having will help you choose. Basically, there are two main serving styles: sit-down and buffet.

Sit-Down

Just like the name says, your guests sit down at a table. If you're having spaghetti, a sit-down meal will be more comfortable for your guests than "lapping it." At a sit-down meal, you have a few serving options:

You can pass the food around the table, family style.

You can dish up the plates in the kitchen and serve them. This is especially nice for garnishing or arranging the food in a special way.

You can do a combination of the two: serve the salad, but pass the rest of the dishes.

Pay attention to the pacing of the meal. At a long meal, there should be a comfortable amount of time between courses so guests don't feel rushed but not so much that guests start to get restless.

When guests are finished or have almost finished eating, that's your cue to get ready for the next course, but don't clear the table until everyone is done eating.

If you are serving drinks and appetizers before the meal, don't wait too long before serving dinner or your guests may fill up on nibbles and have no room left.

Buffet

Buffet-style dining can be very casual (think picnics) or elegant (think dessert parties) and adapts to just about any menu. With a buffet, all the food is set out in a central place and guests take a plate and help themselves. A buffet also can be combined with sit-down dining: guests serve themselves from a buffet set up on a side table or counter, then sit at the main table.

Here are some things to keep in mind when you're planning a buffet-style meal:

Consider your menu. Lasagna is a good buffet food, but spaghetti may be too messy if your guests have to balance a plate on their laps. Keep in mind that your guests will be juggling a plate, glass and silverware, so the food should be easy to eat and require little or no cutting.

If you're inviting a large group, plan to have two platters for each food. When one platter is almost empty, you can fix up the next one and make a quick switch. If the food you are serving is cold or room temperature, you can even prepare the second platter ahead of time.

Remember to have enough places for everyone to sit. Buffets are great if you don't have one table that's big enough to seat all of your guests. But you still need enough spots for people to sit down, unless you're planning a cocktail party and serving just appetizers and finger foods. Kids may think it's cool, but your great-aunt probably won't love sitting cross-legged on the floor!

Setting the Table

You probably learned how to set the table when you were a kid. But if the basics have escaped you, here's a quick refresher course for setting the table for a sit-down meal:

Plates should be placed about 1 inch from the edge of the table with the forks on the left and the knife (blade toward the plate) and spoon to the right.

Bread-and-butter plates, if used, should be placed above the forks. If bread or rolls are not being served, you can replace the bread-and-butter plate with the salad plate.

Salad plates are placed to the left of the forks if salad is served *with* the main course. The salad fork can be placed on either side of the dinner fork.

Flatware pieces used first are placed farthest from the plate. For example, if salad is served first, the salad fork goes to the left of the dinner fork. As you use your utensils for each course, you work your way in toward the plate.

Dessert flatware is usually brought to the table with dessert. If you want to leave it on the table throughout the meal, place it above the top of the dinner plate.

Glassware is arranged above the knife. The water glass is usually at the tip of the knife, with beverage and/or wine glasses to the right of the water glass.

Cups and saucers for coffee and tea, if serving with the main meal, are placed slightly above and to the right of the spoons. Or they can be brought out later when dessert is served.

Napkins can be placed either on the center of the dinner plate, to the left of the forks at each place setting or tucked inside the water glass. (Check out pages 22 to 23 for some great napkin folding suggestions.)

Place Setting for a Casual Meal

Place Setting for a Formal Meal

An Elegant Place Setting

Setting a Buffet Table

Set up the buffet where it's most convenient—on the dining room table, a picnic table, two card tables placed together, a kitchen counter or desk. Or set up "stations" at smaller tables: guests get the main course at one table, dessert and coffee at another.

If your table is small you can use a separate table or counter to lay out the glasses, flatware and napkins.

Table placement is the secret to a guest-friendly buffet. Put the buffet in the center of the room, so guests can help themselves from all sides of the table. For a large group, set up identical lines on each side of the table. Or push the table against the wall to save space, leaving three sides open for serving.

Avoid a traffic jam by setting up a separate area for beverages where guests can serve themselves.

For a multilevel buffet table use upside-down boxes or turned-over pans or bowls (make sure they're sturdy). Cover them with a tablecloth, large pieces of fabric or napkins, and place serving platters, plates or bowls securely on top.

Place the centerpiece where it can be admired but where it won't get in the way as guests help themselves to the food.

Arrange the food so that items that go together (think chips and dip or mashed potatoes and gravy) are near each other. This way, guests can help themselves without backtracking.

Set out name cards by unusual foods or ones that contain nuts.

Pretend you're a guest and walk through your set up buffet table. You'll quickly find out what adjustments you need to make!

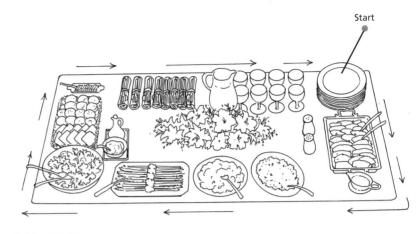

Full-Meal Buffet

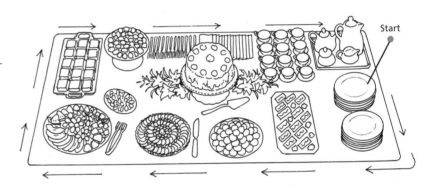

Dessert Buffet

A Multilevel Dessert Buffet

Mixing and Matching

Don't worry if you're short of dishes, silverware or glassware. It's great to use old with new, such as casual pottery plates for the main course and your grandmother's special dessert service to show off your cake. You can add to your collection by:

Shopping garage and estate sales or consignment shops where you can find full or partial sets at terrific bargains. You can also pick up inexpensive plates, bowls and glassware at restaurant supply, discount and outlet stores or by shopping post-holiday sales.

Choosing white for your basic plates. They can be mixed-and-matched more easily with your other dishes, and can be dressed up or down.

Borrowing. That's what parents and friends are for! You have four yellow plates, and your neighbor across the hall has four white ones. Perfect—service for eight! Or if you're short a place setting, give the guest of honor the "special" mismatched one.

Renting. If you're hosting a large bash, you may need to supplement the dishes you have with rentals. Your local party rental center should offer a selection of dishes, flatware and serving pieces to choose from.

Mixing and Matching

Choosing a Serving Piece

Serving pieces don't need to be fancy—they don't even need to match. But keep some things in mind when pairing food to the serving piece:

Start thinking about serving pieces and utensils when you plan the menu, not five minutes before your guests arrive. That gives you time to borrow or buy.

Consider the shape, size and type of food. A platter with a rim will keep food from slipping over the edge; a shallow bowl works best for dips. Serving pieces need to be large enough to hold at least one serving for each of your guests. Will it be placed on a buffet or passed at the table? If you're passing it, make sure it's not too heavy or cumbersome.

Set out the serving pieces, along with the serving utensils, where you plan to serve the food so you can see if the dishes fit in the space—and if you've forgotten anything. You can even jot down the name of the dish on a note and put it in the dish as a reminder.

Don't forget food items when you're scouting for serving pieces. A bell pepper makes a great bowl for dips. Bread and tortilla bowls are super chili holders. And a coconut, cracked in half, can be a marvelous container for macadamia nuts or other crunchy snacks.

More Great Ideas

Where Should Everyone Sit?

Planning the seating arrangement is a great idea for all but the most casual get-togethers. You could just tell your guests where to sit, but place cards can add a personal touch:

Write names on stationery cut to business card size. Use a fountain pen or felt tip for pretty script.

Attach a gift tag to a party favor like cookies or chocolates wrapped in pretty tissue paper, write names on the tags and put one at each place.

Snap a Polaroid of each guest when he/she arrives. Prop the photo in front of the glass at each place. If this is a gathering of close friends and you have old pictures, copy them and have everyone search for their younger selves at the table!

Dressing Up the Table

If you have a linen closet filled with lovely matching tablecloths, special runners for the holidays, decorative place mats and fancy napkins, great, by all means use them! If you don't, here are some ideas for setting a festive table:

Tablecloths and Table Runners

Use a tablecloth for casual or more formal occasions, but especially if your table isn't in good condition. A tablecloth should be big enough so that it hangs 18 to 20 inches over the edge on all sides.

Check out your tablecloth ahead so you have time to iron out any creases.

Improvise with lengths of inexpensive colorful fabric *(1)* or even with a clean, pretty sheet. (Try layering them too.)

Wrapping paper or white butcher paper are great for birthday parties or picnics—don't forget the crayons!

Table runners *(2)* are another way to dress up your table. A runner can be used on its own or layered with a coordinating tablecloth.

Place Mats

Place mats tend to be more casual than a tablecloth, but they can be used along with a tablecloth or table runner to add pizzazz to your table setting. They're also a great way to show off a beautiful wood table. Here are some ideas if your place mats don't all match or you're short a place mat or two:

Put "odd" place mats at each end of the table or set the "odd" place mat in front of the guest of honor. (This lets you mix and match your dishes, too).

Check out the selection of fabulous paper place mats available at paper goods and party supply stores.

Use squares of fabric or decorative art paper that coordinate with your theme or color scheme, mirrored glass squares or simple picture frames.

Layer place mats with different textures and colors *(3)* for a casual look.

For the holidays, use large gold or silver doilies. Place doilies underneath the dinner plates on the tablecloth or on each place mat. Sprinkle the table with gold and silver confetti.

Fun Napkin Folds

Dress (your table) to impress your guests with these three easy ways to fold napkins. These napkin folds work best if you use large, square fabric or heavier paper napkins. You don't have to iron napkins before folding them, but they turn out a little nicer and hold their shape better if you do.

Silverware Holder

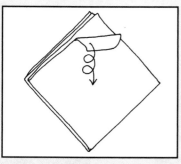

1 Fold the napkin into quarters. Position napkin so the four points are at the top; roll down top layer about half way.

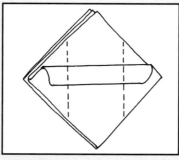

2 Fold the opposite corners under.

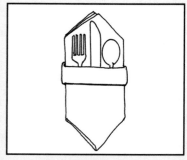

3 Tuck silverware into the napkin's "pocket."

The Fan

1 Open the napkin to full size. Fold in half, bringing the left edge to the right edge. Starting at the bottom, make accordion pleats two-thirds of the way up.

2 Fold in half with the accordion pleating on the outside. Fold on the dotted line, laying the right side along the accordion pleat.

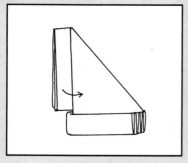

3 Fold the overlap on the left toward the front.

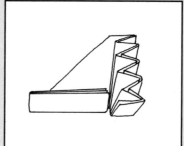

4 Rest the overlap on the table or plate, and let the fan open so it's facing toward you.

Goblet Twist

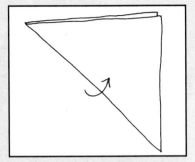

1 Fold napkin in half diagonally into a triangle.

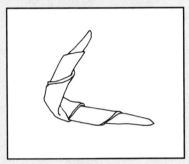

2 Roll up tightly from the diagonal fold. Fold in half and place in goblet.

Easy Centerpiece Ideas

The dishes and flatware are in place, you've ironed out the wrinkles in the tablecloth and there are enough chairs for everyone. So what's missing? A centerpiece adds that finishing touch to your table!

We've created lots of easy-to-make table decorations to give you fresh ideas. Look for them throughout the book with the recipes. Centerpieces don't need to be expensive or time-consuming to make. You don't even need to make a special run to the store—most can be assembled with things you already have around the house or can pick up at the supermarket:

Fill a wooden bowl *(1)* with natural items such as dried berries, fruit, flowers or leaves, pinecones and whole nuts.

Place whole lemons and limes *(2)* and lemon leaves in a clear tall container, vase or wide bowl.

Fill a wire basket with an assortment of shiny, metallic ornaments.

Drape strands of twinkling white Christmas lights (battery operated) down the center of your table.

More Great Ideas

How Can I Make My Party Fun?

For most parties, just getting together is all you'll need to do. But if your guests don't know each other well, here are some ways to break the ice:

Introduce guests to each other as soon as they arrive. Get the conversation rolling by bringing up some topics you know your friends have in common.

Let your guests help by pouring drinks or lighting candles. Some people are more comfortable if they're helping instead of being waited on.

Don't forget the music! It could be jazz, classical, blues . . . or how about salsa or r&b? Just keep the sound level at low to moderate so everyone can enjoy the conversation.

Plan a fun activity for everyone to do together—it could be games like charades or Trivial Pursuit; singing; or a sport if your party is outdoors.

Flowers

There's no rule that says you need a centerpiece to make your table special. A bunch of flowers or a few simple stems add instant color to your table. Buy flowers from a florist or at the farmers' market or pick them from your garden. Have all your vases somehow vanished? Look around your house for creative containers. Drinking glasses, jelly jars, large or small mixing bowls, olive oil and perfume bottles make instant flower holders. Just make sure your guests can see easily around and over the arrangement:

Arrange colorful spring flowers (*3*) in a tea kettle or small watering can.

Wrap a vase (*4*) with fabric or decorative art paper, and tie with a ribbon to match your bouquet.

Cut sweetheart roses down to size and tuck into short glasses or teacups.

Float a flower in a dish at each person's place.

Tuck fresh herbs and flowers into small bottles or juice glasses filled with water. (Pharmacies and natural-food stores often sell small bottles for pills, herbs or spices at a relatively low cost.)

Candles

Whether you want your get-together to be bright and festive or cozy and romantic, candles are one of the simplest ways to set the stage for a memorable evening. From short and stubby votives to tall and skinny tapers, the shape, size and color possibilities are endless. One tip: Be sure to use unscented candles at the dinner or buffet table so a fragrance doesn't overpower the taste and smell of the food. Just about any container you have in your kitchen cupboard can double as a candleholder—coffee cup saucers, martini or wine glasses, empty salt and pepper shakers (with the tops removed), small baking tins or decorative molds:

Fill a large cast-iron skillet (*5*) with candles and whole spices or whole nuts.

Place rings of tea light candles (*6*), small flower blossoms and sprigs of greenery on a tiered cake stand.

Cluster different sizes and shapes of candles in the center of the table on a square of mirrored glass.

Float candles and flowers in a shallow bowl.

Good Planning

Now that you've decided what your party is all about and thought of what you'd like to serve, it's time to move on to the final part of the Entertaining Equation—Good Planning. So what is good planning? It's all the things you'll learn about in this section, like plotting out a time schedule, shopping, and most important, making lots of lists. In short, planning is the key to any party's success.

Now's the time for a reality check, too. How much time do you *really* have to get ready for your event? If you're in a business meeting until 5:00 and guests are coming over at 7:00, the answer is "not much." You may have to rethink your original idea; cocktails with some make-ahead appetizers are probably a better bet than a sit-down, multicourse dinner. But whether you have two hours or two weeks to get ready, you can do it without becoming stressed out. Here are some things to keep in mind that will save you anxiety later on:

Pull together all of the recipes you'll be using before you start. If you have recipes from several cookbooks or magazines, put sticky notes on the pages so you can find them quickly.

Read your recipes. This will help you avoid choosing foods that all need last-minute preparation or two dishes that need to go into the oven at the same time but at different temperatures. Reading your recipes also will help you decide on serving pieces and draw up your timetable, "to do" list and shopping list.

Sketch out a preparation timetable (like the ones you'll find with the menus in this book). Recipes will tell you what foods can be made ahead of time and what you need to do just before serving. For instance, if your dessert has to cool for twelve hours, plan on making it the day before. Minutes before serving you might be beating the whipping cream or scooping the ice cream. This may seem awfully picky, but the day of your get-together, you'll be glad you took the time to plan. Tack your timetable in a place you'll be likely to see it—like on the fridge!

Work with your space. Don't overestimate the amount of cooking space you have. Are you planning on cooking the turkey and the potatoes in the same oven at the same time? Before the big day, you'll want to put the roasting pan for the turkey and the casserole for the potatoes in the oven to make sure they will fit side by side. How about your range-top? Will all the saucepans you need fit on the burners? Do you have enough refrigerator or freezer space, or should you stash a cooler packed with ice on the back porch for beverages and cold foods?

Reality check complete, one of the best ways to organize your thoughts and schedule your time is to make good, old-fashioned lists. If you write everything down, you won't forget anything. Plus, you'll get a better sense of the "big picture" of your party and how to fit everything into your schedule. Store your lists in a handy folder or tape them to the door of the fridge. This will help you keep track of where you are in the grand plan of your gathering.

So, what are the essential lists that you should make?

Guest List

Even with terrific food and a fabulous table setting, it's the people that really make the party. There's no right or wrong answer when it comes to choosing how many guests to invite, but there are some general guidelines. First, consider what kind of get-together you are having and how much space you have. Think about your comfort and energy levels, too. A few friends over for drinks will be much less draining than a house full of people.

Making a guest list will give you a basic idea of who's coming to your party and help you plan all the next steps. Once you have an approximate head count, you'll know the quantity of food, beverages and other supplies to buy. (To determine the amounts of food you'll need, see the chart on page 14 for How Much Food Should I Make?) You'll also have an idea of how many places to set at the table or how many chairs to have on hand if you're serving buffet style.

Before the Party "To Do" List

These are the things that you can get done ahead of time, from two weeks to the day before your party. This list may include: shopping, preparing recipes ahead of time, cleaning the house, ordering flowers, setting the table, decorating, etc. Jot down key dates on your calendar (like when to order the cake from the bakery and flowers from the florist). Check items off your list as you get them done (doesn't that feel good?).

Day of the Party "To Do" List

Although much of your party preparation can be done prior to the actual day, there are some things that can't be done in advance. Some of the tasks that should definitely be on the "day of the party" timetable include: making a shopping run for last-minute items, defrosting food, chopping vegetables, decorating the cake, lighting the candles, etc. Don't forget to schedule some time for yourself! Be sure to leave enough time to relax and get ready so you aren't just hopping out of the shower when the first guests arrive.

More Great Ideas

How Do I Make my Guests Comfortable?

Sometimes it's just little thoughtful touches that make a party seem so special. Here are a few you might want to consider:

If it's coat weather, remember to have a place set aside for guests' coats. If they're going in the closet, make sure to have enough hangers available.

Offer your guests a drink, whether it's wine, punch or soft drinks. Or set out a tray of glasses and a bottle of wine or pitcher of drinks and ask guests to help themselves.

If you're serving coffee, offer regular and decaf. For tea drinkers, it's nice to offer a few different varieties, including some herbal teas like mint or chamomile.

Leave dirty dishes alone while the guests are still there. You can soak the plates, pots and pans in soapy water or put them into the dishwasher, but wash them later.

Shopping List

Once you've thought of all the tasks you need to do, it's time to pull together your actual shopping list. A well-thought-out list is a must for keeping you cool, calm and collected. Here's a foolproof way to draw one up:

Jot down your complete menu. Be sure to include beverages and other fixings you might need, such as mustard for the burgers or ice for the lemonade.

Read through the recipes and write down the ingredients and the amounts you'll need for each one. Then look for repeated ingredients and add them up. For example, 2 cups sour cream for the dip, about 1 cup for topping the baked potatoes and 1/2 cup for the cake you're baking makes a grand total of 3 1/2 cups. (Round that up to 4 cups. It's better to have a little extra just to be on the safe side.)

Double-check your pantry to find out what staples (flour, sugar, canned tomatoes, chicken broth, paper towels) you have on hand and what you'll need to stock up on.

Clip any coupons right onto your list.

Write down any prepared foods that you plan to pick up: fresh bread, salads from the deli, a sheet cake from the bakery. You'll probably have to pick these up at the last minute, so make sure they're also on your "day of the party" list.

Write down all the extras you'll need: wine and beer, cocktail napkins, toothpicks with frilly ends, paper birthday decorations, flowers, candles. Next to each item or group of items, write down where you need to go to get them: the liquor store, paper goods warehouse, florist, etc. You'll probably be able to pick up lots of these ahead of time—just cross them off the list when you're done!

Group your list by the places you'll need to go to pick up your items. If you're shopping all at once, use your list to plan your route. Buy nonrefrigerated stuff first, and save the ice for last. If it's a hot day, you may want to bring along a cooler, especially if you're making more than one food stop.

That's all it takes—now you're good to go. Your get-together will be terrific, so why wait? Go ahead and invite some friends over tonight!

Appetizers and Beverages

2

Poached Salmon Appetizer

MAKES 8 servings • **COOK** 10 minutes • **REFRIGERATE** 2 hours

INGREDIENTS

Essential Equipment:
10- or 12-inch skillet; serving plate

1 small lemon

1 small onion

4 cups water

1/4 cup small parsley sprigs

1/2 teaspoon salt

1/4 teaspoon coarsely ground pepper

1-pound salmon fillet

Honey-Mustard Sauce (below)

1/4 teaspoon salt

Cocktail bread slices or crackers, if desired

Honey-Mustard Sauce

2 tablespoons lemon juice

1 tablespoon honey

1 tablespoon Dijon mustard

1 tablespoon olive or vegetable oil

DIRECTIONS

1 Cut the lemon crosswise in half. Cut one half into 1/4-inch slices. Wrap remaining half in plastic wrap, and refrigerate for another use. Peel the onion, and cut in half. Cut one half into 1/4-inch slices. Wrap remaining half in plastic wrap, and refrigerate for another use.

2 Add the lemon slices, onion slices, water, parsley sprigs, 1/2 teaspoon salt and the pepper to the skillet. Heat to boiling over high heat. Boil 3 minutes, stirring occasionally.

3 Reduce the heat to medium-low. Add the salmon, with the skin side down, to the skillet. Cover and cook 5 to 6 minutes or until salmon flakes easily with a fork.

4 Remove the salmon from the liquid in the skillet, using a slotted spatula. Discard liquid from skillet. Cool salmon completely.

5 Cover the salmon with plastic wrap and refrigerate at least 2 hours but no longer than 24 hours. While salmon is chilling, make Honey-Mustard Sauce (below).

6 Carefully remove the skin from the salmon. Place salmon on the serving plate. Sprinkle with 1/4 teaspoon salt. Drizzle the sauce over salmon. Serve with bread slices.

HONEY-MUSTARD SAUCE Stir the lemon juice, honey, mustard and oil until well mixed.

1 Serving: Calories 105 (Calories from Fat 45); Fat 5g (Saturated 1g); Cholesterol 30mg; Sodium 220mg; Carbohydrate 4g (Dietary Fiber 0g); Protein 11g **% Daily Value:** Vitamin A 2%; Vitamin C 2%; Calcium 0%; Iron 2% **Diet Exchanges:** 1 1/2 Lean Meat

Tip **FOR A PRETTY GARNISH,** mix 1/4 cup chopped fresh parsley, 2 tablespoons finely chopped red onion, 2 teaspoons capers and 1 teaspoon grated lemon peel. Sprinkle the parsley mixture over top of salmon. Garnish with quartered lemon slices.

A Special Touch Glitter and Bead Vase

Clear glass vase (any size)
Spray adhesive or glue
Fine or ultra-fine glitter or small glitter beads
Optional: Round self-adhesive stickers

1 Clean vase, and dry thoroughly.

2 Cover work surface with newspaper. Spray one side of the vase with adhesive. Sprinkle glitter onto vase while vase is still wet. Shake off excess glitter. Repeat with other side of vase. If using beads, brush all sides of vase with glue. Roll vase in beads.

3 Let stand until vase is completely dry and glitter is set.

Optional: To make a polka dot vase, place round stickers onto clean vase. Then spray and apply glitter.

Jamaican Shrimp

MAKES about 60 appetizers • **REFRIGERATE** 1 hour

INGREDIENTS

Essential Equipment:
large glass or plastic bowl

1 can (4 ounces) chopped
jalapeño chilies

3 tablespoons lime juice

2 tablespoons honey

2 teaspoons Jerk seasoning

2 pounds cooked peeled and
cleaned large shrimp

1 medium mango or 2 medium
peaches

1 medium papaya

DIRECTIONS

1 Drain the chilies in a strainer. Make a marinade by mixing the chilies, lime juice, honey and Jerk seasoning in the bowl. Stir in the shrimp until coated. Cover and refrigerate 1 hour, stirring occasionally. While the shrimp are marinating, continue with the recipe.

2 Cut the mango lengthwise in half, sliding a sharp knife along the flat side of the seed on one side. Repeat on the other side, which will give you two large pieces plus the seed. Cut away any flesh from the seed. Make lengthwise and crosswise cuts, 1/2 inch apart, in the flesh of each mango half in a crisscross pattern. Be careful not to cut through the peel. Turn each mango half inside out, and cut off mango pieces.

3 Cut the papaya lengthwise in half, and scoop out the seeds using a spoon. Remove the peel, and cut papaya into 1/2-inch pieces.

4 Add the mango and papaya to the shrimp. Mix all the ingredients. Serve with toothpicks.

1 Appetizer: Calories 15 (Calories from Fat 0); Fat 0g (Saturated 0g); Cholesterol 15mg; Sodium 20mg; Carbohydrate 2g (Dietary Fiber 0g); Protein 2g **% Daily Value:** Vitamin A 2%; Vitamin C 4%; Calcium 0%; Iron 0% **Diet Exchanges:** 1 Serving is free

Tip **TO MAKE YOUR OWN JERK SEASONING,** mix 1/2 teaspoon ground allspice, 1/2 teaspoon garlic powder and 1/2 teaspoon dried thyme leaves. Add 1/8 teaspoon each of ground red pepper (cayenne), salt and sugar.

Tip **TO SAVE TIME,** purchase already peeled mango and papaya slices available in jars in the produce section of your supermarket.

Cutting a Mango

Cut the mango length-wise in half, sliding a knife along the flat side of the seed on one side. Repeat on the other side. Cut away any flesh from the seed. Cut a crisscross pattern in the flesh of each mango half, being careful not to cut through the peel. Turn each mango half inside out; cut off mango pieces.

Cutting a Papaya

Cut the papaya length-wise in half, and scoop out seeds using a spoon. Remove peel, using a sharp knife. Cut papaya into 1/2-inch pieces.

Marinated Peppers, Olives and Cheese

MAKES 10 servings • **BROIL** 7 minutes • **LET STAND** 20 minutes • **REFRIGERATE** 4 hours

INGREDIENTS

DIRECTIONS

Essential Equipment:
large glass or plastic bowl

6 large red or green bell peppers

1 cup whole Greek or pitted ripe olives

4 ounces mozzarella or provolone cheese

2 large cloves garlic

1/4 cup olive or vegetable oil

1/4 cup lemon juice

2 tablespoons chopped fresh parsley

1 teaspoon chopped fresh or 1/4 teaspoon dried oregano leaves

1 teaspoon chopped fresh or 1/4 teaspoon dried basil leaves

1/2 teaspoon salt

1/8 teaspoon pepper

1 Move the oven rack so the tops of peppers will be about 5 inches from the broiler. Set the oven control to broil.

2 Place the bell peppers on rack in broiler pan or directly on the oven rack. Broil 5 to 7 minutes, turning occasionally, until the skin is blistered and evenly browned but not burned. Place peppers in a plastic bag and close tightly. Let stand 20 minutes.

3 Peel the skin from the peppers, using a paring knife or your fingers, and remove the stems, seeds and membranes. Cut each pepper into 1/2-inch pieces. Place in the bowl.

4 Add olives to the peppers in bowl. Cut the cheese into 1/2-inch cubes, and add to peppers and olives.

5 Peel and finely chop the garlic. Place the garlic, oil, lemon juice, parsley, oregano, basil, salt and pepper in a tightly covered container. Shake well to mix ingredients, and pour over pepper mixture. Gently stir the mixture.

6 Cover and refrigerate at least 4 hours, stirring occasionally.

1 Serving: Calories 95 (Calories from Fat 70); Fat 8g (Saturated 3g); Cholesterol 10mg; Sodium 320mg; Carbohydrate 6g (Dietary Fiber 2g); Protein 2g **% Daily Value:** Vitamin A 14%; Vitamin C 64%; Calcium 8%; Iron 4% **Diet Exchanges:** 1 Vegetable, 1 1/2 Fat

Tip **WHEN STORED TIGHTLY COVERED** in the refrigerator, this appetizer will keep up to 2 weeks. Make it ahead to keep on hand for drop-in guests.

Tip **THESE PARTY NIBBLES LOOK GREAT** when served in footed dessert dishes, stemmed martini glasses or wine goblets. Using peppers with different colors is a pretty touch, but green peppers will not be as sweet as red or yellow.

Broiling Bell Peppers

Broil peppers with tops about 5 inches from heat 5 to 7 minutes, turning occasionally, until the skin is blistered and evenly browned but not burned.

Veggie Tortilla Roll-Ups

MAKES about 30 appetizers • **REFRIGERATE** 3 hours

INGREDIENTS

DIRECTIONS

Essential Equipment:
serving plate or tray

2 tablespoons sliced ripe olives
(from 2 1/4-ounce can)

1 small red bell pepper

1/2 cup sour cream

1/2 cup finely shredded
Cheddar cheese (2 ounces)

1 tablespoon chopped fresh
parsley

1 package (3 ounces) cream
cheese at room temperature

3 flavored or plain flour
tortillas (8 to 10 inches in
diameter)

1 Chop the olives. Cut the bell pepper lengthwise in half, and cut out seeds and membrane. Finely chop enough of the bell pepper to measure 1/4 cup. Wrap remaining bell pepper in plastic wrap, and refrigerate for another use.

2 Mix the olives, bell pepper, sour cream, Cheddar cheese, parsley and cream cheese in a medium bowl. Spread about 1/2 cup of the cheese mixture over one side of each tortilla. Roll tortilla up tightly. Repeat with the remaining tortillas and cheese mixture.

3 Wrap each tortilla roll individually in plastic wrap. Refrigerate at least 3 hours but no longer than 24 hours. To serve, cut each tortilla roll into 1-inch slices.

1 Appetizer: Calories 45 (Calories from Fat 25); Fat 3g (Saturated 2g); Cholesterol 10mg; Sodium 45mg; Carbohydrate 3g (Dietary Fiber 0g); Protein 1g **% Daily Value:** Vitamin A 2%; Vitamin C 8%; Calcium 2%; Iron 0% **Diet Exchanges:** 1 Vegetable, 1/2 Fat

Tip **FOR MORE FLAVOR AND VARIETY,** use a combination of flavored tortillas for the roll-ups. Spinach and tomato, for example, are a perfect pair on a holiday appetizer platter.

A Special Touch Picture Frame Tray

A multiphoto picture frame acts as an instant, elegant tray for appetizers or desserts. To catch any food drips or crumbs, line the sections of the frame with pieces of vellum paper, waxed paper or cooking parchment paper.

For appetizers with a dry crust, such tartlets or mini pizzas, fill the photo areas with coarse salt, uncooked couscous, lentils or rice, small seeds or nuts, whole spices or dried herbs.

Roasted Vegetables with Creamy Caesar Dip

MAKES 8 servings • **REFRIGERATE** 30 minutes • **BAKE** 20 minutes

INGREDIENTS

DIRECTIONS

Essential Equipment:
*large shallow baking pan
(about 15×10 inches); serving plate*

Creamy Caesar Dip (below)

**Olive oil-flavored or regular
cooking spray**

**1 medium yellow or red
bell pepper**

1/2 pound green beans

2 cups cauliflowerets

**1 tablespoon olive or
vegetable oil**

**1/4 teaspoon peppered
seasoned salt**

Creamy Caesar Dip

1 cup sour cream

**1/2 cup mayonnaise or salad
dressing**

1/2 cup creamy Caesar dressing

**1/4 cup shredded Parmesan
cheese**

1 Make Creamy Caesar Dip (below). While the dip is chilling, continue with the recipe.

2 Heat the oven to 450°. Spray the baking pan with cooking spray.

3 Cut the bell pepper lengthwise in half, and cut out seeds and membrane. Cut bell pepper into 1-inch pieces. Cut off ends of beans and discard.

4 Spread the bell pepper, beans and cauliflowerets in the sprayed pan.

5 Drizzle the oil over the vegetables, and turn vegetables so all sides are coated. Sprinkle the seasoned salt over the vegetables, and stir the vegetables.

6 Bake uncovered 15 to 20 minutes or until vegetables are crisp-tender when pierced with a fork.

7 Arrange the vegetables on the serving plate. Serve warm with the dip.

CREAMY CAESAR DIP Mix the sour cream, mayonnaise and Caesar dressing in a large bowl. Stir in the cheese. Cover and refrigerate at least 30 minutes to blend flavors.

1 Serving: Calories 260 (Calories from Fat 225); Fat 25g (Saturated 7g); Cholesterol 30mg; Sodium 370mg; Carbohydrate 7g (Dietary Fiber 2g); Protein 3g **% Daily Value:** Vitamin A 14%; Vitamin C 34%; Calcium 8%; Iron 2% **Diet Exchanges:** 1 Vegetable, 2 Fat

Tip **TO SAVE TIME,** serve the dip with assorted raw veggies instead of roasting them. Besides bell peppers, beans and cauliflowerets, you'll find ready-to-eat vegetables such as whole baby-cut carrots, broccoli flowerets and cherry tomatoes in the produce section of your supermarket. Try placing the raw veggies in clear bowls or glasses for a colorful display.

Cutting a Bell Pepper

Cut the bell pepper lengthwise in half, and cut out seeds and membrane.

Spinach Dip

MAKES about 3 1/2 cups dip • **REFRIGERATE** 4 hours

Essential Equipment:
serving plate

1 package (10 ounces) frozen chopped spinach, thawed

1 can (8 ounces) sliced water chestnuts

2 medium green onions with tops

1 cup mayonnaise or salad dressing

1 cup sour cream

1 package (1.4 ounces) vegetable soup and recipe mix

1-pound unsliced round bread loaf, if desired

1 Drain the thawed spinach in a strainer, then squeeze out the excess moisture from the spinach, using paper towels or a clean kitchen towel, until spinach is dry. Place in a large bowl.

2 Drain the water chestnuts in a strainer. Chop them into small pieces, and add to the bowl.

3 Cut and discard the tip of the green onion with the stringy end. Cut green onions into thin slices, including some of the green part and add onion to the bowl.

4 Add the mayonnaise, sour cream and soup mix to the bowl. Mix all ingredients thoroughly. Cover and refrigerate at least 4 hours to blend flavors.

5 Just before serving, cut a 1- to 2-inch slice from the top of the loaf of bread. Hollow out the loaf by cutting along the edge with a serrated knife, leaving about a 1-inch shell, and pulling out large chunks of bread. Cut or tear the top slice and the hollowed-out bread into bite-size pieces.

6 Fill the bread loaf with the spinach dip, and place on the serving plate. Arrange the bread pieces around the loaf to use for dipping.

1 Tablespoon: Calories 40 (Calories from Fat 35); Fat 4g (Saturated 1g); Cholesterol 5mg; Sodium 80mg; Carbohydrate 1g (Dietary Fiber 0g); Protein 0g **% Daily Value:** Vitamin A 4%; Vitamin C 2%; Calcium 0%; Iron 0% **Diet Exchanges:** 1 Fat

Tip **FOR CRUNCHY DIP SCOOPERS,** use Belgian endive leaves. Belgian endive becomes bitter when exposed to light, so be sure to keep it refrigerated, wrapped in a slightly damp paper towel inside a plastic bag, for no more than a day or two.

Tip **FOR QUICK PARTY SNACKS,** set out bowls of nuts, candies and other munchies that can easily be refilled throughout the party.

Draining Frozen Spinach

Squeeze excess moisture from spinach, using paper towels or a clean kitchen towel, until spinach is dry.

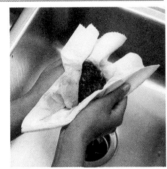

Making a Bread Bowl

Cut a 1- to 2-inch slice from top of loaf. Hollow it out by cutting along the edge with a serrated knife, leaving about a 1-inch shell, and pulling out large chunks of bread. Cut or tear top slice and hollowed-out bread into bite-size pieces for dipping.

Tex-Mex Layered Dip

MAKES 16 servings

Essential Equipment:
12- or 13-inch round serving plate or pizza pan

1 can (16 ounces) refried beans

2 tablespoons salsa

1 1/2 cups sour cream

1 cup purchased guacamole

1 cup shredded Cheddar cheese
(4 ounces)

2 medium green onions
with tops

Tortilla chips, if desired

1 Mix the refried beans and salsa in a small bowl. Spread in a thin layer over the serving plate.

2 Spread the sour cream over the beans, leaving about a 1-inch border of beans around the edge. Spread the guacamole over the sour cream, leaving a border of sour cream showing.

3 Sprinkle the cheese over the guacamole. Cut and discard the tip of the green onion with the stringy end. Cut green onions into thin slices, including some of the green part. Sprinkle onions over the cheese. Cover with plastic wrap and refrigerate until serving time.

4 Serve the dip with tortilla chips.

1 Serving: Calories 115 (Calories from Fat 80); Fat 9g (Saturated 5g); Cholesterol 25mg; Sodium 210mg; Carbohydrate 7g (Dietary Fiber 2g); Protein 4g **% Daily Value:** Vitamin A 8%; Vitamin C 14%; Calcium 6%; Iron 4% **Diet Exchanges:** 1 Vegetable, 2 Fat

Tip **ADD A TWIST** to this kickin' dip by sprinkling sliced jalapeño chilies, ripe pitted olives or chopped fresh cilantro over the top.

Spreading Layers for Dip

Spread sour cream over beans, leaving about a 1-inch border of beans around the edge. Spread guacamole over sour cream, leaving a border of sour cream showing.

Hot Crab Dip

MAKES about 2 1/2 cups dip • **BAKE** 20 minutes

INGREDIENTS

DIRECTIONS

Essential Equipment:
1 1/2-quart casserole or 9-inch pie pan

4 medium green onions
   with tops

1 clove garlic

1 package (8 ounces) cream
   cheese at room temperature

1/4 cup grated Parmesan
   cheese

1/4 cup mayonnaise or
   salad dressing

1/4 cup dry white wine or
   apple juice

2 teaspoons sugar

1 teaspoon ground mustard

1 can (6 ounces) crabmeat

1/3 cup sliced almonds

Assorted crackers or sliced raw
   vegetables, if desired

1 Heat the oven to 375°.

2 Cut and discard the tip of the green onion with the stringy end. Cut green onions into thin slices, including some of the green part. Peel and finely chop the garlic.

3 Mix the onions, garlic, cream cheese, Parmesan cheese, mayonnaise, wine, sugar and mustard in the ungreased casserole.

4 Drain the crabmeat in a strainer. Flake crabmeat with a fork, and remove any tiny pieces of shell. Stir the crabmeat into the cheese mixture in casserole. Sprinkle with the almonds.

5 Bake uncovered 15 to 20 minutes or until hot and bubbly. Serve with crackers.

1 Tablespoon: Calories 45 (Calories from Fat 35); Fat 4g (Saturated 2g); Cholesterol 10mg; Sodium 50mg; Carbohydrate 1g (Dietary Fiber 0g); Protein 2g **% Daily Value:** Vitamin A 2%; Vitamin C 0%; Calcium 2%; Iron 0% **Diet Exchanges:** 1 Fat

HOT ARTICHOKE-CRAB DIP Drain 1 can (14 ounces) artichoke heart quarters in a strainer, then coarsely chop. Stir into cheese mixture with the crabmeat.

Tip **YOU CAN USE** 6 ounces imitation crabmeat, coarsely chopped, for the canned crabmeat in this recipe.

Flaking Crabmeat

Use a fork to flake the crabmeat, and remove any tiny pieces of shell.

Buffalo Chicken Wings

MAKES 24 appetizers • **BAKE** 30 minutes

INGREDIENTS

DIRECTIONS

Essential Equipment:
13×9-inch rectangular pan

12 chicken wings (about
   2 pounds)

2 tablespoons margarine or
   butter

1/2 cup all-purpose flour

1/2 teaspoon salt

1/4 teaspoon pepper

1 cup barbecue sauce

1 tablespoon red pepper sauce

1/2 teaspoon Cajun seasoning

1/4 teaspoon ground cumin

1 bottle (8 ounces) blue cheese
   dressing, if desired

Celery sticks, if desired

1 If the chicken is frozen, place it in the refrigerator the night before you plan to use it or for at least 12 hours until thawed. Cut each chicken wing at joints to make 3 pieces. Discard the tips. Cut and discard excess skin from chicken with kitchen scissors or knife.

2 Heat the oven to 425°. Place the margarine in the rectangular pan and place in the oven about 1 minute or until melted.

3 Mix the flour, salt and pepper in a large heavy-duty resealable plastic bag. Place the chicken in the bag, seal the bag and shake until chicken is completely coated with the flour mixture. Place the chicken in a single layer in the pan.

4 Bake uncovered 20 minutes. While the chicken is baking, mix the barbecue sauce, pepper sauce, Cajun seasoning and cumin in a small bowl.

5 Remove the chicken from the oven, and turn the pieces over with tongs. Pour the sauce mixture over chicken, spooning sauce over chicken pieces if necessary to coat them completely.

6 Continue baking uncovered about 10 minutes longer or until juice of chicken is no longer pink when you cut into the center of the thickest pieces. Serve with blue cheese dressing and celery sticks.

1 Appetizer: Calories 70 (Calories from Fat 35); Fat 4g (Saturated 1g); Cholesterol 15mg; Sodium 170mg; Carbohydrate 3g (Dietary Fiber 0g); Protein 5g **% Daily Value:** Vitamin A 2%; Vitamin C 0%; Calcium 0%; Iron 2% **Diet Exchanges:** 1 Medium-Fat Meat

Tip **YOU CAN SUBSTITUTE** chicken drummettes for the chicken wings. Drummettes are cut up and ready for baking. You will need about 24 drummettes for this recipe.

Tip **FOR AN EDIBLE "DIP" HOLDER,** use a hollowed-out bell pepper for the blue cheese dressing.

Cutting a Chicken Wing

Use a sharp knife or kitchen scissors to cut chicken wing at joints to make 3 pieces. Discard tip.

Mediterranean Chicken Quesadillas

MAKES 16 appetizers • **BAKE** 5 minutes

INGREDIENTS

Essential Equipment:
*cookie sheet or large shallow baking pan
(about 15×10 inches)*

**1/2 pound cooked chicken
or turkey (from the deli)
(about 1 cup cut up)**

3 roma (plum) tomatoes

**4 flour tortillas (8 to 10 inches
in diameter)**

**1/4 cup soft cream cheese
with roasted garlic
(from 8-ounce tub)**

**1 cup shredded mozzarella
cheese (4 ounces)**

**1/2 cup crumbled feta cheese
(2 ounces)**

**Chopped fresh cilantro or
parsley, if desired**

Sliced ripe olives, if desired

Sliced jalapeño chili, if desired

Salsa, if desired

DIRECTIONS

1 Heat the oven to 450°.

2 Cut the chicken into 1/2-inch pieces. Chop the tomatoes.

3 Place 2 tortillas on the ungreased cookie sheet. Spread about 2 tablespoons of the cream cheese over each tortilla. Top with the chicken, tomatoes, mozzarella cheese and feta cheese. Top with the 2 remaining tortillas.

4 Bake about 5 minutes or just until the cheese is melted.

5 To serve, cut each quesadilla into 8 wedges. Sprinkle with cilantro. Garnish each wedge with an olive or jalapeño chili slice, using a toothpick to hold the olive or chili in place. Serve with salsa.

1 Appetizer: Calories 95 (Calories from Fat 45); Fat 5g (Saturated 2g); Cholesterol 20mg; Sodium 160mg; Carbohydrate 7g (Dietary Fiber 0g); Protein 6g **% Daily Value:** Vitamin A 2%; Vitamin C 0%; Calcium 8%; Iron 2% **Diet Exchanges:** 1/2 Starch, 1/2 High-Fat Meat

IF YOU CAN'T FIND roasted garlic cream cheese, use 1/4 cup regular cream cheese at room temperature, and stir in 1/4 teaspoon garlic powder.

IF YOU BUY COOKED CHICKEN pieces or cook your own chicken, you will need 2 or 3 chicken breast halves.

A Special Touch   Menu, Buffet or Place Cards

Selected image to copy
8 1/2×11-inch sheets overhead transparency film
 (available at copy center or office supply store)
Blank cards or card stock
Adhesive tape

1 Photocopy an image onto transparency film.

2 Cut out desired shape in card.

3 Tape image onto back of card.

Tip: Before cutting out the desired shape in the cards,
you can print a menu or other names on the cards using
a computer.

Sweet-and-Sour Meatballs

MAKES 30 appetizers • **BAKE** 15 minutes • **COOK** 20 minutes

INGREDIENTS

DIRECTIONS

Essential Equipment:
13×9-inch rectangular pan; medium saucepan (about 2-quart size)

1 medium onion

1 pound ground beef

1/3 cup dry bread crumbs

1/4 cup milk

1/4 teaspoon salt

1/8 teaspoon pepper

1 egg

1 jar (9 1/2 ounces) sweet-and-sour sauce

1 Heat the oven to 400°.

2 Peel and finely chop the onion. Mix the onion, beef, bread crumbs, milk, salt, pepper and egg in a large bowl. Shape the mixture into thirty 1-inch meatballs.

3 Place the meatballs in the ungreased rectangular pan. Bake uncovered about 15 minutes or until beef in center of meatball is no longer pink and juice of beef is clear.

4 Place the meatballs and sweet-and-sour sauce in the saucepan. Heat to boiling over medium-high heat, stirring occasionally. Once mixture is boiling, reduce heat just enough so mixture bubbles gently. Cover and cook about 15 minutes or until sauce and meatballs are hot. Serve hot with toothpicks.

1 Appetizer: Calories 40 (Calories from Fat 20); Fat 2g (Saturated 1g); Cholesterol 15mg; Sodium 70mg; Carbohydrate 2g (Dietary Fiber 0g); Protein 3g **% Daily Value:** Vitamin A 0%; Vitamin C 2%; Calcium 0%; Iron 2% **Diet Exchanges:** 1/2 Medium-Fat Meat

SALSA MEATBALLS Substitute 1 jar (12 ounces) salsa for the sweet-and-sour sauce. Garnish with sliced green onions if desired.

Tip **TO SAVE TIME,** make and bake the meatballs and freeze them up to 3 months, or purchase frozen meatballs from your supermarket. Heat sauce ingredients to boiling, then stir in frozen meatballs. Simmer uncovered for about 20 minutes or until meatballs are hot.

Tip **WHEN SERVING APPETIZERS,** consider using two trays for each appetizer served. When one tray is on the buffet table, the empty tray can be refilled in the kitchen to quickly replace the other when needed.

Shaping Meatballs

Use your hands to shape beef mixture into thirty 1-inch meatballs.

Italian Stuffed Mushrooms

MAKES 36 appetizers • **COOK** 5 minutes • **BAKE** 15 minutes • **BROIL** 2 minutes

INGREDIENTS

Essential Equipment:
10-inch skillet; large shallow baking pan (about 15×10 inches)

36 medium mushrooms
(about 1 pound)

4 medium green onions
with tops

1 small red bell pepper

2 tablespoons margarine
or butter

2 slices bread

2 teaspoons chopped fresh or
1/2 teaspoon dried oregano
leaves

1/4 teaspoon salt

1/4 teaspoon pepper

Grated Parmesan cheese,
if desired

DIRECTIONS

1 Move the oven racks so one is in the middle of the oven and one is near the broiler so tops of mushrooms will be 3 to 4 inches from the heat. Heat the oven to 350°.

2 Twist the mushroom stems to remove them from the mushroom caps. Set aside the mushroom caps. Finely chop enough of the mushroom stems to measure 1/3 cup.

3 Cut green onions into thin slices, using some of the green part. Discard the tip with the stringy end. Cut the bell pepper lengthwise in half, and cut out seeds and membrane. Chop half of the bell pepper. Wrap remaining bell pepper in plastic wrap, and refrigerate for another use.

4 Melt the margarine in the skillet over medium-high heat. Cook mushroom stems, onions and bell pepper in margarine about 3 minutes, stirring frequently, until onions are softened.

5 Remove the skillet from the heat. Tear the bread into small pieces, and stir into the vegetable mixture in the skillet. Stir in the oregano, salt and pepper.

6 Fill the mushroom caps with the bread crumb mixture. You can use a small melon baller for this if you have one. Place the mushrooms, filled sides up, in the ungreased baking pan. Sprinkle with the cheese.

7 Bake uncovered on middle oven rack 15 minutes. Set the oven control to broil. Move the pan to the top oven rack. Broil about 2 minutes or until the tops are light brown. Serve hot.

1 Appetizer: Calories 20 (Calories from Fat 10); Fat 1g (Saturated 0g); Cholesterol 0mg; Sodium 30mg; Carbohydrate 2g (Dietary Fiber 0g); Protein 1g **% Daily Value:** Vitamin A 2%; Vitamin C 4%; Calcium 0%; Iron 2% **Diet Exchanges:** 1 Serving is free

Tip **TO DO AHEAD,** stuff mushrooms, then cover and refrigerate up to 24 hours before baking. Heat the oven to 350°, and continue as directed in step 7.

Tip **WHEN PLANNING YOUR MENU,** select a few hot appetizers and a few cold appetizers. Having a combination will be easier for you to manage, and it gives your guests more variety.

Filling Mushroom Caps

Fill mushroom caps with bread crumb mixture. Using a small melon baller is an easy way to fill the caps.

Baked Brie with Sun-Dried Tomatoes

MAKES 8 servings • **BAKE** 10 minutes

INGREDIENTS

Essential Equipment:
shallow baking pan or 8- or 10-inch heavy skillet; 8-inch round pan or ovenproof plate

1 tablespoon pine nuts

Vegetable oil to grease pan

1 round or wedge (8 ounces) Brie cheese (with herbs or plain)

3 tablespoons julienne strips sun-dried tomatoes packed in oil and herbs (from 8-ounce jar)

1 tablespoon chopped fresh basil leaves, if desired

Crackers, if desired

DIRECTIONS

1 Heat the oven to 350°.

2 Spread the nuts in the ungreased shallow pan. Bake uncovered about 10 minutes, stirring occasionally, until golden brown and fragrant. Watch carefully because nuts brown quickly. (Or cook nuts in the ungreased heavy skillet over medium-low heat 5 to 7 minutes, stirring frequently until browning begins, then stirring constantly until golden brown and fragrant.) Set nuts aside.

3 Lightly brush the round pan with the vegetable oil. Do not peel the white rind from the cheese. Place the cheese in center of the pan. Bake uncovered 8 to 10 minutes or until the cheese is warm and soft but not runny. (Or place cheese on a microwavable plate and microwave uncovered on High about 40 seconds.)

4 Remove the cheese from the oven. Carefully move cheese to serving plate using wide spatula or pancake turner. Sprinkle the toasted nuts, tomatoes and basil over the cheese. Serve with crackers.

1 Serving: Calories 100 (Calories from Fat 70); Fat 8g (Saturated 4g); Cholesterol 20mg; Sodium 250mg; Carbohydrate 1g (Dietary Fiber 0g); Protein 6g **% Daily Value:** Vitamin A 8%; Vitamin C 2%; Calcium 10%; Iron 0% **Diet Exchanges:** 1 High-Fat Meat

BAKED BRIE WITH CRANBERRIES AND PISTACHIOS Omit the pine nuts, tomatoes and basil. Spread 1/4 cup whole berry cranberry sauce over the warm cheese. Sprinkle with 1 tablespoon chopped pistachio nuts.

Tip **YOU CAN SUBSTITUTE** an 8-ounce block of cream cheese if you don't care for Brie cheese. Do not heat the cream cheese. Just top with the toasted nuts, tomatoes and basil.

Tip **YOU CAN SERVE BAKED BRIE** as a first course for a sit-down dinner or as part of an all-appetizer buffet.

Toasting Nuts in Oven

Spread nuts in un-greased shallow pan. Bake uncovered in 350° oven about 10 minutes, stirring occasionally, until golden brown and fragrant.

Tomato-Basil Bruschetta

MAKES about 30 appetizers • **BAKE** 8 minutes

INGREDIENTS

Essential Equipment:
cookie sheet

2 large tomatoes

2 cloves garlic

1/4 cup chopped fresh basil
 leaves

1/4 cup shredded Parmesan
 cheese

2 tablespoons olive or
 vegetable oil

1/2 teaspoon salt

1/2 teaspoon pepper

1 baguette, 14 to 16 inches
 long

DIRECTIONS

1 Heat the oven to 450°.

2 Chop the tomatoes. Peel and finely chop the garlic.

3 Mix the tomatoes, garlic, basil, cheese, oil, salt and pepper in a medium bowl.

4 Cut the baguette into 1/2-inch slices. Place the slices on the ungreased cookie sheet. Spoon tomato mixture onto bread.

5 Bake 6 to 8 minutes or until edges of the bread are golden brown. Serve warm.

1 Appetizer: Calories 25 (Calories from Fat 10); Fat 1g (Saturated 0g); Cholesterol 0mg; Sodium 75mg; Carbohydrate 3g (Dietary Fiber 0g); Protein 1g **% Daily Value:** Vitamin A 0%; Vitamin C 2%; Calcium 0%; Iron 0% **Diet Exchanges:** 1 Serving is free

ROASTED RED PEPPER BRUSCHETTA Substitute 2 jars (7 ounces each) roasted red bell peppers, drained, for the tomatoes and 1/4 cup chopped fresh parsley for the basil. Sprinkle with 2 tablespoons capers if desired.

Tip **TO KEEP APPETIZERS WARM LONGER,** heat oven-proof serving plates on the lowest oven setting 5 to 10 minutes before serving. Or, just before using, warm plate by rinsing in hot water; dry with kitchen towel.

Chopping Garlic

Hit garlic clove with flat side of heavy knife to crack the skin, which will then slip off easily. Finely chop garlic with knife.

Hot Spiced Cider

MAKES 8 servings (about 3/4 cup each) • **COOK** 15 minutes

INGREDIENTS

DIRECTIONS

Essential Equipment:
large saucepan (about 3–quart size)

6 cups apple cider

1/2 teaspoon whole cloves

1/4 teaspoon ground nutmeg

3 sticks cinnamon

1 Heat the apple cider, cloves, nutmeg and cinnamon sticks to boiling in the saucepan over medium-high heat. Once the mixture is boiling, reduce heat just enough so mixture bubbles gently. Cook uncovered 10 minutes.

2 Pour the cider mixture through a strainer into a heatproof container to remove the cloves and cinnamon if desired. Or use a slotted spoon to remove cloves and cinnamon if desired. Serve hot.

1 Serving: Calories 90 (Calories from Fat 0); Fat 0g (Saturated 0g); Cholesterol 0mg; Sodium 10mg; Carbohydrate 22g (Dietary Fiber 0g); Protein 0g **% Daily Value:** Vitamin A 0%; Vitamin C 0%; Calcium 0%; Iron 4% **Diet Exchanges:** 1 1/2 Fruit

PEACHY SPICED CIDER Substitute 3 cups peach nectar or juice for 3 cups of the apple cider. Omit the cloves. Add 1 teaspoon chopped crystallized ginger and 4 orange slices to the mixture before boiling.

Tip **WHEN SERVING HOT CIDER** at a buffet, pour heated cider into a slow cooker set on low. Or use an attractive saucepan kept right on the stove-top over low heat, and invite guests into the kitchen to ladle cider into their own mugs.

A Special Touch   Cast-Iron Candleholder

3 or 4 pillar candles
Cast-iron skillet (8 to 10 inches in diameter)
Whole spices (nutmeg, coriander seed, rose hips, star
  anise) or mixed whole nuts (Brazil nuts, hazelnuts,
  pecans, walnuts)
Raffia, twine or ribbon
Cinnamon sticks

1   Arrange candles in skillet.

2   Fill skillet with spices.

3   Tie cinnamon sticks to handle of skillet with raffia.
Light candles just before guests arrive.

Old-Fashioned Lemonade

MAKES 8 servings (about 1 cup each)

INGREDIENTS

DIRECTIONS

Essential Equipment:
juicer; 2- or 4-cup measuring cup; large glass or plastic pitcher

8 to 10 medium lemons

6 cups cold water

1 cup sugar

Ice

Lemon slices for garnish, if desired

Maraschino cherries with stems, if desired

1 Cut the lemons in half. Squeeze the juice from the lemon halves using a juicer set on a measuring cup. Stop when you have 2 cups of juice. Pour juice through a strainer into the pitcher to remove any seeds and pulp.

2 Add the cold water and sugar to the lemon juice in the pitcher. Stir until sugar is dissolved.

3 Serve the lemonade over ice. Garnish each serving with a lemon slice and cherry.

1 Serving: Calories 130 (Calories from Fat 0); Fat 0g (Saturated 0g); Cholesterol 0mg; Sodium 10mg; Carbohydrate 33g (Dietary Fiber 0g); Protein 0g **% Daily Value:** Vitamin A 0%; Vitamin C 20%; Calcium 0%; Iron 0% **Diet Exchanges:** 2 Fruit

TO GET THE MOST JUICE from the lemons, let them stand at room temperature or microwave on High for a few seconds before squeezing them. Rolling the lemons on a counter while pushing down firmly to break the tissues inside will also release more juice.

TASTES FOR SWEETNESS OF LEMONADE VARY, so feel free to adjust the sugar to your taste. You may want to make this on the tart side and let guests add sugar if they prefer it sweeter.

Squeezing Juice from Lemons

Squeeze and measure juice from lemon halves by placing the juicer over a measuring cup. The juicer also strains out most of the seeds and pulp.

Frozen Strawberry Margaritas

MAKES 10 servings (about 1 cup each) • **FREEZE** 24 hours

INGREDIENTS

DIRECTIONS

Essential Equipment:
blender; large plastic container (about 2-quart size)

3/4 cup frozen (thawed) limeade concentrate (from 12-ounce can)

1 package (10 ounces) frozen strawberries in syrup, thawed

3 cups water

3/4 cup tequila

1 bottle (1 liter) lemon-lime soda pop, chilled

1 Place the limeade concentrate and strawberries with syrup in the blender. Cover and blend on medium speed about 30 seconds or until smooth.

2 Add the water and tequila to the strawberry mixture. Stir all ingredients until well mixed. Pour the strawberry mixture into the plastic container. Cover and freeze at least 24 hours, stirring occasionally, until mixture is slushy.

3 For each serving, place about 2/3 cup of the slush mixture and about 1/3 cup soda pop in each glass. Stir until mixed.

1 Serving: Calories 125 (Calories from Fat 0); Fat 0g (Saturated 0g); Cholesterol 0mg; Sodium 15mg; Carbohydrate 31g (Dietary Fiber 0g); Protein 0g **% Daily Value:** Vitamin A 0%; Vitamin C 24%; Calcium 0%; Iron 0% **Diet Exchanges:** 2 Fruit

FROZEN RASPBERRY MARGARITAS Substitute 1 package (10 ounces) frozen raspberries in syrup, thawed, for the strawberries.

Tip **DRESS UP THESE FROSTY DRINKS** by rubbing a slice of lime around the rims of the margarita glasses to moisten, then dipping rims in plain or colored sugar.

Tip **TO QUICKLY CHILL BOTTLED DRINKS,** completely submerge them in a bucket or large pot filled with half ice and half water for about 20 minutes.

A Special Touch Ruffled Paper Baskets

Heavy or thick decorative art paper
Large taco shell baking pan (7 to 8 inches in
  diameter)
Spray bottle filled with water
Tortilla chips, purchased snack mix or candies

1 Cut art paper into 12-inch circles (circles should be about 2 inches wider than diameter of baking pan used).

2 Lightly spray paper with water. Place paper in baking pan, pressing into ridges; let stand until completely dry.

3 Fill baskets with chips.

Tip: The art paper must be thick to hold its shape when dry. A little spray starch misted on the back of the paper before pressing it in the pan can help to make it stiffer.

Citrus Spritzers

MAKES 8 servings (about 3/4 cup each)

INGREDIENTS | DIRECTIONS

Essential Equipment:
large glass or plastic pitcher

2 cups cold water

1 can (6 ounces) frozen orange juice concentrate, thawed

3/4 cup frozen (thawed) grapefruit juice concentrate (from 12-ounce can)

1 bottle (1 liter) sparkling water, chilled

Ice

Orange slices, if desired

Fresh mint leaves, if desired

1 Mix the cold water, orange juice concentrate, grapefruit juice concentrate and sparkling water in the pitcher.

2 Serve the spritzers over ice. Garnish each serving with an orange slice and mint leaf.

1 Serving: Calories 80 (Calories from Fat 0); Fat 0g (Saturated 0g); Cholesterol 0mg; Sodium 10mg; Carbohydrate 19g (Dietary Fiber 0g); Protein 1g **% Daily Value:** Vitamin A 0%; Vitamin C 100%; Calcium 2%; Iron 0% **Diet Exchanges:** 1 1/2 Fruit

Tip **FOR AN ALCOHOLIC VERSION** of this party drink, use one chilled bottle (750 ml) of champagne or dry white wine instead of the sparkling water.

Tip **ADD A SPECIAL TOUCH** to these spritzers with minted ice cubes. Freeze fresh mint leaves in water in ice-cube trays.

A Special Touch Wine Glass ID Bracelets

Have you ever been to a party, set down your glass and forgotten which one is yours? To solve the "where's my glass?" mystery, attach different identifying objects (colored beads, buttons, small ornaments, charms) to wire, ribbon or raffia and twist around glass stems. Or choose one kind of wire or ribbon and vary the beads or charms only. For a quick on-hand solution, use various colors of rubber bands.

Sparkling Cranberry Punch

MAKES 24 servings (about 3/4 cup each)

INGREDIENTS

DIRECTIONS

Essential Equipment:
large pitcher; large punch bowl (about 1 1/2-gallon size)

Ice Ring (below), if desired or ice cubes

1 can (12 ounces) frozen lemonade concentrate, thawed

1 1/2 cups cold water

1 bottle (64 ounces) cranberry juice cocktail, chilled

4 cans (12 ounces each) ginger ale, chilled

Ice Ring

Sliced fruit, berries, strips of orange, lemon or lime peel and mint leaves

Water or fruit juice

1 Make Ice Ring (below). Mix the lemonade concentrate and cold water in the pitcher. Stir in the cranberry juice cocktail. Pour into the punch bowl.

2 Just before serving, stir in the ginger ale. Add the ice ring or ice cubes.

ICE RING Choose a ring mold or bundt cake pan that fits inside your punch bowl. For color, arrange sliced fruit, berries, strips of orange, lemon or lime peel and mint leaves in mold. Slowly add just enough water or fruit juice to partially cover fruit (too much water will make the fruit float); freeze. When frozen, add enough water or fruit juice to fill mold three-fourths full; freeze overnight or at least 12 hours to make sure ice ring is solid. Unmold ring and place in punch bowl fruit side up.

1 Serving: Calories 110 (Calories from Fat 0); Fat 0g (Saturated 0g); Cholesterol 0mg; Sodium 10mg; Carbohydrate 27g (Dietary Fiber 0g); Protein 0g **% Daily Value:** Vitamin A 0%; Vitamin C 54%; Calcium 0%; Iron 2% **Diet Exchanges:** 1 Fruit

Tip IF YOU DON'T HAVE A PUNCH BOWL, mix all ingredients in a large mixing bowl, and serve punch in tall glasses filled with ice.

Unmolding an Ice Ring

When ready to serve punch, run hot water over bottom of mold to loosen ice ring. Carefully turn over mold and catch the ice ring as it slips from the mold. Float ice ring in punch.

Tip TO SAVE REFRIGERATOR SPACE, consider placing punch ingredients and other beverages in a large ice-filled cooler.

Tip WHEN SERVING DRINKS AT A BUFFET, it helps to set up a separate table for drinks, ice and glasses so guests can fill and refill their drinks without going back to the food table.

Main Dishes

3

Beef Kabobs with Chilied Plum Sauce

MAKES 8 servings (2 kabobs each) • **COOK** 30 minutes • **GRILL** 15 minutes

INGREDIENTS

Essential Equipment:
blender; medium saucepan (about 2-quart size); charcoal or gas grill; sixteen 10- to 12-inch metal skewers

Chilied Plum Sauce (below)

1 1/2 pounds beef boneless sirloin or round steak, 1 inch thick

3 medium zucchini or yellow summer squash

2 medium bell peppers

1 large onion

24 whole medium mushrooms

About 1/2 cup Italian dressing

Chilied Plum Sauce

1 small onion

1 can (16 1/2 ounces) purple plums

1 can (6 ounces) frozen lemonade concentrate, thawed

1/4 cup (1/2 stick) margarine or butter

1/4 cup chili sauce

1 tablespoon Dijon mustard

DIRECTIONS

1 Make Chilied Plum Sauce (below). Prepare the coals or a gas grill for direct heat (page 264). Heat to medium heat, which will take about 40 minutes for charcoal or about 10 minutes for a gas grill.

2 Cut and discard most of the fat from the beef. Cut beef into 1-inch pieces. Cut zucchini into 1-inch slices. Cut bell peppers in half lengthwise, and cut out seeds and membrane. Cut bell peppers into 1 1/2-inch pieces. Peel the onion, and cut into 1-inch pieces.

3 Thread 4 or 5 pieces of the beef on the skewers, alternating with the zucchini, bell peppers, onion and mushrooms, leaving a 1/2-inch space between each piece.

4 Place the kabobs on the grill 4 to 5 inches from medium heat. Cover and grill 10 to 15 minutes for medium beef doneness, turning and brushing 2 or 3 times with the Italian dressing. Serve kabobs with sauce for dipping.

CHILIED PLUM SAUCE Peel and finely chop the onion. Drain the plums in a strainer. Remove the pits, then finely chop the plums. Place the plums and lemonade concentrate in the blender. Cover and blend on medium speed until smooth, and set aside. Melt the margarine in the saucepan over medium heat 1 to 2 minutes. Cook the onion in margarine about 2 minutes, stirring occasionally, until tender. Stir in the plum mixture, chili sauce and mustard. Heat to boiling over medium-high heat. Once mixture is boiling, reduce heat just enough so mixture bubbles gently. Cook uncovered 15 minutes, stirring occasionally. Serve warm, or cover and refrigerate up to 48 hours.

1 Serving: Calories 355 (Calories from Fat 135); Fat 14g (Saturated 3g); Cholesterol 55mg; Sodium 440mg; Carbohydrate 34g (Dietary Fiber 3g); Protein 22g **% Daily Value:** Vitamin A 14%; Vitamin C 48%; Calcium 4%; Iron 18% **Diet Exchanges:** 2 Medium-Fat Meat, 4 Vegetable, 1 Fruit, 1 Fat

Tip **IF YOU DON'T HAVE A GRILL,** you can broil the kabobs. Place kabobs on the rack in a broiler pan. Broil with tops about 3 inches from heat 8 to 10 minutes for medium beef doneness, turning and brushing 2 or 3 times with the Italian dressing.

Tip **FOR AN IMPRESSIVE PRESENTATION,** line a large serving platter or tray with hot cooked rice or couscous and serve the kabobs on top.

Threading the Kabobs

Thread 4 or 5 beef pieces on the skewers, alternating with zucchini, bell peppers, onion and mushrooms, leaving a 1/2-inch space between each piece.

Beef Enchiladas

MAKES 4 servings • **COOK** 20 minutes • **BAKE** 20 minutes

INGREDIENTS

Essential Equipment:
10-inch skillet; small saucepan (about 1-quart size); pie pan or shallow dish; 11×7-inch rectangular pan

1 pound ground beef

1 medium onion

1 small green bell pepper

1 clove garlic

1/2 cup sour cream

1 cup shredded Cheddar cheese (4 ounces)

2 tablespoons chopped fresh parsley

1/4 teaspoon pepper

2/3 cup water

1 tablespoon chili powder

1 1/2 teaspoons chopped fresh or 1/2 teaspoon dried oregano leaves

1/4 teaspoon ground cumin

1 can (15 ounces) tomato sauce

8 corn tortillas (5 or 6 inches in diameter)

Sour cream, if desired

Chopped green onions, if desired

DIRECTIONS

1 Heat the oven to 350°.

2 Cook the beef in the skillet over medium heat 8 to 10 minutes, stirring occasionally, until beef is brown. While the beef is cooking, continue with the recipe.

3 Peel and chop the onion. Cut the bell pepper lengthwise in half, and cut out seeds and membrane. Chop enough of the bell pepper to measure 1/3 cup. Wrap remaining bell pepper in plastic wrap, and refrigerate for another use. Peel and finely chop the garlic.

4 Place a strainer over a medium bowl, or place a colander in a large bowl. Spoon beef into strainer to drain the fat. Discard fat. Return the beef to the skillet. Stir in the onion, sour cream, cheese, parsley and pepper. Cover and set aside.

5 Place the bell pepper, garlic, water, chili powder, oregano, cumin and tomato sauce in the saucepan. Heat to boiling over medium heat, stirring occasionally. Once mixture is boiling, reduce heat just enough so that mixture bubbles gently. Cook uncovered 5 minutes. Pour mixture into the ungreased pie pan.

6 Place 2 tortillas between dampened microwavable paper towels or microwavable plastic wrap and microwave on High 15 to 20 seconds to soften them. Dip each tortilla into the sauce mixture to coat both sides.

7 Spoon about 1/4 cup of the beef mixture down one side of each softened tortilla to within 1 inch of edge. Roll tortilla around filling, and place seam side down in the ungreased rectangular pan. Repeat with remaining tortillas and beef mixture. Pour any remaining sauce over enchiladas.

8 Bake uncovered about 20 minutes or until hot and bubbly. Garnish with sour cream and green onions.

1 Serving: Calories 565 (Calories from Fat 295); Fat 33g (Saturated 16g); Cholesterol 110mg; Sodium 1000mg; Carbohydrate 39g (Dietary Fiber 6g); Protein 34g **% Daily Value:** Vitamin A 36%; Vitamin C 30%; Calcium 30%; Iron 24% **Diet Exchanges:** 2 Starch, 3 High-Fat Meat, 2 Vegetable, 1 Fat

CHEESE ENCHILADAS Substitute 2 cups shredded Monterey Jack cheese (8 ounces) for the beef. Add the onion, sour cream, 1 cup Cheddar cheese, parsley and pepper to Monterey Jack cheese. Sprinkle 1/4 cup shredded Cheddar cheese over enchiladas before baking.

Tip **TO SAVE TIME,** omit the bell pepper, garlic, chili powder, oregano, cumin and tomato sauce. Instead, use a 16-ounce jar of salsa, which is about 2 cups.

Filling Tortillas

Spoon about 1/4 cup of the beef mixture down one side of each softened tortilla to within 1 inch of edge. Roll tortilla around filling, and place seam side down in baking dish.

Chili for a Crowd

MAKES 12 servings • **COOK** 1 hour 45 minutes

INGREDIENTS

DIRECTIONS

Essential Equipment:
Dutch oven (about 4-quart size)

4 medium onions

2 pounds ground beef

2 cans (28 ounces each) diced tomatoes, undrained

1 can (8 ounces) tomato sauce

1 1/2 tablespoons chili powder

1 tablespoon sugar

2 teaspoons salt

2 cans (15 to 16 ounces each) kidney beans, undrained

1 Peel and chop the onions. Cook the onions and beef in the Dutch oven over medium heat about 15 minutes, stirring occasionally, until beef is brown. Place a large strainer over a medium bowl, or place a colander in a large bowl. Spoon beef mixture into strainer to drain the fat. Discard fat.

2 Return the beef mixture to the Dutch oven. Stir in the tomatoes with their liquid, tomato sauce, chili powder, sugar and salt. Heat to boiling over high heat. Once mixture is boiling, reduce heat just enough so mixture bubbles gently. Cook uncovered 1 hour 15 minutes.

3 Stir the beans with their liquid into the chili. Heat to boiling over high heat. Once chili is boiling, reduce heat just enough so chili bubbles gently. Cook uncovered about 15 minutes longer, stirring occasionally, until chili is thickened.

1 Serving: Calories 280 (Calories from fat 110); Fat 12g (Saturated 4g); Cholesterol 45mg; Sodium 960mg; Carbohydrate 28g (Dietary Fiber 7g); Protein 22g **% Daily Value:** Vitamin A 12%; Vitamin C 20%; Calcium 8%; Iron 24% **Diet Exchanges:** 1 Starch, 2 Medium-Fat Meat, 2 Vegetable

Tip **IF YOU'RE SERVING A SMALLER BUNCH,** you can cut the ingredient amounts in half and cook the chili in a 3-quart saucepan. Decrease the cooking time by about 10 minutes.

Tip **FOR A COOL ZING,** mix a tablespoon or 2 of fresh lime juice into 1 cup of sour cream to spoon on top of the chili. Sprinkle with chopped fresh cilantro or sliced green onions.

Tip **GATHER THE GANG** and serve a "make it your way" chili bar. Provide toppings of sour cream, salsa, shredded cheeses, chopped red onion, chopped ripe olives and chopped avocado. Have baskets filled with croutons, tortilla chips, crackers, corn muffins and breadsticks for chili dipping. For an extra treat, offer purchased bread bowls or tortilla bowls (available at your supermarket) to serve the chili in.

A Special Touch — Tortilla Holders

Aluminum foil
Empty soup or vegetable cans (2 or 3 inches in
  diameter)
Cooking spray
6 flour tortillas (12 inches in diameter)
1/3 cup olive or vegetable oil
3 tablespoons chili powder, ground cinnamon or
  ground nutmeg

1 Heat the oven to 325°. Wrap aluminum foil around
outside of cans. Spray foil with cooking spray.

2 Cut each tortilla in half. Mix oil and chili powder.
Brush about 1 1/2 teaspoons oil mixture over 1 side of
each tortilla half. Roll uncoated side of tortilla around
foil-wrapped can.

3 Place tortilla, rolled edge down, in a baking pan. Bake
5 minutes. While still warm, unwrap tortilla slightly to
remove from can. Repeat with remaining tortillas. Cool.

*Tip: Use these edible containers to hold breadsticks, pretzel
rods or carrot and celery sticks.*

Cider-Glazed Stuffed Pork Roast

MAKES 8 servings • **BAKE** 1 hour 30 minutes

INGREDIENTS

Essential Equipment:
four 18-inch pieces of kitchen string; shallow roasting pan (about 13×9-inch rectangle) and rack; small saucepan (about 1-quart size); meat thermometer

1/2 cup dried cherries or cranberries

1/2 cup dried apricots

1 medium tart cooking apple, such as Granny Smith, Rome Beauty or Greening

2 tablespoons dry bread crumbs

2 teaspoons chopped fresh or 1/2 teaspoon dried rosemary leaves, crumbled

1/4 teaspoon salt

3-pound pork boneless loin roast

1/4 cup apple cider

Cider Sauce (below)

Cider Sauce

1 1/4 cups apple cider

2 teaspoons cornstarch

DIRECTIONS

1 Heat the oven to 350°.

2 Chop the cherries and apricots. Peel and finely chop the apple. To make the stuffing, mix the cherries, apricots, apple, dry bread crumbs, rosemary and salt.

3 Starting at the narrow side of the pork roast and holding the blade of the knife parallel to the work surface, cut lengthwise almost to the inside edge of the pork. Do not cut all the way through. The pork will open like a book. Place the 4 pieces of string on a cutting board at even intervals. Lay the pork on top of string. Spoon the stuffing evenly into the opening of the pork. Close the opening, and tie at even intervals with the pieces of string so pork resumes its original shape.

4 Place the pork, fat side up, on the rack in the roasting pan. Insert the meat thermometer so the tip is in center of thickest part of pork. Bake uncovered 1 hour to 1 hour 30 minutes, brushing occasionally with the apple cider, until thermometer reads 155° and pork is slightly pink when you cut into the center. Cover pork loosely with a tent of aluminum foil and let stand 10 to 15 minutes or until thermometer reads 160°.

5 While the pork is baking, make Cider Sauce (below). Serve the pork with sauce.

CIDER SAUCE Mix the apple cider and cornstarch in the saucepan. Heat to boiling over medium heat, stirring constantly. Boil and stir about 1 minute or until sauce thickens slightly.

1 Serving: Calories 360 (Calories from Fat 125); Fat 14g (Saturated 5g); Cholesterol 110mg; Sodium 160mg; Carbohydrate 23g (Dietary Fiber 4g); Protein 39g **% Daily Value:** Vitamin A 6%; Vitamin C 8%; Calcium 2%; Iron 12% **Diet Exchanges:** 5 Lean Meat, 1 1/2 Fruit

Tip **WHEN CHOPPING** the dried cherries and apricots, spray the knife with a little cooking spray so the fruit won't stick. You can also use a kitchen scissors to snip the dried cherries and apricots into small pieces.

Tip **SERVE WITH** Buttermilk Corn Bread (page 152) and a side of tender green peas for a hearty winter meal with family or friends.

Cutting the Pork Roast

Starting at narrow side of pork roast and holding the blade of the knife parallel to the work surface, cut lengthwise almost to the inside edge of the pork. Do not cut all the way through. The pork will open like a book.

Stuffing the Pork Roast

Spoon stuffing evenly into opening of pork. Close opening, and tie at even intervals with pieces of string so pork resumes its original shape.

Roasted Pork Tenderloin

MAKES 6 servings • **BAKE** 30 minutes

INGREDIENTS

Essential Equipment:
shallow roasting pan (about 13×9-inch rectangle) and rack; meat thermometer

Cooking spray to grease rack

1 clove garlic

1 teaspoon olive or vegetable oil

1/2 teaspoon salt

1/2 teaspoon fennel seed, crushed

1/4 teaspoon pepper

2 pork tenderloins (about 3/4 pound each)

DIRECTIONS

1 Heat the oven to 450°. Spray the roasting pan rack with cooking spray.

2 Peel and finely chop the garlic. Mix the garlic, oil, salt, fennel and pepper in a small bowl until a paste forms. Rub the paste on the pork.

3 Place pork on the rack in the roasting pan. Insert the meat thermometer so the tip is in the thickest part of the pork.

4 Bake uncovered 25 to 30 minutes or until thermometer reads 155° and pork is slightly pink when you cut into the center. Cover pork loosely with a tent of aluminum foil and let stand 10 to 15 minutes or until thermometer reads 160°. Cut pork crosswise into thin slices.

1 Serving: Calories 140 (Calories from Fat 45); Fat 5g (Saturated 2g); Cholesterol 65mg; Sodium 240mg; Carbohydrate 0g (Dietary Fiber 0g); Protein 24g **% Daily Value:** Vitamin A 0%; Vitamin C 0%; Calcium 0%; Iron 6% **Diet Exchanges:** 3 Lean Meat

Tip **YOU CAN SUBSTITUTE** 1 1/2 teaspoons finely chopped rosemary or 1/2 teaspoon dried rosemary leaves, crumbled, for the fennel seed if you like.

Slicing Pork

Use a sharp knife to cut pork crosswise into thin slices.

Pecan-Crusted Pork Chops

MAKES 6 servings • **BROIL** 25 minutes

INGREDIENTS

Essential Equipment:
blender or food processor; shallow bowl or pie pan; broiler pan with rack

6 pork loin or rib chops,
 about 3/4 inch thick
 (about 2 pounds total)

2 tablespoons Dijon mustard

2 tablespoons mayonnaise
 or salad dressing

1 tablespoon vegetable oil

1 slice bread

1/2 cup chopped pecans

1/2 teaspoon salt

4 sprigs fresh parsley or
 1 tablespoon parsley flakes

DIRECTIONS

1 Cut and discard most of the fat from the pork chops.

2 Mix the mustard, mayonnaise and oil.

3 Tear the bread into small pieces. Place the bread, pecans, salt and parsley in a blender or food processor. Cover and blend on high speed, using quick on-and-off motions, until the pecans are finely chopped. Place pecan mixture in the shallow bowl.

4 Move the oven rack so the tops of pork chops will be about 6 inches from the broiler. Set the oven control to broil.

5 Spread the mustard mixture over all sides of pork. Then coat all sides with the pecan mixture.

6 Place the pork on the rack in the broiler pan. Broil about 10 minutes or until brown. Turn pork, and broil 10 to 15 minutes longer or until pork is slightly pink when you cut into the center.

1 Serving: Calories 280 (Calories from Fat 180); Fat 20g (Saturated 4g); Cholesterol 70mg; Sodium 350mg; Carbohydrate 4g (Dietary Fiber 1g); Protein 24g **% Daily Value:** Vitamin A 0%; Vitamin C 0%; Calcium 2%; Iron 6% **Diet Exchanges:** 3 1/2 Medium-Fat Meat, 1/2 Fat

Tip **FOR EASY CLEANUP,** line the broiler pan with aluminum foil before placing the pork on the rack.

A Special Touch Simple Fruit Topiary

Floral foam block
Small terra-cotta pot (4 to 6 inches in diameter)
Fresh pear or apple
6- to 7-inch stick or branch
About 1 foot 1/4-inch-wide ribbon
Glue
Moss, pebbles, nuts or small candies
Additional ribbon, if desired
Optional: Spray paint

1 Cut foam into pieces to fit in pot. Press foam firmly in pot. Add water (foam will absorb water which helps to weight down the pot).

2 Pierce small hole in bottom of pear; firmly insert stick. Insert other end of stick into foam in middle of pot. Wrap ribbon around stick. Glue ends of ribbon to stick.

3 Cover foam with moss or pebbles, or line with plastic wrap or tissue and place nuts or candies on top. Tie additional ribbon into bow around top of pot.

Optional: *Spray paint the pot to coordinate with your color scheme.*

Saucy Barbecued Ribs

MAKES 6 servings • **BAKE** 1 hour 45 minutes • **COOK** 18 minutes

INGREDIENTS

Essential Equipment:
shallow roasting pan (about 13×9-inch rectangle); small saucepan (about 1-quart size)

4 1/2 pounds pork spareribs

Smoky Barbecue Sauce (below)

Smoky Barbecue Sauce

1/2 cup ketchup

1/4 cup water

3 tablespoons packed
　brown sugar

2 tablespoons white vinegar

2 teaspoons celery seed

1/4 teaspoon liquid smoke

1/4 teaspoon red pepper sauce

DIRECTIONS

1 Heat the oven to 325°.

2 Cut the ribs into 6 serving pieces. Place the ribs, meaty sides up, in the roasting pan.

3 Bake uncovered 1 hour. While the ribs are baking, make Smoky Barbecue Sauce (below).

4 Brush the sauce over the ribs. Bake uncovered about 45 minutes longer, brushing frequently with sauce, until tender.

SMOKY BARBECUE SAUCE Place the ketchup, water, brown sugar, vinegar, celery seed, liquid smoke and pepper sauce in the saucepan. Heat to boiling over high heat, stirring occasionally. Once mixture is boiling, reduce heat just enough so mixture bubbles gently. Cook uncovered 15 minutes, stirring occasionally.

1 Serving: Calories 615 (Calories from Fat 360); Fat 40g (Saturated 15g); Cholesterol 160mg; Sodium 360mg; Carbohydrate 12g (Dietary Fiber 0g); Protein 39g **% Daily Value:** Vitamin A 2%; Vitamin C 2%; Calcium 8%; Iron 16% **Diet Exchanges:** 1 Starch, 5 High-Fat Meat

Tip **TO SAVE TIME,** use 2/3 cup of your favorite bottled barbecue sauce instead of preparing the Smoky Barbecue Sauce recipe.

Tip **SERVE WITH** Tangy Coleslaw (page 140) and watermelon slices for a stick-to-your-ribs summer feast.

Cutting Ribs

Use kitchen scissors or a sharp knife to cut pork ribs into serving-size pieces.

Italian Sausage Lasagna

MAKES 8 servings • **COOK** 55 minutes • **BAKE** 45 minutes • **LET STAND** 15 minutes

INGREDIENTS

Essential Equipment:
10-inch skillet; Dutch oven (about 4-quart size); 13×9-inch rectangular pan

1 medium onion

1 clove garlic

1 pound bulk Italian sausage or ground beef

3 tablespoons chopped fresh parsley

1 tablespoon chopped fresh or 1 teaspoon dried basil leaves

1 teaspoon sugar

1 can (15 ounces) tomato sauce

1 can (14 1/2 ounces) whole tomatoes, undrained

8 uncooked lasagna noodles (from 16-ounce package)

1 container (15 ounces) ricotta cheese or small curd creamed cottage cheese (2 cups)

1/2 cup grated Parmesan cheese

1 tablespoon chopped fresh or 1 1/2 teaspoons dried oregano leaves

2 cups shredded mozzarella cheese (8 ounces)

DIRECTIONS

1 Peel and chop the onion. Peel and finely chop the garlic.

2 Cook the sausage, onion and garlic in the skillet over medium heat about 5 minutes, stirring occasionally, until the sausage is no longer pink. Place a strainer over a medium bowl, or place a colander in a large bowl. Spoon sausage mixture into strainer to drain the fat. Discard fat.

3 Return the sausage mixture to the skillet. Stir in 2 tablespoons of the parsley, the basil, sugar, tomato sauce and tomatoes with their liquid. Break up the tomatoes with a spoon or fork.

4 Heat the mixture to boiling over medium-high heat, stirring occasionally. Once mixture is boiling, reduce heat just enough so mixture bubbles gently. Cook uncovered about 45 minutes, stirring occasionally, until the sauce is slightly thickened.

5 After the sauce has been cooking about 25 minutes, fill the Dutch oven about half full with water. Add 1/2 teaspoon salt if desired. Cover and heat over high heat until the water is boiling rapidly. Add the noodles. Heat to boiling again. Boil uncovered 12 to 15 minutes, stirring frequently, until tender.

6 While the noodles are cooking, mix the ricotta cheese, 1/4 cup of the Parmesan cheese, the oregano and remaining 1 tablespoon parsley.

7 Heat the oven to 350°. Drain the noodles in a strainer or colander. Spread half of the sauce (about 2 cups) in the ungreased rectangular pan. Top with 4 noodles. Spread half of the ricotta cheese mixture (about 1 cup) over the noodles. Sprinkle with 1 cup of the mozzarella cheese.

8 Repeat layers by adding remaining sauce, noodles, ricotta cheese mixture and mozzarella cheese. Sprinkle with remaining 1/4 cup Parmesan cheese.

9 Cover with aluminum foil and bake 30 minutes. Carefully remove the foil, and continue baking about 15 minutes longer or until lasagna is bubbly around the edges and looks very hot. Remove from the oven and let stand 15 minutes, so lasagna will become easier to cut and serve.

---

1 Serving: Calories 415 (Calories from Fat 200); Fat 22g (Saturated 10g); Cholesterol 65mg; Sodium 1090mg; Carbohydrate 28g (Dietary Fiber 2g); Protein 28g **% Daily Value:** Vitamin A 18%; Vitamin C 14%; Calcium 46%; Iron 14% **Diet Exchanges:** 2 Starch, 3 Medium-Fat Meat, 1 Fat

Tip **TO DO AHEAD,** cover the unbaked lasagna with aluminum foil and refrigerate up to 24 hours or freeze up to 2 months. Bake covered 45 minutes. Uncover and bake refrigerated lasagna 15 to 20 minutes longer or frozen lasagna 35 to 45 minutes longer until hot and bubbly.

Layering the Lasagna

Spread 2 cups sauce in the pan. Top with 4 noodles. Spread 1 cup ricotta cheese mixture over noodles. Sprinkle with 1 cup mozzarella cheese. Repeat layers by adding remaining sauce, noodles, ricotta cheese mixture and mozzarella cheese.

Honey-Mustard Chicken

MAKES 6 servings • **BAKE** 1 hour

INGREDIENTS

Essential Equipment:
13×9-inch rectangular pan

3- to 3 1/2-pound cut-up
  broiler-fryer chicken

1/3 cup country-style
  Dijon mustard

3 tablespoons honey

1 tablespoon mustard seed

1/2 teaspoon freshly ground
  pepper

DIRECTIONS

1 If the chicken is frozen, place it in the refrigerator the night before you plan to use it or for at least 12 hours until thawed. Cut and discard fat from chicken with kitchen scissors or knife. Rinse chicken under cold water, and pat dry with paper towels.

2 Heat the oven to 375°.

3 Place the chicken, skin side down, in a single layer in the ungreased rectangular pan.

4 Mix the mustard, honey, mustard seed and pepper. Brush half of the mustard mixture on all sides of chicken.

5 Cover the pan with aluminum foil and bake 30 minutes. Remove the chicken from the oven, and turn the pieces over with tongs. Brush with remaining mustard mixture.

6 Bake uncovered about 30 minutes longer or until juice of chicken is no longer pink when you cut into the center of the thickest pieces.

1 Serving: Calories 285 (Calories from Fat 135); Fat 15g (Saturated 4g); Cholesterol 85mg; Sodium 250mg; Carbohydrate 10g (Dietary Fiber 0g); Protein 28g **% Daily Value:** Vitamin A 4%; Vitamin C 0%; Calcium 2%; Iron 8% **Diet Exchanges:** 1/2 Starch, 4 Lean Meat, 1/2 Fat

SERVE WITH Do-Ahead Mashed Potatoes (page 134) and a side of steamed veggies for an easy weeknight get-together. Keep it simple for dessert by serving ice cream sundaes topped with warm caramel or chocolate sauce.

A Special Touch Gift Wrap Tablecloth

Gift wrap is an easy and inexpensive way to create a fun tablecloth. First, cover your table with a plain white table-cloth. Then, cut gift-wrap paper slightly smaller than the plain tablecloth, and place on top.

Thai Peanut Chicken

MAKES 6 servings • **BAKE** 1 hour

INGREDIENTS

DIRECTIONS

Essential Equipment:
13×9-inch rectangular pan

3- to 3 1/2-pound cut-up
  broiler-fryer chicken

Cooking spray

1 1/2 cups hot salsa

1/2 cup peanut butter

1/4 cup lime juice

2 tablespoons soy sauce

2 teaspoons grated fresh
  gingerroot

1/4 cup chopped peanuts

1/4 cup chopped fresh cilantro

1 If the chicken is frozen, place it in the refrigerator the night before you plan to use it or for at least 12 hours. Cut and discard fat from chicken with kitchen scissors or knife. Rinse chicken under cold water, and pat dry with paper towels.

2 Heat the oven to 375°. Spray the rectangular pan with cooking spray. Place the chicken, skin side down, in a single layer in the sprayed pan.

3 Mix the salsa, peanut butter, lime juice, soy sauce and gingerroot. Spoon salsa mixture over the chicken.

4 Cover the pan with aluminum foil and bake 30 minutes. Remove the chicken from the oven, and turn the pieces over with tongs. Spoon sauce from pan over chicken pieces to coat them.

5 Continue baking uncovered 20 to 30 minutes longer or until juice of chicken is no longer pink when you cut into the center of the thickest pieces. Sprinkle with the peanuts and cilantro.

1 Serving: Calories 440 (Calories from Fat 270); Fat 20g (Saturated 7g); Cholesterol 85mg; Sodium 700mg; Carbohydrate 11g (Dietary Fiber 4g); Protein 36g **% Daily Value:** Vitamin A 8%; Vitamin C 12%; Calcium 6%; Iron 12% **Diet Exchanges:** 4 1/2 Medium-Fat Meat, 2 Vegetable, 1 Fat

Tip **FRESH GINGERROOT** can be wrapped tightly and frozen for up to 4 months if you don't use it very often. Grate it straight from the freezer as needed.

Tip **SERVE WITH** Hot Cooked Rice (page 98) that has been made with canned coconut milk instead of water (don't use cream of coconut). Stir in a dash of ground turmeric for a rich golden color. Add a side salad of sliced cucumbers drizzled with vinaigrette and sprinkled with chopped red onion for a true Thai-inspired meal.

A Special Touch Crinkled Paper Chargers

Lightweight decorative art paper, lightweight gift
 wrap, tissue paper or gold foil
Spray adhesive
Large flat plates or serving platters

1 Cut paper into circles 1 inch larger in diameter than
the plates to be covered.

2 Spray adhesive onto back of paper; press onto
plates and over edges. Smooth paper, pressing from
the center out.

3 For serving, place dinner plates on top of papered
charger plates.

Smoked Gouda–Spinach Stuffed Chicken

MAKES 4 servings • **BAKE** 55 minutes

INGREDIENTS

Essential Equipment:
9-inch square pan

4 bone-in, skin-on chicken breast halves (2 1/2 to 3 pounds total)

Cooking spray

Smoked Gouda–Spinach Stuffing (below)

1/2 teaspoon salt

1/4 teaspoon pepper

2 teaspoons margarine or butter, melted

Smoked Gouda–Spinach Stuffing

1 package (10 ounces) frozen chopped spinach, thawed

1/2 cup shredded smoked Gouda or Swiss cheese (2 ounces)

1/4 teaspoon ground nutmeg

DIRECTIONS

1 If the chicken is frozen, place it in the refrigerator the night before you plan to use it or for at least 12 hours until thawed.

2 Heat the oven to 375°. Spray the square pan with cooking spray. Make Smoked Gouda–Spinach Stuffing (below).

3 Rinse chicken under cold water, and pat dry with paper towels. Loosen the skin from the chicken breasts by inserting fingers between the skin and flesh. Gently separate in center, leaving the skin attached at ends.

4 Spread one-fourth of the stuffing evenly between meat and skin of each chicken breast, using your fingers. Smooth skin over breasts, tucking under loose areas. Place chicken, skin side up, in the sprayed pan. Sprinkle the salt and pepper evenly over chicken. Drizzle with the margarine.

5 Bake uncovered 45 to 55 minutes or until juice of chicken is no longer pink when you cut into the center of the thickest pieces.

SMOKED GOUDA–SPINACH STUFFING Drain the thawed spinach in a strainer, then squeeze out the excess moisture from the spinach, using paper towels or a clean kitchen towel, until the spinach is dry. Place in medium bowl. Add the cheese and nutmeg. Mix all ingredients thoroughly.

1 Serving: Calories 225 (Calories from Fat 90); Fat 10g (Saturated 5g); Cholesterol 90mg; Sodium 550mg; Carbohydrate 3g (Dietary Fiber 1g); Protein 32g **% Daily Value:** Vitamin A 42%; Vitamin C 4%; Calcium 18%; Iron 8% **Diet Exchanges:** 4 Lean Meat

APPLE-HAZELNUT STUFFED CHICKEN Omit Smoked Gouda–Spinach Stuffing. Mix 1/4 cup chopped hazelnuts (filberts), 1 medium apple, chopped (1 cup) and 1 package (3 ounces) cream cheese at room temperature. Stuff and bake chicken as directed.

Tip **YOU CAN ALSO MAKE THIS RECIPE** with boneless, skinless chicken breast halves. Instead of spreading stuffing between meat and skin of chicken, cut a horizontal slit through the thickest part of each chicken breast to make a pocket. Spoon about 2 tablespoons of the stuffing into each pocket.

Loosening Chicken Skin

Loosen skin from chicken breasts by inserting fingers between the skin and flesh. Gently separate in center, leaving the skin attached at ends.

Stuffing Chicken

Using your fingers, spread one-fourth of the stuffing evenly between meat and skin of each chicken breast. Smooth skin over breasts, tucking under loose areas.

Crunchy Herb Baked Chicken

MAKES 6 servings • **FREEZE** 30 minutes • **BAKE** 35 minutes

INGREDIENTS

DIRECTIONS

Essential Equipment:
9-inch square pan; 2 shallow bowls or pie pans

6 boneless, skinless chicken breast halves (about 1/4 pound each)

1 clove garlic, finely chopped

1/4 cup (1/2 stick) margarine or butter at room temperature

1 tablespoon chopped fresh chives or parsley

Cooking spray

1 1/2 cups cornflakes cereal, crushed (3/4 cup)

2 tablespoons chopped fresh parsley

1/2 teaspoon paprika

1/4 cup buttermilk or milk

1 If the chicken is frozen, place it in the refrigerator the night before you plan to use it or for at least 12 hours until thawed. Cut and discard fat from chicken with kitchen scissors or knife. Rinse chicken under cold water, and pat dry with paper towels.

2 Peel and finely chop the garlic. Mix the garlic, margarine and chives. Shape the mixture into a rectangle, about 3×2 inches. Cover and freeze about 30 minutes or until firm.

3 Heat the oven to 425°. Spray the square pan with cooking spray. Flatten each chicken breast half to 1/4-inch thickness between sheets of plastic wrap or waxed paper, lightly pounding with the flat side of a meat mallet.

4 Remove the margarine mixture from the freezer, and cut crosswise into 6 pieces. Place 1 piece on the center of each chicken breast half. Fold each chicken breast lengthwise over margarine. Fold the ends up, and secure each end with a toothpick.

5 Mix the cornflakes, parsley and paprika in a shallow bowl. Pour the buttermilk into another shallow bowl. Dip the chicken, one piece at a time, into the milk, coating all sides. Then coat all sides with cornflakes mixture. Place the chicken, seam sides down, in the sprayed pan.

6 Bake uncovered about 35 minutes or until chicken is no longer pink when you cut into the center of the thickest pieces. Remove the toothpicks before serving.

1 Serving: Calories 230 (Calories from Fat 110); Fat 12g (Saturated 6g); Cholesterol 95mg; Sodium 160mg; Carbohydrate 4g (Dietary Fiber 0g); Protein 27g **% Daily Value:** Vitamin A 10%; Vitamin C 2%; Calcium 2%; Iron 12% **Diet Exchanges:** 4 Lean Meat

Tip **IF YOU DON'T HAVE A MEAT MALLET** for flattening the chicken, you can use the bottom of a heavy 1-quart saucepan, a rolling pin or the side of an unopened soup can that you've wrapped in plastic wrap.

Tip **TO CRUSH CORNFLAKES** put them in a sealable plastic bag. You can squeeze the cornflakes to crush them, or roll over them with a rolling pin, glass or jar. If you have a food processor, you can quickly make crumbs by pulsing the flakes a few times.

Flattening Chicken Breasts

Flatten each chicken breast to 1/4-inch thickness between sheets of plastic wrap or waxed paper, lightly pounding with the flat side of a meat mallet.

Folding Chicken

Fold chicken lengthwise over margarine. Fold ends up, and secure each end with a toothpick.

Dilled Chicken with Lemon Basmati Rice

MAKES 4 servings • **COOK** 25 minutes

INGREDIENTS

DIRECTIONS

Essential Equipment:
12-inch skillet

4 boneless, skinless chicken breast halves (about 1/4 pound each)

1 medium onion, finely chopped

2 tablespoons margarine or butter

2 cups chicken broth

1 cup uncooked basmati or regular long-grain white rice

1 teaspoon grated lemon peel

1 tablespoon lemon juice

2 tablespoons chopped fresh dill weed

1 If the chicken is frozen, place it in the refrigerator the night before you plan to use it or for at least 12 hours until thawed. Cut and discard fat from chicken with kitchen scissors or knife. Rinse chicken under cold water, and pat dry with paper towels.

2 Peel and finely chop the onion, and set aside.

3 Melt the margarine in the skillet over medium-high heat. Cook chicken in the margarine about 5 minutes, turning chicken over with tongs, until chicken is brown. Remove the chicken from the skillet.

4 Add the onion to the hot skillet. Cook 30 seconds, stirring constantly. Stir in the broth, uncooked rice, lemon peel and lemon juice. Heat the mixture to boiling over high heat, stirring constantly.

5 Once mixture is boiling, reduce heat just enough so mixture bubbles gently. Return the chicken to the skillet. Cover and cook 15 to 20 minutes, without stirring, until rice is tender, liquid is absorbed and chicken is no longer pink when you cut into the center of the thickest pieces. Stir in the dill weed.

1 Serving: Calories 400 (Calories from fat 100); Fat 11g (Saturated 2g); Cholesterol 75mg; Sodium 670mg; Carbohydrate 43g (Dietary Fiber 1g); Protein 33g **% Daily Value:** Vitamin A 8%; Vitamin C 2%; Calcium 4%; Iron 16% **Diet Exchanges:** 3 Starch, 3 Very Lean Meat, 1 Fat

Tip GRATE ONLY THE YELLOW OUTER LAYER, or the "zest," of the lemon peel. The bright yellow peel provides the best flavor without bitterness. Also, grate the lemon peel before you squeeze the lemon for juice.

Tip YOU CAN PURCHASE basmati rice in most large supermarkets. Basmati rice has a slightly sweet and nutty flavor, which is wonderful in this dish, but regular long-grain rice will also work just fine.

Grating Lemon Peel

Grate lemon peel by rubbing the lemon across the small rough holes of a grater.

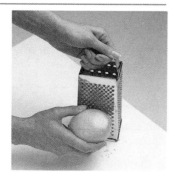

Chicken Manicotti

MAKES 7 servings • **BAKE** 1 hour 30 minutes

INGREDIENTS

Essential Equipment:
13×9-inch rectangular pan

1 jar (26 to 30 ounces) tomato
pasta sauce (any variety)

1 teaspoon garlic salt

1 1/2 pounds chicken breast
tenders (not breaded)

14 uncooked manicotti shells
(8 ounces)

2 cups shredded mozzarella
cheese (8 ounces)

Chopped fresh basil leaves,
if desired

DIRECTIONS

1 Heat the oven to 350°. Spread about 1 cup of the pasta sauce in the ungreased rectangular pan.

2 Sprinkle the garlic salt over the chicken. Fill the uncooked manicotti shells with chicken, stuffing chicken from each end of shell. Place filled shells on pasta sauce in the pan.

3 Pour the remaining pasta sauce evenly over the shells, covering shells completely with sauce. Sprinkle with the cheese.

4 Cover the pan with aluminum foil and bake about 1 hour 30 minutes or until shells are tender. Sprinkle with basil.

1 Serving: Calories 435 (Calories from Fat 115); Fat 13g (Saturated 5g); Cholesterol 75mg; Sodium 880mg; Carbohydrate 46g (Dietary Fiber 3g); Protein 36g **% Daily Value:** Vitamin A 12%; Vitamin C 12%; Calcium 28%; Iron 18% **Diet Exchanges:** 3 Starch, 3 Lean Meat, 1 Vegetable, 1 Fat

Tip **TO DO AHEAD,** tightly wrap pan of unbaked manicotti (before adding cheese) with aluminum foil, and freeze up to 1 month. Thaw, wrapped, in refrigerator 12 hours or until completely thawed. Sprinkle with cheese, and bake as directed.

A Special Touch   Fall Harvest Bowl

Clean peat pot liner (10 to 12 inches in diameter)
Natural excelsior (wood shavings), straw or hay
Variety of fresh fall fruits and vegetables
  (apples, baby artichokes, beets, bell peppers,
  garlic, mushrooms, pears, mini pumpkins,
  squash, turnips)
About 1 yard 2-inch-wide ribbon

1 Line peat pot with excelsior.

2 Arrange fruits and vegetables in pot.

3 Tie ribbon around pot into bow.

*Tip: Peat pot liners are used in hanging flowerpots and
are available at your local nursery. You'll find them in
many sizes.*

Chicken Stir-Fry with Broccoli

MAKES 4 servings • **COOK** 10 minutes

INGREDIENTS

Essential Equipment:
medium saucepan (about 2-quart size);
12-inch skillet, stir-fry pan or wok

**1 pound boneless, skinless
chicken breast halves**

2 green onions with tops

1 clove garlic

Hot Cooked Rice (below)

1/3 cup chicken broth

1 tablespoon cornstarch

3 tablespoons vegetable oil

3 cups broccoli flowerets

1/2 teaspoon dark sesame oil

Hot Cooked Rice

2 cups water

**1 cup uncooked regular
long-grain white rice**

DIRECTIONS

1 If the chicken is frozen, place it in the refrigerator the night before you plan to use it or for at least 12 hours until thawed. Cut and discard fat from chicken with kitchen scissors or knife. Rinse chicken under cold water, and pat dry with paper towels. Cut chicken into 1-inch pieces.

2 Cut and discard the tip of the green onion with the stringy end. Cut green onions into thin slices, including some of the green part. Peel and finely chop the garlic.

3 Make Hot Cooked Rice (below). While the rice is cooking, continue with the recipe. Gradually stir the broth into the cornstarch in a measuring cup until the mixture is smooth.

4 About 10 minutes before rice is done, heat the skillet over high heat 1 to 2 minutes. Add the oil to the hot skillet. If using a stir-fry pan or wok, rotate it to coat the side with oil.

5 Add the chicken to the skillet. Stir-fry with a turner or large spoon 3 to 4 minutes, lifting and stirring constantly, until chicken is no longer pink in center. Add the broccoli and garlic. Stir-fry 1 minute.

6 Stir the broth mixture into the chicken mixture. Heat to boiling over high heat, stirring constantly. Continue boiling 1 minute, stirring constantly. Stir in the onions and sesame oil. Cook 1 minute, stirring constantly. Serve chicken mixture over rice.

HOT COOKED RICE Heat the water and rice to boiling in the saucepan over high heat, stirring occasionally to prevent sticking. Once mixture is boiling, reduce heat just enough so mixture bubbles gently. Cover and cook about 15 minutes or until rice is fluffy and tender.

1 Serving: Calories 395 (Calories from Fat 125); Fat 14g (Saturated 3g); Cholesterol 50mg; Sodium 150mg; Carbohydrate 45g (Dietary Fiber 2g); Protein 24g **% Daily Value:** Vitamin A 8%; Vitamin C 42%; Calcium 6%; Iron 16% **Diet Exchanges:** 2 Starch, 2 Lean Meat, 3 Vegetable, 1 Fat

 **YOU CAN SUBSTITUTE** 1 bag (16 ounces) frozen broccoli cuts, thawed, for the fresh broccoli flowerets.

Stir-Frying Chicken

Stir-fry chicken over high heat with a turner or large spoon, lifting and stirring constantly.

Baked Salmon with Mango Salsa

MAKES 8 servings • **BAKE** 20 minutes

INGREDIENTS

Essential Equipment:
13×9-inch rectangular pan

Cooking spray to grease pan

1 large salmon fillet
  (about 2 pounds)

1/2 cup lemon juice

2 medium mangoes

1 medium jalapeño chili

1/2 cup chopped fresh cilantro

DIRECTIONS

1 Heat the oven to 400°. Spray the pan with cooking spray.

2 Cut the salmon fillet into 8 serving pieces. Place salmon in the pan. Drizzle 1/4 cup of the lemon juice over salmon.

3 Bake uncovered 15 to 20 minutes or until salmon flakes easily with a fork. While the salmon is baking, continue with the recipe.

4 Cut each mango lengthwise in half, sliding a sharp knife along the flat side of the seed on one side. Repeat on the other side, which will give you two large pieces plus the seed. Cut away any flesh from the seed. Make lengthwise and crosswise cuts, 1/2 inch apart, in the flesh of each mango half in a crisscross pattern. Be careful not to cut through the peel. Turn each mango half inside out, and cut off mango pieces.

5 Cut the stem off the jalapeño chili, then cut off the sides along the ribs, avoiding the seeds. The flesh, ribs and seeds of chilies contain irritating, burning oils, so wash hands (or wear protective gloves) and utensils in soapy water, and be especially careful not to rub your face or eyes. Chop enough of the chili to measure 2 teaspoons. Wrap any remaining chili in plastic wrap and refrigerate for another use.

6 Mix the mango, chili, cilantro and remaining 1/4 cup lemon juice. Serve over the salmon.

1 Serving: Calories 180 (Calories from Fat 55); Fat 6g (Saturated 2g); Cholesterol 65mg; Sodium 60mg; Carbohydrate 11g (Dietary Fiber 1g); Protein 21g **% Daily Value:** Vitamin A 34%; Vitamin C 34%; Calcium 2%; Iron 4% **Diet Exchanges:** 3 Very Lean Meat, 1 Fruit, 1/2 Fat

Tip **INSTEAD OF USING MANGO,** you can substitute 4 medium peaches or nectarines if you like.

Cutting and Seeding a Jalapeño Chili

Cut the stem off the jalapeño chili, then cut off the sides along the ribs, avoiding the seeds. The flesh, ribs and seeds of chilies contain burning, irritating oils. Be sure to wash your hands in soapy water (or wear protective gloves), and be especially careful not to rub your face or eyes until the oils have been washed away.

Grilled Tuna Steaks with Ginger-Lime Marinade

MAKES 6 servings • **REFRIGERATE** 1 hour • **GRILL** 20 minutes

INGREDIENTS

Essential Equipment:
shallow glass or plastic dish; charcoal or gas grill

1 1/2 pounds tuna steaks, 3/4 to 1 inch thick

1 clove garlic

1/4 cup lime juice

2 tablespoons olive or vegetable oil

1 teaspoon finely chopped gingerroot

1/4 teaspoon salt

Dash of ground red pepper (cayenne)

Lime wedges, if desired

DIRECTIONS

1 Cut the tuna steaks into 6 serving pieces if needed. Place tuna in the shallow dish.

2 Peel and crush the garlic. Make a marinade by mixing the garlic, lime juice, oil, gingerroot, salt and red pepper. Pour marinade over tuna, turning tuna to coat with marinade. Cover and refrigerate, turning tuna over once, at least 1 hour but no longer than 24 hours.

3 Prepare the coals or gas grill for direct heat (page 264). Heat to medium heat, which will take about 40 minutes for charcoal or about 10 minutes for a gas grill.

4 Remove the tuna from the marinade, reserving marinade. Place tuna on the grill about 4 inches from medium heat. Grill uncovered 7 to 10 minutes, brushing once with the marinade.

5 Carefully turn the tuna over with a turner. If tuna sticks to the grill, loosen with a turner. Brush marinade on tuna. Grill uncovered 7 to 10 minutes longer or until the tuna flakes easily with a fork. Discard any remaining marinade. Serve the tuna with lime wedges.

1 Serving: Calories 150 (Calories from fat 80); Fat 9g (Saturated 2g); Cholesterol 45mg; Sodium 150mg; Carbohydrate 1g (Dietary Fiber 0g); Protein 26g **% Daily Value:** Vitamin A 6%; Vitamin C 4%; Calcium 0%; Iron 6% **Diet Exchanges:** 2 1/2 Lean Meat

Tip **FOR VARIETY,** try this recipe using swordfish or halibut steaks instead of the tuna steaks.

Tip **IF YOU DON'T HAVE A GRILL,** you can broil the tuna steaks. Place tuna on the rack in a broiler pan. Brush marinade on tuna. Broil with tops about 4 inches from heat 5 minutes. Carefully turn tuna over with a turner. Brush marinade on tuna. Broil 4 to 6 minutes longer or until tuna flakes easily with a fork.

Crushing Garlic

Garlic can be crushed in a garlic press, or by pressing with the side of a knife or mallet to break into small pieces.

Crab Cakes

MAKES 4 servings • **COOK** 10 minutes

INGREDIENTS

Essential Equipment:
shallow dish or pie pan; 12-inch skillet

Mustard-Dill Sauce or Cilantro-Sour Cream (below)

1/4 cup mayonnaise or salad dressing

1 egg

2 slices bread (without crust)

2 medium green onions with tops

2 cans (6 ounces each) crabmeat

1 teaspoon ground mustard

1/4 teaspoon salt

1/8 teaspoon pepper

1/4 cup dry bread crumbs

2 tablespoons vegetable oil

Mustard-Dill Sauce

1/4 cup mayonnaise or salad dressing

1/4 cup sour cream

1 tablespoon Dijon mustard

3/4 teaspoon chopped fresh or 1/4 teaspoon dried dill weed

Cilantro-Sour Cream

1/2 cup sour cream

2 tablespoons chopped fresh cilantro

DIRECTIONS

1 Make Mustard-Dill Sauce or Cilantro-Sour Cream (below).

2 Mix the mayonnaise and egg in a medium bowl. Tear the bread into small pieces. You should have about 1 1/4 cups of soft bread crumbs. Add the soft bread crumbs to mayonnaise mixture. Cut and discard the tip of the green onion with the stringy end. Cut green onions into thin slices, including some of the green part and add onions to mayonnaise mixture. Mix all ingredients thoroughly.

3 Drain the crabmeat in a strainer. Flake crabmeat with a fork, and remove any tiny pieces of shell. Add crabmeat to mayonnaise mixture. Stir in the ground mustard, salt and pepper. Shape the crabmeat mixture into 4 patties.

4 Place the dry bread crumbs in the shallow dish. Place each patty in this dish of bread crumbs, and turn once to coat both sides. Use your hands to gently press bread crumbs onto patties.

5 Heat the oil in the skillet over medium heat 1 to 2 minutes. Cook patties in oil about 10 minutes, gently turning patties over once with a turner, until golden brown on both sides. You may need to reduce the heat to medium-low if the crab cakes become brown too quickly. Serve crab cakes with sauce.

MUSTARD-DILL SAUCE Mix the mayonnaise, sour cream, Dijon mustard and dill weed. Cover and refrigerate until serving time.

CILANTRO-SOUR CREAM Mix the sour cream and cilantro. Cover and refrigerate until serving time.

1 Serving: Calories 430 (Calories from Fat 295); Fat 33g (Saturated 7g); Cholesterol 155mg; Sodium 780mg; Carbohydrate 12g (Dietary Fiber 1g); Protein 22g **% Daily Value:** Vitamin A 6%; Vitamin C 2%; Calcium 14%; Iron 10% **Diet Exchanges:** 1 Starch, 3 High-Fat Meat, 1 Fat

 **YOU CAN SUBSTITUTE** 3/4 pound cooked crabmeat, flaked, for the canned crabmeat.

Coating Crab Cakes

Place each patty in the dish of dry bread crumbs, and turn once to coat both sides. Use your hands to gently press bread crumbs onto patties.

Garlic Shrimp

MAKES 4 servings • **COOK** 5 minutes

INGREDIENTS

Essential Equipment:
10-inch skillet, stir-fry pan or wok

3 large cloves garlic

1 large carrot

1 pound uncooked medium
shrimp, thawed if frozen

1 tablespoon olive or
vegetable oil

2 tablespoons chopped
fresh cilantro

DIRECTIONS

1 Peel and finely chop the garlic. Peel the carrot, then shred carrot by rubbing it across the largest holes of a grater. You will need about 2/3 cup.

2 Peel the shrimp (leave tail intact if you like). Make a shallow cut lengthwise down the back of each shrimp, and wash out the vein.

3 Heat the skillet over medium-high heat 1 to 2 minutes. Add the oil to the hot skillet. If using a stir-fry pan or wok, rotate it to coat the side with oil.

4 Add the garlic. Stir-fry with a turner or large spoon 1 minute, lifting and stirring constantly. Add the shrimp. Stir-fry 1 minute.

5 Add the carrot. Stir-fry about 3 minutes or until shrimp are pink and firm. Do not overcook the shrimp or they will become tough. Remove the skillet from the heat. Stir in the cilantro.

1 Serving: Calories 90 (Calories from Fat 35); Fat 4g (Saturated 1g); Cholesterol 105mg; Sodium 130mg; Carbohydrate 3g (Dietary Fiber 1g); Protein 12g **% Daily Value:** Vitamin A 30%; Vitamin C 2%; Calcium 2%; Iron 10% **Diet Exchanges:** 2 Very Lean Meat, 1/2 Vegetable

Tip **SERVE WITH** hot cooked fettuccine noodles tossed with a little olive oil. Add a mixed-greens salad topped with sliced tomatoes and drizzled with Italian dressing, and you have an impressive, throw-together meal for friends. Dessert can be as simple as a dish of ice cream or sorbet topped with sliced fresh strawberries and a dollop of whipped cream.

Tip **TO SAVE TIME,** purchase already peeled shrimp so you don't have to peel and clean them yourself.

Peeling Shrimp

Starting at the large end of shrimp, use your fingers to peel off the shell. Leave tail intact if you like.

Deveining (Cleaning) Shrimp

Use a paring knife to make a shallow cut lengthwise down the back of each shrimp, and wash out the vein.

Shrimp and Feta Pizza

MAKES 1 pizza (8 slices) • **BAKE** 15 minutes

INGREDIENTS	DIRECTIONS

Essential Equipment:
cookie sheet; 10-inch skillet

1 package (16 ounces) ready-to-serve pizza crust (12 to 14 inches in diameter)

1/2 pound uncooked medium shrimp, thawed if frozen

1 clove garlic, finely chopped

1 tablespoon olive or vegetable oil

2 cups shredded mozzarella cheese (8 ounces)

1 can (2 1/4 ounces) sliced ripe olives

1 cup crumbled feta cheese (4 ounces)

1 tablespoon chopped fresh or 1 teaspoon dried rosemary leaves, crumbled

1 Heat the oven to 400°. Place the pizza crust on the ungreased cookie sheet.

2 Peel the shrimp. Make a shallow cut lengthwise down the back of each shrimp, and wash out the vein. If the shrimp have tails, pull them off. Peel and finely chop the garlic.

3 Heat the oil in the skillet over medium heat 1 to 2 minutes. Cook the shrimp and garlic in oil about 3 minutes, stirring frequently, until shrimp are pink and firm. Do not overcook the shrimp or they will become tough.

4 Sprinkle 1 cup of the mozzarella cheese over the pizza crust. Top with the shrimp and garlic.

5 Drain the olives in a strainer, then sprinkle over pizza. Top with remaining 1 cup mozzarella cheese and the feta cheese. Sprinkle with the rosemary.

6 Bake about 15 minutes or until cheese is melted. To serve, cut pizza into wedges.

1 Slice: Calories 435 (Calories from Fat 170); Fat 19g (Saturated 9g); Cholesterol 95mg; Sodium 960mg; Carbohydrate 43g (Dietary Fiber 2g); Protein 25g **% Daily Value:** Vitamin A 10%; Vitamin C 0%; Calcium 42%; Iron 22% **Diet Exchanges:** 3 Starch, 2 High-Fat Meat

Tip **FOR A FUN GET-TOGETHER IDEA,** consider buying individual-size pizza crusts and inviting friends over for a pizza-topping party. Set out bowls of flavored cheeses, veggies, cooked meats and sauce, and let guests assemble their own personal pizzas to pop in the oven.

A Special Touch · Iced Wine Bottle

Empty green or clear wine bottle
Uncooked rice
1 bunch (about 12 inches long) flexible branches
   (willow or grapevine)
1 bunch (18 to 20 inches long) flexible branches
   (willow or grapevine)
Twine
Empty half-gallon milk carton

1 Clean and completely dry inside of bottle. Fill bottle with rice to prevent cracking. Cork or cover top with plastic wrap. Wrap and tie each branch bunch in middle and at both ends, using twine. Wrap 12-inch bunch around middle of bottle, and tie with twine to secure. Secure ends of longer bunch to opposite sides of the bunch on the bottle to make a handle, using twine.

2 Cut milk carton to a height of 7 inches. Place bottle inside carton. Fill carton with water; freeze overnight or until solid.

3 To remove frozen bottle from carton, place carton briefly in warm water. Pour rice out of bottle. Fill bottle with chilled wine or water. Place on liner or plate to catch the water as the ice melts.

Pizza Margherita

MAKES 1 pizza (8 slices) • **BAKE** 20 minutes

INGREDIENTS

DIRECTIONS

Essential Equipment:
cookie sheet

Shortening to grease cookie sheet

1 can (10 ounces) refrigerated pizza crust dough

2 cups shredded mozzarella cheese (8 ounces)

2 roma (plum) tomatoes

1/4 teaspoon salt

1/8 teaspoon pepper

1/4 cup chopped fresh basil leaves

1 tablespoon olive or vegetable oil

1 Heat the oven to 425°. Lightly grease the cookie sheet with the shortening.

2 Unroll the pizza crust dough. Press the dough into a 12-inch circle on the greased cookie sheet, pressing from center to edge so edge is slighter thicker than center.

3 Sprinkle 1 cup of the cheese over the dough, leaving about a 1/2-inch border of dough showing.

4 Slice the tomatoes, and arrange on cheese. Sprinkle the salt, pepper and 2 tablespoons of the basil over tomatoes and cheese. Sprinkle with remaining 1 cup cheese. Drizzle with the oil.

5 Bake about 20 minutes or until the crust is golden brown and cheese is melted. Sprinkle with remaining 2 tablespoons basil. To serve, cut pizza into wedges.

1 Slice: Calories 190 (Calories from Fat 70); Fat 8g (Saturated 4g); Cholesterol 15mg; Sodium 380mg; Carbohydrate 30g (Dietary Fiber 1g); Protein 11g **% Daily Value:** Vitamin A 4%; Vitamin C 2%; Calcium 20%; Iron 8% **Diet Exchanges:** 1 Starch, 1 Medium-Fat Meat, 1 Vegetable

YOU CAN ALSO SERVE this Italian classic mozzarella and tomato pizza as an appetizer. For bite-size portions, cut the pizza into small squares instead of wedges.

Pressing Pizza Crust Dough

Use your hands to press dough into a 12-inch circle on the cookie sheet, pressing from center to edge so edge is slighter thicker than center.

Lasagna Primavera

MAKES 8 servings • **BAKE** 1 hour • **LET STAND** 15 minutes

INGREDIENTS

Essential Equipment:
*Dutch oven (about 4-quart size);
13×9-inch rectangular pan*

9 uncooked lasagna noodles
(from 16-ounce package)

3 large carrots

2 medium green or red
bell peppers

3 cups fresh or frozen (thawed)
broccoli flowerets

1 can (14 1/2 ounces) diced
tomatoes

1 container (15 ounces)
ricotta cheese

1/2 cup grated Parmesan
cheese

1 egg

2 containers (10 ounces each)
refrigerated Alfredo sauce

3 1/2 cups shredded mozzarella
cheese (14 ounces)

DIRECTIONS

1 Heat the oven to 350°. Fill the Dutch oven about half full with water. Add 1/2 teaspoon salt if desired. Cover and heat over high heat until the water is boiling rapidly. Add the noodles. Heat to boiling again. Boil uncovered 12 to 15 minutes, stirring frequently, until noodles are tender. While the water is heating and noodles are cooking, continue with the recipe.

2 Peel the carrots, then shred carrots by rubbing them across the largest holes of a grater. You will need about 2 cups.

3 Cut the bell peppers lengthwise in half, and cut out seeds and membrane. Chop the bell peppers. Cut the broccoli flowerets into bite-size pieces if needed.

4 Drain the tomatoes in a strainer. Mix the tomatoes, carrots, bell peppers and broccoli.

5 Stir the ricotta cheese, Parmesan cheese and egg until well mixed. Drain the noodles in a strainer or colander.

6 Spread 2/3 cup of the Alfredo sauce in the ungreased rectangular pan. Top with 3 noodles. Spread half of the cheese mixture, one-third of the vegetable mixture and 2/3 cup of the sauce over the noodles. Sprinkle with 1 cup of the mozzarella cheese.

7 Top cheese with 3 noodles. Spread remaining cheese mixture, one-third of the vegetable mixture and 2/3 cup of the sauce over the noodles. Sprinkle with 1 cup of the mozzarella cheese.

8 Top with remaining 3 noodles and vegetable mixture. Pour remaining sauce evenly over the top. Sprinkle with remaining 1 1/2 cups mozzarella cheese.

9 Cover with aluminum foil and bake 30 minutes. Carefully remove the foil, and continue baking about 30 minutes longer or until lasagna is hot in center. Remove from the oven and let stand 15 minutes, so lasagna will become easier to cut and serve.

1 Serving: Calories 610 (Calories from Fat 350); Fat 39g (Saturated 24g); Cholesterol 145mg; Sodium 840mg; Carbohydrate 35g (Dietary Fiber 4g); Protein 33g **% Daily Value:** Vitamin A 80%; Vitamin C 50%; Calcium 80%; Iron 12% **Diet Exchanges:** 2 Starch, 3 1/2 High-Fat Meat, 1 Vegetable, 2 Fat

Tip **USE A SHARP SERRATED KNIFE** to cut the lasagna into serving pieces. Go over the cuts again with the knife to make serving easier.

Shredding a Carrot

Peel the carrot, then shred the carrot by rubbing it across the largest holes of a grater.

Gorgonzola Linguine with Toasted Walnuts

MAKES 4 servings • **COOK** 15 minutes

INGREDIENTS

Essential Equipment:
8- or 10-inch heavy skillet or shallow baking pan; Dutch oven (about 4-quart size); 10-inch skillet

8 ounces uncooked linguine

1/4 cup chopped walnuts

1 clove garlic

1 tablespoon margarine or butter

1 1/2 cups whipping (heavy) cream

1/4 cup dry white wine or chicken broth

1/4 teaspoon salt

1/2 cup crumbled Gorgonzola cheese (about 2 ounces)

DIRECTIONS

1 Fill the Dutch oven about half full with water. Add 1/2 teaspoon salt if desired. Cover and heat over high heat until the water is boiling rapidly. Add the linguine. Heat to boiling again. Boil uncovered 11 to 13 minutes, stirring frequently, until pasta is tender. While the water is heating and linguine is cooking, continue with the recipe.

2 Cook the walnuts in the ungreased heavy skillet over medium-low heat 5 to 7 minutes, stirring frequently until browning begins, then stirring constantly until golden brown and fragrant. Watch carefully; times vary greatly between gas and electric ranges. (Or heat the oven to 350°, and spread walnuts in the ungreased shallow pan. Bake uncovered about 10 minutes, stirring occasionally, until golden brown and fragrant.) Set walnuts aside.

3 Peel and finely chop the garlic. Melt the margarine in the 10-inch skillet over low heat. Cook the garlic in margarine, stirring occasionally, until garlic is golden.

4 Stir the whipping cream, wine and salt into the skillet with the garlic. Cook about 6 minutes, stirring constantly, until mixture is smooth and slightly thickened. Remove the skillet from the heat. Stir in the cheese until melted.

5 Drain the linguine in a strainer or colander, and place in a large bowl or back in the Dutch oven. Pour the sauce over hot linguine, and stir until linguine is well coated. Sprinkle with the toasted walnuts.

1 Serving: Calories 615 (Calories from Fat 370); Fat 41g (Saturated 23g); Cholesterol 120mg; Sodium 290mg; Carbohydrate 50g (Dietary Fiber 2g); Protein 14g **% Daily Value:** Vitamin A 26%; Vitamin C 0%; Calcium 16%; Iron 14% **Diet Exchanges:** 3 Starch, 7 Fat, 1/2 Skim Milk

Tip **HOW MUCH IS 8 OUNCES OF LINGUINE?** All bundled up, 8 ounces of uncooked linguine is about 1 1/2 inches in diameter.

Tip **DID YOU KNOW** that frozen nuts are easier to chop than room-temperature nuts? Put nuts in the freezer for at least an hour before chopping them.

Toasting Nuts in Skillet

Cook nuts in ungreased heavy skillet over medium-low heat 5 to 7 minutes, stirring frequently until browning begins, then stirring constantly until golden brown and fragrant.

Penne Pasta with Marinara Sauce

MAKES 8 servings • **COOK** 35 minutes

INGREDIENTS

DIRECTIONS

Essential Equipment:
large saucepan (about 3-quart size);
Dutch oven (about 4-quart size)

2 medium onions

2 large cloves garlic

1 small green bell pepper

2 tablespoons olive or
  vegetable oil

1 can (28 ounces) whole
  tomatoes, undrained

1 can (15 ounces) tomato sauce

2 tablespoons chopped fresh
  or 2 teaspoons dried basil
  leaves

1 tablespoon chopped fresh
  or 1 teaspoon dried oregano
  leaves

1/2 teaspoon salt

1/2 teaspoon fennel seed

1/4 teaspoon pepper

1 package (16 ounces) penne
  pasta (about 5 1/3 cups)

Grated Parmesan cheese,
  if desired

1 Peel and chop the onions. Peel and finely chop the garlic. Cut the bell pepper lengthwise in half, and cut out seeds and membrane. Chop enough of the bell pepper into small pieces to measure 1/4 cup. Wrap remaining bell pepper in plastic wrap, and refrigerate for another use.

2 Heat the oil in the saucepan over medium heat 1 to 2 minutes. Cook the onion, garlic and bell pepper in the oil 2 minutes, stirring occasionally.

3 Stir in the tomatoes with their liquid, and break them up with a spoon or fork. Stir in the tomato sauce, basil, oregano, salt, fennel seed and pepper. Heat to boiling over high heat. Once mixture is boiling, reduce heat just enough so mixture bubbles gently and does not spatter.

4 Cover and cook 35 minutes, stirring about every 10 minutes to make sure mixture is just bubbling gently and to prevent sticking. Lower the heat if the sauce is bubbling too fast.

5 After the tomato sauce has been cooking about 20 minutes, fill the Dutch oven about half full with water. Add 1/2 teaspoon salt if desired. Cover and heat over high heat until the water is boiling rapidly. Add the pasta. Heat to boiling again. Boil uncovered 10 to 12 minutes, stirring frequently, until pasta is tender.

6 Drain the pasta in a strainer or colander. Serve with the marinara sauce. Sprinkle with cheese.

1 Serving: Calories 290 (Calories from Fat 45); Fat 5g (Saturated 1g); Cholesterol 0mg; Sodium 620mg; Carbohydrate 56g (Dietary Fiber 5g); Protein 10g **% Daily Value:** Vitamin A 12%; Vitamin C 34%; Calcium 6%; Iron 18% **Diet Exchanges:** 3 Starch, 2 Vegetable

Tip **SERVE WITH** Hot Cheese Bread (page 150), a crisp green salad and a bottle of red wine for an impromptu dinner with friends.

A Special Touch — Pasta Bowl Basket Charger

A shallow basket or large terra-cotta saucer makes a perfect pasta bowl charger. For a rustic touch, line the basket first with natural excelsior or straw.

Asian Noodle Bowl

MAKES 4 servings • **COOK** 15 minutes

INGREDIENTS

DIRECTIONS

Essential Equipment:
*12-inch skillet; Dutch oven
(about 4-quart size)*

1/4 cup barbecue sauce

2 tablespoons hoisin sauce

1 tablespoon peanut butter

Dash of ground red pepper
(cayenne), if desired

1 small onion

1 small red bell pepper

1 tablespoon vegetable oil

2 cups broccoli flowerets or
1 bag (14 ounces) frozen
broccoli flowerets, thawed

3/4 cup water

1 package (10 ounces) Chinese
curly noodles

1 can (14 ounces) baby corn
nuggets

1/4 cup chopped peanuts

1 Mix the barbecue sauce, hoisin sauce, peanut butter and ground red pepper in a medium bowl, and set aside.

2 Peel the onion, and cut into thin wedges. Cut the bell pepper lengthwise in half, and cut out seeds and membrane. Chop enough bell pepper to measure 1/4 cup. Wrap remaining bell pepper in plastic wrap, and refrigerate for another use.

3 Heat the oil in the skillet over medium heat 1 to 2 minutes. Cook the onion and bell pepper in oil 2 minutes, stirring frequently. Stir in the broccoli and 3/4 cup water. Cover and cook 4 to 6 minutes, stirring occasionally, until broccoli is crisp-tender when pierced with a fork. While the vegetables are cooking, heat the water for the noodles.

4 Fill the Dutch oven about half full with water. Add 1/2 teaspoon salt if desired. Cover and heat over high heat until the water is boiling rapidly. Add the noodles. Heat to boiling again. Boil uncovered 4 to 5 minutes, stirring frequently, until noodles are tender. While water is heating and noodles are cooking, continue with the recipe.

5 Drain the corn in a strainer. Stir the corn and sauce mixture into the vegetable mixture. Cook uncovered 3 to 4 minutes, stirring occasionally, until mixture is hot and bubbly.

6 Drain the noodles in a strainer or colander. Spoon the noodles into 4 individual serving bowls. Spoon vegetable mixture over noodles. Sprinkle with the peanuts.

1 Serving: Calories 325 (Calories from Fat 45); Fat 5g (Saturated 1g); Cholesterol 0mg; Sodium 510mg; Carbohydrate 67g (Dietary Fiber 6g); Protein 9g **% Daily Value:** Vitamin A 20%; Vitamin C 72%; Calcium 6%; Iron 16% **Diet Exchanges:** 2 Starch, 4 Vegetable, 1 Fruit

Tip **TO SERVE THIS DISH FAMILY STYLE,** spoon the hot cooked noodles into one large bowl and the vegetable mixture into another bowl. Pass both bowls around the table so everyone can help themselves. Pass the peanuts separately in case someone does not want them.

A Special Touch — Vellum Place Mats

Spray adhesive
8 1/2×11-inch sheets lightweight decorative
  art paper
11×17-inch sheets vellum paper
Skeleton leaves (available at art store) or
  dried leaves

1 Spray adhesive onto back side of lightweight paper;
place on vellum and press lightly.

2 Spray adhesive onto backs of leaves; press lightly onto
vellum in desired design.

Vegetables, Salads and Sides

4

Hazelnut-Parmesan Asparagus

MAKES 4 servings • **COOK** 10 minutes

INGREDIENTS

DIRECTIONS

Essential Equipment:
10-inch skillet

1 pound asparagus spears

1 cup water

1 tablespoon margarine or butter

4 ounces sliced mushrooms (about 1 1/2 cups)

3/4 teaspoon chopped fresh or 1/4 teaspoon dried basil leaves

1/8 teaspoon salt

1/8 teaspoon coarsely ground pepper

2 tablespoons shredded Parmesan cheese

2 tablespoons chopped hazelnuts (filberts)

1 Break off the tough ends of asparagus stalks where they snap easily. Discard ends.

2 Heat the water in the skillet to boiling over high heat. Add the asparagus. Cover and heat to boiling again. Once water is boiling, reduce heat just enough so water bubbles gently. Cook covered 4 to 6 minutes or until asparagus is crisp-tender when pierced with a fork. Remove asparagus from water with tongs, allowing extra water to drip off; set aside.

3 While the asparagus is cooking, melt the margarine in the skillet over medium-high heat. Stir in the mushrooms. Cook 2 to 3 minutes, stirring frequently, until mushrooms are light brown.

4 Add the asparagus, basil, salt and pepper to mushrooms in skillet. Stir until vegetables are coated with seasonings. Sprinkle with the cheese and hazelnuts.

1 Serving: Calories 85 (Calories from Fat 55); Fat 6g (Saturated 1g); Cholesterol 2mg; Sodium 160mg; Carbohydrate 5g (Dietary Fiber 1g); Protein 4g **% Daily Value:** Vitamins A 8%; Vitamin C 12%; Calcium 6%; Iron 4% **Diet Exchanges:** 1 Vegetable, 1 Fat

Tip **YOU CAN SUBSTITUTE** 2 packages (10 ounces each) frozen asparagus spears for the fresh asparagus. Cook the asparagus as directed on the package.

Tip **IF YOUR SPACE FOR ENTERTAINING** is limited, use light to create the illusion of a different room. Keep the lights on during drinks and appetizers for a lively look, then dim the lights and use candles during the main meal for a more subdued atmosphere.

Preparing Asparagus for Cooking

Break off tough ends of asparagus stalks where they snap easily. Discard ends.

Baked Corn-on-the-Cob with Herbs

MAKES 4 servings • **BAKE** 20 minutes

INGREDIENTS

DIRECTIONS

Essential Equipment:
heavy-duty aluminum foil

4 ears corn

Butter-flavored cooking spray

1/4 teaspoon salt

1/8 teaspoon pepper

8 to 12 sprigs fresh dill weed

8 to 12 sprigs fresh thyme

1 Heat the oven to 450°.

2 Pull the green husks off the ears of corn and remove the silk. If there are any bad spots on the ears, cut them out.

3 Place each ear of corn on a 12-inch square of heavy-duty aluminum foil. Spray all sides of the corn with cooking spray. Sprinkle with salt and pepper. Place 2 or 3 sprigs each of dill weed and thyme around each ear of corn. Wrap foil securely around corn.

4 Place the corn directly on the oven rack. Bake about 20 minutes or until corn is tender when pierced with a fork.

1 Serving: Calories 100 (Calories from Fat 20); Fat 2g (Saturated 0g); Cholesterol 0mg; Sodium 160mg; Carbohydrate 25g (Dietary Fiber 3g); Protein 3g **% Daily Value:** Vitamin A 2%; Vitamin C 4%; Calcium 0%; Iron 2% **Diet Exchanges:** 1 Starch, 1 Vegetable

Tip **INSTEAD OF USING** dill weed and thyme, try fresh basil and rosemary for another delicious combination.

Tip **TRY GRILLING THE CORN** if you're hosting a barbecue with all the fixings. Place the foil-wrapped corn on the grill 4 to 5 inches from medium heat. Grill uncovered about 20 minutes, turning frequently, until corn is tender when pierced with a fork.

Husking Corn

Pull the green husks off the ears and remove the silk. Do not put corn husks or silk in your garbage disposal.

Sesame Green Beans

MAKES 6 servings • **COOK** 15 minutes

INGREDIENTS

Essential Equipment:
*large saucepan (about 3-quart size);
6- or 8-inch heavy skillet*

1 1/2 pounds green beans

1 tablespoon sesame seed

**2 tablespoons rice vinegar or
white wine vinegar**

2 tablespoons soy sauce

2 teaspoons sugar

1 teaspoon crushed red pepper

DIRECTIONS

1 Cut off ends of beans and discard.

2 Add 1 inch of water to the saucepan. Heat to boiling over high heat. Add the beans. Boil uncovered 5 minutes. Cover and boil about 5 minutes longer or until beans are crisp-tender when pierced with a fork. While the beans are cooking, continue with the recipe.

3 Cook the sesame seed in the ungreased heavy skillet over medium heat about 2 minutes, stirring frequently until browning begins, then stirring constantly until golden brown. Remove the skillet from the heat. Stir in the vinegar, soy sauce, sugar and red pepper. Cook 1 to 2 minutes longer or until mixture is hot.

4 Drain the beans in a strainer. Place beans in a large bowl. Pour the sesame mixture over beans. Gently toss with a fork until beans are evenly coated.

1 Serving: Calories 35 (Calories from Fat 10); Fat 1g (Saturated 0g); Cholesterol 0mg; Sodium 240mg; Carbohydrate 8g (Dietary Fiber 0g); Protein 2g **% Daily Value:** Vitamin A 4%; Vitamin C 2%; Calcium 4%; Iron 6% **Diet Exchanges:** 1 1/2 Vegetable

Tip **FOR A PARTY-SIZE PORTION,** double all the ingredients and cook beans in a Dutch oven (about 4-quart size).

Toasting Sesame Seed

Cook sesame seed in ungreased heavy skillet over medium heat about 2 minutes, stirring frequently until browning begins, then stirring constantly until golden brown.

Curried Vegetables

MAKES 6 servings • **COOK** 20 minutes

INGREDIENTS

Essential Equipment:
Dutch oven (about 4-quart size)

1 medium onion

1 clove garlic

1 medium carrot

1 small bell pepper

1 medium zucchini

1 tablespoon olive or
  vegetable oil

2 teaspoons curry powder

1 teaspoon grated gingerroot

3/4 cup water

3/4 cup apple juice

1 tablespoon soy sauce

1 tablespoon cornstarch

2 cups cauliflowerets

1/2 cup raisins

DIRECTIONS

1 Peel the onion, and cut into thin slices. Peel and finely chop the garlic. Peel the carrot, and cut into 1/2-inch slices. Cut the bell pepper lengthwise in half, and cut out seeds and membrane. Cut the bell pepper into thin strips. Cut the zucchini into 1/2-inch slices.

2 Heat the oil in the Dutch oven over medium-high heat 1 to 2 minutes. Cook the onion, garlic, curry powder and gingerroot in oil, stirring frequently, until onion is tender when pierced with a fork.

3 Stir in the water, 1/2 cup of the apple juice, the soy sauce and carrot. Heat to boiling over high heat. Once mixture is boiling, reduce heat just enough so mixture bubbles gently. Cover and cook 10 minutes.

4 Mix the cornstarch and remaining 1/4 cup apple juice until cornstarch is dissolved. Stir the bell pepper, zucchini, cauliflowerets and raisins into the carrot mixture. Stir in the cornstarch mixture.

5 Cover and cook 3 to 5 minutes longer, stirring occasionally, until zucchini is tender when pierced with a fork.

1 Serving: Calories 115 (Calories from Fat 25); Fat 3g (Saturated 0g); Cholesterol 0mg; Sodium 170mg; Carbohydrate 23g (Dietary Fiber 3g); Protein 2g **% Daily Value:** Vitamin A 18%; Vitamin C 26%; Calcium 2%; Iron 6% **Diet Exchanges:** 2 Vegetable, 1 Fruit

Tip **SERVE WITH** a big bowl of Hot Cooked Rice (page 98) for an impressively simple vegetarian dinner. Let everyone add his or her special touch by passing small bowls of traditional curry toppers, such as chopped peanuts, toasted shredded coconut, chopped fresh cilantro and mango chutney.

Grating Gingerroot

Grate gingerroot by rubbing it across the small rough holes of a grater.

Maple-Glazed Acorn Squash

MAKES 8 servings • **BAKE** 1 hour

INGREDIENTS

DIRECTIONS

Essential Equipment:
13×9-inch rectangular pan

4 small acorn squash
  (1 pound each)

1/3 cup maple-flavored syrup

1/4 cup whipping (heavy)
  cream

1/2 teaspoon salt

1/4 teaspoon ground
  cinnamon, if desired

1 Heat the oven to 350° (or follow Microwave Directions below).

2 Cut each squash lengthwise in half. You will need to do this on a cutting board using your biggest knife because the shell is quite tough. Place a paper towel on the cutting board to keep the squash from slipping while you cut. Scrape out the seeds and fibers with a soup spoon.

3 Place squash halves, cut sides up, in the ungreased rectangular pan. Spoon about 2 teaspoons of the maple syrup and 1 1/2 teaspoons of the whipping cream into each half.

4 Bake uncovered about 1 hour or until squash is tender when pierced with a fork. Sprinkle with the salt and cinnamon.

1 Serving: Calories 210 (Calories from Fat 45); Fat 5g (Saturated 3g); Cholesterol 15mg; Sodium 10mg; Carbohydrate 47g (Dietary Fiber 5g); Protein 3g **% Daily Value:** Vitamin A 12%; Vitamin C 18%; Calcium 10%; Iron 10% **Diet Exchanges:** 1 Starch, 2 Fruit

MICROWAVE DIRECTIONS Pierce whole squash with knife in several places to allow steam to escape. Place on a paper towel and microwave on High 6 to 8 minutes or until rind is firm but easy to cut; cool slightly. Cut squash as directed in step 2. Place 4 squash halves on large microwavable plate. Fill squash as directed in step 3. Microwave uncovered on High 6 to 8 minutes or until squash is tender when pierced with a fork. Repeat with remaining 4 squash halves.

Tip **FOR A SPECIAL TOUCH,** fill the squash with chopped crisp red apples and coarsely chopped toasted walnuts. Just add them to the sauce in the centers of the squash halves. Sprinkle chopped crystallized ginger around the edge of the squash for added flavor.

Tip **TO DO AHEAD,** you can cut and seed the squash, then cover and refrigerate up to two days before baking.

Cutting a Squash

Cut the squash lengthwise in half on a cutting board, using your biggest knife. Place a paper towel on the cutting board to keep the squash from slipping while you cut it.

Pecan Sweet Potatoes

MAKES 8 servings • **BAKE** 1 hour • **COOK** 2 minutes

INGREDIENTS

Essential Equipment:
12-inch skillet

8 medium sweet potatoes or yams (about 3 pounds)

1/2 cup packed brown sugar

1/4 cup (1/2 stick) margarine or butter

1/4 cup water

3/4 teaspoon salt

1/3 cup chopped pecans

DIRECTIONS

1 Heat the oven to 350°. Scrub the sweet potatoes thoroughly with a vegetable brush, but do not peel. Pierce potatoes on all sides with a fork to allow steam to escape while potatoes bake. Place potatoes directly on oven rack.

2 Bake potatoes about 1 hour or until tender when pierced with a fork. Be sure to use a pot holder because potatoes will be very hot to the touch.

3 When potatoes are cool enough to handle, gently peel off the skins using a paring knife. Cut potatoes into 1/2-inch slices.

4 Heat the brown sugar, margarine, water and salt in the skillet over medium heat about 2 minutes, stirring constantly, until mixture is smooth and bubbly. Add the potatoes and pecans. Gently stir until potatoes are coated with sauce.

1 Serving: Calories 255 (Calories from Fat 80); Fat 9g (Saturated 1g); Cholesterol 0mg; Sodium 290mg; Carbohydrate 41g (Dietary Fiber 4g); Protein 2g **% Daily Value:** Vitamin A 100%; Vitamin C 22%; Calcium 4%; Iron 4% **Diet Exchanges:** 2 Starch, 1 Fruit, 1 Fat

ORANGE SWEET POTATOES Substitute orange juice for the water. Add 1 table-spoon grated orange peel to the brown sugar sauce in step 4. Omit the pecans.

Tip **YOU CAN SUBSTITUTE** three 23-ounce cans of sweet potatoes or yams, drained and cut into 1/2-inch slices, for the fresh sweet potatoes. Omit steps 1, 2 and 3. In step 4, heat until potatoes are hot and coated with sauce.

A Special Touch Pear Glasses

4 large martini or margarita glasses or footed
  dessert dishes
Straw, hay or moss
4 fresh pears
Optional: Short pillar or votive candles and
  uncooked rice or popcorn

1 Line glasses with straw.

2 Place 1 pear in each glass. Arrange glasses along center
of table.

*Optional: Fill 2 glasses with uncooked rice. Place candles in
glasses. Alternate glasses with pears and candles on table.*

Do-Ahead Mashed Potatoes

MAKES 8 servings • **COOK** 30 minutes • **REFRIGERATE** up to 24 hours • **BAKE** 45 minutes

INGREDIENTS

DIRECTIONS

Essential Equipment:
large saucepan (about 3-quart size);
potato masher or electric mixer;
small saucepan (about 1-quart size);
2-quart casserole

**9 medium potatoes
(about 3 pounds)**

3/4 cup milk

**1/2 cup whipping (heavy)
cream**

**1/2 cup (1 stick) margarine
or butter**

1 teaspoon salt

Dash of pepper

Cooking spray to grease pan

1 Wash and peel the potatoes, and cut into large pieces.

2 Add 1 inch of water and 1/4 teaspoon salt if desired to the large saucepan. Cover and heat to boiling over high heat. Add potato pieces. Cover and heat to boiling again. Once the water is boiling, reduce heat just enough so water bubbles gently.

3 Cook covered 20 to 25 minutes or until potatoes are tender when pierced with a fork. The cooking time will vary, depending on the size of the potato pieces and the type of potato used. Drain potatoes in a strainer.

4 Return the drained potatoes to the saucepan, and cook over low heat about 1 minute to dry them. While cooking, shake the pan often to keep the potatoes from sticking and burning, which can happen very easily once the water has been drained off.

5 Place the potatoes in a medium bowl to be mashed. Or mash them in the same saucepan they were cooked in if the saucepan will not be damaged by the potato masher or electric mixer. Mash the potatoes with a potato masher or electric mixer until no lumps remain.

6 Heat the milk, whipping cream, margarine, salt and pepper in the small saucepan over medium-low heat, stirring occasionally, until margarine is melted. Measure out 1/4 cup of the milk mixture; cover and refrigerate.

7 Add the remaining milk mixture in small amounts to potatoes, mashing after each addition. You may not use all the milk because the amount needed to make potatoes smooth and fluffy depends on the type of potato used. Beat vigorously until potatoes are light and fluffy.

8 Spray the casserole with cooking spray. Spoon the potatoes into the sprayed casserole. Bake immediately, or cover and refrigerate up to 24 hours.

9 Heat the oven to 350°. Pour the reserved milk mixture over potatoes. Bake uncovered 40 to 45 minutes or until potatoes are hot. Just before serving, stir the potatoes.

1 Serving: Calories 280 (Calories from Fat 155); Fat 17g (Saturated 5g); Cholesterol 20mg; Sodium 470mg; Carbohydrate 29g (Dietary Fiber 2g); Protein 4g **% Daily Value:** Vitamin A 20%; Vitamin C 8%; Calcium 4%; Iron 2% **Diet Exchanges:** 2 Starch, 3 Fat

DO-AHEAD GARLIC MASHED POTATOES Peel and finely chop 1 or 2 cloves garlic. Add to the potatoes before mashing in step 5.

FOR EXTRA FLAVOR, sprinkle 1 cup crushed herb-seasoned croutons or shredded Parmesan cheese over mashed potatoes. Or place purchased basil pesto in a resealable plastic bag, snip off a tiny corner and drizzle pesto over potatoes.

Mashing Potatoes

Use a handheld potato masher for the fluffiest mashed potatoes. If using an electric mixer, do not mix too long; overmixing releases more starch from the potatoes and they can become gummy.

Cheddar Twice-Baked Potatoes

MAKES 8 servings • **BAKE** 1 hour 35 minutes

INGREDIENTS

DIRECTIONS

Essential Equipment:
potato masher or electric mixer;
cookie sheet

8 large baking potatoes
   (russet or Idaho),
   8 to 10 ounces each

About 1/3 cup milk

1/4 cup (1/2 stick) margarine or
   butter at room temperature

1/4 teaspoon salt

Dash of pepper

1 cup shredded Cheddar cheese
   (4 ounces)

1 tablespoon chopped
   fresh chives

Additional chopped fresh
   chives for garnish, if desired

1 Heat the oven to 375°. Scrub the potatoes thoroughly with a vegetable brush, but do not peel. Pierce the potatoes on all sides with a fork to allow steam to escape while the potatoes bake. Place potatoes directly on the oven rack.

2 Bake potatoes 1 hour to 1 hour 15 minutes or until potatoes feel tender when squeezed gently. Be sure to use a pot holder because potatoes will be very hot to the touch.

3 When potatoes are cool enough to handle, cut them lengthwise in half. Scoop out the insides into a medium bowl, leaving about a 1/4-inch shell in the potato skin.

4 Increase the oven temperature to 400°.

5 Mash the potatoes with a potato masher or electric mixer until no lumps remain. Add the milk in small amounts, beating after each addition. The amount of milk needed to make potatoes smooth and fluffy depends on the type of potato used.

6 Add the margarine, salt and pepper. Beat vigorously until potatoes are light and fluffy. Stir in the cheese and 1 tablespoon chives. Fill the potato shells with the mashed potato mixture. Place on the ungreased cookie sheet. Bake potatoes uncovered about 20 minutes or until hot. Sprinkle with additional chives.

1 Serving: Calories 305 (Calories from Fat 100); Fat 11g (Saturated 4g); Cholesterol 15mg; Sodium 260mg; Carbohydrate 47g (Dietary Fiber 4g); Protein 8g **% Daily Value:** Vitamin A 10%; Vitamin C 20%; Calcium 10%; Iron 14% **Diet Exchanges:** 3 Starch, 2 Fat

HORSERADISH TWICE-BAKED POTATOES Omit the cheese and chives. Stir 1/4 cup sour cream and 2 tablespoons prepared horseradish into the mashed potato mixture in step 6. Garnish with fresh dill weed if desired.

Tip **TO DO AHEAD,** wrap filled potato shells airtight and refrigerate up to 24 hours or freeze up to 2 months. Unwrap potatoes and place on a cookie sheet. Bake in a 400° oven about 30 minutes for refrigerated potatoes, about 40 minutes for frozen potatoes, until hot.

Tip **FOR A DRESSED-UP DISH,** tuck sprigs of fresh herbs, such as chives, oregano, thyme and rosemary, around the potatoes on the serving platter or tray.

Scooping Potato from Shells

Using a soup spoon, carefully scoop out the inside of each potato half, leaving about a 1/4-inch shell.

Pear and Blue Cheese Salad

MAKES 4 servings

INGREDIENTS

Essential Equipment:
large salad or mixing bowl

Cider Vinaigrette (below)

1 medium bunch romaine

2 medium red or green pears

1/4 cup crumbled blue cheese
   (1 ounce)

2 tablespoons chopped
   walnuts

Cider Vinaigrette

1/4 cup olive or vegetable oil

2 tablespoons cider vinegar

1/2 teaspoon Dijon mustard

1/4 teaspoon salt

Dash of ground pepper

DIRECTIONS

1 Make Cider Vinaigrette (below).

2 Remove any limp outer leaves from the romaine and discard. Break remaining leaves off the core, and rinse with cool water. Shake off excess water and blot to dry, or roll up the leaves in a clean kitchen towel or paper towel to dry. Or use a spinner to dry leaves. Tear the leaves into bite-size pieces. You will need about 8 cups of romaine pieces. Place romaine pieces in the bowl.

3 Cut each pear into fourths. Cut the core and seeds from the center of each fourth. Cut each fourth into 1/4-inch slices, and add to romaine. Add the cheese and walnuts to romaine.

4 Pour the vinaigrette over the salad ingredients, and toss with 2 large spoons or salad tongs. To keep salad crisp, serve immediately.

CIDER VINAIGRETTE Shake the oil, vinegar, mustard, salt and pepper in a tightly covered jar or container. Shake again before pouring over salad.

1 Serving: Calories 95 (Calories from Fat 55); Fat 6g (Saturated 2g); Cholesterol 4mg; Sodium 180mg; Carbohydrate 10g (Dietary Fiber 2g); Protein 2g **% Daily Value:** Vitamin A 8%; Vitamin C 6%; Calcium 4%; Iron 2% **Diet Exchanges:** 1 Fruit, 1 Fat

Tip **TO SAVE TIME,** purchase romaine already washed, torn and ready to use. You will need 8 cups, which is about 10 ounces.

Tip **TO MAKE SERVING EASIER,** arrange the salad on small plates and place them on the table before your guests are seated.

Drying Romaine

Shake off excess water and blot to dry, or roll up the leaves in a clean kitchen towel or paper towel to dry. Or use a spinner to dry greens.

Slicing a Pear

Cut the pear into fourths. Cut the core and seeds from the center of each fourth. Cut each fourth into 1/4-inch slices.

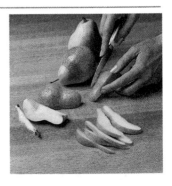

Tangy Coleslaw

MAKES 8 servings • **REFRIGERATE** 30 minutes

INGREDIENTS

DIRECTIONS

Essential Equipment:
large salad or mixing bowl

1 bag (16 ounces) coleslaw mix

4 medium green onions
   with tops

1/3 cup orange marmalade

1/4 cup rice vinegar or white
   wine vinegar

1 tablespoon sugar

1 tablespoon dark sesame oil

1 1/2 teaspoons grated
   gingerroot

1 teaspoon salt

1 Place the coleslaw mix in the bowl. Cut and discard the tip of the green onion with the stringy end. Cut green onions into thin slices, including some of the green part and add to the coleslaw mix.

2 Add the marmalade, vinegar, sugar, oil, gingerroot and salt to the coleslaw mix. Mix with a large spoon until coleslaw is evenly coated with the dressing.

3 Cover and refrigerate at least 30 minutes to blend flavors.

1 Serving: Calories 70 (Calories from Fat 20); Fat 2g (Saturated 0g); Cholesterol 0mg; Sodium 310mg; Carbohydrate 14g (Dietary Fiber 2g); Protein 1g **% Daily Value:** Vitamin A 0%; Vitamin C 34%; Calcium 4%; Iron 2% **Diet Exchanges:** 1 Vegetable, 1/2 Fruit, 1/2 Fat

Tip **ADD A TWIST** to this picnic favorite by stirring in 1 cup canned mandarin orange segments, drained. Sprinkle with 2 tablespoons toasted sliced almonds.

Tip **IF YOU DON'T HAVE A BAG OF COLESLAW MIX,** you can use 7 cups shredded cabbage and 2 shredded carrots instead.

A Special Touch Water or Punch Fishbowl

Small decorative molds, small paper cups or muffin
    pan with regular-size muffin cups
Large fresh flowers (such as carnations, daisies or
    zinnias)
Large clear tray, platter or liner with rim
1-gallon fishbowl (available at pet store)
Lemonade or ice water

1 Fill molds with water. Place flowers in molds. Freeze
until solid.

2 Fill tray 1/2 full with water. Fill fishbowl with lemonade or ice water, and place in tray.

3 Dip bottoms of molds in warm water to loosen frozen
flowers. Remove frozen flowers from molds; float in tray.

*Tip: Distilled water will keep the ice molds clear when they
are frozen. You can use tap water if you like, but the
molds will be more opaque.*

Seven-Layer Salad

MAKES 6 servings • **REFRIGERATE** 2 hours

INGREDIENTS

Essential Equipment:
12-inch skillet; large salad or mixing bowl

12 slices bacon

8 medium radishes

5 medium green onions with tops

2 medium stalks celery

6 cups ready-to-eat mixed salad greens (from 10-ounce bag)

1 package (10 ounces) frozen green peas, thawed

1 1/2 cups mayonnaise or salad dressing

1/2 cup shredded Cheddar cheese or grated Parmesan cheese (2 ounces)

DIRECTIONS

1 Cook the bacon in the skillet over low heat 8 to 10 minutes, turning occasionally, until bacon is evenly browned and crisp. Drain bacon on paper towels. When bacon is cool enough to handle, crumble into small pieces.

2 Cut the radishes into thin slices. Cut and discard the tip of the green onion with the stringy end. Cut green onions into thin slices, including some of the green part. Cut the celery into thin slices.

3 Place the salad greens in the bowl. Layer the radishes, onions, celery, bacon and peas on salad greens.

4 Spread the mayonnaise over the peas, covering top completely and sealing to edge of bowl. Sprinkle with the cheese.

5 Cover and refrigerate at least 2 hours to blend flavors but no longer than 12 hours. Just before serving, toss if desired with 2 large spoons. Store any remaining salad covered in refrigerator.

1 Serving: Calories 535 (Calories from Fat 470); Fat 52g (Saturated 10g); Cholesterol 48mg; Sodium 700mg; Carbohydrate 11g (Dietary Fiber 4g); Protein 10g **% Daily Value:** Vitamin A 10%; Vitamin C 18%; Calcium 14%; Iron 10% **Diet Exchanges:** 1/2 Medium-Fat Meat, 2 Vegetable, 10 Fat

Tip **TO KEEP SALADS COLD** at a picnic or other outdoor event, place the serving container in a bowl filled with ice.

Spreading Mayonnaise over Peas

Spread mayonnaise over peas, covering top completely and sealing to edge of bowl.

Couscous-Pesto Salad

MAKES 6 servings • **COOK** 5 minutes

INGREDIENTS

DIRECTIONS

Essential Equipment:
medium saucepan (about 2-quart size); 10-inch skillet; large salad or mixing bowl

2 medium zucchini

1 large red bell pepper

1 medium red onion

2 cups water

1 1/2 cups uncooked couscous

1 tablespoon olive or vegetable oil

1 container (7 ounces) refrigerated basil pesto

2 tablespoons balsamic or red wine vinegar

1 Cut the zucchini lengthwise in half. Cut each half into 1/4-inch slices. Cut the bell pepper lengthwise in half, and cut out seeds and membrane. Cut bell pepper into 1/2-inch pieces. Cut the onion lengthwise in half. Cut one half into 8 wedges. Wrap remaining onion in plastic wrap, and refrigerate for another use.

2 Heat the water and 1/2 teaspoon salt if desired to boiling in the saucepan over high heat. Stir in the couscous. Cover and remove from heat. Let stand 5 minutes. Meanwhile, continue with the recipe.

3 Heat the oil in the skillet over medium-high heat 1 to 2 minutes. Cook the zucchini, bell pepper and onion in oil about 5 minutes, stirring frequently, until vegetables are crisp-tender when pierced with a fork.

4 Mix the couscous, vegetable mixture, pesto and vinegar in the bowl. Serve warm, or cover and refrigerate about 30 minutes until chilled.

1 Serving: Calories 350 (Calories from Fat 180); Fat 20g (Saturated 4g); Cholesterol 5mg; Sodium 270mg; Carbohydrate 41g (Dietary Fiber 5g); Protein 9g **% Daily Value:** Vitamin A 20%; Vitamin C 50%; Calcium 14%; Iron 10% **Diet Exchanges:** 2 Starch, 2 Vegetable, 3 Fat

Cutting a Zucchini

Cut the zucchini lengthwise in half. Cut each half into slices.

Artichoke-Pepper Pasta Salad

MAKES 6 servings • **COOK** 15 minutes

INGREDIENTS

DIRECTIONS

Essential Equipment:
Dutch oven (about 4-quart size; large salad or mixing bowl

2 2/3 cups uncooked fusilli (corkscrew) pasta (8 ounces)

1 jar (7 ounces) roasted red bell peppers

1 jar (2 ounces) sliced mushrooms

1 jar (6 to 7 ounces) marinated artichoke hearts, undrained

2 tablespoons shredded Parmesan cheese

1/2 teaspoon pepper

2 tablespoons pine nuts

3 tablespoons chopped fresh basil leaves, if desired

1 Fill the Dutch oven about half full with water. Add 1/2 teaspoon salt if desired. Cover and heat over high heat until the water is boiling rapidly. Add the pasta. Heat to boiling again. Boil uncovered 10 to 12 minutes, stirring frequently, until pasta is tender. While the water is heating and pasta is cooking, continue with the recipe.

2 Drain the bell peppers in a strainer, then cut them into small pieces. Place peppers in the large bowl. Drain the mushrooms in strainer, and add to peppers.

3 Add the artichoke hearts with their liquid, cheese and pepper to vegetables in bowl. Mix all ingredients thoroughly.

4 Drain the pasta in a strainer or colander, and rinse thoroughly with cold water. Add pasta to vegetable mixture, and toss with 2 large spoons. Sprinkle with the nuts and basil.

1 Serving: Calories 195 (Calories from Fat 35); Fat 4g (Saturated 1g); Cholesterol 0mg; Sodium 180mg; Carbohydrate 36g (Dietary Fiber 4g); Protein 8g **% Daily Value:** Vitamin A 14%; Vitamin C 50%; Calcium 4%; Iron 12% **Diet Exchanges:** 2 Starch, 1 Vegetable

Tip **SERVE THIS SALAD** as a side dish, at any time. All the ingredients are pantry items that you can keep on hand indefinitely. For 4 main-dish servings, add 1 cup chopped cooked chicken or turkey.

A Special Touch Lined Salad Plates

For an appealing way to serve salad or dessert, use clear glass plates. For each place setting, choose two plates: one dinner size (about 10 inches) and the other salad size (about 8 inches). Place cards, photographs, torn art paper, flowers, leaves, or other flat objects between the two plates. If you like, let guests take home the plate decorations as a memento of their visit.

Summer Citrus Fruit Salad

MAKES 8 servings

INGREDIENTS

Essential Equipment:
large salad or mixing bowl

1 cup vanilla yogurt

1 tablespoon mayonnaise or salad dressing

1/4 teaspoon grated orange peel

2 tablespoons orange juice

1 pint (2 cups) strawberries

1 kiwifruit

1 small bunch seedless green grapes

1 can (11 ounces) mandarin orange segments

DIRECTIONS

1 Mix the yogurt, mayonnaise, orange peel and orange juice in the bowl.

2 Rinse the strawberries with cool water, and pat dry with paper towels. Cut out the hull, or "cap," with the point of a paring knife. Cut the strawberries lengthwise into slices.

3 Peel the kiwifruit. Cut lengthwise in half, then cut into pieces. Wash the grapes, and cut in half.

4 Drain the oranges in a strainer.

5 Add the fruits to the yogurt mixture. Gently stir until fruits are coated with yogurt mixture. Cover and refrigerate until serving time.

1 Serving: Calories 90 (Calories from Fat 20); Fat 2g (Saturated 1g); Cholesterol 5mg; Sodium 35mg; Carbohydrate 18g (Dietary Fiber 2g); Protein 2g **% Daily Value:** Vitamin A 6%; Vitamin C 56%; Calcium 6%; Iron 2% **Diet Exchanges:** 1 Fruit, 1/2 Fat

Tip **THE YOGURT MIXTURE** also makes a wonderful party dip to serve with fruit. Try it with strawberries, sliced peaches and chunks of melon.

Tip **IF YOU'RE ENTERTAINING OUTDOORS,** wait until the last minute to set out any perishable food. Dishes made with mayonnaise, eggs, meat, seafood, poultry or dairy products should be kept in the refrigerator or placed on ice until you're ready to serve them.

Peeling a Kiwifruit

Cut the fuzzy brown skin from the fruit with a paring knife.

Hot Cheese Bread

MAKES 1 loaf (24 slices) • **BAKE** 20 minutes

INGREDIENTS

DIRECTIONS

Essential Equipment:
heavy-duty aluminum foil

1/2 cup (1 stick) margarine or butter at room temperature

1/4 cup crumbled blue cheese (1 ounce)

1/4 cup shredded mozzarella cheese (1 ounce)

1 loaf (1 pound) French bread

1 Heat the oven to 350°.

2 Mix the margarine, blue cheese and mozzarella cheese.

3 Cut the bread horizontally in half. Spread cheese mixture over cut sides of bread. Reassemble the loaf.

4 Cut the bread crosswise into 1-inch slices. Reassemble the loaf, and wrap securely in heavy-duty aluminum foil.

5 Bake about 20 minutes or until cheese is melted. Serve hot.

1 Slice: Calories 180 (Calories from Fat 90); Fat 10g (Saturated 6g); Cholesterol 25mg; Sodium 320mg; Carbohydrate 19g (Dietary Fiber 1g); Protein 5g **% Daily Value:** Vitamin A 6%; Vitamin C 0%; Calcium 6%; Iron 6% **Diet Exchanges:** 1 Starch, 2 Fat

Tip **FOR A QUICKER BREAD FIX-UP,** spread cheese mixture on French bread slices, and place slices, cheese sides up, on the rack in a broiler pan. Broil with tops 2 to 3 inches from heat 1 to 2 minutes or until cheese is melted.

Assembling Loaf of Bread

Spread cheese mixture over cut sides of bread. Reassemble loaf. Cut bread crosswise into 1-inch slices. Reassemble loaf, and wrap securely in heavy-duty aluminum foil.

Buttermilk Corn Bread

MAKES 8 servings • **BAKE** 30 minutes

INGREDIENTS

DIRECTIONS

Essential Equipment:
8-inch square pan

Shortening to grease pan

1 1/3 cups buttermilk

1/3 cup margarine or butter,
melted

2 eggs

1 1/4 cups cornmeal

3/4 cup all-purpose flour

1 tablespoon sugar

2 teaspoons baking powder

1 teaspoon salt

1/2 teaspoon baking soda

1 Heat the oven to 450°. Grease the bottom and sides of the pan with the shortening.

2 Beat the buttermilk, margarine and eggs in a large bowl with a fork or wire whisk until well mixed. Stir in the cornmeal, flour, sugar, baking powder, salt and baking soda all at once just until the flour is moistened. The batter will be lumpy. Pour the batter into the greased pan.

3 Bake 25 to 30 minutes or until golden brown and when a tooth-pick inserted in the center comes out clean. Serve warm.

1 Serving: Calories 220 (Calories from Fat 90); Fat 10g (Saturated 2g); Cholesterol 55mg; Sodium 650mg; Carbohydrate 29g (Dietary Fiber 2g); Protein 6g **% Daily Value:** Vitamin A 14%; Vitamin C 0%; Calcium 12%; Iron 10% **Diet Exchanges:** 2 Starch, 1 1/2 Fat

CHIPOTLE-CHEESE CORN BREAD Stir 1 tablespoon chopped canned chipotle chilies in adobo sauce and 1/2 cup shredded Monterey Jack cheese into the batter in step 2.

Tip **IF USING MARGARINE,** purchase regular margarine or a spread that contains at least 65 percent vegetable oil and is in a stick form. Spreads with less fat do not work well for many quick breads, muffins, cakes and other baked goods.

Testing Corn Bread for Doneness

If corn bread is not fully baked, a toothpick inserted in the center will have uncooked batter clinging to it.

Baking Powder Biscuits

MAKES 12 biscuits • **BAKE** 12 minutes

INGREDIENTS

Essential Equipment:
cookie sheet

**Shortening to grease
  cookie sheet**

2 cups all-purpose flour

1 tablespoon sugar

3 teaspoons baking powder

1 teaspoon salt

1/2 cup shortening

1 cup milk

DIRECTIONS

1 Heat the oven to 450°. Grease the cookie sheet with the shortening.

2 Mix the flour, sugar, baking powder and salt in a medium bowl. Cut the 1/2 cup shortening into the flour mixture, using a pastry blender or crisscrossing 2 knives, until the mixture looks like fine crumbs.

3 Stir the milk into the crumb mixture just until blended and a dough forms. Drop the dough by 12 spoonfuls onto the greased cookie sheet.

4 Bake 10 to 12 minutes or until golden brown. Immediately remove biscuits from the cookie sheet to a wire cooling rack. Serve warm.

1 Biscuit: Calories 160 (Calories from Fat 80); Fat 9g (Saturated 2g); Cholesterol 5mg; Sodium 310mg; Carbohydrate 18g (Dietary Fiber 0g); Protein 2g **% Daily Value:** Vitamin A 0%; Vitamin C 0%; Calcium 10%; Iron 6% **Diet Exchanges:** 1 Starch, 2 Fat

SAVORY HERB BISCUITS Add 2 teaspoons chopped fresh or 3/4 teaspoon dried dill weed or basil leaves to the flour mixture in step 2.

Tip BISCUITS ARE BEST SERVED WARM, but if you are lucky enough to have leftovers, wrap them in aluminum foil and store at room temperature. To reheat, put the foil-wrapped biscuits in a 300° oven for about 10 minutes or until warm.

Cutting in Shortening

Cut shortening into flour mixture, using a pastry blender or criss-crossing 2 knives, until mixture looks like fine crumbs.

Sour Cream Breadstick Twists

MAKES 12 breadsticks • **BAKE** 12 minutes

INGREDIENTS

Essential Equipment:
cookie sheet

2 cups all-purpose flour

3 teaspoons baking powder

1/2 teaspoon salt

1/3 cup shortening

1 1/4 cups sour cream

2 tablespoons chopped fresh or freeze-dried chives

2 tablespoons margarine or butter, melted

About 1/4 cup poppy seed

DIRECTIONS

1 Heat the oven to 450°.

2 Mix the flour, baking powder and salt in a large bowl. Cut in the shortening, using a pastry blender or crisscrossing 2 knives, until mixture looks like fine crumbs.

3 Stir in the sour cream and chives until the dough leaves the side of the bowl and forms a ball.

4 Sprinkle a clean surface, such as a kitchen counter or breadboard, with a small amount of flour. Place the dough on the lightly floured surface. Gently roll dough in flour to coat all sides. Shape the dough into a ball. Knead the dough by curving your fingers around and folding dough toward you, then pushing it away with the heels of your hands, using a quick rocking motion. Repeat 10 times, turning dough each time.

5 Roll the dough with a rolling pin into a 12×8-inch rectangle. Cut the rectangle crosswise into 12 breadsticks, each about 1 inch wide.

6 Carefully pick up both ends of each breadstick, and twist the dough. Place breadsticks about 1 inch apart on the ungreased cookie sheet. Brush the breadsticks lightly with the margarine. Sprinkle with the poppy seed.

7 Bake 10 to 12 minutes or until golden brown. Immediately remove breadsticks from the cookie sheet to a wire cooling rack. Serve warm.

1 Breadstick: Calories 195 (Calories from Fat 115); Fat 13g (Saturated 6g); Cholesterol 20mg; Sodium 240mg; Carbohydrate 17g (Dietary Fiber 1g); Protein 3g **% Daily Value:** Vitamin A 4%; Vitamin C 0%; Calcium 10%; Iron 6% **Diet Exchanges:** 1 Starch, 2 1/2 Fat

Tip **FOR A FLAVOR TWIST,** get creative with other toppers on these breadsticks. Instead of sprinkling with poppy seed, try sesame seed, grated Parmesan cheese or coarse salt.

Rolling Dough

Use a rolling pin to roll the dough into a 12×8-inch rectangle.

Cutting and Shaping Breadsticks

Use a sharp knife to cut rectangle of dough crosswise into 12 breadsticks, each about 1 inch wide. Carefully pick up both ends of each breadstick, and twist dough.

Desserts

Rich Chocolate Fudge Cake

MAKES 12 servings • **BAKE** 35 minutes • **COOL** 1 hour

INGREDIENTS

Essential Equipment:
9-inch round pan; medium saucepan (about 2-quart size); electric mixer or hand beater

Shortening to grease pan

1 cup semisweet chocolate chips

1/2 cup (1 stick) margarine or butter

1/2 cup all-purpose flour

4 eggs, separated into yolks and whites

1/2 cup sugar

1/2 cup semisweet chocolate chips

2 tablespoons margarine or butter

2 tablespoons corn syrup

DIRECTIONS

1 Heat the oven to 325°. Grease the bottom and side of the round pan with the shortening.

2 Heat 1 cup chocolate chips and 1/2 cup margarine in the saucepan over low heat, stirring constantly, until chocolate is melted. Cool 5 minutes.

3 Stir the flour into the melted chocolate mixture until smooth. Stir in the egg yolks until well blended

4 Beat the egg whites in a large bowl with the electric mixer on high speed until foamy. Beat in the sugar, 1 tablespoon at a time, until soft peaks form. Soft peaks should be rounded or curled when beaters are lifted from bowl, while still being moist and glossy.

5 Gently stir the chocolate mixture into the egg whites. Spread in the greased pan. Bake 30 to 35 minutes or until a thin crust forms and a toothpick inserted in the center comes out clean.

6 Place the pan on a wire cooling rack, and cool 10 minutes. Run a knife around the edge of the pan to loosen cake. Remove the cake from the pan. To remove cake from pan, place wire cooling rack upside down onto cake. Using pot holders, turn rack and pan over, and remove pan. Place another rack upside down on bottom of cake, and turn racks and cake over so cake is right side up. Trim top edges of cake where crust overhangs side. Cool cake completely, about 1 hour.

7 Place the cooled cake on a serving plate, using a second plate and the method in step 6.

8 Heat 1/2 cup chocolate chips, 2 tablespoons margarine and the corn syrup in the saucepan over low heat, stirring constantly, until chocolate is melted and mixture is smooth.

9 Spread the melted chocolate mixture over the top of the cake, allowing some of it to drizzle down side of cake.

1 Serving: Calories 360 (Calories from Fat 205); Fat 23g (Saturated 9g); Cholesterol 75mg; Sodium 150mg; Carbohydrate 36g (Dietary Fiber 2g); Protein 4g **% Daily Value:** Vitamin A 14%; Vitamin C 0%; Calcium 2%; Iron 6% **Diet Exchanges:** Not Recommended

Tip **TO ADD A LITTLE PIZZAZZ,** drizzle the top of the glazed cake with melted white baking chips. Melt 1/4 cup white baking chips and 1 teaspoon shortening in a small saucepan over low heat, stirring constantly, until chips are melted and mixture is smooth. Drizzle over cake.

Beating Egg Whites

Beat egg whites in a large bowl with electric mixer on high speed until foamy. Beat in sugar, 1 tablespoon at a time, until soft peaks form. Peaks should be rounded or curled when beaters are lifted from bowl, while still being moist and glossy.

Vanilla Cheesecake with Cherry-Berry Topping

MAKES 8 servings • **BAKE** 40 minutes • **COOL** 30 minutes • **REFRIGERATE** 3 hours

INGREDIENTS | DIRECTIONS

Essential Equipment:
9-inch pie pan; electric mixer or hand beater

Graham Cracker Crust (below)

2 packages (8 ounces each) cream cheese at room temperature

1/2 cup sugar

1/2 teaspoon vanilla

2 eggs

Cherry-Berry Topping (below)

Graham Cracker Crust

1 1/2 cups graham cracker crumbs (about 20 squares)

1/4 cup sugar

1/3 cup margarine or butter, melted

Cherry-Berry Topping

1 pint (2 cups) strawberries

1 can (21 ounces) cherry pie filling

1 teaspoon lemon juice

1 Heat the oven to 325°. Make Graham Cracker Crust (below). While crust is chilling, continue with the recipe.

2 Beat the cream cheese in a large bowl with the electric mixer on medium speed until smooth. Gradually beat in the sugar and vanilla until smooth. Beat in the eggs, one at a time.

3 Pour the cheesecake mixture into the crust, and spread evenly. Bake about 40 minutes or until filling is set. Place pan on a wire cooling rack. Cool 30 minutes.

4 Cover the cheesecake and refrigerate at least 3 hours but no longer than 48 hours. While the cheesecake is chilling, make Cherry-Berry Topping (below).

5 Serve the cheesecake with the topping. Store covered in refrigerator.

GRAHAM CRACKER CRUST Mix the cracker crumbs, sugar and margarine. Press firmly and evenly against bottom and side of the ungreased pie pan. Cover and refrigerate about 30 minutes or until firm.

CHERRY-BERRY TOPPING Rinse the strawberries with cool water, and pat dry with paper towels. Cut out the hull, or "cap," with the point of a paring knife. Cut the strawberries lengthwise into slices. Mix the strawberries, pie filling and lemon juice in a medium bowl. Cover and refrigerate topping until you are ready to serve the cheesecake.

1 Serving: Calories 450 (Calories from Fat 295); Fat 31g (Saturated 18g); Cholesterol 135mg; Sodium 360mg; Carbohydrate 52g (Dietary Fiber 2g); Protein 8g **% Daily Value:** Vitamin A 34%; Vitamin C 28%; Calcium 8%; Iron 8% **Diet Exchanges:** Not Recommended

TURTLE CHEESECAKE Omit Cherry-Berry Topping. Drizzle 2 tablespoons each of caramel topping and hot fudge topping, warmed, over the baked and chilled cheesecake. Sprinkle with chopped pecans.

IF YOU DON'T HAVE a package of graham cracker crumbs, you can use 20 graham cracker squares and crush them yourself. Place a few crackers at a time in a plastic bag. Seal the bag, and crush crackers into fine crumbs with a rolling pin or bottle.

FOR AN INFORMAL PARTY WITH FRIENDS, try a dessert potluck. Invite your guests to prepare and share their favorite sweet treat. You can supply the beverages, dishes and one or two desserts, as well.

Removing Hull from Strawberries

Cut out the hull, or "cap," with the point of a paring knife.

Caramelized-Peach Shortcakes

MAKES 6 servings • **COOK** 10 minutes • **COOL** 10 minutes

INGREDIENTS

Essential Equipment:
10-inch skillet; electric mixer or hand beater

2 medium peaches

3 tablespoons margarine
 or butter

1/4 cup packed brown sugar

2 tablespoons amaretto or
 1 teaspoon almond extract

1 cup raspberries

Amaretto Whipped Cream
 (below)

6 sponge shortcake cups

Sliced almonds, if desired

Amaretto Whipped Cream

1 cup whipping (heavy) cream

2 tablespoons packed brown
 sugar

1 teaspoon cornstarch

1 teaspoon amaretto or
 1/4 teaspoon almond extract

DIRECTIONS

1 Cut each peach lengthwise in half around the pit. Twist the peach halves in opposite directions, and remove pit. Peel the peach halves, and cut into 1/4-inch slices.

2 Melt the margarine in the skillet over medium-low heat 1 to 2 minutes. Stir in the brown sugar. Cook 2 minutes, stirring constantly.

3 Stir in the amaretto and peaches. Cook 3 to 4 minutes, stirring occasionally, until peaches are coated with brown sugar mixture.

4 Remove the skillet from the heat, and cool peach mixture 10 minutes. Gently stir in the raspberries.

5 Just before serving, make Amaretto Whipped Cream (below). Top each shortcake cup with peach-raspberry mixture and whipped cream. Sprinkle with almonds.

AMARETTO WHIPPED CREAM Beat the whipping cream, brown sugar, cornstarch and amaretto in a chilled medium bowl with the electric mixer on high speed until stiff peaks form.

1 Serving: Calories 320 (Calories from Fat 170); Fat 19g (Saturated 9g); Cholesterol 80mg; Sodium 105mg; Carbohydrate 36g (Dietary Fiber 2g); Protein 3g **% Daily Value:** Vitamin A 20%; Vitamin C 14%; Calcium 4%; Iron 4% **Diet Exchanges:** Not Recommended

Tip **TO EASE LAST-MINUTE PARTY PREPARATIONS,** make the Amaretto Whipped Cream up to 24 hours in advance. Cover and refrigerate until serving time.

Tip **THE WHIPPING CREAM** will beat up more easily if the bowl and beaters for the mixer are chilled in the freezer or refrigerator for 15 to 20 minutes before beating.

Cutting a Peach

Cut the peach lengthwise in half around the pit. Twist peach halves in opposite directions, and remove pit. Peel the peach halves, and cut into 1/4-inch slices.

Fresh Berry Cobbler

MAKES 6 servings • **BAKE** 15 minutes

INGREDIENTS

DIRECTIONS

Essential Equipment:
medium saucepan (about 2-quart size);
2-quart casserole

1/2 cup sugar

1 tablespoon cornstarch

4 cups raspberries or blueberries

2 tablespoons water

1 teaspoon lemon juice

1 cup Original Bisquick®

1/4 cup milk

1 tablespoon sugar

1 tablespoon margarine or butter, melted

1 Heat the oven to 425°.

2 Mix the 1/2 cup sugar and the cornstarch in the saucepan. Stir in the raspberries, water and lemon juice. Heat to boiling over medium heat, stirring constantly. Continue boiling 1 minute, stirring constantly. Pour berry mixture into the ungreased casserole.

3 Stir the Bisquick, milk, 1 tablespoon sugar and the melted margarine just until blended and a dough forms. Drop the dough by 6 spoonfuls onto the hot berry mixture.

4 Bake about 15 minutes or until the berry mixture is bubbly and the topping is light brown.

5 Place the casserole on a wire cooling rack. Cool slightly. Serve warm.

1 Serving: Calories 205 (Calories from Fat 45); Fat 5g (Saturated 1g); Cholesterol 0mg; Sodium 310mg; Carbohydrate 39g (Dietary Fiber 1g); Protein 2g **% Daily Value:** Vitamin A 2%; Vitamin C 4%; Calcium 4%; Iron 4% **Diet Exchanges:** 1 Starch, 1 1/2 Fruit, 1 Fat

STORE RASPBERRIES AND BLUEBERRIES in their original container or spread them out in a dish or pan lined with paper towels. Raspberries especially are very fragile, so plan to use them within a day or so to avoid moldy berries.

FOR A SPLASHING FINISH, pass a pitcher of whipping (heavy) cream, half-and-half or eggnog, when it is available, to pour over bowls of warm cobbler. Sprinkle a little ground cinnamon or nutmeg on top for just a hint of spiciness.

Dropping Dough onto Berry Mixture

Drop dough by 6 spoonfuls onto hot berry mixture.

Cinnamon-Apple Crisp

MAKES 6 servings • **BAKE** 35 minutes

INGREDIENTS

Essential Equipment:
8-inch square pan or 9-inch round pan

Shortening to grease pan

6 medium tart cooking apples, such as Granny Smith, Rome Beauty or Greening

1 tablespoon lemon juice

1 teaspoon ground cinnamon

1 cup quick-cooking or old-fashioned oats

1 cup packed brown sugar

3/4 cup all-purpose flour

1/2 cup margarine or butter at room temperature

Ice cream or cream, if desired

DIRECTIONS

1 Heat the oven to 375°. Peel the apples if desired. Cut each apple into fourths. Cut the core and seeds from the center of each fourth. Cut each fourth into slices. You will need about 6 cups of apple slices.

2 Spread the apples in the pan. Drizzle the lemon juice over the apples. Sprinkle with cinnamon.

3 Mix the oats, brown sugar, flour and margarine with a fork. The mixture will be crumbly. Sprinkle this mixture evenly over the apples.

4 Bake 30 to 35 minutes or until the topping is golden brown and the apples are tender when pierced with a fork.

5 Place the pan on a wire cooling rack. Cool slightly. Serve warm with ice cream.

1 Serving: Calories 450 (Calories from Fat 145); Fat 16g (Saturated 10g); Cholesterol 40mg; Sodium 120mg; Carbohydrate 78g (Dietary Fiber 6g); Protein 4g **% Daily Value:** Vitamin A 14%; Vitamin C 6%; Calcium 6%; Iron 12% **Diet Exchanges:** Not Recommended

Tip **TO SERVE A CROWD OF 12,** double all of the ingredients and bake in a 13×9-inch rectangular pan about 40 minutes.

Tip **FOR A FUN WAY TO SERVE** this yummy dessert, spoon the crisp into individual shallow bowls and top each serving with a big scoop of ice cream. For a festive finish, sprinkle ground cinnamon around the edge of each bowl.

Slicing an Apple

Cut the apple into fourths. Cut the core and seeds from the center of each fourth. Cut each fourth into slices.

Mixed-Fruit Tart with Coconut Crust

MAKES 12 servings • **BAKE** 25 minutes • **COOL** 30 minutes

INGREDIENTS

Essential Equipment:
12-inch pizza pan; small saucepan (about 1-quart size)

Coconut Crust (below)

1 package (8 ounces) cream cheese at room temperature

3/4 cup marshmallow creme

3 cups assorted fruit (blueberries, raspberries or sliced kiwifruit, nectarines or strawberries)

1/4 cup apricot preserves

1 tablespoon water

Coconut Crust

1 cup all-purpose flour

6 tablespoons margarine or butter at room temperature

2 tablespoons sugar

1 egg yolk

3/4 cup shredded coconut

DIRECTIONS

1 Heat the oven to 350°. Bake and cool Coconut Crust (below).

2 Mix the cream cheese and marshmallow creme until smooth. Spread over cooled crust.

3 Arrange the fruit on the cream cheese mixture.

4 Heat the apricot preserves and water in the saucepan over low heat, stirring occasionally, until preserves are melted; cool slightly. Spoon over fruit.

5 To serve, cut tart into wedges. Store covered in refrigerator.

COCONUT CRUST Mix the flour, margarine, sugar and egg yolk in a small bowl, using a pastry blender or fork, until a soft dough forms. Stir in the coconut. Press the dough firmly in the ungreased pizza pan to the edge of the pan. Prick the crust all over with a fork so the crust won't puff up. Bake 20 to 25 minutes or until golden. Cool completely, about 30 minutes.

1 Serving: Calories 250 (Calories from Fat 135); Fat 15g (Saturated 7g); Cholesterol 40mg; Sodium 160mg; Carbohydrate 28g (Dietary Fiber 2g); Protein 3g **% Daily Value:** Vitamin A 14%; Vitamin C 14%; Calcium 2%; Iron 6% **Diet Exchanges:** 1 Starch, 1 Fruit, 2 1/2 Fat

Tip **FOR A CASUAL GET-TOGETHER,** serve this tart right from the pizza pan. For a more elegant presentation, you may want to transfer the cooled crust to a large round serving platter before topping it with the cream cheese mixture and fruit.

Pressing Coconut Crust Dough in Pan

Press dough firmly in ungreased pizza pan to the edge of the pan.

Praline Pumpkin Dessert

MAKES 12 servings • **BAKE** 1 hour

INGREDIENTS

DIRECTIONS

Essential Equipment:
13×9-inch rectangular pan; electric mixer or hand beater

Shortening to grease pan

1 can (15 ounces) pumpkin
(not pumpkin pie mix)

1 can (12 ounces) evaporated
milk

3 eggs

1 cup granulated sugar

4 teaspoons pumpkin pie spice

1 package (1 pound 2.25
ounces) golden vanilla cake
mix with pudding

1 1/2 cups chopped pecans or
walnuts

3/4 cup (1 1/2 sticks) margarine
or butter, melted

Sweetened Whipped Cream
(below) or 1 1/2 cups frozen
(thawed) whipped topping

Additional pumpkin pie spice,
if desired

Sweetened Whipped Cream

3/4 cup whipping (heavy)
cream

2 tablespoons granulated or
powdered sugar

1 Heat the oven to 350°. Grease the bottom and sides of the rectangular pan with the shortening.

2 Beat the pumpkin, milk, eggs, sugar and 4 teaspoons pumpkin pie spice in a medium bowl with a wire whisk until smooth. Pour into the greased pan.

3 Sprinkle the dry cake mix over the pumpkin mixture. Sprinkle with the pecans. Pour the melted margarine evenly over top of the dessert.

4 Bake 50 to 60 minutes or until a knife inserted in the center comes out clean. Place pan on a wire cooling rack. Cool slightly.

5 Just before serving, make Sweetened Whipped Cream (below). To serve, cut dessert into 4 rows by 3 rows. Serve warm or chilled with whipped cream. Sprinkle with additional pumpkin pie spice. Cover and refrigerate any remaining dessert.

SWEETENED WHIPPED CREAM Beat the whipping cream and sugar in a chilled medium bowl with the electric mixer on high speed until stiff peaks form. The whipping cream will beat up more easily if the bowl and beaters for the mixer are chilled in the freezer or refrigerator for 15 to 20 minutes before beating.

1 Serving: Calories 510 (Calories from Fat 250); Fat 28g (Saturated 5g); Cholesterol 60mg; Sodium 510mg; Carbohydrate 61g (Dietary Fiber 3g); Protein 7g **% Daily Value:** Vitamin A 98%; Vitamin C 2%; Calcium 16%; Iron 0% **Diet Exchanges:** Not Recommended

Tip TO SIMPLIFY LAST-MINUTE PREPARATIONS, whip up this dessert a day or two ahead of your meal. Cover the dessert with plastic wrap and refrigerate up to 48 hours.

Tip FOR FUN FALL PLACE CARDS, use mini pumpkins or small gourds. Write name on tag and tie to pumpkin or gourd stem with ribbon or raffia.

Beating Whipping Cream

Beat whipping cream and sugar in a chilled medium bowl with electric mixer on high speed until stiff peaks form.

Tiramisu-Toffee Dessert

MAKES 12 servings • **REFRIGERATE** 1 hour

INGREDIENTS

Essential Equipment:
*11×7-inch rectangular pan; electric mixer
or hand beater*

1 package (10 3/4 ounces)
   frozen pound cake, thawed

3/4 cup strongly brewed
   coffee or espresso at
   room temperature

1 cup sugar

1/2 cup chocolate-flavored
   syrup

1 package (8 ounces)
   mascarpone cheese or
   cream cheese at room
   temperature

2 cups whipping (heavy) cream

2 bars (1.4 ounces each)
   chocolate-covered toffee
   candy

DIRECTIONS

1 Cut the cake crosswise into 9 slices. Arrange cake slices on the bottom of the ungreased rectangular pan, cutting cake slices if necessary to cover bottom of pan. Drizzle the coffee over the cake slices.

2 Beat the sugar, chocolate syrup and mascarpone cheese in a large bowl with the electric mixer on medium speed until smooth. Add the whipping cream. Beat on medium speed until light and fluffy. Spread the cheese mixture over the cake slices.

3 Chop the candy into small pieces. Sprinkle chopped candy over top of dessert.

4 Cover and refrigerate at least 1 hour to set dessert and blend flavors but no longer than 24 hours.

1 Serving: Calories 430 (Calories from Fat 250); Fat 28g (Saturated 16g); Cholesterol 95mg; Sodium 130mg; Carbohydrate 42g (Dietary Fiber 1g); Protein 4g **% Daily Value:** Vitamin A 16%; Vitamin C 0%; Calcium 6%; Iron 0% **Diet Exchanges:** Not Recommended

Arranging Cake Slices

Arrange cake slices on bottom of ungreased pan, cutting cake slices if necessary to cover bottom of pan.

Party Ice-Cream Cake

MAKES 16 servings • **BAKE** 33 minutes • **COOL** 1 hour • **FREEZE** 4 hours

INGREDIENTS

Essential Equipment:
13×9-inch rectangular pan; electric mixer or hand beater

Cooking spray to grease pan

1 package (1 pound 2.25 ounces) party rainbow chip cake mix

1 1/4 cups water

1/3 cup vegetable oil

3 eggs

1 quart ice cream or frozen yogurt (any flavor), slightly softened

Candy decorations, if desired

DIRECTIONS

1 Heat the oven to 350°. Spray just the bottom of the pan with the cooking spray.

2 Beat the cake mix, water, oil and eggs in a large bowl with the electric mixer on low speed 2 minutes. Pour batter into the sprayed pan.

3 Bake 28 to 33 minutes or until a toothpick inserted in the center comes out clean. Place pan on a wire cooling rack. Cool completely, about 1 hour.

4 Spread the ice cream over the top of the cooled cake. Immediately cover and freeze at least 4 hours or until firm.

5 Just before serving, top the cake with the candy decorations. Cover and freeze any remaining cake.

1 Serving: Calories 265 (Calories from Fat 90); Fat 10g (Saturated 2g); Cholesterol 0mg; Sodium 300mg; Carbohydrate 40g (Dietary Fiber 0g); Protein 4g **% Daily Value:** Vitamin A 0%; Vitamin C 0%; Calcium 12%; Iron 4% **Diet Exchanges:** 1 1/2 Starch, 1 Fruit, 2 Fat

Tip **FEEL FREE TO USE YOUR FAVORITE FLAVOR** of ice cream, frozen yogurt, or sherbet to top the cake. Instead of candy decorations, you can use colored sugars, edible flowers, sliced fresh fruit or ice-cream topping for a special finish.

Tip **SO THE FROZEN CAKE WON'T BE TOO HARD TO CUT,** remove it from the freezer 20 to 30 minutes before serving.

A Special Touch Floral Gift Vase

Vase (8 to 10 inches high)
20-inch-square piece lightweight fabric
About 1 1/2 yards 1 1/2-inch-wide ribbon
Fresh flowers to coordinate with fabric and ribbon

1 Place vase on center of fabric. Wrap fabric around vase by pulling up the four corners first and then the sides.

2 Wrap ribbon around neck of vase to secure fabric; tie bow.

3 Fill vase with water. Arrange flowers in vase.

Tip: If fabric is very thin, you can use spray starch to stiffen it. Let fabric dry before wrapping.

Frosty Key Lime Pie

MAKES 8 servings • **FREEZE** 6 hours • **LET STAND** 5 minutes

INGREDIENTS

Essential Equipment:
9-inch pie pan; electric mixer or hand beater

Crunchy Pretzel Crust (below)
 or 1 package (6 ounces)
 ready-to-use graham cracker
 pie crust

2 packages (8 ounces each)
 cream cheese at room
 temperature

1 teaspoon grated lime peel

1/2 cup Key lime juice or
 regular lime juice

1 can (14 ounces) sweetened
 condensed milk

Few drops of green food color,
 if desired

Sweetened Whipped Cream
 (below) or 1 cup frozen
 (thawed) whipped topping

Crunchy Pretzel Crust

3 cups small pretzel twists
 (about 40)

1/2 cup (1 stick) margarine or
 butter, melted

1/4 cup granulated sugar

Sweetened Whipped Cream

1/2 cup whipping (heavy)
 cream

1 tablespoon granulated or
 powdered sugar

DIRECTIONS

1 Make Crunchy Pretzel Crust (below). While crust is chilling, continue with the recipe.

2 Beat the cream cheese, lime peel, lime juice, milk and food color in a large bowl with the electric mixer on medium speed about 1 minute or until smooth.

3 Pour the lime mixture into the crust. Cover and freeze about 6 hours or until the filling is firm.

4 Let the pie stand at room temperature about 5 minutes before cutting into slices. Make Sweetened Whipped Cream (below); serve with pie. Cover and freeze any remaining pie.

CRUNCHY PRETZEL CRUST Place a few pretzels at a time in a plastic bag. Seal the bag, and crush pretzels into fine crumbs with a rolling pin. You should have 1 1/4 cups of crumbs. Mix the crumbs, margarine and sugar in a medium bowl. Press firmly and evenly against bottom and side of the pie pan. Cover and refrigerate about 30 minutes or until firm.

SWEETENED WHIPPED CREAM Beat the whipping cream and sugar in a chilled medium bowl with the electric mixer on high speed until stiff peaks form.

1 Serving: Calories 590 (Calories from Fat 335); Fat 37g (Saturated 18g); Cholesterol 85mg; Sodium 570mg; Carbohydrate 53g (Dietary Fiber 0g); Protein 11g **% Daily Value:** Vitamin A 38%; Vitamin C 10%; Calcium 24%; Iron 6% **Diet Exchanges:** Not Recommended

Tip **FOR A SOFTER TEXTURE,** cover and refrigerate the pie for 6 to 8 hours instead of freezing it.

Tip **THE WHIPPING CREAM** will beat up more easily if the bowl and beaters for the mixer are chilled in the freezer or refrigerator for 15 to 20 minutes before beating.

Crushing Pretzels

Place a few pretzels at a time in a plastic bag. Seal the bag, and crush pretzels into fine crumbs with a rolling pin.

Chocolate-Mint Mousse

MAKES 8 servings • **FREEZE** 4 hours

INGREDIENTS

Essential Equipment:
electric mixer or hand beater;
9-inch square pan

2 cups whipping (heavy) cream

1/4 cup crème de menthe

1/2 cup chocolate-flavored syrup

Baking cocoa, if desired

Chopped rectangular chocolate mints or crushed chocolate wafer cookies, if desired

DIRECTIONS

1 Beat the whipping cream in a chilled large bowl with the electric mixer on high speed until stiff peaks form. The whipping cream will beat up more easily if the bowl and beaters for the mixer are chilled in the freezer or refrigerator for 15 to 20 minutes before beating.

2 Gently pour the crème de menthe and chocolate syrup over the whipped cream. To fold ingredients together, use a rubber spatula to cut down vertically through the whipped cream, then slide the spatula across the bottom of the bowl and up the side, turning the whipped cream over. Rotate the bowl one-fourth turn, and repeat this down-across-up motion. Continue mixing in this way just until ingredients are blended.

3 Spread the whipped cream mixture into the ungreased square pan. Cover and freeze at least 4 hours or until mousse is firm.

4 Sprinkle the cocoa over the top of the mousse. If you have a small strainer, place the cocoa in the strainer and shake it over the mousse. Otherwise, shake the cocoa from a spoon. To serve, cut mousse into 4 rows by 2 rows. Garnish with chopped candies. Cover and freeze any remaining mousse.

1 Serving: Calories 240 (Calories from Fat 170); Fat 19g (Saturated 12g); Cholesterol 65mg; Sodium 40mg; Carbohydrate 15g (Dietary Fiber 0g); Protein 2g **% Daily Value:** Vitamin A 14%; Vitamin C 0%; Calcium 4%; Iron 2% **Diet Exchanges:** 1 Starch, 3 1/2 Fat

MOCHA MOUSSE Substitute coffee-flavored liqueur for the crème de menthe. Omit the crushed candies. Garnish each serving with a chocolate-covered coffee bean.

FROZEN MOUSSE PIE Spread the whipped cream mixture in a ready-to-use chocolate-flavored pie crust instead of spreading in the pan. Freeze as directed.

Tip **THE CRÈME DE MENTHE KEEPS** this dessert from freezing totally solid. That's why the mousse can be served immediately after taking it from the freezer.

Tip **COVER THE PAN TIGHTLY** with a double layer of heavy-duty aluminum foil and this dessert will keep up to 1 month in the freezer. Perfect for those unexpected holiday guests!

Folding Ingredients into Whipped Cream

To fold ingredients together, use a rubber spatula to cut down vertically through the whipped cream, then slide the spatula across the bottom of the bowl and up the side, turning the whipped cream over. Rotate the bowl one-fourth turn, and repeat this down-across-up motion.

Raspberry Custard Cream

MAKES 4 servings

INGREDIENTS

Essential Equipment:
electric mixer or hand beater

2 containers (6 ounces each) raspberry yogurt (1 1/3 cups)

1 package (4-serving size) vanilla instant pudding and pie filling mix

1 cup whipping (heavy) cream

1 cup fresh or frozen (thawed) raspberries

Additional fresh raspberries for garnish, if desired

DIRECTIONS

1 Beat the yogurt and dry pudding mix in a medium bowl with the electric mixer on low speed 30 seconds.

2 Add the whipping cream to the pudding mixture. Beat on medium speed 3 to 5 minutes, scraping bowl occasionally, until soft peaks form. Soft peaks should be rounded or curled when beaters are lifted from bowl.

3 Gently stir 1 cup raspberries into custard.

4 Spoon custard mixture into 4 stemmed glasses, dessert dishes or small bowls. Garnish with fresh raspberries. Store covered in refrigerator.

1 Serving: Calories 370 (Calories from Fat 180); Fat 20g (Saturated 12g); Cholesterol 70mg; Sodium 430mg; Carbohydrate 45g (Dietary Fiber 2g); Protein 5g **% Daily Value:** Vitamin A 14%; Vitamin C 14%; Calcium 18%; Iron 2% **Diet Exchanges:** Not Recommended

ORANGE-BLUEBERRY CUSTARD CREAM Substitute orange yogurt for the raspberry yogurt. Omit raspberries. Stir in 1 cup blueberries.

LEMON-STRAWBERRY CUSTARD CREAM Substitute lemon yogurt for the raspberry yogurt. Omit raspberries. Stir in 1 cup sliced strawberries.

Tip **ADD VARIETY** to this elegant dessert by using a mix of fresh raspberries, blueberries and strawberries. Wondering what to serve it in? Wine or juice glasses, sundae dishes or clear small bowls all will show off the pretty fruit and custard. And even if they don't match, it will still look great.

A Special Touch — Intertwined Pillars

2 pillar candles (about 8 inches high)
About 1 yard colored string, ribbon or raffia
Heart button or charm
1 sheet (8×10 inches) clear glass (from picture frame)
Adhesive tape
4 round napkin rings

1 Wrap candles together with string. Tie ends of string; attach button.

2 Clean glass; tape edges if sharp.

3 Place glass on napkin rings, making sure 1 ring is under each corner of glass. Arrange candles on glass.

Tip: *Color coordinate the tape to match your color scheme. You can use natural masking tape for cream or tan colors or colored tapes for others. You can also color the tape with permanent markers.*

Milk Chocolate Fondue

MAKES 8 servings

INGREDIENTS

Essential Equipment:
*medium saucepan (about 2-quart size);
fondue pot or heatproof serving bowl*

1 package (11 1/2 ounces) milk chocolate chips (2 cups)

2/3 cup half-and-half

2 tablespoons liqueur (almond, cherry, coffee, hazelnut, Irish cream, orange or raspberry), if desired

Dippers (below)

Dippers

Angel food cake cubes

Apple wedges

Banana slices

Brownie cubes

Grapes

Kiwifruit pieces

Mandarin orange segments

Maraschino cherries

Marshmallows

Miniature cream puffs

Pineapple cubes

Pound cake cubes

Strawberries

DIRECTIONS

1 Heat the chocolate chips and half-and-half in the saucepan over low heat, stirring constantly, until chocolate is melted and mixture is smooth. Remove the saucepan from the heat.

2 Stir in the liqueur. Pour the mixture into the fondue pot and keep warm over low heat.

3 Spear the Dippers with wooden picks or fondue forks, and dip into fondue. If the fondue becomes too thick, stir in a small amount of half-and-half.

1 Serving: Calories 255 (Calories from Fat 135); Fat 15g (Saturated 9g); Cholesterol 15mg; Sodium 45mg; Carbohydrate 27g (Dietary Fiber 1g); Protein 4g **% Daily Value:** Vitamin A 4%; Vitamin C 0%; Calcium 10%; Iron 2% **Diet Exchanges:** 1 Starch, 1 Fruit, 2 1/2 Fat

DARK CHOCOLATE FONDUE Substitute 1 package (12 ounces) semisweet chocolate chips for the milk chocolate chips.

WHITE ALMOND FONDUE Substitute 12 ounces vanilla-flavored candy coating (almond bark), chopped, for the milk chocolate chips and decrease half-and-half to 1/3 cup.

Tip **TO KEEP FRUIT FROM DARKENING,** dip apples and bananas into lemon juice after slicing them.

A Special Touch Screen Luminaria

8×5-inch and 15×10-inch rectangles fine metal mesh
  window screening
Glass votive (about 2 1/2 inches high) and glass
  cylinder (about 6 inches high) candleholders
Votive (about 2 inches high) and pillar
  (about 4 to 5 inches high) candles
Colored string or thin ribbon

1 Fold over 1/2 inch on 1 short edge and 1 long edge of each
small rectangle of screening. Fold over 1 inch on both short
edges and 1 long edge of each large rectangle of screening.

2 Mold each rectangle of screening around candleholder
to form cylinder shape; remove candleholder. Staple short
edges of screening together, tucking the unfolded short
edge into the corner of the long folded edge.

3 Add votive candles to votive candleholders; place small
luminaria screen, folded edge up, over candleholders. Add
taller candles to cylinder candleholders; place large luminaria screen, folded edge up, over candleholders. Tie
string around centers of luminarias.

Tip: Window screening is sold in rolls at hardware stores.
Cut screening to desired size with scissors or wire cutters.

White Chocolate–Dipped Strawberries

MAKES 18 to 24 strawberries • **REFRIGERATE** 30 minutes

INGREDIENTS

Essential Equipment:
cookie sheet; 2 small saucepans
(about 1-quart size)

**18 to 24 large strawberries
with leaves**

**1 bag (12 ounces) white baking
chips (2 cups)**

1 tablespoon shortening

**1/2 cup semisweet chocolate
chips**

1 teaspoon shortening

DIRECTIONS

1 Cover the cookie sheet with waxed paper.

2 Rinse the strawberries with cool water, and pat dry with paper towels.

3 Heat the white baking chips and 1 tablespoon shortening in the saucepan over low heat, stirring constantly, until the chips are melted.

4 For each strawberry, poke a fork into the stem end, and dip three-fourths of the way into the melted white chips, leaving the top of the strawberry and leaves uncoated. Place dipped strawberries on the waxed paper-covered cookie sheet.

5 Heat the semisweet chocolate chips and 1 teaspoon shortening in another small saucepan over low heat, stirring constantly, until chocolate chips are melted. (Or place chocolate chips and shortening in a small microwavable bowl. Microwave uncovered on Medium 1 minute; stir. Microwave 2 to 3 minutes longer, until mixture can be stirred smooth.)

6 Drizzle the melted chocolate chips over the dipped strawberries, using a small spoon. Refrigerate uncovered about 30 minutes or until coating is set.

1 Strawberry: Calories 125 (Calories from Fat 65); Fat 8g (Saturated 5g); Cholesterol 5mg; Sodium 15mg; Carbohydrate 15g (Dietary Fiber 1g); Protein 1g **% Daily Value:** Vitamin A 0%; Vitamin C 16%; Calcium 4%; Iron 0% **Diet Exchanges:** 1 Fruit, 1 1/2 Fat

DOUBLE CHOCOLATE-DIPPED STRAWBERRIES Substitute 1 package (12 ounces) semisweet or milk chocolate chips for the white baking chips.

Tip **RINSE STRAWBERRIES** just before you are ready to use them. If you wash and then refrigerate the strawberries ahead of time, they will turn mushy.

Dipping Strawberries

For each strawberry, poke a fork into the stem end, and dip three-fourths of the way into the melted white chips, leaving the top of the strawberry and leaves uncoated.

Luscious Lemon Bars

MAKES 16 bars • **BAKE** 50 minutes • **COOL** 1 hour

INGREDIENTS

DIRECTIONS

Essential Equipment:
8- or 9-inch square pan; electric mixer or hand beater

1 cup all-purpose flour

1/2 cup (1 stick) margarine or
    butter at room temperature

1/4 cup powdered sugar

1 cup granulated sugar

2 teaspoons grated lemon peel,
    if desired

2 tablespoons lemon juice

1/2 teaspoon baking powder

1/4 teaspoon salt

2 eggs

1 Heat the oven to 350°.

2 Mix the flour, margarine and powdered sugar. Press in the bottom and 1/2 inch up the sides of the ungreased square pan.

3 Bake the crust 20 minutes. While the crust is baking, continue with the recipe.

4 Beat the granulated sugar, lemon peel, lemon juice, baking powder, salt and eggs in a medium bowl with the electric mixer on high speed about 3 minutes or until light and fluffy.

5 Carefully pour the lemon filling over the hot crust.

6 Bake 25 to 30 minutes or until no indentation remains when touched lightly in the center. Place pan on a wire cooling rack. Cool completely, about 1 hour. For bars, cut into 4 rows by 4 rows.

1 Bar: Calories 160 (Calories from Fat 55); Fat 6g (Saturated 1g); Cholesterol 26mg; Sodium 80mg; Carbohydrate 21g (Dietary Fiber 0g); Protein 2g **% Daily Value:** Vitamin A 8%; Vitamin C 0%; Calcium 0%; Iron 2% **Diet Exchanges:** 1 Fruit, 1 Fat

Tip **IF THE DOUGH IS STICKY** when pressing the crust into the pan, try dipping your fingers in a little flour.

Tip **TO DRESS UP** these lemony bars, sprinkle them with a delicate dusting of powdered sugar. Just place a small amount of powdered sugar in a small strainer, and shake it over the pan of cooled lemon bars.

A Special Touch Screen and Lemon Bowl

1 square (14 to 15 inches) fine metal mesh window
  screening
1 square (10 to 11 inches) fine metal mesh window
  screening
1 large white plate (10 or 11 inches in diameter)
1 large white shallow bowl (9 or 10 inches in diameter)
7 or 8 fresh whole lemons
Optional: Whole cloves and star anise

1 Fold over 1 inch on edges of squares of screening so
edges are smooth.

2 Set plate on center of table. Place large screen on
plate; set bowl on top of screen.

3 Place 4 or 5 lemons in bowl. Place small screen over
lemons; top with remaining lemons.

*Optional: You can stud the lemons with whole cloves and
place star anise on screens.*

*Tip: Use any size plate and bowl, and cut the screen into
squares slightly larger than your plate and bowl. Window
screening is sold in rolls at hardware stores. Cut screening
to desired size with scissors or wire cutters.*

Gooey Caramel Brownies

MAKES 48 brownies • **BAKE** 30 minutes • **COOL** 1 hour

INGREDIENTS

Essential Equipment:
13×9-inch rectangular pan;
large saucepan (about 3-quart size);
small saucepan (about 1-quart size)

Shortening to grease pan

2 packages (4 ounces each)
    sweet baking chocolate

1/2 cup (1 stick) margarine or
    butter

1 1/2 cups all-purpose flour

1 cup sugar

1/2 teaspoon baking powder

1/2 teaspoon vanilla

1/4 teaspoon salt

2 eggs

1 package (14 ounces) vanilla
    caramels

1/4 cup milk

1 package (6 ounces) semi-
    sweet chocolate chips (1 cup)

1 cup coarsely chopped nuts,
    if desired

DIRECTIONS

1 Heat the oven to 350°. Grease the bottom and sides of the rectangular pan with the shortening.

2 Heat the sweet baking chocolate and margarine in the large saucepan over low heat, stirring frequently, until chocolate is melted. Remove the saucepan from the heat.

3 Stir the flour, sugar, baking powder, vanilla, salt and eggs into the chocolate mixture until well mixed. Spread the batter in the greased pan. Bake 15 minutes. While the brownies are baking, continue with the recipe.

4 Heat the caramels and milk in the small saucepan over low heat, stirring frequently, until melted and smooth.

5 Remove the brownies from the oven. Spread the caramel mixture over the warm brownies. Sprinkle with the chocolate chips and nuts.

6 Bake 10 to 15 minutes or just until brownies begin to pull away from the sides of the pan. Place pan on a wire cooling rack. Cool completely, about 1 hour. For brownies, cut into 8 rows by 6 rows.

1 Brownie: Calories 130 (Calories from Fat 55); Fat 6g (Saturated 3g); Cholesterol 15mg; Sodium 55mg; Carbohydrate 19g (Dietary Fiber 1g); Protein 1g **% Daily Value:** Vitamin A 2%; Vitamin C 0%; Calcium 2%; Iron 2% **Diet Exchanges:** 1 Starch, 1 Fat

Tip **FOR EASY CUTTING AND SERVING,** line your pan with aluminum foil, leaving edge of foil above rim of pan; grease foil instead of pan with the shortening. The cooled brownies will lift right out, so you can cut them easily.

A Special Touch Cabinet Door Tray

12×15-inch cabinet door
Decorative drawer pulls or handles
1 sheet (8 1/2×11 inches) decorative paper, if desired
Optional: Four 4- or 6-inch fence post end caps

1 Drill holes (if needed) on short sides of door.

2 Attach drawer pulls.

3 Line tray with decorative paper.

Optional: To add height and dimension to your buffet table, place the tray on fence post end caps.

Tip: Cabinet door and fence post end caps are available at hardware stores.

Breakfast and Brunch

Streusel Berry Muffins

MAKES 12 muffins • **BAKE** 25 minutes • **LET STAND** 5 minutes

INGREDIENTS

DIRECTIONS

Essential Equipment:
muffin pan with 12 regular-size muffin cups

Shortening to grease muffin cups

Streusel Topping (below)

1 egg

1/2 cup milk

1/2 cup (1 stick) margarine or butter, melted

1 3/4 cups all-purpose flour

1/4 cup granulated sugar

1/4 cup packed brown sugar

2 teaspoons baking powder

1 1/2 teaspoons grated lemon peel

1 teaspoon ground cinnamon

1/2 teaspoon salt

1 cup raspberries or blackberries

Streusel Topping

1/4 cup packed brown sugar

1/4 cup chopped pecans

2 tablespoons all-purpose flour

1 tablespoon margarine or butter at room temperature

1 teaspoon grated lemon peel

1 Heat the oven to 400°. Grease just the bottoms of the muffin cups with the shortening, or line each cup with a paper baking cup.

2 Make Streusel Topping (below), and set aside.

3 Beat the egg in a large bowl with a fork or wire whisk until yolk and white are well mixed. Stir in the milk and margarine Stir in the flour, granulated sugar, brown sugar, baking powder, lemon peel, cinnamon and salt all at once just until flour is moistened. The batter will be lumpy.

4 Gently stir in the raspberries. Spoon the batter into the greased muffin cups, dividing batter evenly among them.

5 Sprinkle the topping evenly over the muffins. Bake 20 to 25 minutes or until golden brown. Let the muffins stand 5 minutes in the pan. Transfer muffins from the pan to a wire cooling rack. Serve warm or cool.

STREUSEL TOPPING Mix the brown sugar, pecans, flour, margarine and lemon peel with a fork. The mixture will be crumbly.

1 Muffin: Calories 230 (Calories from Fat 100); Fat 11g (Saturated 6g); Cholesterol 40mg; Sodium 250mg; Carbohydrate 31g (Dietary Fiber 1g); Protein 3g **% Daily Value:** Vitamin A 8%; Vitamin C 2%; Calcium 8%; Iron 8% **Diet Exchanges:** 1 Starch, 1 Fruit, 2 Fat

 **BE CAREFUL NOT TO OVERMIX** the batter. If the batter is mixed too much, the muffins will have high peaks instead of being nicely rounded.

 **FOR PRETTY TABLE TOPPER,** float flowers in clear glasses or small bowls, and set on the table at each place setting.

Stirring Raspberries into Muffin Batter

Gently stir raspberries into the muffin batter.

Filling Muffin Cups

Using an ice-cream scoop is an easy way to fill muffin cups with batter.

Lemon–Poppy Seed Scones

MAKES 8 scones • **BAKE** 18 minutes

INGREDIENTS

DIRECTIONS

Essential Equipment:
cookie sheet

1 3/4 cups all-purpose flour

1/4 cup sugar

2 teaspoons baking powder

1/4 teaspoon salt

1/3 cup margarine or butter

Grated peel of 1 medium
  lemon (1 1/2 to 3 teaspoons)

1 tablespoon poppy seed

1 egg

1/4 cup half-and-half

1 Heat the oven to 400°.

2 Mix the flour, sugar, baking powder and salt in a medium bowl. Cut the margarine into the flour mixture, using a pastry blender or crisscrossing 2 knives, until the mixture looks like fine crumbs.

3 Stir in the lemon peel, poppy seed, egg and half-and-half just until mixed and a dough forms. If the dough mixture is not completely moistened, stir in an additional 1 to 2 tablespoons half-and-half.

4 Sprinkle a clean surface, such as a kitchen counter or breadboard, with a small amount of flour. Place the dough on the lightly floured surface. Gently roll dough in flour to coat all sides. Shape the dough into a ball. Knead the dough by curving your fingers around and folding dough toward you, then pushing it away with the heels of your hands, using a quick rocking motion. Repeat 10 times, turning dough each time.

5 Place the dough on the ungreased cookie sheet. Pat the dough into an 8-inch circle. Cut dough into 8 wedges, but do not separate.

6 Bake 16 to 18 minutes or until golden brown. Carefully separate the wedges. Transfer the scones from the cookie sheet to a wire cooling rack. Serve warm.

1 Scone: Calories 225 (Calories from Fat 90); Fat 10g (Saturated 6g); Cholesterol 50mg; Sodium 360mg; Carbohydrate 31g (Dietary Fiber 1g); Protein 4g **% Daily Value:** Vitamin A 10%; Vitamin C 0%; Calcium 10%; Iron 10% **Diet Exchanges:** 1 1/2 Starch, 1 Fruit, 1 Fat

GOLDEN ALMOND SCONES Omit lemon peel and poppy seed. Stir in 1/4 cup chopped almonds with the egg and half-and-half in step 3. Brush tops of scones with melted margarine, and sprinkle with sliced almonds before baking.

CHERRY-CHIP SCONES Omit lemon peel and poppy seed. Stir in 1/3 cup chopped dried cherries and 1/3 cup white baking chips with the egg and half-and-half in step 3.

Tip EMBELLISH THESE SCONES by sprinkling with coarse decorating sugar crystals or granulated sugar before you bake them.

Tip SERVE THESE SCONES on a cake platter with clusters of sugared champagne grapes. To sugar the grapes, brush them with a little corn syrup and lightly sprinkle with granulated sugar.

Kneading Dough

Knead the dough by curving your fingers around and folding dough toward you, then pushing it away with the heels of your hands, using a quick rocking motion.

Cutting Dough into Wedges

Use a sharp knife to cut dough into 8 wedges. Do not separate wedges.

Banana-Nut Bread

MAKES 1 loaf (18 slices) • **BAKE** 1 hour 15 minutes • **COOL** 1 hour

INGREDIENTS

DIRECTIONS

Essential Equipment:
9×5-inch loaf pan

Shortening to grease pan

1 1/4 cups sugar

1/2 cup (1 stick) margarine or
    butter at room temperature

2 eggs

3 medium very ripe bananas

1/2 cup buttermilk

1 teaspoon vanilla

2 1/2 cups all-purpose flour

1 teaspoon baking soda

1 teaspoon salt

1 cup chopped nuts

1 Heat the oven to 350°. Grease just the bottom of the loaf pan with the shortening.

2 Mix the sugar and margarine in a large bowl. Stir in the eggs until well mixed.

3 Mash the bananas with a potato masher or fork in a medium bowl. You should have about 1 1/2 cups mashed bananas. Add the bananas, buttermilk and vanilla to the egg mixture. Stir until smooth. Stir in the flour, baking soda and salt all at once just until flour is moistened. Stir in the nuts. Pour the batter into the greased pan.

4 Bake about 1 hour 15 minutes or until a toothpick inserted in the center comes out clean.

5 Place the pan on a wire cooling rack, and cool 5 minutes. Loosen the sides of bread from the pan, using a knife. Carefully tip pan on its side and tap gently to remove bread from pan. Place the bread top side up on a wire cooling rack. Cool completely, about 1 hour, before slicing.

1 Slice: Calories 245 (Calories from Fat 100); Fat 11g (Saturated 2g); Cholesterol 25mg; Sodium 280mg; Carbohydrate 33g (Dietary Fiber 1g); Protein 4g **% Daily Value:** Vitamin A 8%; Vitamin C 0%; Calcium 2%; Iron 6% **Diet Exchanges:** 1 Starch, 1 Fruit, 2 Fat

Tip **TO DO AHEAD,** wrap cooled bread tightly in plastic wrap and store at room temperature up to 4 days or refrigerate up to 10 days.

Mashing Bananas

Use a potato masher or fork to mash bananas.

Vanilla-Glazed Sour Cream Coffee Cake

MAKES 16 servings • **BAKE** 1 hour • **COOL** 15 minutes

INGREDIENTS

DIRECTIONS

Essential Equipment:
12-cup bundt cake pan or 10×4-inch angel food cake pan (tube pan); electric mixer or hand beater

Shortening to grease pan

1/2 cup packed brown sugar

1/2 cup finely chopped nuts

1 1/2 teaspoons ground cinnamon

1 1/2 cups granulated sugar

3/4 cup (1 1/2 sticks) margarine or butter at room temperature

1 1/2 teaspoons vanilla

3 eggs

3 cups all-purpose flour

1 1/2 teaspoons baking powder

1 1/2 teaspoons baking soda

3/4 teaspoon salt

1 1/2 cups sour cream

Vanilla Glaze (below)

Vanilla Glaze

1/2 cup powdered sugar

1/4 teaspoon vanilla

2 to 3 teaspoons milk

1 Heat the oven to 350°. Grease the bottom and side of the bundt cake pan with the shortening.

2 Mix the brown sugar, nuts and cinnamon, and set aside.

3 Beat the granulated sugar, margarine, vanilla and eggs in a large bowl with the electric mixer on medium speed 2 minutes, scraping bowl occasionally.

4 Mix the flour, baking powder, baking soda and salt in a medium bowl. Beat about one-third of the flour mixture into the sugar mixture on low speed until blended. Beat in about 1/2 cup of the sour cream until blended. Repeat with remaining flour mixture and sour cream.

5 Spread one-third of the batter (about 2 cups) in the greased pan. Sprinkle with half of the brown sugar mixture. Repeat layers once. Spread with remaining batter.

6 Bake about 1 hour or until a toothpick inserted near the center comes out clean. While the cake is baking, make Vanilla Glaze (below).

7 Place the pan on a wire cooling rack, and cool 5 minutes. Run a knife around the edge of the pan to loosen cake. Remove the cake from the pan. To remove cake from pan, place wire cooling rack upside down onto cake. Using pot holders, turn rack and pan over, and remove pan. Cool 10 minutes.

8 Dip a small spoon into glaze. Spread glaze over top of cake, letting glaze drip down sides of cake. Serve cake warm or cool.

VANILLA GLAZE Mix the powdered sugar, vanilla and milk until smooth and spreadable.

1 Serving: Calories 370 (Calories from Fat 145); Fat 16g (Saturated 5g); Cholesterol 55mg; Sodium 410mg; Carbohydrate 57g (Dietary Fiber 1g); Protein 5g **% Daily Value:** Vitamin A 16%; Vitamin C 0%; Calcium 6%; Iron 8% **Diet Exchanges:** Not Recommended

IF YOU DON'T HAVE a bundt pan, you can bake this cake in two 9×5-inch loaf pans. Spread one-fourth of the batter (about 1 1/2 cups) in each pan, then sprinkle each with one-fourth of the filling. Repeat layers once. You'll need to decrease the baking time to about 45 minutes or until a toothpick inserted in center comes out clean.

Removing Cake from Pan

Place wire cooling rack upside down onto cake. Using pot holders, turn rack and pan over, and remove pan.

Spreading Glaze over Cake

Dip a small spoon into glaze. Spread glaze over top of cake letting glaze drip down sides of cake.

Caramel Sticky Rolls

MAKES 12 rolls • **BAKE** 30 minutes

INGREDIENTS

DIRECTIONS

Essential Equipment:
13×9-inch rectangular pan; large heatproof serving plate or cookie sheet

1 cup pecan halves

2/3 cup packed brown sugar

1/2 cup corn syrup

1/4 cup (1/2 stick) margarine or butter, melted

4 cups Original Bisquick

1 cup milk

2 tablespoons margarine or butter at room temperature

1/2 cup packed brown sugar

1 teaspoon ground cinnamon

1 Heat the oven to 400°.

2 Mix the pecans, 2/3 cup brown sugar, the corn syrup and 1/4 cup margarine in the ungreased rectangular pan, and set aside.

3 Stir the Bisquick and milk until a dough forms. Sprinkle a clean surface, such as a kitchen counter or breadboard, with a small amount of Bisquick. Place the dough on the surface. Gently roll dough in Bisquick to coat all sides. Shape the dough into a ball. Knead the dough by curving your fingers around and folding dough toward you, then pushing it away with the heels of your hands, using a quick rocking motion. Repeat 10 times, turning dough each time.

4 Roll the dough with a rolling pin into a 15×9-inch rectangle. Spread 2 tablespoons margarine evenly over dough.

5 Mix 1/2 cup brown sugar and the cinnamon. Sprinkle the cinnamon-sugar mixture evenly over the dough. Roll up dough tightly, starting at one of the short ends. Pinch the edge of dough into the roll to seal in the filling.

6 Cut the dough into 12 slices, each about 1 1/4 inches thick. Arrange dough slices with cut sides down on top of the pecan mixture in the pan.

7 Bake 25 to 30 minutes or until golden brown. Immediately place the heatproof plate upside down onto the pan, and turn plate and pan over. Leave the pan over the rolls for a few minutes, so sauce will drizzle over rolls. Serve warm.

1 Roll: Calories 405 (Calories from Fat 160); Fat 18g (Saturated 3g); Cholesterol 0mg; Sodium 680mg; Carbohydrate 58g (Dietary Fiber 1g); Protein 4g **% Daily Value:** Vitamin A 8%; Vitamin C 0%; Calcium 12%; Iron 10% **Diet Exchanges:** 2 Starch, 2 Fruit, 3 Fat

Tip **TO CUT THIS RECIPE IN HALF,** use an 8-inch round pan, and divide the ingredient amounts in half. Roll the dough into a 9×7-inch rectangle, and cut into 6 slices, each about 1 1/4 inches thick.

Rolling Up Dough

Roll up dough tightly, starting at one of the short ends. Pinch edge of dough into the roll to seal in filling.

Cutting Dough into Slices

Using dental floss is an easy way to cut the roll into slices. To cut, place a length of dental floss under roll where you want to cut a slice. Bring ends of floss up and crisscross them at top of roll, then pull ends in opposite directions.

Brunch Bread Pudding

MAKES 6 servings • **BAKE** 55 minutes • **COOK** 5 minutes

INGREDIENTS

Essential Equipment:
9-inch square pan; medium saucepan (about 2-quart size)

Shortening to grease pan

1 loaf (8 ounces) or 1/2 loaf (1-pound size) French bread

2 tablespoons raisins, if desired

3 eggs

1/3 cup granulated sugar

1/2 teaspoon ground cinnamon

Dash of salt

1 1/2 cups milk

2 tablespoons packed brown sugar

Cran-Raspberry Topping (below)

Cran-Raspberry Topping

1 package (10 ounces) frozen raspberries in syrup, thawed

1 cup granulated sugar

1 cup cranberries

DIRECTIONS

1 Heat the oven to 325°. Grease the bottom and sides of the square pan with the shortening.

2 Tear the bread into 1-inch pieces. You should have about 8 cups of bread pieces. Spread the bread pieces evenly in the greased pan. Sprinkle with the raisins.

3 Beat the eggs, granulated sugar, cinnamon and salt in a medium bowl with a fork or wire whisk. Beat in the milk. Pour the milk mixture over bread in pan. Sprinkle with the brown sugar.

4 Bake uncovered 50 to 55 minutes or until golden brown. While the bread pudding is baking, make Cran-Raspberry Topping (below). Serve bread pudding warm with topping.

CRAN-RASPBERRY TOPPING Drain the raspberries in a strainer, reserving 1/2 cup of the syrup. Mix the syrup and sugar in the saucepan. Cook over medium heat, stirring constantly, until the mixture thickens and boils. Continue boiling 1 to 2 minutes, stirring constantly. Stir in the raspberries and cranberries. Reduce heat just enough so mixture bubbles gently. Cook about 3 minutes, stirring occasionally, until cranberries are tender but do not burst.

1 Serving: Calories 410 (Calories from Fat 45); Fat 5g (Saturated 2g); Cholesterol 110mg; Sodium 280mg; Carbohydrate 86g (Dietary Fiber 4g); Protein 9g **% Daily Value:** Vitamin A 6%; Vitamin C 8%; Calcium 12%; Iron 10% **Diet Exchanges:** 3 Starch, 3 Fruit

Tip **TO SERVE A CROWD OF 10,** double all ingredients in the recipe except the French bread. Bake in a greased 13×9-inch rectangular pan. There's no need to double the Cran-Raspberry Topping.

A Special Touch   Sticker Garland

12 to 16 round or same-shape self-adhesive stickers
About 1 yard thin ribbon or string

1   Place 1 sticker on ribbon; back with another sticker.

2   Repeat with remaining stickers, spacing them evenly
along length of ribbon.

3   Arrange garland along center of table.

Apricot-Stuffed French Toast

MAKES 6 servings (2 slices each) • **REFRIGERATE** 30 minutes • **BAKE** 25 minutes

INGREDIENTS

Essential Equipment:
rectangular baking pan (about 13×9 inches); electric mixer or hand beater

Cooking spray to grease pan

1 loaf (8 ounces) or 1/2 loaf (1-pound size) French bread

1 package (3 ounces) cream cheese at room temperature

3 tablespoons apricot preserves

1/4 teaspoon grated lemon or orange peel

3 eggs

3/4 cup half-and-half

2 tablespoons granulated sugar

1 teaspoon vanilla

1/8 teaspoon salt

1/8 teaspoon ground nutmeg, if desired

2 tablespoons margarine or butter, melted

Powdered sugar, if desired

DIRECTIONS

1 Spray the rectangular pan with the cooking spray.

2 Cut the bread crosswise into 1-inch slices. Cut a horizontal slit in the side of each bread slice, cutting to but not through to the other edge.

3 Beat the cream cheese, preserves and lemon peel in a medium bowl with the electric mixer on medium speed about 1 minute or until well mixed. Spread about 2 teaspoons of the cream cheese mixture inside slit in each bread slice. Place stuffed bread slices in the pan.

4 Beat the eggs, half-and-half, granulated sugar, vanilla, salt and nutmeg in a medium bowl with a fork or wire whisk until well mixed. Pour egg mixture over bread slices in pan, and turn slices carefully to coat. Cover and refrigerate at least 30 minutes but no longer than 24 hours.

5 Heat the oven to 425°. Uncover the French toast. Drizzle with the melted margarine. Bake 20 to 25 minutes or until golden brown. Sprinkle with powdered sugar.

1 Serving: Calories 305 (Calories from Fat 145); Fat 16g (Saturated 9g); Cholesterol 145mg; Sodium 380mg; Carbohydrate 41g (Dietary Fiber 1g); Protein 9g **% Daily Value:** Vitamin A 14%; Vitamin C 0%; Calcium 8%; Iron 8% **Diet Exchanges:** 2 Starch, 1/2 Medium-Fat Meat, 2 1/2 Fat

Tip **YOU CAN SUBSTITUTE** any flavor of fruit preserves or orange marmalade for the apricot preserves in this recipe.

A Special Touch — Carrots and Flower Pitcher

Clear glass pitcher (3- to 4-quart size or 9 to
 10 inches high)
1 bunch carrots with tops
Yellow or white fresh flowers

1   Fill pitcher about 3/4 full with water.

2   Clean carrots; place in pitcher.

3   Add flowers to pitcher.

*Tip: Keep this arrangement in the refrigerator until you're
ready to set it on your table. The carrot tops will stay
fresher and prettier longer this way.*

Blueberry Pancakes with Maple-Orange Syrup

MAKES 4 servings (two 4-inch pancakes each) • **COOK** 20 minutes

INGREDIENTS

Essential Equipment:
small saucepan (about 1-quart size); griddle or 10- or 12-inch skillet

Maple-Orange Syrup (below)

1 egg

1 cup all-purpose flour

3/4 cup milk

1 tablespoon sugar

2 tablespoons vegetable oil

1 1/2 teaspoons baking powder

1/4 teaspoon salt

1/2 cup fresh or frozen (thawed and well drained) blueberries

Margarine, butter or shortening to grease griddle

Maple-Orange Syrup

1 cup maple-flavored syrup

3 tablespoons orange juice

3 tablespoons margarine or butter

DIRECTIONS

1 Make Maple-Orange Syrup (below).

2 Beat the egg in a medium bowl with a fork or wire whisk until yolk and white are well mixed. Beat in the flour, milk, sugar, oil, baking powder and salt just until smooth. Gently stir in the blueberries.

3 Heat the griddle to 375° or heat the skillet over medium heat. To test the heat, sprinkle the griddle with a few drops of water. If the bubbles jump around, heat is just right. If the griddle or skillet is non-stick, you can cook the pancakes without any margarine. Otherwise, melt 1 to 2 teaspoons of margarine each time, before pouring the pancake batter onto the hot griddle.

4 For each pancake, pour a little less than 1/4 cup batter from a measuring cup or pitcher onto the hot griddle. Cook 2 to 4 minutes or until edge of pancake is golden brown and slightly dry and bubbles begin to appear on the surface. Run a turner under edge of pancake, and flip pancake over. Cook other side of pancake about 2 minutes or until golden brown. Repeat with remaining batter.

5 Serve pancakes immediately, or keep warm by placing pancakes in a single layer on a wire rack in a 200° oven for up to 15 minutes. Serve pancakes with syrup.

MAPLE-ORANGE SYRUP Heat the maple syrup, orange juice and margarine in the saucepan over medium heat, stirring occasionally, until warm.

1 Serving: Calories 580 (Calories from Fat 180); Fat 20g (Saturated 5g); Cholesterol 60mg; Sodium 780mg; Carbohydrate 94g (Dietary Fiber 1g); Protein 7g **% Daily Value:** Vitamin A 18%; Vitamin C 4%; Calcium 28%; Iron 12% **Diet Exchanges:** 3 Starch, 3 Fruit, 4 Fat

BUTTERMILK PANCAKES Substitute 1 cup buttermilk for the 3/4 cup milk. Decrease baking powder to 1 teaspoon, and beat in 1/2 teaspoon baking soda.

 **FOR THINNER PANCAKES,** stir in an additional 1 to 2 tablespoons milk.

 **TO SAVE TIME,** mix the batter right in a 4- or 8- cup glass measure with a handle and spout, which makes pouring batter onto the griddle easy.

Cooking Pancakes

For each pancake, pour a little less than 1/4 cup batter from a measuring cup or pitcher onto hot griddle. Cook 2 to 4 minutes or until edge of pancake is golden brown and slightly dry and bubbles begin to appear on the surface.

Waffles with Caramel-Apple Topping

MAKES 6 servings (one 7-inch-round waffle each) • **BAKE** 30 minutes

INGREDIENTS

Essential Equipment:
10-inch skillet; waffle iron

Caramel-Apple Topping (below)

Vegetable oil or cooking spray
 to grease waffle iron

2 eggs

2 cups all-purpose flour

1 3/4 cups milk

1/2 cup vegetable oil

1 tablespoon granulated sugar

4 teaspoons baking powder

1/4 teaspoon salt

Caramel-Apple Topping

2 tablespoons margarine or
 butter

3 medium eating apples, such
 as Gala, Golden Delicious or
 Red Delicious

1/4 cup caramel topping

DIRECTIONS

1 Make Caramel-Apple Topping (below).

2 Heat the waffle iron. If the waffle iron is nonstick, you can cook the waffles without any oil. Otherwise, brush the waffle iron lightly with oil before you heat it.

3 Beat the eggs in a large bowl with a fork or wire whisk until yolks and whites are well mixed. Beat in the flour, milk, oil, sugar, baking powder and salt just until smooth.

4 For each waffle, pour a little less than 2/3 cup batter from a measuring cup or pitcher onto the center of hot waffle iron. Check the manufacturer's directions for the recommended amount of batter to use. Close the lid of the waffle iron.

5 Bake about 5 minutes or until the steaming stops. Carefully remove waffle. Repeat with remaining batter. Serve immediately, or keep warm by placing waffles in a single layer on a wire rack in a 200° oven for up to 15 minutes. Serve waffles with topping.

CARAMEL-APPLE TOPPING Peel the apples. Cut each apple into fourths. Cut the core and seeds out of the center of each fourth. Cut each fourth into slices. Melt the margarine in the skillet over medium heat. Stir in the apples. Cook about 3 minutes, stirring frequently, until apples are crisp-tender when pierced with a fork. Pour the caramel topping over apples. Cook, stirring frequently, until topping is warm. Remove the skillet from the heat.

1 Serving: Calories 500 (Calories from Fat 245); Fat 27g (Saturated 5g); Cholesterol 75mg; Sodium 580mg; Carbohydrate 57g (Dietary Fiber 2g); Protein 9g **% Daily Value:** Vitamin A 12%; Vitamin C 2%; Calcium 28%; Iron 14% **Diet Exchanges:** 3 Starch, 1 Fruit, 5 Fat

CRUNCHY NUT WAFFLES After pouring the batter onto the hot waffle iron, immediately sprinkle with about 2 tablespoons coarsely chopped nuts for each 7-inch waffle.

FOR EXTRA-SPECIAL WAFFLES, top with a dollop of Sweetened Whipped Cream (pages 172 or 178) and a sprinkle of toasted nuts.

Pouring Waffle Batter onto Waffle Iron

For each waffle, pour a little less than 2/3 cup batter from a measuring cup or pitcher onto the center of hot waffle iron. Check manufacturer's directions for the recommended amount of batter to use.

Savory Sausage and Egg Bake

MAKES 12 servings • **BAKE** 35 minutes

INGREDIENTS

DIRECTIONS

Essential Equipment:
13×9-inch rectangular pan; 10-inch skillet

Shortening to grease pan

1 pound bulk pork sausage

1/4 pound mushrooms

8 medium green onions
with tops

2 medium tomatoes

2 cups shredded mozzarella
cheese (8 ounces)

1 1/4 cups Original Bisquick

1 cup milk

1 1/2 teaspoons salt

1/2 teaspoon pepper

1 1/2 teaspoons chopped
fresh or 1/2 teaspoon
dried oregano leaves

12 eggs

1 Heat the oven to 350°. Grease the bottom and sides of the rectangular pan with the shortening.

2 Cook the sausage in the skillet over medium heat 8 to 10 minutes, stirring occasionally, until sausage is no longer pink. Place a strainer over a medium bowl, or place a colander in a large bowl. Spoon the sausage into strainer to drain the fat. Discard fat.

3 Cut the mushrooms into slices. Cut and discard the tip of the green onion with the stringy end. Cut green onions into thin slices, including some of the green part. Chop the tomatoes. Layer the sausage, mushrooms, onions, tomatoes and cheese in the greased pan.

4 Beat the Bisquick, milk, salt, pepper, oregano and eggs in a large bowl with a fork or wire whisk until well mixed. Pour over cheese in the pan.

5 Bake uncovered 30 to 35 minutes or until golden brown and filling is firm.

1 Serving: Calories 255 (Calories from Fat 145); Fat 16g (Saturated 6g); Cholesterol 240mg; Sodium 880mg; Carbohydrate 12g (Dietary Fiber 1g); Protein 17g **% Daily Value:** Vitamin A 12%; Vitamin C 4%; Calcium 22%; Iron 8% **Diet Exchanges:** 1/2 Starch, 2 High-Fat Meat, 1/2 Vegetable

Tip **TO DO AHEAD,** cover and refrigerate this dish up to 24 hours. Bake uncovered 40 to 45 minutes or until golden brown and filling is firm.

Draining Sausage

Place a strainer over a medium bowl. Spoon the sausage into strainer to drain the fat. Discard fat in the garbage (not down your drain).

Bacon and Swiss Quiche

MAKES 6 servings • **BAKE** 45 minutes • **LET STAND** 10 minutes

INGREDIENTS

Essential Equipment:
9-inch pie pan; 12-inch skillet

Pat-in-the-Pan Pastry (below)

8 slices bacon

1 small onion

1 cup shredded Swiss cheese
   (4 ounces)

4 eggs

2 cups whipping (heavy) cream

1/2 teaspoon salt

1/4 teaspoon pepper

1/8 teaspoon ground
   red pepper (cayenne)

Pat-in-the-Pan Pastry

1 1/3 cups all-purpose flour

1/3 cup vegetable oil

1/2 teaspoon salt

2 tablespoons cold water

DIRECTIONS

1 Move the oven rack to its lowest position. Heat the oven to 425°. Make Pat-in-the-Pan Pastry (below).

2 Cook the bacon in the skillet over low heat 8 to 10 minutes, turning occasionally, until bacon is evenly browned and crisp. Drain bacon on paper towels. When bacon is cool enough to handle, crumble into small pieces.

3 Peel and finely chop the onion. Sprinkle bacon, cheese and onion in pastry-lined pie pan.

4 Beat the eggs slightly in a large bowl with a wire whisk or hand beater. Beat in the whipping cream, salt, pepper and ground red pepper. To prevent spilling, place pastry-lined pie pan on oven rack before adding filling. Carefully pour the egg filling into the pie pan. Bake uncovered 20 minutes.

5 Reduce the oven temperature to 300°. Bake about 25 minutes longer or until a knife inserted in the center comes out clean. Place the pan on a wire cooling rack. Let stand 10 minutes before cutting. Store covered in refrigerator.

PAT-IN-THE-PAN PASTRY Mix the flour, oil and salt with a fork in a medium bowl until all flour is moistened. Sprinkle with cold water, 1 tablespoon at a time, tossing with fork until all water is absorbed. Shape pastry into a ball, using your hands. Press pastry in bottom and up side of the pie pan.

1 Serving: Calories 620 (Calories from Fat 450); Fat 50g (Saturated 23g); Cholesterol 255mg; Sodium 640mg; Carbohydrate 26g (Dietary Fiber 1g); Protein 17g **% Daily Value:** Vitamin A 26%; Vitamin C 0%; Calcium 24%; Iron 10% **Diet Exchanges:** 2 Starch, 2 High-Fat Meat, 6 Fat

Tip **SERVE WITH** a fruit platter of sliced apples, sliced pears and grapes for a casual breakfast or brunch. Pick up an assortment of muffins or rolls from your local bakery, or if you have a bit more time, make a batch of Streusel Berry Muffins (page 194).

Tip **TO SAVE TIME,** use half of a 15-ounce package of frozen pie crust shells (one 9 5/8-inch shell) instead of making the Pat-in-the-Pan Pastry.

Pressing Pastry in Pan

Press pastry in bottom and up side of pie pan.

Vegetable Frittata

MAKES 6 servings • **COOK** 15 minutes • **BROIL** 2 minutes

INGREDIENTS

Essential Equipment:
ovenproof 10-inch nonstick skillet

2 medium bell peppers

1 medium onion

2 tablespoons margarine or butter

8 eggs

1/2 teaspoon salt

1/8 teaspoon pepper

1/2 cup shredded Monterey Jack cheese (2 ounces)

DIRECTIONS

1 Cut the bell peppers lengthwise in half, and cut out seeds and membrane. Chop the bell peppers. Peel and chop the onion.

2 Melt the margarine in the skillet over medium heat.

3 Cook the bell peppers and onion in margarine, stirring occasionally, until onion is tender when pierced with a fork.

4 Beat the eggs, salt and pepper in a medium bowl with a fork or wire whisk until yolks and whites are well mixed. Stir in the cheese.

5 Pour egg mixture over vegetable mixture. Cover and cook over medium-low heat 8 to 10 minutes or until eggs are set and light brown on bottom.

6 Move the oven rack so the top of the frittata will be 4 to 6 inches from the broiler. Set the oven control to broil. Broil frittata about 2 minutes or until golden brown. Cut frittata into wedges. Serve immediately.

1 Serving: Calories 185 (Calories from Fat 125); Fat 14g (Saturated 6g); Cholesterol 300mg; Sodium 370mg; Carbohydrate 5g (Dietary Fiber 1g); Protein 11g **% Daily Value:** Vitamin A 16%; Vitamin C 30%; Calcium 10%; Iron 6% **Diet Exchanges:** 1 Medium-Fat Meat, 1 Vegetable, 2 Fat

IF THE HANDLE OF YOUR SKILLET IS MADE OF PLASTIC, it is not ovenproof. But don't worry! Just wrap the handle completely in several layers of heavy-duty aluminum foil before broiling.

Broiling a Frittata

Broil frittata with top 4 to 6 inches from heat about 2 minutes or until golden brown. The distance between the heat and the food is important. If the food is too close to the heat, it will burn.

Country Egg Scramble

MAKES 8 servings • **COOK** 20 minutes

INGREDIENTS

Essential Equipment:
*large saucepan (about 3-quart size);
12-inch skillet*

10 to 12 new potatoes
  (about 1 1/2 pounds)

8 eggs

1/2 cup milk

1/2 teaspoon salt

1/4 teaspoon pepper

6 medium green onions
  with tops

1/3 cup margarine or butter

DIRECTIONS

1 Scrub the potatoes thoroughly with a vegetable brush to remove all the dirt, but do not peel. Cut potatoes into 1/2-inch pieces.

2 Add 1 inch of water to the saucepan. Cover and heat the water to boiling over high heat. Add potatoes. Cover and heat to boiling again. Once water is boiling, reduce heat just enough so water bubbles gently.

3 Cook covered 6 to 8 minutes or until potatoes are tender when pierced with a fork. While potatoes are cooking, beat the eggs, milk, salt and pepper in a large bowl with a fork or wire whisk until well mixed, and set aside. Cut and discard the tip of the green onion with the stringy end. Cut green onions into thin slices, including some of the green part.

4 Drain the potatoes in a strainer. Heat the margarine in the skillet over medium-high heat. As margarine melts, tilt skillet to coat bottom.

5 Cook the potatoes in the margarine 3 to 5 minutes, turning potatoes occasionally with a spatula, until light brown. Stir in the onions. Cook 1 minute, stirring constantly.

6 Pour the egg mixture over the potatoes in the skillet. The egg mixture will become firm at the bottom and sides very quickly. When this happens, gently lift the cooked portions around the edge with a spatula so that the thin, uncooked portion can flow to the bottom. Avoid constant stirring, but continue to lift the cooked portion and allow the thin uncooked portions to flow to the bottom. Cook 3 to 4 minutes or until eggs are thickened throughout but still moist and creamy.

1 Serving: Calories 205 (Calories from Fat 115); Fat 13g (Saturated 3g); Cholesterol 215mg; Sodium 330mg; Carbohydrate 16g (Dietary Fiber 2g); Protein 8g **% Daily Value:** Vitamin A 18%; Vitamin C 6%; Calcium 6%; Iron 8% **Diet Exchanges:** 1 Starch, 1 Medium-Fat Meat, 1 Fat

Tip **TO WARM PLATES** for serving the eggs, run hot water over the serving plates, then dry them thoroughly right before serving.

A Special Touch — Green Onion and Flower Bundle

1 bunch fresh green onions
Fresh flowers
Clear drinking glass (6 to 8 inches high)
Twine

1 Trim ends of tops of onions. Trim stems of flowers so they are shorter than onions.

2 Tie twine around onions and flowers to form a bundle.

3 Fill glass about 1/2 full with water. Place bundle in glass.

Home-Style Hash Browns

MAKES 6 servings • **BAKE** 40 minutes

INGREDIENTS

DIRECTIONS

Essential Equipment:
13×9-inch rectangular pan

2 small bell peppers

1 medium onion

1 bag (1 pound 4 ounces) refrigerated shredded hash brown potatoes

2 tablespoons grated Parmesan cheese

1/2 teaspoon salt

1/4 teaspoon pepper

1 tablespoon margarine or butter, melted

1 tablespoon vegetable oil

Additional grated Parmesan cheese, if desired

1 Heat the oven to 325°.

2 Cut each bell pepper lengthwise in half, and cut out seeds and membrane. Finely chop the bell peppers. Peel and finely chop the onion.

3 Mix the bell peppers, onion, potatoes, 2 tablespoons cheese, the salt and pepper in a large bowl.

4 Pour the margarine and oil into the rectangular pan. Tilt the pan to coat the bottom. Spread the potato mixture in the pan.

5 Bake uncovered about 35 minutes. Remove pan from oven. Run a spatula under the edge of the potato mixture. Turn the potato mixture over to other side. Bake uncovered about 5 minutes longer or until golden brown. Sprinkle with additional cheese before serving.

1 Serving: Calories 160 (Calories from Fat 35); Fat 4g (Saturated 2g); Cholesterol 5mg; Sodium 610mg; Carbohydrate 29g (Dietary Fiber 3g); Protein 4g **% Daily Value:** Vitamin A 2%; Vitamin C 26%; Calcium 4%; Iron 4% **Diet Exchanges:** 2 Starch, 1 Vegetable

Tip **TO DO AHEAD,** spread potato mixture in pan. Cover and refrigerate up to 24 hours before baking.

A Special Touch Bird Feeder Vase

Suet bird feeder (about 6 inches wide) with chain
Sphagnum moss
3 floral water tubes
Fresh flowers

1 Fill bird feeder with moss.

2 Fill tubes with water; place in moss. Place one flower stem in each tube.

3 Hang feeder from chain, or remove chain and place feeder on table.

Holiday Menus

7

Thanksgiving Dinner

Filled with the fall harvest flavors of squash, cranberry and pumpkin, as well as the perfect roasted bird, this menu is sure to satisfy your family and friends. Once you've cooked a traditional Thanksgiving dinner with all the trimmings, like this one, you'll feel like you've arrived as a cook—and as a host!

This dinner isn't difficult to prepare, but it does take some planning. Don't worry—our timetable will walk you through all the steps. Keep in mind that you don't have to do it all yourself. Take guests up on their offers to bring something, such as an appetizer, salad or a bottle of wine. And if you don't have time to make the dessert, you can always pick up a pumpkin pie from your favorite bakery. When it's time for dinner, a few guests can pitch in to help you with last-minute tasks like carving the turkey and bringing the food to the table.

Although the dinner is traditional, the setting can be casual (so you can watch the football games) or more formal. It doesn't matter if your dishes all match, but if you have a matching set, now's the time to bring it out. Use napkins and napkin rings to make a festive table runner (page 231). Martini glasses or footed dessert dishes filled with fresh pears and candles (page 133) will add the finishing touch to your table.

Menu

SERVES 8

Mixed Nuts, if desired

Mixed-Greens Salad

Roast Turkey with Bread Stuffing, pages 226, 231

Do-Ahead Mashed Potatoes, page 134

Turkey Gravy, page 228

Maple-Glazed Squash, page 130

Cranberry-Orange Sauce, page 230

Small Croissants or Dinner Rolls with Butter

Praline Pumpkin Dessert, page 172

Coffee and Tea

Wine, if desired

A Special Touch

Napkin Table Runner and Pear Glasses, pages 231, 133

PARTY COUNTDOWN

1 week before dinner
Buy supplies for Napkin Table Runner (page 231); make table runner.

3 days before dinner
Buy groceries plus supplies for Pear Glasses (page 133).

Thaw turkey, if frozen, in refrigerator.

Wrap croissants in aluminum foil; freeze to keep them fresh.

Make Cranberry-Orange Sauce (page 230); cover and refrigerate.

2 days before dinner
Make Praline Pumpkin Dessert (page 172); cover and refrigerate.

Put nuts in serving bowl; cover and leave at room temperature.

1 day before dinner
Make Bread Stuffing (page 231); cover and refrigerate immediately. ***Don't stuff the turkey ahead of time.***

Prepare Do-Ahead Mashed Potatoes (page 134) up to the point of baking; cover and refrigerate.

Choose serving dishes and utensils.

Arrange table runner and pear glasses on table.

Morning of the dinner
Take croissants out of freezer.

Set the table.

5 hours before dinner
Wash turkey; pat dry with paper towels. Stuff with Bread Stuffing.

Place turkey in oven for roasting immediately after stuffing.

1 hour before dinner

Microwave and cut squash for Maple-Glazed Squash (page 130), following the Microwave Directions; cover with aluminum foil to keep warm.

Make Sweetened Whipped Cream (pages 172 or 178) for the dessert; cover and refrigerate.

Chill the wine.

45 minutes before dinner

Remove mashed potatoes from the refrigerator and bake.

Set out bowl of nuts.

Set butter and Cranberry-Orange Sauce on the table.

30 minutes before dinner

Remove turkey from the oven; place on carving board or platter. Loosely cover with aluminum foil and let stand 15 minutes.

Place croissants in aluminum foil in oven to heat.

Make Turkey Gravy (page 228).

20 minutes before dinner

Fill and microwave squash; cover with aluminum foil to keep warm.

15 minutes before dinner

Remove stuffing from turkey; place in serving bowl and cover with aluminum foil to keep warm.

Carve the turkey, if desired, and arrange on a platter. If you aren't serving immediately, cover with aluminum foil to keep warm, and serve within 10 minutes. Or carve the turkey at the table if you are comfortable doing so.

10 minutes before dinner

Fill water glasses.

Place salad greens in a serving bowl, and toss with dressing.

Remove croissants from oven, and put in serving basket.

Place gravy in serving bowl.

Pour wine.

Place the food on the table.

Make coffee and tea for dessert.

After dinner

Clear the table.

Cut Praline Pumpkin Dessert, and serve on small plates. Top with whipped cream.

Serve coffee and tea.

Roast Turkey

MAKES 8 to 10 servings • **BAKE** 3 hours 30 minutes • **LET STAND** 15 minutes

INGREDIENTS

Essential Equipment:
shallow roasting pan (about 13×9-inch rectangle) and rack; meat thermometer (not instant-read)

8- to 12-pound turkey

Bread Stuffing (page 230), if desired

2 tablespoons margarine or butter, melted

DIRECTIONS

1 If the turkey is frozen, thaw it either slowly in the refrigerator, in cold water or quickly in the microwave. A turkey weighing 8 to 12 pounds will thaw in about 2 days in the refrigerator. A whole frozen turkey also can be safely thawed in cold water. Leave the turkey in its original wrap, free from tears or holes. Place in cold water, allowing 30 minutes per pound for thawing, and change the water often. Or thaw turkey in the microwave following the manufacturer's directions for your oven.

2 Heat the oven to 325°. Remove the package of giblets (gizzard, heart and neck), if present, from the neck cavity of the turkey, and discard. Rinse both the neck and body cavities, or inside of the turkey, with cool water; pat dry with paper towels. Rub both cavities lightly with salt if desired. Do not salt the cavities if you will be stuffing the turkey.

3 Stuff the turkey with Bread Stuffing (page 230) just before roasting—not ahead of time. Fill the neck cavity lightly with stuffing. Fasten the neck skin to the back of the turkey with a skewer. Fold the wings across the back so the tips are touching. Fill the body cavity lightly with stuffing. It is not necessary to pack the stuffing because it will expand during roasting. Tuck the drumsticks under the band of skin at the tail, or tie or skewer the drumsticks to the tail.

4 Place the turkey, breast side up, on a rack in a shallow roasting pan. Brush the margarine over the turkey. It is not necessary to add water or to cover the turkey. Insert the meat thermometer so the tip is in the thickest part of thigh muscle and thermometer does not touch bone.

5 Bake uncovered about 2 hours. Place a tent of aluminum foil loosely over the turkey when it begins to turn golden. Cut the band of skin or remove the tie or skewer holding the drumsticks; this will allow the interior part of the thighs to cook through.

6 Bake 1 hour to 1 hour 30 minutes longer or until thermometer reads 180° and juice is no longer pink when you cut into the center of the thigh. The drumstick should move easily when lifted or twisted. Remove the turkey from the oven and let stand about 15 minutes for easiest carving. Keep turkey covered with aluminum foil so it will stay warm.

1 Serving: Calories 385 (Calories from Fat 205); Fat 23g (Saturated 6g); Cholesterol 140mg; Sodium 170mg; Carbohydrate 0g (Dietary Fiber 0g); Protein 44g **% Daily Value:** Vitamin A 14%; Vitamin C 0%; Calcium 4%; Iron 22% **Diet Exchanges:** 6 Lean Meat, 1 Fat

Tip **SELECT A TURKEY** that is plump and meaty with smooth, moist-looking skin. The skin should be creamy colored. The cut ends of the bones should be pink to red in color.

Timetable for Roasting Whole Stuffed Turkey
at 325°

Ready-to-Cook Weight	Roasting Time*
8 to 12 pounds	3 to 3 1/2 hours
12 to 14 pounds	3 1/2 to 4 hours
14 to 18 pounds	4 to 4 1/4 hours
8 to 20 pounds	4 1/4 to 4 3/4 hours
20 to 24 pounds	4 3/4 to 5 1/4 hours

*Begin checking turkey for doneness about one hour before end of recommended roasting time.
For prestuffed turkeys, follow package directions very carefully—do not use this timetable.*

Turkey Gravy

MAKES 1 cup gravy • **COOK** 5 minutes

INGREDIENTS

DIRECTIONS

Essential Equipment:
the pan the turkey was roasted in

**Drippings from cooked turkey
(fat and juices)**

2 tablespoons all-purpose flour

1 cup chicken broth or water

Browning sauce, if desired

Salt and pepper to taste

1 Place the turkey on a carving board or warm platter, and cover with aluminum foil while preparing gravy. Pan and drippings will be hot, so be careful when handling. Pour drippings from roasting pan into a glass measuring cup or bowl, leaving the brown particles stuck to the bottom of the pan.

2 Skim 2 tablespoons of fat from the top of the drippings and return to the pan. Measuring accurately is important because too little fat makes the gravy lumpy and too much fat makes the gravy greasy. Skim off any remaining fat from the drippings and discard. Set aside remaining juices.

3 Stir the flour into the fat in the pan, using a long-handled fork or spoon. Cooking with the roasting pan on top of the burner may be awkward, so keep a pot holder handy to steady the pan. Cook over low heat, stirring constantly, until the mixture is smooth and bubbly. As you stir, the brown particles will be loosened from the bottom of the pan; they add more flavor to the gravy. Remove the pan from the heat.

4 Stir enough broth or water into the reserved turkey juices to measure 1 cup. Add to mixture in pan. Heat to boiling over high heat, stirring constantly. Continue boiling 1 minute, stirring constantly. Stir in a few drops of browning sauce if you want the gravy to have a richer, deeper color. Taste the gravy, and add a desired amount of salt and pepper.

1 Tablespoon: Calories 20 (Calories from Fat 20); Fat 2g (Saturated 1g); Cholesterol 0mg; Sodium 65mg; Carbohydrate 1g (Dietary Fiber 0g); Protein 0g **% Daily Value:** Vitamin A 0%; Vitamin C 0%; Calcium 0%; Iron 0% **Diet Exchanges:** 1 Serving is free

Tip THIS RECIPE CAN EASILY be doubled or tripled if there are enough drippings. Sprinkle with a little salt and pepper and taste before adding more. The amount of seasoning will not need to be doubled or tripled.

Thickening Gravy

Stir enough broth or water into the reserved turkey juices to measure 1 cup. Heat to boiling, stirring constantly. Continue boiling 1 minute, stirring constantly.

Carving the Turkey

Use a sharp carving knife for best results when carving a whole turkey. While carving, keep the turkey from moving by holding it in place with a meat fork. Carve on a stable cutting surface, such as a cutting board, meat carving board or platter. Carving is easier if the turkey is allowed to stand for about 15 minutes after roasting.

Place the turkey, breast up and with its legs to your right if you're right-handed or to the left if left-handed. Remove the ties or skewers.

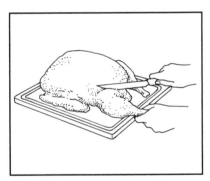

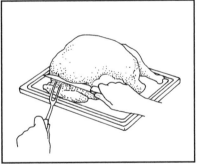

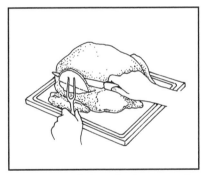

1 While gently pulling the leg and thigh away from the body, cut through the joint between leg and body. Separate the drumstick and thigh by cutting down through the connecting joint. Serve the drumstick and thighs whole, or carve them.

2 Make a deep horizontal cut into the breast just above the wing.

3 Insert a fork in the breast, and starting halfway up the breast, carve thin slices down to the horizontal cut, working upward. Repeat steps 1 through 3 on the other side of the turkey.

Bread Stuffing

MAKES 10 servings (about 1/2 cup each)

INGREDIENTS

Essential Equipment:
*Dutch oven (about 4-quart size)
or 12-inch skillet*

2 large celery stalks
(with leaves)

1 medium onion

3/4 cup (1 1/2 sticks) margarine
or butter

9 cups soft bread cubes
(about 15 slices bread)

2 tablespoons chopped fresh or
1 1/2 teaspoons dried sage
leaves

1 tablespoon chopped fresh or
1 teaspoon dried thyme
leaves

1 1/2 teaspoons salt

1/2 teaspoon pepper

DIRECTIONS

1 Chop the celery, including the leaves. Peel and chop the onion.

2 Melt the margarine in the Dutch oven over medium-high heat. Cook the celery and onion in margarine 6 to 8 minutes, stirring occasionally, until celery is tender when pierced with a fork. Remove the Dutch oven from the heat.

3 Gently toss the celery mixture with the bread cubes, sage, thyme, salt and pepper, using a spoon, until bread cubes are evenly coated. You should have about 9 cups of stuffing, enough to stuff a 10- to 12-pound turkey.

1 Serving: Calories 215 (Calories from Fat 135); Fat 15g (Saturated 9g); Cholesterol 0mg; Sodium 510mg; Carbohydrate 18g (Dietary Fiber 1g); Protein 3g **% Daily Value:** Vitamin A 10%; Vitamin C 2%; Calcium 4%; Iron 6% **Diet Exchanges:** 1 Starch, 3 Fat

APPLE-CRANBERRY STUFFING Stir in 3 cups finely chopped apples and 1 cup fresh or frozen (thawed) cranberries with the bread cubes in step 3.

CORN BREAD STUFFING Substitute corn bread cubes for the soft bread cubes.

ORANGE-APPLE STUFFING Stir in 1 cup diced orange sections or mandarin orange segments and 1 cup finely chopped apples with the bread cubes in step 3.

Filling Neck Cavity

Fill neck cavity with stuffing. Fasten neck skin to back with skewer. Fold wings across back with tips touching.

Filling Body Cavity

Fill body cavity lightly with stuffing. Do not pack; stuffing will expand. Tuck drumsticks under band of skin at tail, or skewer to tail.

YOU CAN BAKE THE STUFFING separately if you like. Place stuffing in a greased 3-quart casserole or 13×9-inch rectangular baking dish. Cover with lid or aluminum foil and bake in a 325° oven for 30 minutes; uncover and bake 15 minutes longer.

Cranberry-Orange Sauce

MAKES about 2 cups sauce • **COOK** 10 minutes • **REFRIGERATE** 3 hours

INGREDIENTS

DIRECTIONS

Essential Equipment:
medium saucepan (about 2-quart size)

1 bag (12 ounces) fresh or frozen cranberries (3 cups)

1/2 cup water

1 1/2 cups sugar

2 teaspoons grated orange peel

1 Rinse the cranberries in a strainer with cool water, and remove any stems or blemished berries.

2 Heat the water and sugar to boiling in the saucepan over medium heat, stirring occasionally.

3 Stir in the cranberries and orange peel. Heat to boiling over medium heat, stirring occasionally. Continue boiling about 5 minutes longer, stirring occasionally, until cranberries begin to pop. Remove the saucepan from the heat, and pour the sauce into a bowl or container. Refrigerate about 3 hours or until chilled.

1/4 Cup: Calories 110 (Calories from Fat 0); Fat 0g (Saturated 0g); Cholesterol 0mg; Sodium 55mg; Carbohydrate 29g (Dietary Fiber 1g); Protein 0g **% Daily Value:** Vitamin A 0%; Vitamin C 2%; Calcium 0%; Iron 0% **Diet Exchanges:** 2 Fruit

A Special Touch Napkin Table Runner

4 square matching-fabric napkins or 4-foot length
lightweight cloth
Fabric glue or needle and thread
2 or 3 napkin rings

1 Glue or sew edges of napkins together.

2 Place napkin rings around seams or evenly spaced along length of fabric.

3 Arrange runner down center of table.

Christmas Dinner

The warm glow of candles, a crackling fire and cheerful Christmas decorations set the stage for this festive dinner. The menu is elegant, but there's nothing tricky to prepare, so you'll be able to relax and enjoy the company of your guests.

A rib roast is an impressive entrée, and a simple herb rub makes it especially delicious. Purchase two 10-ounce bags of ready-to-eat salad greens, bottled dressing and a loaf of crusty bread from the supermarket along with all of the other ingredients you need, and let our timetable and recipes take away the guesswork. When time is running short, an assortment of Christmas cookies (purchased or homemade) arranged on a pretty serving platter makes a great stand-in for the dessert.

How you serve the meal is up to you. It works beautifully as a buffet dinner or served family style, or you can assemble the plates in the kitchen and bring them out to your guests. Christmas is an excellent time to use your best plates, glasses, silverware and serving pieces. Or if your everyday dishes are white, they'll look great on richly colored place mats or a tablecloth. If you're serving buffet style, wrap napkins around each setting of silverware and tie with ribbon or a string of beads that coordinates with your color scheme. If you are having a sit-down dinner, you may want to get creative and try some fun napkin folds (page 22). Complete the scene with a Wrapped Rose Topiary (page 236), or purchase an arrangement of fresh flowers and seasonal greenery for the table.

Menu

SERVES 8

Baked Brie with Cranberries and Pistachios, page 54

Mixed-Greens Salad

Herb-Rubbed Rib Roast with Peppery Horseradish Sauce, pages 234, 236

Cheddar Twice-Baked Potatoes, page 136

Crusty French Bread with Butter

Chocolate-Mint Mousse, page 180

Coffee and Tea

Wine, if desired

A Special Touch
Wrapped Rose Topiary, page 236

PARTY COUNTDOWN

3 days before dinner
Buy groceries.

Wrap bread in aluminum foil; freeze to keep it fresh.

Chop pistachio nuts for Baked Brie (page 54); cover and leave at room temperature.

Make Peppery Horseradish Sauce (page 236); cover and refrigerate.

2 days before dinner
Make Chocolate-Mint Mousse (page 180); cover and freeze.

Chop candies or crush chocolate wafer cookies to garnish mousse; cover and leave at room temperature.

1 day before dinner
Buy flowers and supplies for Wrapped Rose Topiary (page 236), or order a pretty, low floral centerpiece for the table.

Prepare potatoes for Cheddar Twice-Baked Potatoes (page 136), and fill the potato shells; cover and refrigerate.

Chill the wine.

Choose serving pieces and utensils.

Morning of the dinner
Prepare herb mixture for Herb-Rubbed Rib Roast (page 234); cover and refrigerate.

Make topiary, or arrange centerpiece on table.

Set the table.

3 hours before dinner

Prepare roast, and place in oven (about 2 to 2 1/2 hours before you plan to serve the meal).

1 hour before dinner

Bake Brie.

Set butter on the table.

45 minutes before dinner

Remove Brie from oven, and top with cranberry sauce and pistachios; serve with crackers.

Pour wine and serve.

30 minutes before dinner

Remove roast from the oven; place on carving board or platter. Loosely cover with aluminum foil and let stand 15 minutes.

Place horseradish sauce in a serving bowl, and set on the table.

Remove potatoes from refrigerator; sprinkle with cheese and pop in the oven.

15 minutes before dinner

Slice the roast, and arrange on a platter. If you aren't serving it immediately, cover with aluminum foil to keep warm, and serve within 15 minutes.

Fill the water glasses.

Place salad greens in a serving bowl, and toss with dressing.

Slice bread, and place in a serving basket or on a serving platter.

Place the food on the table.

Refill wine glasses if needed.

Make coffee and tea for dessert.

After dinner

Clear the table.

Cut Chocolate-Mint Mousse, and serve on small plates. Garnish each serving with chopped candies or crushed chocolate wafer cookies.

Serve coffee and tea.

Herb-Rubbed Rib Roast

MAKES 8 servings • **BAKE** 2 hours • **LET STAND** 15 minutes

INGREDIENTS

Essential Equipment:
shallow roasting pan (about 13×9-inch rectangle) and rack; meat thermometer (not instant-read)

4-pound beef rib roast

3 cloves garlic

1/4 cup Dijon mustard

3/4 cup chopped fresh parsley

1 1/2 tablespoons chopped fresh or 1 1/2 teaspoons dried thyme leaves

1 1/2 tablespoons chopped fresh or 1 1/2 teaspoons dried rosemary leaves

1 tablespoon olive or vegetable oil

DIRECTIONS

1 Heat the oven to 325°. Place the beef, fat side up, on the rack in the roasting pan.

2 Peel 1 clove of garlic, and cut in half. Rub the garlic over the beef. Spread the mustard over top and sides of beef.

3 Peel and finely chop remaining 2 cloves of garlic. Mix the chopped garlic, parsley, thyme and rosemary in a small bowl. Stir in the oil. Spread herb mixture over the top and sides of beef.

4 Insert the meat thermometer so the tip is in the thickest part of the beef and does not touch bone or rest in fat.

5 Bake uncovered 1 hour 30 minutes to 2 hours for medium done-ness or until thermometer reads 155°.

6 Remove the beef from the oven. Cover beef loosely with a tent of aluminum foil and let stand about 15 minutes or until thermometer reads 160°. After standing, the beef also will be easier to carve.

1 Serving: Calories 265 (Calories from Fat 155); Fat 17g (Saturated 6g); Cholesterol 80mg; Sodium 170mg; Carbohydrate 1g (Dietary Fiber 1g); Protein 28g **% Daily Value:** Vitamin A 2%; Vitamin C 6%; Calcium 2%; Iron 20% **Diet Exchanges:** 4 Lean Meat, 1 Fat

Tip **LETTING THE ROAST STAND** for 15 minutes makes it easier to carve because the juices will set up. Avoid covering the roast too tightly, which will create steam and soften the surface of the beef.

Tip **ALWAYS USE A SHARP KNIFE** and cut beef across the grain at a slanted angle into slices.

Carving a Beef Rib Roast

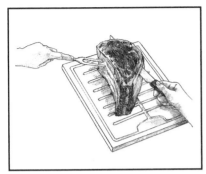

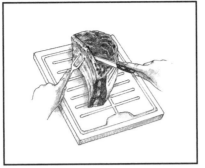

1 Place roast, large side down, on a carving board or platter. Remove wedge-shaped slice from large end, if necessary, so roast will stand firmly on this end. Insert meat fork below top rib. Slice from outside of roast toward rib side.

2 After making several slices, cut along inner side of rib bone with tip of knife. As each slice is released, slide knife under and lift to plate.

Peppery Horseradish Sauce

MAKES 1 cup sauce • **REFRIGERATE** 1 hour

INGREDIENTS

1 cup sour cream

1 tablespoon plus 1 teaspoon horseradish sauce (not prepared horseradish)

1 tablespoon plus 1 teaspoon Dijon mustard

1/4 teaspoon coarsely ground pepper

DIRECTIONS

1 Mix the sour cream, horseradish sauce, mustard and pepper in a small glass or plastic bowl.

2 Cover and refrigerate at least 1 hour to blend flavors. Cover and refrigerate any remaining sauce.

1 Tablespoon: Calories 30 (Calories from fat 20); Fat 2g (Saturated 1g); Cholesterol 5mg; Sodium 25mg; Carbohydrate 2g (Dietary Fiber 0g); Protein 1g **% Daily Value:** Vitamin A 2%; Vitamin C 0%; Calcium 2%; Iron 0% **Diet Exchanges:** 1/2 Fat

Tip **HERE'S ANOTHER EASY** horseradish sauce that's so quick to make: Beat 1/2 cup whipping (heavy) cream in a chilled bowl until stiff. Fold in 3 tablespoons well-drained prepared horseradish and 1/2 teaspoon salt. Easy and delicious—enjoy!

Tip **HORSERADISH SAUCE** is a white cream sauce with grated horseradish that looks like mayonnaise—and that's what you want to choose for this recipe. Prepared horseradish is grated horseradish that is preserved in vinegar so it's much stronger in flavor than the sauce.

A Special Touch Wrapped Rose Topiary

Floral foam block
Decorative pot (8 to 10 inches high)
5 to 7 fresh long-stemmed roses
Sphagnum moss
About 1 1/2 yards 2-inch-wide sheer ribbon

1 Cut foam into pieces to fit in pot. Press foam firmly in pot; add water.

2 Bunch roses together. Insert stems of roses into foam. Trim leaves as needed.

3 Arrange moss over foam. Wrap ribbon around stems of roses and tie into bow.

Tip: You can use any sturdy stemmed flowers such as tulips, lilies or gerbera daisies instead of the roses if you like.

More Great Ideas

What Are Some Extra-Special Christmas Drinks?

When you welcome family and friends to your home for the holidays, you may want to greet them with a fun and festive drink. Great drinks add to the spirit of the occasion—here are some super sippers that are sure to add more merriment to your Christmas moments:

Cider—Turn to page 58 for our warming recipe for Hot Spiced Cider. For serving, try one of these handy hints:

Pull out the slow cooker to help you with the holiday rush. When serving hot cider at a holiday buffet, pour heated cider into a slow cooker set on low and let guests help themselves.

If you prefer to keep the hot cider in the kitchen, invite in guests to ladle cider into their own mugs. Use an attractive saucepan kept right on the stove top over low heat.

You can make a glass punch bowl safer for hot beverages by filling it first with hot water and letting it stand about 30 minutes. Pour out water, and slowly add hot cider.

Punch—Turn to page 66 for a knockout recipe for Sparkling Cranberry Punch. For a finishing touch, try these delightful additions:

Garnish holiday drinks with a slice of starfruit on the rim of each glass.

Freeze fresh mint leaves and whole cranberries in water in ice-cube trays.

Make ice cubes with juice instead of water. When the juice cubes melt, they won't dilute the punch.

Eggnog—Don't have time to make your own eggnog? That's just fine because you can dress up purchased eggnog instead! Here's the best way, plus some fun flavor variations:

Place eggnog in punch bowl and stir in some rum, if desired, to taste. Scoop dollops of cinnamon or French vanilla ice cream over the nog and sprinkle with freshly grated nutmeg.

For coffee lovers, make Hot Cappuccino Eggnog: substitute coffee liqueur for the rum and stir in 1 cup hot espresso coffee. Don't worry if you don't have brewed espresso coffee; any strongly brewed cup of coffee (regular or decaf) will do.

Freeze small dollops of sweetened whipped cream (see pages 172 or 178) by scooping them out onto a cookie sheet and freezing until firm. Keep them handy in a resealable plastic freezer bag. Place one dollop on each drink just before serving and sprinkle lightly with ground cinnamon or nutmeg.

Place plain or chocolate-dipped pirouette cookies on a serving plate next to the punch bowl—guests can use them as edible stirring spoons!

Easter Easter Brunch

Spring brings tulips, daffodils and Easter. It's a lovely time for a brunch, and this menu captures all the fresh flavors of the season—cherry, lemon and strawberry. Plus it showcases that Easter favorite—ham.

The Glazed Baked Ham recipe calls for a 6- to 8-pound bone-in ham, which is enough for twelve people, or for eight with leftovers. Bone-in hams have marvelous flavor, and the leftovers are great in ham sandwiches, casseroles and salads. Freeze some of the ham in slices, or cut into chunks or strips for casseroles and salads. All of the other recipes serve eight, so if you are entertaining a group of twelve, you will want to make each recipe one and one-half times.

This menu is ideal for serving buffet style. If the weather pleasant, your guests can wander out to the deck or yard to eat. And think spring as you plan your color scheme— lavender, pastel pinks, blues, greens and yellows. For a showstopping centerpiece, make the Wok Skimmer Basket (page 243). Or keep it simple by setting out a wire basket of colored Easter eggs, several small baskets full of pretty Easter candy or a big vase filled with tulips and daffodils. For more ideas with spring flowers, turn to page 243.

Menu

SERVES 8

Glazed Baked Ham with Tangy Cherry Sauce, pages 240, 242

Country Egg Scramble, page 218

Lemon–Poppy Seed Scones, page 196

Fresh Strawberries and Cut-Up Kiwifruit

Coffee, Tea and Orange Juice

A Special Touch
Wok Skimmer Basket, page 243

PARTY COUNTDOWN

1 week before brunch
Buy supplies for Wok Skimmer Basket (page 243), and assemble centerpiece.

3 days before brunch
Buy groceries.

1 day before brunch
Make Tangy Cherry Sauce (page 242); cover and refrigerate.

Make Lemon-Poppy Seed Scones (page 196); wrap cooled scones in aluminum foil and leave at room temperature. Or purchase scones from your favorite bakery.

Arrange buffet table, and choose serving dishes and utensils.

Morning of the brunch
Set the table.

Prepare potatoes for Country Egg Scramble (page 218); cover with cold water in saucepan to keep them from turning brown. Slice the green onions; cover and refrigerate.

3 hours before brunch
Prepare Glazed Baked Ham (page 240). Place ham in oven (about 2 1/2 hours before you plan to serve the meal).

Make brown sugar mixture for ham; cover and leave at room temperature.

1 hour before brunch
Wash and dry strawberries. Peel and cut up kiwifruit. Arrange fruit on a platter or place in serving bowl; cover and refrigerate.

Pour orange juice into a pitcher; refrigerate.

45 minutes before brunch

Remove ham from oven; cut diamond pattern in ham and insert whole cloves. Pat or spoon brown sugar mixture over ham, and continue baking.

Cook potatoes for Country Egg Scramble (page 218).

30 minutes before brunch

Remove ham from the oven; place on carving board or platter. Cover with aluminum foil and let stand for 10 minutes.

20 minutes before brunch

Carve the ham and arrange on a platter; cover with aluminum foil to keep warm.

Place scones in oven to heat.

Make coffee and tea.

Finish making Country Egg Scramble; place in serving bowl and cover with aluminum foil to keep warm.

10 minutes before brunch

Reheat the cherry sauce, and place in serving bowl.

Remove scones from oven, and place in serving basket.

Place the food on the table.

Serve coffee, tea and juice.

Glazed Baked Ham

MAKES 12 servings • **BAKE** 2 hours 15 minutes • **LET STAND** 10 minutes

INGREDIENTS

Essential Equipment:
shallow roasting pan (about 13×9-inch rectangle) and rack; meat thermometer (not instant-read)

6- to 8-pound fully cooked bone-in ham

1/2 cup packed brown sugar

2 tablespoons orange or pineapple juice

1/2 teaspoon ground mustard (dry)

Whole cloves, if desired

DIRECTIONS

1 Heat the oven to 325°. Place the ham, fat side up, on the rack in the roasting pan. The rack keeps the ham out of the drippings and prevents scorching. It is not necessary to brush the ham with pan drippings while it bakes.

2 Insert the meat thermometer so the tip is in the thickest part of the ham and does not touch bone or rest in fat.

3 Bake uncovered 1 hour 15 minutes to 2 hours 15 minutes (13 to 17 minutes per pound) or until thermometer reads 135° (see step 5).

4 While the ham is baking, mix brown sugar, orange juice and mustard until smooth.

5 Remove the ham from the oven 30 minutes before it is done. Remove any skin from the ham. Make cuts about 1/2 inch apart and 1/4 inch deep in a diamond pattern in the fat surface of the ham, without cutting into the meat. Insert a whole clove into the corner of each diamond. Pat or spoon brown sugar mixture over the top and sides of ham.

6 Bake about 30 minutes longer or until thermometer reads 135°. Remove the ham from the oven. Cover ham loosely with a tent of aluminum foil and let stand about 10 minutes or until thermometer reads 140°. After standing, the ham also will be easier to carve.

1 Serving: Calories 195 (Calories from Fat 80); Fat 9g (Saturated 3g); Cholesterol 55mg; Sodium 1450mg; Carbohydrate 7g (Dietary Fiber 0g); Protein 22g **% Daily Value:** Vitamin A 0%; Vitamin C 0%; Calcium 0%; Iron 8% **Diet Exchanges:** 3 Lean Meat, 1/2 Fruit

Tip **FOR EASY CLEANUP,** line bottom of roasting pan with aluminum foil before placing ham on rack.

Cutting Diamond Pattern in Ham

Make cuts about 1/2 inch apart and 1/4 inch deep in diamond pattern in fat surface of ham, without cutting into the meat.

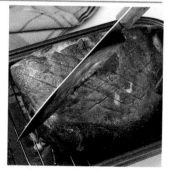

Carving Bone-in Ham

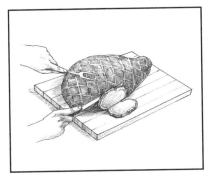

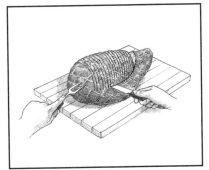

1 Place ham, fat side up and bone to your right, on a carving board or platter. Cut a few slices from thin side. Turn ham cut side down, so it rests firmly.

2 Make vertical slices down to the leg bone, then cut horizontally along bone to release slices.

Tangy Cherry Sauce

MAKES about 1 cup sauce • **COOK** 8 minutes

INGREDIENTS

Essential Equipment:
medium saucepan (about 2-quart size)

1/2 cup packed brown sugar

2 tablespoons cornstarch

1 teaspoon ground mustard

1 cup dried sour cherries

1 1/2 cups water

1 teaspoon grated lemon peel

1/4 cup lemon juice

DIRECTIONS

1 Mix the brown sugar, cornstarch and mustard in the saucepan. Stir in the cherries, water, lemon peel and lemon juice.

2 Cook over low heat 6 to 8 minutes, stirring constantly, until mixture is thickened.

1 Tablespoon: Calories 55 (Calories from Fat 10); Fat 1g (Saturated 0g); Cholesterol 0mg; Sodium 5mg; Carbohydrate 16g (Dietary Fiber 3g); Protein 0g **% Daily Value:** Vitamin A 0%; Vitamin C 8%; Calcium 0%; Iron 2% **Diet Exchanges:** 1 Fruit

Tip **TO DO AHEAD,** make this sauce up to 3 days before. Store the sauce covered in the refrigerator. Reheat in a microwave-safe dish 1 or 2 minutes or until hot.

Tip **SOUR CHERRIES** are too tart to eat raw when fresh. However when they are dried, their sugar becomes more concentrated. Dried sour cherries are excellent to use in sauces and desserts and for baking. They make a great snack as well.

Tip **TO SAVE TIME,** serve ham with purchased sauce such as a special mustard or horseradish sauce.

More Great Ideas

Welcome Easter with Spring Flowers

For a change of pace, serve this lovely spring brunch somewhere unexpected, like a sunroom or enclosed porch. Or else bring some of spring's blooming bounty indoors. Special flowers and plants will enhance both your table and the room where you serve your brunch. Here are a few ideas:

Arrange small potted blooming plants or forced bulbs such as hyacinths, daffodils and crocuses on the table. Intersperse white or pale pastel votive candles in glass holders.

Place a small basket of cut spring flowers at each place setting. Fresh violets, snowdrops, scilla, primrose or crocus are lovely choices. Invite your guests to take their baskets home after the brunch.

Force branches of early spring shrubs or trees into bloom to use as a centerpiece. Forsythia in its cheering shades of yellow is widely available at florist shops. Or cut crab apple or cherry branches for their pink and white blossoms. Pussy willow and cattails in neutral grays and browns are also lovely. If you're not sure how to force branches, most flower arranging or gardening books will tell you how. Arrange the branches in a simple pitcher or large vase.

Use your favorite vase and fill it to almost overflowing with such lovely spring flowers as tulips, iris, lily of the valley and daffodils—roses are delightful too. Use flowers in any combination or alone, whatever suits your table and budget.

A Special Touch Wok Skimmer Basket

6- to 8-inch stick
3 bamboo wok skimmers (available at kitchen stores or Asian markets)
Twine
4- to 5-inch ivy plant
Terra-cotta saucer (4 to 6 inches in diameter)
Glue
Straw
Colored eggs
About 1 1/2 yards 2-inch-wide wired ribbon

1 Tie stick and skimmers together, weaving twine through holes at top of skimmer handles to secure.

2 Place plant in center of saucer. Press stick into center of plant. Glue bottoms of skimmers to edge of saucer to secure. (Bend the baskets of the skimmers down a little to level them if needed before gluing.)

3 Place straw and eggs in baskets. Wrap ribbon around top of handles and tie into bow.

Beyond the Basics

Seven Great Menus

Birthday Celebration Dinner for 8

Remember how much fun birthdays were when you were a kid? Your best friends came over, you ate your favorite foods and there was a magnificent cake at the end. Well, whether you're 20, 30, 40 or more, nothing's changed, especially with this menu for an informal birthday buffet dinner.

Menu

Lasagna Primavera (page 112)
or Italian Sausage Lasagna (page 84)

Mixed-greens salad (from a purchased salad mix)
with choice of bottled dressing

Sour Cream Breadstick Twists (page 156)
or purchased soft breadsticks

Party Ice-Cream Cake (page 170)
or Rich Chocolate Fudge Cake (page 160)

Citrus Spritzers (page 64), soft drinks and water

Coffee and tea

Tip **WHEN SETTING THE BUFFET TABLE,** place the plates and flatware (no knives needed!) at the beginning, followed by the lasagna, salad and breadsticks.

SET UP a separate drinks station for the spritzers, soft drinks and water.

AFTER GUESTS HAVE HELPED THEMSELVES to seconds, clear the table and set out dessert plates, forks and extra napkins. Decorate the cake with colored sugars, edible flowers or candy decorations, and place birthday candles on cake just before serving.

IF YOU DON'T HAVE TIME to make a cake, purchase one at the bakery, or ask a guest to bring one instead.

Party Countdown

Up to 2 weeks before
Bake and cool Sour Cream Breadstick Twists; wrap in aluminum foil and freeze.

The day before
Make Lasagna Primavera up to the baking step; cover and refrigerate.

Make Party Ice-Cream Cake; freeze tightly covered.

Make or buy ice.

The morning of
Remove breadsticks from freezer.

Chill soft drinks.

About 1 1/2 hours before
Bake Lasagna Primavera, covered, in 350° oven 45 minutes; uncover and bake 30 minutes longer or until lasagna is hot in center.

About 20 minutes before
Make Citrus Spritzers.

Heat breadsticks in 400° oven for 5 minutes.

Make coffee.

Mix salad greens and dressing; place in serving bowl.

Cocktails and Appetizers for 12

Good conversation and tasty nibbles are the hallmarks of a great cocktail party with good friends. The food in this menu is perfect for a stand-up-and-mingle party. You can eat it with your fingers or with toothpicks and nothing's hard to balance on a plate. Yet the flavors, colors and shapes are a treat for the eye and the taste buds.

Menu

Assorted nuts, pretzels or purchased snack mix

Marinated Peppers, Olives and Cheese (page 34)

Veggie Tortilla Roll-Ups (page 36)

Sweet-and-Sour Meatballs (page 50)
or Buffalo Chicken Wings (page 46)

Hot Crab Dip (page 44) or Spinach Dip (page 40)

Cut-up fresh vegetables

White Chocolate–Dipped Strawberries (page 186)

Assorted cookies or purchased candies

Champagne or wine, beer and mixed drinks,
if desired

Tip **IF TIME'S SHORT,** choose two or three recipes and double them. Or pick up an appetizer or two from your supermarket deli, such as meatballs or veggies and dip.

BUY the nuts, pretzels, snack mix, cookies, candies and beverages ahead of time—they keep!

SET UP THE BAR in the kitchen or on a table close to where your guests will be mingling.

PLAN ON FOUR OR FIVE APPETIZERS per hour per guest (more if your party is over the dinner hour).

Party Countdown

Up to 2 weeks before
Make Marinated Peppers, Olives and Cheese; cover and refrigerate.

The day before
Make and bake Sweet-and-Sour Meatballs; cover and refrigerate.

Prepare Hot Crab Dip up to the baking step; cover and refrigerate.

Make White Chocolate–Dipped Strawberries; cover and refrigerate.

Cut up the veggies; put in plastic bags and refrigerate.

Chill champagne, wine and beer.

The morning of
Make Veggie Tortilla Roll-Ups; cover and refrigerate.

Put candies, pretzels, nuts and snack mix in serving dishes; cover and set on table.

Arrange cookies on serving plate; cover and set on table.

About 20 minutes before
Heat meatballs and sauce for Sweet-and-Sour Meatballs.

Bake Hot Crab Dip.

Uncover candies, pretzels, nuts, snack mix and cookies.

Cut tortilla rolls into slices; arrange on serving plate.

Arrange cut-up veggies in serving containers or on serving plate.

Backyard Barbecue for 8

Aah, summertime. It's the perfect time for a backyard barbecue. And this barbecue menu's perfect because you never have to turn on the oven and heat up your kitchen! The menu stars tender beef kabobs, a different and more sophisticated choice for grilling, and the accompaniments are all-American favorites.

Menu

Pretzels and chips

Beef Kabobs with Chilied Plum Sauce (page 70)

Hot cooked rice or couscous

Tangy Coleslaw (page 140)

Sliced Watermelon

Frosty Key Lime Pie (page 178)

Old-Fashioned Lemonade (page 60)

Beer or wine, if desired

 BREAK OUT THE COOLERS and plenty of ice to keep the cold food cold.

FOR THE KIDS, throw some chicken breasts on the grill and serve with the chilied plum sauce—it's tangy sweet and not too spicy. Kids will enjoy all the other sides just as much as the adults.

FOR ICE-COLD LEMONADE, put an empty glass pitcher in the freezer for about 30 minutes before filling with lemonade.

THE FOODS ARE EASY TO PASS, or you can set up a buffet on a picnic table.

Party Countdown

Up to 2 days before
Make Frosty Key Lime Pie; freeze tightly covered.

The day before
Make Chilied Plum Sauce for Beef Kabobs; cover and refrigerate.

Chill beer and wine.

The morning of
Assemble Beef Kabobs; cover and refrigerate.

Make Tangy Coleslaw, and put in serving bowl; cover and refrigerate.

Make Old-Fashioned Lemonade; refrigerate.

About 1 hour before
If using a charcoal grill, light the coals.

About 20 minutes before
Light gas grill, if using.

Cook rice.

Cut watermelon into slices; place on serving platter.

About 15 minutes before
Grill kabobs.

Put pretzels and chips in serving bowls.

Casual Get-Together with Friends for 6

A promotion, an anniversary, a great new video or no particular reason at all. There's always a good excuse for getting friends together for dinner. This easy, casual, sit-down dinner won't leave you frazzled but will give you plenty of time to talk and catch up. Some tips for making this get-together a success:

YOU HAVE SEVERAL OPTIONS for serving the meal: Set up a buffet on the kitchen counter, pass the dishes family style or dish up the manicotti on each plate and pass the remaining foods.

IF YOU CAN'T FIND CAESAR SALAD MIX, buy a bunch of romaine, a bottle of Caesar dressing and a package of croutons. Grate some fresh Parmesan cheese over the salad at the last minute and toss.

MAKE COFFEE AND TEA when you clear the table and take the apple crisp out of the oven.

> ### *Menu*
>
> Chicken Manicotti (page 96)
>
> Caesar salad (from a purchased salad mix)
>
> Sesame Green Beans (page 126)
>
> Hot Cheese Bread (page 150)
>
> Cinnamon-Apple Crisp (page 168)
>
> Coffee and tea
>
> Wine, if desired

Party Countdown

Up to 2 weeks before
Make Chicken Manicotti up to the baking step and before sprinkling with cheese; tightly cover and freeze.

The day before
Remove manicotti from freezer; thaw in refrigerator at least 12 hours.

Chill wine.

The morning of
Make Cinnamon-Apple Crisp up to baking step; cover and refrigerate.

Prepare green beans and assemble ingredients for Sesame Green Beans.

About 1 1/2 hours before
Sprinkle manicotti with cheese; bake.

Make Hot Cheese Bread up to baking step; wrap in heavy-duty aluminum foil and refrigerate.

About 20 minutes before
Bake bread.

Cook green beans.

Mix salad with dressing; place in serving bowl.

Right before
Bake apple crisp (so it's nice and warm when you are ready to serve dessert).

Decadent Dessert Buffet for 12

An easy, elegant and often less expensive way to entertain is with a dessert buffet. It's perfect after a concert, or for a holiday gathering, baby shower or any number of special occasions.

Tip **IF TIME'S TIGHT,** make just one "star" dessert, and pick up "supporting" desserts at your favorite bakery.

FRESH FRUIT AND CHEESES are perfect alongside sweet desserts.

IT WILL BE EASIER FOR EVERYONE to help themselves if you cut the lemon bars and the tiramisu dessert into small squares ahead of time, and arrange on platters or on individual plates. Your guests will want to sample everything, so keep pieces small.

THE CHOCOLATE CAKE is a beautiful showstopper. Place it, uncut, on a pretty serving plate or cake stand, and arrange the other desserts around it. Cut it into slices once your guests have oohed and aahed.

Party Countdown

The day before
Bake and cool Rich Chocolate Fudge Cake up to the glazing step; place on serving plate and cover.

Bake and cool lemon bars; cover and keep at room temperature.

Make White Chocolate–Dipped Strawberries; cover and refrigerate.

Chill cranberry juice cocktail and ginger ale for Sparkling Cranberry Punch.

Make ice ring or ice.

The morning of
Make Tiramisu-Toffee Dessert; cover and refrigerate.

Glaze cake; loosely cover and keep at room temperature.

Mix ingredients except for ginger ale for punch; refrigerate.

About 1 hour before
Wash and slice fruit (dip apples and pears in lemon juice so they don't turn brown). Arrange on serving plate with cheeses; cover and refrigerate.

About 20 minutes before
Make coffee and tea.

Cut tiramisu dessert; arrange on individual plates.

Cut lemon bars; arrange on serving plate with dipped strawberries.

Add ginger ale and ice ring to punch.

Menu

Rich Chocolate Fudge Cake (page 160)

Tiramisu-Toffee Dessert (page 174)

Luscious Lemon Bars (page 188)

White Chocolate–Dipped Strawberries (page 186)

Assorted fresh fruit (raspberries, apples, pears, kiwifruit) and cheeses

Assorted purchased cookies, if desired

Sparkling Cranberry Punch (page 66)

Coffee and tea

Lazy Weekend Brunch for 6

You won't have to leap out of bed at the crack of dawn to put this brunch on the table. Sleep in or stay through the whole church service because you've made the main dish the night before.

Menu

Apricot-Stuffed French Toast (page 206)
with strawberry sauce or maple syrup

Bacon and sausage

Hash browns

Red or green grapes

Coffee, tea and orange juice

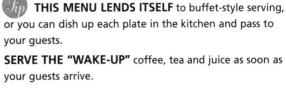 **THIS MENU LENDS ITSELF** to buffet-style serving, or you can dish up each plate in the kitchen and pass to your guests.

SERVE THE "WAKE-UP" coffee, tea and juice as soon as your guests arrive.

FOR THIS MENU, purchase a bag of hash browns in the refrigerated section of the supermarket and cook them in a skillet according to package directions. If you have two ovens, you may want to try Home-Style Hash Browns (page 220) that can be prepared up to baking the night before. They are cooked at a lower temperature than the French Toast, so it is best to bake them separately.

THE "MAGIC FORMULA" FOR GREAT COFFEE is 2 level tablespoons of ground coffee per 3/4 cup of water. Use freshly ground beans and cold water for the best flavor.

Party Countdown

The day (night) before
Make Apricot-Stuffed French Toast up to the baking step; cover and refrigerate.

Wash and dry grapes; refrigerate.

About 30 minutes before
Bake French toast.

About 20 minutes before
Make coffee and tea.

Cook bacon and sausage.

Cook hash browns.

Candlelight Dinner for 2

Surprise your guest with this elegant dinner, or if you both love to cook, hand over an apron! For this meal, you'll want to break out your best of everything: dishes, linens, glassware and flatware.

Menu

Tomato-Basil Bruschetta (page 56)

Pear and Blue Cheese Salad (page 138)

Garlic Shrimp (page 106) with fettuccine or
Dilled Chicken with Lemon Basmati Rice (page 94)

Hazelnut-Parmesan Asparagus (page 122)

Raspberry Custard Cream (page 182)

Champagne or sparkling cider

Tip **TURN THE LIGHTS DOWN LOW** and light the candles—not just on the table but all around the room.

PUT YOUR FAVORITE MUSIC ON nice and low.

TO MAKE THIS MENU EASY as well as elegant, forgo the bruschetta appetizer and buy a delectable dessert.

IT'S EASY TO MAKE all of these recipes for two—just cut them in half. Or make the full amount of each recipe and enjoy delicious leftovers the next day.

Party Countdown

The day before
Make Cider Vinaigrette for Pear and Blue Cheese Salad; cover and refrigerate.

Chill champagne.

The morning of
Make tomato mixture for Tomato-Basil Bruschetta; cover and refrigerate. Cut baguette into slices; place in plastic bag and keep at room temperature.

Slice pears (dip in lemon juice so they don't turn brown), and wash and dry romaine for salad; cover and refrigerate.

Peel and devein (clean) shrimp for Garlic Shrimp; cover and refrigerate. Chop garlic and cilantro, and shred carrot.

Prepare asparagus and assemble ingredients for Hazelnut-Parmesan Asparagus; refrigerate asparagus.

About 1 hour before
Make Raspberry Custard Cream, and spoon into glasses; cover and refrigerate.

Make salad and arrange on individual plates; cover and refrigerate.

About 15 minutes before
Assemble and bake bruschetta.

Cook and drain fettuccine; cover and keep warm.

About 10 minutes before
Cook asparagus and finish recipe; cover and keep warm.

After serving bruschetta
Cook shrimp.

Arrange fettuccine on individual plates or in a serving bowl; top with shrimp.

Beverage Basics

An important part of entertaining is making guests feel comfortable, and one of the easiest ways you can do this is by offering your guests something to drink. Punch, tea, coffee, lemonade, soft drinks, sparkling cider, water, juice or alcoholic beverages are all appropriate party drinks. (Nonalcoholic beverages tend to be less expensive if you're planning a get-together on a limited budget.) At the end of a meal, there's nothing better than a fragrant cup of coffee or tea. Serve it with dessert, or after, if you like. And for some parties, such as a dessert buffet or a brunch, coffee and tea will be the favorites. For easy serving, set out a tray of coffee cups and saucers, teaspoons, and sugar bowl and creamer ahead of time.

The Perfect Cup Of Coffee

For a coffee drinker, the perfect cup is always the goal. Here are some tips to get it right every time:

Start with a clean pot. Wash the pot and filter basket after each use with hot, soapy water—but not abrasive scouring pads—to get rid of any bitter oils that may cling to the inside. Rinse well with hot water. Check manufacturer's directions for periodic cleaning of the entire coffeemaker.

Choose the correct grind for your coffeemaker. Check the manufacturer's recommendations if you're not sure.

Use freshly ground beans and fresh cold water. For the best flavor, grind coffee beans just before using. The "magic formula" preferred by many coffee lovers is 2 level tablespoons of ground coffee per 3/4 cup (or 6 ounces) of water—this makes a stronger cup of coffee. For regular strength, decrease the coffee to 1 tablespoon.

Serve hot coffee as soon as it's done brewing. Heat destroys the flavor of coffee if left on the burner too long. If you aren't going to drink it right away, remove the grounds and keep the heat very low, or pour the coffee into an insulated container.

Never reheat coffee, since it becomes very bitter. However, leftover coffee that is covered and refrigerated until cold becomes delicious iced coffee!

A Cozy Cup Of Tea

Tea is a beverage that's steeped in tradition, but brewing tea is as easy as 1-2-3! Here are 3 easy steps to prepare a perfect pot:

1. **Warm a spotlessly clean teapot** by filling it with hot water. Empty it just before adding the tea.
2. **Bring fresh, cold water** to a full boil in a teakettle.
3. **Add tea to the warm pot,** about 1 teaspoon of loose tea or 1 tea bag for each 3/4 cup of water. Pour the boiling water over the tea. Let it steep for 3 to 5 minutes to bring out the full flavor (tea is not ready once the color has changed). Stir the tea once to ensure an even brew. Remove the tea bag or infuser, or strain the tea as you pour. If you prefer weaker tea, add hot water after brewing the tea. Serve with sugar, and milk or cream or thin slices of lemon.

Great Food and Wine Pairs

Remember the old rule of serving red wine with meat and white wine with fish and chicken? Well, wine styles and the rules have changed. Today, pairing wine with food is all about *flavor* and *weight*. Basically, the wine should complement the food and not overpower it, and vice versa.

When choosing a wine to go with your meal, ask yourself: Is the food I'm serving rich and hearty or simple and light? Is it spicy or mild, sweet or sour? Does it have a strongly flavored sauce? How is it prepared—grilled, baked, deep-fried? The answers will help you choose your wine. Here are some pairing pointers:

Hearty foods such as beef and chili need a heavier, more tannic wine that is bold enough to stand up to the food, such as a Cabernet Sauvignon or a Shiraz.

Lighter foods such as grilled fish and chicken, which would be blown away by a heavier wine, marry well with a light wine with some acidity, such as Sauvignon Blanc or some Chardonnays.

Sweet foods and dishes with some degree of sweetness (think teriyaki or fruit-based sauces) are best paired with a wine that also has a touch of sweetness, such as Riesling. If the food is sweeter than the wine, it can make the wine taste dry and "puckery."

Sour foods such as sauces made with lemons, limes and vinegar cut the tartness of a wine and make a full-bodied wine taste sweet and thin. Instead, choose a wine that also has some acidity, such as a Sauvignon Blanc.

Spicy, smoked and heavily seasoned foods are best when served with light, fruity wines such as Pinot Noir and Sauvignon Blanc that tend to cool the heat.

Although there may be lot of *good* matches in the food and wine world, it's important to remember that there is no single perfect wine for any one food. If you like a wine, drink it with food you also like, and you're sure to have a super match. The suggestions that follow give some ideas to guide you, but there are countless other food and wine pairings just waiting to be explored.

Food and Wine Pairings

Food	Wine
Beef	
Burgers	Cabernet, Zinfandel
Roast	Cabernet, Shiraz/Syrah
Stew	Cabernet, Merlot
Cheese	
Blue	Port
Brie	Chardonnay, Champagne
Cheddar	Cabernet, Zinfandel
Feta or goat cheese	Sauvignon Blanc
Chicken	
Barbecued	Shiraz, Cabernet, Zinfandel
Grilled/Roasted	Chardonnay
Chili	Cabernet
Chocolate	Cabernet, Port
Desserts	Champagne, Riesling
Ethnic Dishes	
Chinese	Riesling, Gewürztraminer, Sauvignon Blanc
Indian	Gewürztraminer, Sauvignon Blanc
Mexican	Zinfandel
Thai	Sauvignon Blanc
Fish and Shellfish	
Crab, Lobster, Shrimp	Chardonnay, Sauvignon Blanc
Fish, mild-flavored (halibut, sole)	Sauvignon Blanc
Fish, strong-flavored (tuna, swordfish)	Chardonnay
Salmon	Chardonnay, Pinot Noir
Lamb	Cabernet
Pasta	
Alfredo	Chardonnay
Lasagna	Merlot, Zinfandel
Pesto	Sauvignon Blanc
Tomato and meat sauce	Chianti, Zinfandel
Pizza	Merlot, Zinfandel
Pork	
Chops	Merlot, Shiraz/Syrah
Ribs, barbecued	Zinfandel
Ham	Shiraz, Riesling
Sausage	Cabernet, Zinfandel
Salads	Riesling, Sauvignon Blanc
Turkey	Gewürztraminer, Pinot Noir

Stocking the Bar

You don't need an elaborate selection of alcoholic beverages to have a well-stocked bar. What should you have on hand? Start with a few liquors that you really like, then build from there, adding before- and after-dinner drinks last. Following are some supplies you'd find in a well-stocked bar.

Liquor

Bourbon

Gin

Rum

Scotch

Tequila

Vermouth (sweet and dry)

Vodka

Whiskey

Wine and Beer

Wine (red and white)

Champagne

Beer (regular, light and nonalcoholic)

Before- and After-Dinner Drinks

Brandy

Liqueurs (almond, chocolate, coffee, orange, raspberry)

Port

Sherry

Mixers

Bottled water

Club soda

Cola (regular and diet)

Ginger ale

Grenadine, sweetened lime juice

Lemon-lime soda (regular and diet)

Juice (cranberry, grapefruit, orange)

Margarita mix

Bloody Mary mix or tomato juice

Tonic water

Condiments and Garnishes

Celery stalks

Lemons and limes

Maraschino cherries

Olives

Bar Equipment

Blender

Bottle opener

Coasters

Cocktail napkins

Corkscrew

Ice

Ice bucket

Ice tongs

Pitcher

Shaker

Shot glass

Stirrer

Strainer

Straws

Serving Alcoholic Beverages

Don't feel as though you have to offer guests a full bar, or *any* hard liquor for that matter. Wine and beer will be perfectly acceptable for most of your gatherings. If you want to serve hard liquor but also want to keep it simple, stick to one or two mixed drinks that tie in with the theme of your party—like rum-spiked eggnog at Christmas or margaritas for a south-of-the-border fest.

And don't forget your designated drivers and nondrinking guests. Be sure to have nonalcoholic choices for them, too. One solution that accommodates drinkers and nondrinkers: Serve a fruit punch with a pitcher of rum or whiskey on the side, and let guests spike their own drinks. This works great with holiday eggnog and hot cider too.

Quick Fixes for Unexpected Guests

What happens if a friend brings an unexpected guest to your party? It's not much of a problem at a buffet or open house. But conjuring up more food for a sit-down meal is a bit trickier. First, smile nicely, welcome the guest, then work a little magic. Here's how you can do it:

Stretch a meal by making extra pasta, couscous, rice or potatoes.

Slice some extras by cutting the meat or chicken a little thinner, or cut smaller squares of a casserole.

Make up the plates in the kitchen instead of passing the food. People tend to eat more when they help themselves.

Slip in an extra course by setting out munchies before dinner; or serve an extra plate of store-bought cookies with dessert or coffee.

Take a smaller portion for yourself.

Remember to cook extra next time for that "invisible" guest!

Accommodating Special Diets

What happens if guests tell you they're on a "special" diet, perhaps low-cholesterol, diabetic, salt-restricted or vegetarian?

Well, accommodate them, up to a point. If you have your heart set on serving turkey for Thanksgiving, but one guest is vegetarian, go ahead and roast a turkey. Just make sure there are other meatless dishes your guest can enjoy. For other diets, once again the word is *accommodate*. Here are a few suggestions:

Try using low-fat or nonfat ingredients in some of the dishes (this works really well for dips and toppings).

Go light on the salt when making the meal, and let guests sprinkle it on at the table.

Serve sauces on the side. Let everyone add salad dressing and butter to taste, too.

Make plenty of the food that fits the special diet (like rice, pasta, potatoes, vegetables).

Have a back-up bowl of cut-up fresh fruit or berries as a "light" alternative if you're planning on serving a rich dessert.

Invite the guest to bring something he or she will want to eat if the diet requires something too "special."

Impromptu Party Fare

You won't always have the luxury of weeks to plan your party. Sometimes it just happens—and that's part of the fun! Here are some quick-to-fix ideas that you can pull together in minutes with foods from your pantry, refrigerator or freezer:

An assortment of snacks and munchies are great to keep on hand. Potato and tortilla chips, salsa, bean dip, honey-roasted nuts, crackers, cheese, olives, packaged gourmet cookies—all can be last-minute lifesavers. Arrange them in serving dishes, and voilà! You've assembled a tasty party.

Pasta, olive oil, a little fresh garlic and some Parmesan cheese, can be tossed together for a simple but delicious main dish in minutes.

Flour tortillas can wrap up a variety of fix-it-fast fillings, such as canned black beans, cut-up cooked chicken or sliced deli meats, for a meal in minutes. Salsa, sour cream and shredded cheese all make great toppers.

Eggs—scrambled, fried, filled and folded into an omelet—make a quick any-time-of-day meal.

Ice cream can be topped with a splash of liqueur or maple syrup and sprinkled with fresh berries or coconut for a spur-of-the-moment dessert.

Pick up the phone. Full-meal help is only a phone call away to your favorite restaurant, deli or pizzeria.

Stocking the Party Pantry

You're ready for just about any occasion when you have a well-stocked party pantry. These foods and supplies will let you pull together a spontaneous yet festive meal.

Some of these items may already be part of your everyday pantry. Buy larger quantities of them and you'll be ready for company—anytime!

In the Cupboard

Artichoke hearts (canned or jarred)

Baking cocoa

Baking mix (Bisquick)

Baking powder and baking soda

Bread crumbs (dry)

Broth (beef, chicken, vegetable)

Chips (potato, tortilla)

Chocolate chips

Chutney

Coffee and tea

Cookies and crackers

Cooking spray

Dips (canned such as black bean and cheese)

Graham cracker pie crust (ready-to-use)

Herbs and spices

Flour

French bread

Garlic

Jams and jellies

Ketchup

Mayonnaise

Mustard (yellow, Dijon)

Noodles (Chinese curly, egg, lasagna)

Nuts (almonds, peanuts, pecans, mixed)

Oils (olive, sesame, vegetable)

Olives (green, Kalamata, ripe)

Onions

Pasta (fettuccine, penne, rotini, spaghetti)

Pasta sauces (Alfredo, pesto, spaghetti)

Popcorn

Rice and rice mixtures

Roasted red bell peppers

Salad dressing

Salsa

Salt and pepper

Soft drinks

Soy sauce and marinating sauces

Sugars (brown, granulated, powdered)

Syrups (caramel, chocolate, maple)

Tomato sauce and tomato paste

Tomatoes (diced, peeled whole)

Tortillas (corn, flour)

Vanilla

Vinegars (balsamic, cider, red wine)

Wine (red and white)

In the Refrigerator

Cheeses (Cheddar, cream, mozzarella, Parmesan, ricotta)

Eggs

Fruit juice

Half-and-half

Lemons and limes

Margarine or butter

Milk

Mint leaves, fresh (for garnishing desserts and beverages)

Parsley, fresh (for garnishing)

Salad greens, packaged

Sour cream

Whipping (heavy) cream

In the Freezer

Chicken (boneless, skinless breasts)

Fruit juice concentrate

Ground beef, turkey or sausage

Ice cream or frozen yogurt

Ice (crushed or cubes)

Vegetables (packaged)

Other Essentials

All-purpose spray cleaner

Aluminum foil

Candles (birthday, taper, votive)

Coffee filters

Dishwasher detergent

Dish towels

Food-storage bags

Kitchen string

Liquid detergent

Notepad (for keeping lists)

Paper plates and napkins

Paper towels

Plastic glasses

Plastic wrap

Pot holders

Scrubbing pads (nonabrasive)

Sponges

Storage containers

Toothpicks (plain, colored, with frills)

Trash bags

Waxed paper

Essential Entertaining Equipment and Tools

Once you have stocked your kitchen with basic equipment for cooking and baking, what are some of the must-have tools to make your entertaining easier? Here are just a few to get you started:

CARVING OR ELECTRIC KNIFE
Essential for carving Thanksgiving turkey or a roast.

ICE-CREAM SCOOP
For dishing up perfectly rounded scoops of ice cream, or for filling muffin and cupcake pans with batter quickly and cleanly. Choose a sturdy, spring-loaded scoop that will work well in solidly frozen ice cream, yogurt and sorbet.

CASSEROLE DISHES
Serving from beautiful casserole dishes adds color and interest to your table setting. Look for 2- and 3-quart sizes.

LADLE
Large ones are great for serving soups, stews and chili. A small ladle is perfect for serving sauces.

COFFEEPOT
A 10-cup, drip-style pot will suit most occasions. You can rent or borrow larger ones.

PITCHER, LARGE GLASS OR PLASTIC
For serving water, iced tea, lemonade and punch.

FORK, LONG-HANDLED
Great for holding meat and poultry in place while you are slicing or carving it.

PLATTERS
In a variety of sizes for serving foods from main dishes to desserts.

POT HOLDERS/TRIVETS
To protect table from hot serving plates. Pot holders should be nice enough to bring to the table.

SERVING SPOONS
A large metal spoon is terrific for serving everything from apple crisp to mashed potatoes. A pierced or slotted spoon comes in handy for lifting foods out of liquid.

ROASTING PAN WITH A RACK
A large shallow pan for roasting meat and poultry, it's a must-have for the Thanksgiving turkey or Christmas roast. The rack suspends the meat so it doesn't cook in its own juice or fat.

THERMOMETER, MEAT OR INSTANT-READ
An easy way to be sure meats, poultry and fish are properly cooked. Make sure not to leave an instant-read thermometer (which isn't ovenproof) in the meat while cooking.

SALT AND PEPPER SHAKERS
Take your pick of fun shakers that are both pretty and practical.

TONGS
Serve up salad or spaghetti with ease. Cooking tongs should be made of all metal, in contrast to salad tongs, which may be wooden or plastic and usually have a larger end for tossing a salad.

SERVING BOWLS
Choose a variety of sizes, in ceramic or glass. Use to serve salads, vegetables, mashed potatoes, chips and more.

Not Essential but Nice to Have

If you like entertaining and plan to do more of it, here are some items you may like to add to your party collection:

BASKETS
For serving bread, rolls and muffins. A napkin or pretty dish towel makes a nice basket liner.

CHAFING DISH
A covered dish that has a small warming unit, such as a candle or canned cooking fuel, for keeping foods hot.

BLENDER
Can be used to make frozen drinks as well as to chop certain ingredients.

CHEESE BOARD AND CHEESE PLANE
An attractive way to present cheese and accompaniments including crackers, bread and fruit. The cheese plane has a sharpened slit for shaving off thin slices of cheese.

BUTTER SPREADER
Use to spread butter on bread, rolls and muffins. Place on the table with the butter that's on a butter dish or small plate.

CRUET WITH STOPPER
An elegant way to serve salad dressings, vinegars and oils. Bring it to the table, and let guests dress their salad to their taste.

CAKE STAND
An elegant way to serve cakes as well as pies, tarts, cookies, appetizers, cheese and fruit. (You can also create a beautiful buffet centerpiece by stacking two or three stands on top of one another.) Some cake stands have a domed cover, which helps protect the food and keep it fresh.

DESSERT DISHES, FOOTED
A fun and pretty way to serve ice cream, custard, fruit, nuts and candy, or to use for small table centerpieces (see page 132).

DESSERT SERVER
Use to easily serve cakes, pies and tarts.

ICE BUCKET WITH TONGS
For serving ice with cold beverages.

FONDUE POT AND SKEWERS
Can be used for cheese or dessert fondue, and for keeping dips, sauces and gravies hot.

JUICER
To squeeze fresh juice from lemons, limes, oranges and other citrus fruits.

FOOD PROCESSOR
If you are planning on shredding, chopping or grinding a lot of ingredients, this piece of equipment is a must.

PUNCH BOWL, 1 1/2-GALLON SIZE
For serving large quantities of punch.

GRAVY BOAT
For serving gravies and sauces in style. Use a pitcher or a small bowl and a ladle if you don't have a gravy boat.

SALAD BOWL WITH SERVERS
A nice way to serve salad on a buffet or for passing it at the table.

SERVING FORK
Use to serve meat or poultry.

GRIDDLE
Great for when you're making a pancake breakfast or serving a French toast brunch.

SLOW COOKER
Excellent for keeping foods such as chili and hot dips warm on a buffet.

SPAGHETTI SERVER
Separates long pasta strands for easy serving.

SPINNER FOR SALAD GREENS
After rinsing greens, spinning is a quick way to dry them so you're not left with a bowl of soggy salad.

SQUEEZE BOTTLES
Fill with sauces and toppings. Use to make fancy drizzles and designs over desserts and soups, or on individual plates and serving platters.

STOCKPOT
A large pot, usually 5-quart size or larger, for crowd-size recipes of chili, stew and soup and for cooking pasta.

STRAINER, SMALL
Comes in handy for garnishing desserts with a sprinkling of powdered sugar, baking cocoa or ground cinnamon.

SUGAR AND CREAMER SET
A small, covered bowl and pitcher for serving sugar and cream (or milk) with coffee and tea.

TEAPOT
For serving tea or other hot beverages. Also doubles as a great flower holder.

TRAY
For serving food and carrying dishes to the kitchen.

VASES
In several shapes and sizes.

WAFFLE IRON

Available in both electric and range-top models in a number of shapes, such as square, rectangular, round and heart. Look for waffle irons with a nonstick surface for easy cooking and cleaning.

WARMING TRAY

A plug-in electric tray that keeps food warm at the table or on a buffet.

WINE COOLER

Keeps wine chilled without ice.

WOK

A round-bottomed cooking utensil that can be used instead of a stir-fry pan or skillet to stir-fry or steam meats and vegetables. Both range-top and electric woks are available.

ZESTER

A special tool that can be used instead of a grater to remove the colored portion, or the "zest," of lemon, lime and orange peel. Can also use to make garnishes.

If the Pan Fits . . .

Okay, your recipe calls for a springform pan. But you don't have a springform pan and don't want to go buy one. What's a cook to do? Substitute! When you don't have the right-sized pan or casserole, here are some you can use instead:

Pan Sizes and Substitutions

If you don't have a . . .	Use a . . .
9-inch springform pan	9-inch square pan
9-inch round pan	8-inch square pan
9×5-inch loaf pan	9-inch square pan
12-cup bundt cake pan	10×4-inch angel food (tube) pan
1-quart casserole	9-inch pie pan
1 1/2-quart casserole	8-inch square pan
2-quart casserole	9-inch square pan
3-quart casserole	13×9-inch rectangular pan

Entertain with Grilling

Grilling is great for entertaining because it's easy, your kitchen doesn't get overheated and there's little cleanup. And it's terrific for foods at both ends of the party scale—from hot dogs to salmon and everything in between.

Grilling Tips

When using a charcoal grill, follow the manufacturer's instructions for lighting the coals well before cooking. Most coals take from 30 to 45 minutes to reach the proper temperature. So include this time in your "day-of-party" to-do list.

When using a gas grill, follow the manufacturer's instructions or heat the grill 5 to 10 minutes before cooking.

Grease or oil the grill rack or spray it with cooking spray before lighting the coals or turning on the gas.

Place the grill rack 4 to 6 inches above the coals or burners.

For even cooking, place thicker foods on the center of the grill rack and smaller pieces on the edges.

Turn pieces with metal tongs; don't pierce the food with a fork because it will lose its juices.

Keep the heat as even as possible throughout the grilling period.

If you're not hearing a sizzle, the fire may be too cool. Regulate the heat by spreading the coals or raking them together, opening or closing the vents or adjusting the control on a gas or electric grill. Raising or lowering the grill rack or covering the grill will also help control the heat.

Use long-handled barbecue tools to allow for a safe distance between you and the intense heat of the grill.

Trim visible fat from meat to avoid flare-ups.

Enhance flavors by using wood chips or chunks to add a smoky taste to grilled foods. A covered grill allows the aroma to penetrate the food.

Sprinkle the hot coals with soaked and drained dried herbs, fresh herbs or garlic cloves for a different flavor and aroma when grilling.

Stainless steel flat-bladed skewers make it easy to turn kabobs. Wooden skewers can be used instead; just be sure to soak them in water at least thirty minutes before using to prevent burning.

Grilling Timetable

Food	Approximate Grilling Time*
Beef boneless sirloin steak (1 inch thick)	14 to 20 minutes
Burgers	14 to 18 minutes
Chicken breasts	15 to 20 minutes
Corn on the cob	20 to 30 minutes
Pork chops	12 to 15 minutes
Salmon fillet	20 to 30 minutes
Shrimp	8 to 10 minutes
Tuna steaks	15 to 20 minutes

*Times are given for foods cooked over medium heat.

Aluminum Foil— A Grill's Best Friend!

Aluminum foil has many uses for grilling. From using it to line the firebox to making cleanup easier, to using it as a serving "dish," you'll want to keep a roll of heavy-duty foil handy. Here are some other uses for foil that you may want to try:

Crumple aluminum foil (used foil works fine), and use to scrape cooked-on food bits from the grill rack.

Scoop warm coals onto foil; cool completely. Wrap or tightly fold foil around coals before discarding.

Cover foods after grilling to keep them warm.

Cover the outside of a saucepan or baking pan you plan to use on the grill to keep it from becoming difficult to clean.

If your grill doesn't have a cover and a recipe recommends one, shape two sheets of heavy-duty aluminum foil in a dome shape the same size as the grill rack. Try forming foil over bent coat hangers to easily retain the shape.

Food-Safety Tips and Storage Strategies

You've planned your party, done the shopping and set the table. Now don't let any uninvited "guests"—food-borne bacteria—crash your party. Start by keeping everything in the kitchen clean. Use hard-plastic cutting boards for raw meat, poultry and fish, and wash them with hot, soapy water or other cleaners, such as those labeled "antibacterial," or in the dishwasher. Wash the board, as well as your knives, before using them for cutting any other foods. And make sure to use a clean towel each time you wipe off the counter. Also, be sure to . . .

Keep hot foods hot.

Bacteria thrive at room temperature and in lukewarm food. So don't allow hot foods to stand at room temperature for more than two hours, including prep time. Keeping hot foods hot means keeping them at 140° or higher.

Use chafing dishes, electric skillets, hot trays or slow cookers to keep foods hot if you are holding them for more than two hours. Warming units heated by canned cooking fuel are safe to use, but don't depend on units heated with candles because they don't get hot enough to keep foods safe from bacteria.

Don't partially cook or heat perishable foods, then set them aside or refrigerate to finish cooking later. During cooking, the food may not reach a temperature high enough to destroy bacteria.

Cook meat and poultry completely, following the "doneness" times and temperatures recommended throughout this book. A meat thermometer comes in handy for making sure meat is cooked through.

Keep cold foods cold.

Bacteria thrive at room temperature and in lukewarm food. So don't allow cold foods to stand at room temperature for more than two hours, including prep time. Keeping cold foods cold means keeping them at 40° or lower.

Foods that contain eggs, milk, seafood, fish, meat and poultry or the dishes that contain them, such as cream pies and seafood salad, are the most perishable. When you shop, make your meat, poultry, fish and seafood selections last. Place them in plastic bags to prevent juices from dripping on other foods in your cart.

Take perishable foods straight home, and refrigerate them immediately. If the time from the store to home is longer than 30 minutes or you have other errands on your list, bring a cooler with freezer packs or filled with ice and put perishable groceries inside. Even short stops in hot weather can cause perishable groceries in a hot car to reach unsafe temperatures very quickly.

Foods will chill faster if you allow space between them when stocking your refrigerator and freezer. It also helps to divide large amounts into smaller ones and store the foods in shallow containers.

Never thaw foods at room temperature—thaw only in the refrigerator or microwave. If you thaw foods in the microwave, finish cooking them immediately.

Store cold foods in the fridge or an ice-filled cooler until just before serving.

A few other food-safety tips to keep in mind:

Tightly wrap leftovers in aluminum foil, plastic wrap, plastic food-storage bags or in tightly sealed plastic containers, and put the fridge as soon as possible.

Don't use recipes that call for uncooked eggs (some recipes for Caesar salad or frostings may) unless you use an egg substitute or pasteurized eggs. Store uncooked "do-ahead" recipes containing raw eggs in the refrigerator for no more than 24 hours before cooking.

Refrigerate meat while marinating, and toss any leftover marinade that has touched raw meat, fish or poultry.

Serve food at buffets in small dishes. Rather than adding fresh food to a dish that already has had food in it, wash the dish or use a different one.

Helpful Yields and Equivalents

Knowing how much cheese or chocolate you'll need for a recipe can be difficult. This guide to some common ingredients used when entertaining will help you draw up your shopping list.

Food	If Your Recipe States	You Will Need Approximately
Apples 1 medium apple	1 cup chopped 1 1/3 cups thinly sliced	1 medium
Asparagus	16 to 20 stalks	1 pound
Bacon	1/2 cup crumbled	8 slices, crisply cooked
Bread, white 1 cup dry crumbs	1 cup soft cubes 4 to 5 slices, dried	1 1/2 slices
Broccoli	2 cups flowerets	6 ounces
Carrots 1 cup 1/4-inch slices	1 medium 2 medium	7 inches
Cauliflower 3 cups flowerets	1 medium head 1 pound	2 pounds (with leaves)
Celery	1 cup, chopped or thinly sliced	2 medium stalks
Coleslaw (bag)	7 cups	16 ounces
Cheese Blue, Cheddar, feta, mozzarella, Swiss (crumbled or shredded) Cream Ricotta	 1 cup 1 cup 2 cups	 4 ounces 8 ounces 16 ounces
Chocolate Chips Unsweetened or semisweet baking	 1 cup 1 square or bar	 6 ounces 1 ounce
Cream Sour Whipping	 1 cup 1 cup (2 cups whipped)	 8 ounces 1/2 pint
Eggs, large egg product	1 egg	1/4 cup fat-free cholesterol-free
Garlic	1/2 teaspoon finely chopped	1 medium clove
Graham cracker crumbs	1 1/2 cups	20 squares
Lemon or lime 2 to 3 tablespoons juice	1 1/2 to 3 teaspoons grated peel 1 medium	1 medium
Lettuce, iceberg or romaine 2 cups shredded 6 cups bite-size pieces	1 medium head 5 ounces 1 pound	1 1/2 pounds
Margarine, butter or spread	1/2 cup	1 stick

Food	If Your Recipe States	You Will Need Approximately
Mushrooms, fresh	3 cups sliced	8 ounces
Nuts (shelled)		
Chopped, slivered, or sliced	1 cup	4 ounces
Whole or halves	3 to 4 cups	1 pound
Olives, ripe pitted	1 cup sliced	32 medium
Onions		
Green, with tops	2 tablespoons chopped	2 medium
	1/4 cup sliced	4 medium
Yellow or white	1/2 cup chopped	1 medium
Orange	1 to 2 tablespoons grated peel	1 medium
	1/3 to 1/2 cup juice	1 medium
Pasta		
Penne	4 cups cooked	2 cups uncooked (6 to 7 ounces)
Noodles, egg	4 cups cooked	4 to 5 cups uncooked (7 ounces)
Spaghetti	4 cups cooked	7 to 8 ounces (uncooked)
Peppers, bell	1/2 cup chopped	1 small
	1 cup chopped	1 medium
	1 1/2 cups chopped	1 large
Potatoes		
New	10 to 12 small	1 1/2 pounds
Red, white, sweet, or yams	1 medium	5 to 6 ounces
Rice, regular long-grain	3 cups cooked	1 cup uncooked
Shrimp (uncooked with shells)		
Large	1 pound	15 to 20 count
Medium	1 pound	26 to 30 count
Sugar		
Brown	2 1/4 cup packed	1 pound
Granulated	2 1/4 cups	1 pound
Powdered	4 cups	1 pound
Tomatoes	1 cup chopped	1 large
	3/4 cup chopped	1 medium
	1/2 cup chopped	1 small

If You Don't Have It, Try This!

Uh-oh. You're halfway through the recipe, and you don't have any cornstarch after all. What do you do? Check out this list of handy substitutions!

Emergency Substitutions

Instead of using:	Use:
Balsamic vinegar (1 tablespoon)	1 tablespoon sherry or cider vinegar
Bread crumbs, dry (1/4 cup)	1/4 cup finely crushed cracker crumbs or cornflakes cereal
Broth (1 cup)	1 teaspoon chicken, beef or vegetable bouillon granules (or 1 cube) dissolved in 1 cup boiling water
Buttermilk (1 cup)	1 tablespoon lemon juice or white vinegar plus enough milk to measure 1 cup. Let stand a few minutes. Or use 1 cup plain yogurt.
Chocolate	
Semisweet baking (1 ounce)	1 ounce unsweetened baking chocolate plus 1 tablespoon sugar
Semisweet chips (1 cup)	6 ounces semisweet baking chocolate, chopped
Unsweetened baking (1 ounce)	3 tablespoons baking cocoa plus 1 tablespoon shortening or margarine
Cornstarch (1 tablespoon)	2 tablespoons all-purpose flour
Eggs (1 large)	2 egg whites or 1/4 cup fat-free cholesterol-free egg product
Garlic, finely chopped (1 medium clove)	1/8 teaspoon garlic powder, 1/4 teaspoon instant minced garlic, or 1/2 teaspoon ready-to-use chopped garlic available in jars
Gingerroot, grated or finely chopped (1 teaspoon)	3/4 teaspoon ground ginger or 1/2 teaspoon ready-to-use chopped gingerroot available in jars
Herbs, chopped fresh (1 tablespoon)	3/4 to 1 teaspoon dried herbs
Lemon juice, fresh (1 tablespoon)	1 tablespoon bottled lemon juice or white vinegar
Lemon peel, grated (1 teaspoon)	1 teaspoon dried lemon peel
Mushrooms, fresh cooked (2/3 cup sliced)	1 can (4 ounces) mushroom stems and pieces, drained
Mustard, yellow (1 tablespoon)	1 teaspoon ground mustard
Orange peel, grated (1 teaspoon)	1 teaspoon dried orange peel
Raisins 1/2 cup	1/2 cup currants, dried cherries, dried cranberries or chopped dates
Red pepper sauce (3 or 4 drops)	1/8 teaspoon ground red pepper (cayenne)
Sour cream (1 cup)	1 cup plain yogurt
Sugar	
Brown, packed (1 cup)	1 cup granulated sugar plus 2 tablespoons molasses or dark corn syrup
Granulated (1 cup)	1 cup light brown sugar (packed) or 2 cups powdered sugar
Tomato paste (1/2 cup)	1 cup tomato sauce cooked uncovered until reduced to 1/2 cup
Tomato sauce (2 cups)	3/4 cup tomato paste plus 1 cup water
Whipping cream, whipped (1 cup)	1 cup frozen (thawed) whipped topping or prepared whipped topping mix
Wine	
Red (1 cup)	1 cup apple cider or beef broth
White (1 cup)	1 cup apple juice, apple cider or chicken broth

Essential Cooking Techniques

BEATING WHIPPING CREAM

Beat whipping cream and sugar with electric mixer on high speed until soft or stiff peaks form. The whipping cream will beat up more easily if the bowl and beaters for the mixer are chilled in the freezer or refrigerator for 15 to 20 minutes before beating.

CHOPPING GARLIC

Hit garlic clove with flat side of heavy knife to crack the skin, which will then slip off easily. Finely chop garlic with knife.

CRUSHING GARLIC

Garlic can be crushed in a garlic press, or by pressing with the side of a knife or mallet to break into small pieces.

CUTTING A BELL PEPPER

Cut the bell pepper lengthwise in half, and cut out seeds and membrane.

CUTTING A MANGO

Cut the mango lengthwise in half, sliding a sharp knife along the flat side of the seed on one side. Repeat on the other side, which will give you two large pieces plus the seed. Cut away any flesh from the seed. Cut a crosscross pattern in the flesh of each mango half, being careful not to cut through peel. Turn each mango half inside out; cut off mango pieces.

CUTTING A ZUCCHINI

Cut zucchini lengthwise in half. Cut each half into slices.

CUTTING AND SEEDING A JALAPEÑO CHILI

Cut the stem off the jalapeño chili, then cut off the sides along the ribs, avoiding the seeds. The flesh, ribs and seeds of chilies contain burning, irritating oils. Be sure to wash your hands in soapy water (or wear protective gloves), and be especially careful not to rub your face or eyes until the oils have been washed away.

CUTTING IN SHORTENING

Cut shortening into flour mixture, using a pastry blender or crisscrossing 2 knives, until mixture looks like fine crumbs.

FLATTENING CHICKEN BREASTS

Flatten each chicken breast to 1/4-inch thickness between sheets of plastic wrap or waxed paper, lightly pounding with the flat side of a meat mallet.

DRAINING FROZEN SPINACH

Squeeze excess moisture from spinach, using paper towels or a clean kitchen towel, until spinach is dry.

GRATING GINGERROOT

Grate gingerroot by rubbing it across the small rough holes of a grater.

DRAINING SAUSAGE OR GROUND BEEF

Place a strainer over a medium bowl, or place a colander in a large bowl. Spoon cooked sausage into strainer to drain the fat. Discard fat in the garbage (not down your drain).

GRATING LEMON PEEL

Grate lemon peel by rubbing the lemon across the small rough holes of a grater. The same technique can be used for grating lime and orange peel.

FLAKING CRABMEAT

Use a fork to flake the crabmeat, and remove any tiny pieces of shell.

HUSKING CORN

Pull the green husks off the ears and remove the silk. Do not put corn husks or silk in your garbage disposal.

KNEADING DOUGH

Sprinkle a clean surface, such as a kitchen counter or bread-board, with a small amount of flour. Place dough on the lightly floured surface. Gently roll dough in flour to coat all sides. Shape the dough into a ball. Knead dough by curving your fingers around and folding dough toward you, then pushing it away with the heels of your hands, using a quick rocking motion.

PEELING AND DEVEINING (CLEANING) SHRIMP

Starting at the large end of shrimp, use your fingers to peel off the shell. Leave tail intact if you like.

Use a paring knife to make a shallow cut lengthwise down the back of each shrimp, and wash out the vein.

MASHING POTATOES

Use a handheld potato masher for the fluffiest mashed potatoes. If using an electric mixer, do not mix too long; overmixing releases more starch from the potatoes and they can become gummy.

PREPARING ASPARAGUS FOR COOKING

Break off tough ends of asparagus stalks where they snap easily. Discard ends.

PEELING A KIWIFRUIT

Cut the fuzzy brown skin from the fruit with a paring knife. Cut fruit into slices or wedges.

REMOVING HULL FROM STRAWBERRIES

Cut out the hull, or "cap," with the point of a paring knife.

SHAPING MEATBALLS
Use your hands to shape beef mixture into thirty 1-inch meatballs.

SQUEEZING JUICE FROM LEMONS
Squeeze and measure juice from lemon halves by placing the juicer over a measuring cup. The juicer also strains out most of the seeds and pulp.

SHREDDING A CARROT
Peel the carrot, then shred the carrot by rubbing it across the largest holes of a grater.

TOASTING NUTS IN OVEN
Spread nuts in ungreased shallow pan. Bake uncovered in 350° oven about 10 minutes, stirring occasionally, until golden brown and fragrant. Watch carefully because nuts brown quickly.

SLICING AN APPLE
Cut the apple into fourths. Cut the core and seeds from the center of each fourth. Cut each fourth into slices.

TOASTING NUTS IN SKILLET
Cook nuts in ungreased heavy skillet over medium-low heat 5 to 7 minutes, stirring frequently until browning begins, then stirring constantly until golden brown and fragrant. Watch carefully; times vary greatly between gas and electric ranges.

Metric Conversion Guide

Volume

U.S. Units	Canadian Metric	Australian Metric
1/4 teaspoon	1 mL	1 ml
1/2 teaspoon	2 mL	2 ml
1 teaspoon	5 mL	5 ml
1 tablespoon	15 mL	20 ml
1/4 cup	50 mL	60 ml
1/3 cup	75 mL	80 ml
1/2 cup	125 mL	125 ml
2/3 cup	150 mL	170 ml
3/4 cup	175 mL	190 ml
1 cup	250 mL	250 ml
1 quart	1 liter	1 liter
1 1/2 quarts	1.5 liters	1.5 liters
2 quarts	2 liters	2 liters
2 1/2 quarts	2.5 liters	2.5 liters
3 quarts	3 liters	3 liters
4 quarts	4 liters	4 liters

Measurements

Inches	Centimeters
1	2.5
2	5.0
3	7.5
4	10.0
5	12.5
6	15.0
7	17.5
8	20.5
9	23.0
10	25.5
11	28.0
12	30.5
13	33.0

Temperatures

Fahrenheit	Celsius
32°	0°
212°	100°
250°	120°
275°	140°
300°	150°
325°	160°
350°	180°
375°	190°
400°	200°
425°	220°
450°	230°
475°	240°
500°	260°

Weight

U.S. Units	Canadian Metric	Australian Metric
1 ounce	30 grams	30 grams
2 ounces	55 grams	60 grams
3 ounces	85 grams	90 grams
4 ounces (1/4 pound)	115 grams	125 grams
8 ounces (1/2 pound)	225 grams	225 grams
16 ounces (1 pound)	455 grams	500 grams
1 pound	455 grams	1/2 kilogram

Note: The recipes in this cookbook have not been developed or tested using metric measures. When converting recipes to metric, some variations in quality may be noted.

Nutrition Guidelines

We provide nutrition information for each recipe that includes calories, fat, cholesterol, sodium, carbohydrate, fiber and protein. Individual food choices can be based on this information.

Recommended intake for a daily diet of 2,000 calories as set by the Food and Drug Administration

Total Fat	Less than 65g
Saturated Fat	Less than 20g
Cholesterol	Less than 300mg
Sodium	Less than 2,400mg
Total Carbohydrate	300g
Dietary Fiber	25g

Criteria Used for Calculating Nutrition Information

- The first ingredient was used wherever a choice is given (such as 1/3 cup sour cream or plain yogurt).

- The first ingredient amount was used wherever a range is given (such as 3- to 3-1/2–pound cut-up broiler-fryer chicken).

- The first serving number was used wherever a range is given (such as 4 to 6 servings).

- "If desired" ingredients and recipe variations were not included (such as sprinkle with brown sugar, if desired).

- Only the amount of a marinade or frying oil that is estimated to be absorbed by the food during preparation or cooking was calculated.

Ingredients Used in Recipe Testing and Nutrition Calculations

- Ingredients used for testing represent those that the majority of consumers use in their homes: large eggs, 2% milk, 80%-lean ground beef, canned ready-to-use chicken broth and vegetable oil spread containing not less than 65 percent fat.

- Fat-free, low-fat or low-sodium products were not used, unless otherwise indicated.

- Solid vegetable shortening (not butter, margarine, nonstick cooking sprays or vegetable oil spread as they can cause sticking problems) was used to grease pans, unless otherwise indicated.

Equipment Used in Recipe Testing

We use equipment for testing that the majority of consumers use in their homes. If a specific piece of equipment (such as a wire whisk) is necessary for recipe success, it is listed in the recipe.

- Cookware and bakeware without nonstick coatings were used, unless otherwise indicated.
- No dark-colored, black or insulated bakeware was used.
- When a pan is specified in a recipe, a metal pan was used; a baking dish or pie plate means ovenproof glass was used.
- An electric hand mixer was used for mixing only when mixer speeds are specified in the recipe directions. When a mixer speed is not given, a spoon or fork was used.

Cooking Terms Glossary

Beat: Mix ingredients vigorously with spoon, fork, wire whisk, hand beater or electric mixer until smooth and uniform.

Boil: Heat liquid until bubbles rise continuously and break on the surface and steam is given off. For rolling boil, the bubbles form rapidly.

Chop: Cut into coarse or fine irregular pieces with a knife, food chopper, blender or food processor.

Cube: Cut into squares 1/2 inch or larger.

Dice: Cut into squares smaller than 1/2 inch.

Grate: Cut into tiny particles using small rough holes of grater (citrus peel or chocolate).

Grease: Rub the inside surface of a pan with shortening, using pastry brush, piece of waxed paper or paper towel, to prevent food from sticking during baking (as for some casseroles).

Julienne: Cut into thin, matchlike strips, using knife or food processor (vegetables, fruits, meats).

Mix: Combine ingredients in any way that distributes them evenly.

Sauté: Cook foods in hot oil or margarine over medium-high heat with frequent tossing and turning motion.

Shred: Cut into long thin pieces by rubbing food across the holes of a shredder, as for cheese, or by using a knife to slice very thinly, as for cabbage.

Simmer: Cook in liquid just below the boiling point on top of the stove; usually after reducing heat from a boil. Bubbles will rise slowly and break just below the surface.

Stir: Mix ingredients until uniform consistency. Stir once in a while for stirring occasionally, often for stirring frequently and continuously for stirring constantly.

Toss: Tumble ingredients (such as green salad) lightly with a lifting motion, usually to coat evenly or mix with another food.

Index

M

Complete your cookbook library with these *Betty Crocker* titles

Betty Crocker Baking for Today

Betty Crocker's Best Bread Machine Cookbook

Betty Crocker's Best Chicken Cookbook

Betty Crocker's Best Christmas Cookbook

Betty Crocker's Best of Baking

Betty Crocker's Best of Healthy and Hearty Cooking

Betty Crocker's Best-Loved Recipes

Betty Crocker's Bisquick® Cookbook

Betty Crocker Bisquick® II Cookbook

Betty Crocker Bisquick® Impossibly Easy Pies

Betty Crocker Celebrate!

Betty Crocker's Complete Thanksgiving Cookbook

Betty Crocker's Cook Book for Boys and Girls

Betty Crocker's Cook It Quick

Betty Crocker's Cookbook, 9th Edition *The* **BIG RED** *Cookbook*®

Betty Crocker's Cookbook, Bridal Edition

Betty Crocker's Cookie Book

Betty Crocker's Cooking Basics

Betty Crocker's Cooking for Two

Betty Crocker's Cooky Book, Facsimile Edition

Betty Crocker's Diabetes Cookbook

Betty Crocker Dinner Made Easy with Rotisserie Chicken

Betty Crocker Easy Family Dinners

Betty Crocker's Easy Slow Cooker Dinners

Betty Crocker's Eat and Lose Weight

Betty Crocker's Entertaining Basics

Betty Crocker's Flavors of Home

Betty Crocker 4-Ingredient Dinners

Betty Crocker Grilling Made Easy

Betty Crocker Healthy Heart Cookbook

Betty Crocker's Healthy New Choices

Betty Crocker's Indian Home Cooking

Betty Crocker's Italian Cooking

Betty Crocker's Kids Cook!

Betty Crocker's Kitchen Library

Betty Crocker's Living with Cancer Cookbook

Betty Crocker's Low-Fat, Low-Cholesterol Cooking Today

Betty Crocker More Slow Cooker Recipes

Betty Crocker's New Cake Decorating

Betty Crocker's New Chinese Cookbook

Betty Crocker One-Dish Meals

Betty Crocker's A Passion for Pasta

Betty Crocker's Picture Cook Book, Facsimile Edition

Betty Crocker's Quick & Easy Cookbook

Betty Crocker's Slow Cooker Cookbook

Betty Crocker's Ultimate Cake Mix Cookbook

Betty Crocker's Vegetarian Cooking